Palgrave Studies in Affect Theory and Literary Criticism

Series Editors

Adam Frank
University of British Columbia
Vancouver, British Columbia, Canada

Joel Faflak
Western University
London, Ontario, Canada

Aim of the Series

The recent surge of interest in affect and emotion has productively crossed disciplinary boundaries within and between the humanities, social sciences, and sciences, but has not often addressed questions of literature and literary criticism as such. The first of its kind, Palgrave Studies in Affect Theory and Literary Criticism seeks theoretically informed scholarship that examines the foundations and practice of literary criticism in relation to affect theory. This series aims to stage contemporary debates in the field, addressing topics such as: the role of affective experience in literary composition and reception, particularly in non-Western literatures; examinations of historical and conceptual relations between major and minor philosophies of emotion and literary experience; and studies of race, class, gender, sexuality, age, and disability that use affect theory as a primary critical tool.

More information about this series at
http://www.springer.com/series/14653

Tyler Bradway

Queer Experimental Literature

The Affective Politics of Bad Reading

Tyler Bradway
State University of New York at Cortland
Cortland, USA

Palgrave Studies in Affect Theory and Literary Criticism
ISBN 978-1-349-95554-1   ISBN 978-1-137-59543-0   (eBook)
DOI 10.1057/978-1-137-59543-0

Cover illustration: *She Was Her Own Experiment* by Jen Lightfoot © 2013

Printed on acid-free paper

This Palgrave Macmillan imprint is published by Springer Nature
The registered company is Nature America Inc.
The registered company address is: 1 New York Plaza, New York, NY 10004, U.S.A.

PREFACE

A predominant question for queer literary criticism has been: How can we "queer" a text by reading it aslant of its manifest content? *Queer Experimental Literature* asks instead: How do the affective relations of a text "queer" its readers and the social relations of reading itself? In short, this book argues that literature does not await a *critical* reading to activate its queerness. Rather, I trace a genealogy of writers that turn to experimental aesthetics to queer the affective relations among readers, texts, and their publics. I call these affective relations experiments in *bad reading* because they are infused with affects that do not conform to the protocols of critical reading and other hegemonic, institutionally sanctioned, and socially approved modes of "good reading." Indeed, these texts elicit masturbatory fantasy, perverse titillation, exuberant sentimentality, and other affects that have failed to signify as "critical" within the domains of literary and cultural theory. They appear naïve, solipsistic, and politically retrograde, often leading critics to apologize for or bracket the text's investment in affect. Yet it is precisely through its solicitations of bad reading, I contend, that queer experimental literature contests and redraws the social relations that underpin the heteronormative public sphere. Rather than oppose aesthetics to politics, or affect to the social, then, *Queer Experimental Literature* reveals their complex imbrication within the affective politics of bad reading.

Queerness has often been conceived as a force of subversion—a performative demystification of apparently natural norms, an anti-social drive toward incoherence, or a shattering of the illusory structures of subjectivity and meaning.[1] While I do not dispute the value of queer negativity, its exclusive claim to criticality has tended to eclipse other forces of queerness and other modes of queer critique. When queerness presents itself in an affirmative mode and draws on corollary affective idioms—joy, happiness, love, ecstasy, optimism, or sweetness—it is often collapsed into the politics of "homonormativity."[2] It is perceived as non-oppositional, as either a symptom or an enabler of neoliberalism's narrowing the zones of political life to the realm of consumption.[3] It will not simply be enough to show that queer deployments of positive affect exist or that they might have oppositional force, if they are only to be measured in terms of subversion. We must go further and meet them on their own ground. To glimpse the affective politics of queer experimental literature, we require a conception of *queerness as a creative experiment in relationality*. Following critics such as José Esteban Muñoz and Elizabeth Freeman, I understand the relations of queerness as unfurling into futurity; they are unfinished, open ended, and rife with untapped potential for becoming.[4] At the same time, queer relationality is a historically contingent social form, inextricably bound up, as Michel Foucault teaches us, with the institutions and relations of power.[5] Yet an attention to the creativity of queerness makes it possible to see how queer aesthetic objects are, through their own terms and forces, reconfiguring relational potentialities in excess of the existing codifications of sexuality as identity.[6]

Situated against contestations over queer sexuality in the postwar period, queerness often appears as a figural crisis in relation. This is due to the discursive, representational, and ideological pressure to conceive and narrate queerness as an individual rather than a collective body, as a body politic. All of the writers in *Queer Experimental Literature* contest this reduction of queer relationality, and they utilize the affective relations of reading to experiment with and provoke collective forms of queer belonging. Thus, the crisis in queer relationality should not solely be understood as an example of queer "trouble" or intrinsic destabilization; it is also, as the etymology of crisis implies, a turning point, a moment of becoming pregnant with potentiality. The affective relations fostered through queer experimental literature must therefore be understood as *incipiently social*—pitched between the "merely" affective and the "properly" political. This is due to the representational prohibitions that prevent the figuration of queerness as collectivity, forcing a displacement of this figuration into the ineffable idioms of affect. The incipience of these social imaginings is not "utopian" in any traditional sense, despite their investment in the horizons of queer potentiality that Muñoz has taught us to see. The relations that they configure have been prohibited, destroyed, or gentrified, and thus, these texts meditate on the paradoxical distance between their viscerally immediate intimations of queer relationality and the inability for these relations to become collectively materialized in the text's temporality of reception. Their emphasis falls less on a horizon of futurity, then, and more on experimentations with affective relations in the present, in advance of any idiom that could conceive of them as socially meaningful. The relations of queer experimental literature are incipiently social precisely because they are emergent, or becoming-fomented, in the event of reading.

Clearly, "reading" in this book signifies far more than the subject's interpretive act of decoding. Reading, for my purposes, is not a phenomenology of the reader's consciousness as it processes meaning; it does not refer to a subject position or an existing collective that will be named and studied for their reception practices. Indeed, I tend to stress "reading" rather than "the reader" to preserve the present participle of the affective relation to literature. Reading is virtual—an encounter composed through a text that is not entirely under its own control and is not reducible to a single affective referent. By thinking of affect as a relation unfurled by aesthetic objects—a relation that is as much a part of the object as its content and form—we can sidestep a perennial problem in the convergence of affect theory and literary criticism. At one end, critics think of affect as a purely visceral and unarticulated wave of sensation, which tends to diminish the ability to read qualitatively specific configurations of affect composed within and through a text.[7] In this framework, affective qualities are equivalent to subjective capture—they are codified, personalized, and lacking in potential for becoming. At the other end, critics think of affect as a subjective property the reader or critic brings to the text; they may debate which affective orientation is most appropriate—suspicion or empathy, for example—but the text's own affective coordination is diminished or occluded.[8] In both cases, the affective relation—the qualitatively inflected scene composed by the text and actualized in the event of reading—is overlooked as its own space of potentiality. More recent scholarship on affect and aesthetics has begun to address both the relational dimension of the aesthetic and the possibility of "reading" affect as a form without reference to subjective reception.[9] *Queer Experimental Literature* shares both of these goals. Yet the stakes that it proposes for this theoretical and methodological approach to affect center specifically on understanding the affective politics of queer aesthetics, the way that

aesthetic objects configure affective relations within and against the existing relations of power that fuse scenes of reading into the production of
heteronormative subjects and collectives.

In making this argument, my goal is to forestall the reduction of
"queer reading" to paranoid reading or reparative reading, the two modes
famously identified by Eve Kosofsky Sedgwick.[10] *Queer Experimental
Literature* reveals the limitation of heuristically mapping the many affects
of queer reading into this narrow dichotomy. The dichotomy tends to
miss weak, minor, or simply illegible affective relations that fall to the
side of either of these codified orientations. But more importantly, the
dichotomy prioritizes the critic as the agent of queer reading, as the locus
of both affect and critique. Instead, I trace how queer experimental literature solicits its own singular relations for affective reading, which do
not presume the critical reader (or the literary critic) as the primary hero
in the dramatic scene of reading. While other literary traditions may also
participate in this project, queer experimental literature makes its affective
agencies visible by drawing attention to literary form's capacity to work
on and through the bodies of readers, immanently restructuring our felt
relations to the aesthetic object.

Thus, it is important to resist a methodology for reading queer experimental literature that dictates, in advance, the embodied orientation that
readers must bring to these texts, whether distance or closeness, empathetic care or paranoid suspicion. As Barbara Johnson observes, "[T]he
question is not whether to be or not to be philological but how to read
in such a way as to break through preconceived notions of meaning. ...
To know whether this requires more closeness or more distance, a leap
or a crawl, may very well *itself* be part of the challenge."[11] Similarly, the
question is not whether to be or not be affective in our reading but how
to read in such a way as to break through entrained and hegemonic affective relations of reading. Note that, in Johnson's description, the reader
becomes an immanently embodied figure—leaping over and crawling
through the surface of the text, mindful that the necessary posture cannot
be known in advance. *Queer Experimental Literature* follows Johnson's
cue, and it begins with the challenge that the affects for queer reading
cannot be determined transcendentally above or before the text. In these
pages, reading becomes less an *ethical choice* made by a critic than a *social
encounter* engendered by the text. We may not know how much closeness
or distance is required, whether to leap or crawl, to fantasize or faint, but
the optic of bad reading makes the text's provocation of these postures

both thinkable and meaningful as strategies for contesting the historical conflicts over and representational prohibitions on queer relationality that pre-condition the reception of its queer aesthetics.

The primary historical and representational conflict that cuts across *Queer Experimental Literature* might be called "postmodernity," but as each chapter shows, this context requires more specificity to understand how it inflects the local circumstances of each author and how it intersects with emergent forms of institutionalized hetero- and homonormativity throughout the period. At the outset, however, it is important to stress that "queer experimental literature" is not reducible to postmodern fiction, although it converges with it in several formal and ideological respects. The reason for this caveat is that queerness and postmodernism are often equated to one another, and in many readings of postmodern fiction, queerness—particularly its fragmentation, demystification, and dispersal of identity—is positioned as merely exemplary of a more general postmodern condition. This move eclipses the specifically queer contexts that motivate putatively "postmodern" authors such as Kathy Acker, William S. Burroughs, Jeanette Winterson, Samuel R. Delany, and Chuck Palahniuk. But more problematically, it assimilates queer writing to the postmodern canon and, consequently, makes it difficult to perceive how, precisely, queer writers contest, resist, and even radically reject "postmodernism" as such, particularly postmodernity's atrophied capacity for social imagination.[12] For this reason, this book's archive draws primarily on authors that have been central to debates about postmodernism among scholars of contemporary fiction; it works to repatriate the zones of queerness in these works to make legible their agonistic and, indeed, excitingly fresh aesthetic challenges to postmodernity, which have otherwise been ignored or subordinated as less radical because of their imbrication with affect. This is not to imply that one can no longer read these authors as postmodern or value their use of postmodern aesthetics such as deconstructive resignification and metafictive intertextuality. However, I hope to displace the centrality of those forms as the only index of "critical" aesthetic politics for contemporary literature, thereby drawing attention to formal practices that articulate their social agency through affective idioms.

Queer Experimental Literature also contributes to the recent reconsideration of experimental writing. Long discounted as abstruse and formalist, a number of scholars have turned to experimental writing to reconsider its political and philosophical relevance.[13] Of particular note is Anthony

Reed's incisive *Freedom Time: The Poetics and Politics of Black Experimental Writing*, which shares a similar goal to my own. Reed traces a genealogy of "black experimental writing" in the postwar era and reveals the complex role that formal experimentations plays in a critical politics of race.[14] Much like race, sexuality has been subordinated in scholarly accounts of experimental writing, and *Queer Experimental Literature* seeks to redress this marginalization. At the same time, I do not claim to offer a definitive survey of queer experimental literature. Rather, my purpose is to look to a small archive of writers—and, more specifically, to a handful of works that lie at the literary margins—to chart the para-academic politics of queer reading solicited through formal experimentation.

To see this politics, however, will require a displacement of the predominant affective narrative about experimental writing—namely that its "difficulty" alienates and aggressively attacks the reader. In her survey of postwar experimental literature, for example, Kathryn Hume characterizes these works as "aggressive fictions" that break the conventional author–reader contract, which promises pleasure and edification as the proverbial carrot on the stick for reading.[15] Instead, these texts attack, offend, disturb, and disgust, and in her view, "The reader does not like the feeling of being unable to follow the text and hence of having lost control of it."[16] When Hume speculates about readers that *do* enjoy the feelings stimulated by experimental writing, she imagines a specialized coterie of professional critics that have learned to access pleasure from the interpretative mastery of the text's difficulty. I propose an alternative view. First, I trace how queer experimental literature appeals to neither a mass public nor a special coterie but seeks to conjure new readerly publics that outstrip the existing landscape for the texts' reception. Second, I show that queer experimental literature refuses a pleasure principle for reading, opening up a number of queerer affective relations to the event of reading that do not move toward mastery. Most importantly, these texts do not forsake pleasure but actively solicit it, particularly through figurations of eroticism, sex, and intimate contact. They do not, in other words, equate pleasure with difficulty or primarily seek to alienate and attack readers. Rather, queer experimental literature creates an erotic relationality among texts, readers, and publics that redefines the difference that pleasure can make in the politics of experimental writing.

By encountering the affective relations of these texts on their own terms, *Queer Experimental Literature* partakes in what Rita Felski calls "postcritical reading."[17] I attend to the aesthetic surface of the text rather than rewriting the surface as a symptom of an underlying ideological cause, thereby moving beyond the hermeneutics of suspicion as the privileged index for queer critique and critical reading. Unlike some variants of postcritical reading, however, I do not oppose affect and aesthetic form to political reading. Rather, I show that the affective dimension of the aesthetic compels a rethinking of what political interpretation looks like: where the operative agencies of reading take place, who (or what) deploys the agencies of critique, and what "counts" as critical reading. *Queer Experimental Literature* thus locates the politics of aesthetics in their affective relations, and it traces how the disruptive, seductive, or adhesive relations of reading respond to and intersect with the history of sexuality in the postwar era. To do so, each chapter considers a specific obstacle to the figuration of queer relationality in the postwar period. These obstacles include the obscenity laws governing the literary representation of queerness in pre-Stonewall America; the "epidemic of signification" that shapes the discourse of the AIDS crisis; the neoliberal gentrification of the queer avant-garde and the commodification of its intellectual discourses about radical aesthetics; the convergence of homonormativity and biopower to narrow queerness to a consumer identity; and the entrenchment of suspicion as a disciplinary norm for queer and critical theory. Each chapter traces a writer's turn to queer experimental literature to contest these obstacles and to reimagine the social relations of queer belonging through the affective relations of reading.

Chapter 1 argues that William S. Burroughs innovates an experimental aesthetics of "queer spectrality" in *Naked Lunch* (1959) to challenge the reduction of queerness to an individual pathology. I demonstrate that the stylistic shift from Burroughs's prior figuration of queer spectrality in his long-unpublished novel *Queer* (1985) to his experimental novels hinges on affectively enfolding the reader within the text's perverse fantasies. Although interpreted at the time as the uncritical hallucination of a drug addict, I argue that the aesthetics of queer spectrality enable Burroughs to figure queerness as an erotic and political collectivity in a historical moment when such a representation would otherwise be censored as obscene. Whereas Chap. 1 expands the agency of queer critique by looking to the stylistic manifestation of affect, Chap. 2 displaces the priority of academic genealogies for queer reading to glimpse the proliferation of queer hermeneutics that emerge in response to the AIDS crisis. To do so, I examine Samuel Delany's turn to experimental writing in his AIDS novels, *The Tale of Plagues and Carnivals* (1984) and *The Mad Man* (1994).

I argue that experimental writing affords Delany a "para-academic" mode to elaborate a queer hermeneutic that does not seek paranoid mastery but, instead, attends to the affective history of the crisis, particularly the singular convergence of uncertainty, anxiety, and erotic pleasure. Delany ultimately offers queer hermeneutics as an affective inheritance, a means for readers to remain attached to the enduring and unfinished histories of AIDS. Chapter 3 extends the analysis of how queer experimental literature contests academic discourses of reading, focusing in particular on Kathy Acker's rejection of the discourses of deconstruction and poststructural theory. The chapter follows Acker's turn from deconstructive aesthetics toward a sensuous "language of the body," which she hopes will make her work "unreadable" within the increasingly commodified hermeneutic frameworks for postmodern fiction. Looking to *Bodies of Work* (1997) and *In Memoriam to Identity* (1990), where Acker makes this turn, I argue that the languages of the body—in which literature stimulates a masturbatory encounter with queer becoming—strive to recover the critical agency of queer aesthetics within the context of the gentrification of the queer avant-garde. Through her provocation of an affective *becoming-unreadable*, Acker hopes to clear a space for a future community of radical readers and artists to emerge.

In Chap. 4, I move from the margins of cult and para-academic queer experimentation to an experimental writer that has achieved mainstream success, Jeanette Winterson. While often critiqued for her unrepentant sentimentality, I argue that Winterson's "queer exuberance" presses back against the homonormative reduction of queerness to a privatized, consumer identity. Focusing in particular on *Art and Lies* (1994) and *Art Objects* (1995), I demonstrate how Winterson develops a concept of visceral aesthetics, in which the transmission of affect disrupts the identitarian consumer categories (i.e., lesbian fiction, queer writing) that have been mapped onto her fiction. By dynamizing positive affects, Winterson refuses the stigmatization of exuberance as a degraded form of false consciousness or a capitulation to normativity. Instead, Winterson queers exuberance in the hopes of provoking the desire for a more radically relational conception of queerness in her readers. Chapter 5 looks to Eve Kosofsky Sedgwick's experimental memoir *A Dialogue on Love* (1999) as the locus for her development of new practices of queer reading, revealing the unacknowledged influence that queer experimental literature has on queer theory's rediscovery of affective reading. I argue that the memoir's formal composition of permeability illuminates the ethical values that inspire

Sedgwick's late-career shift away from "paranoid reading" to "reparative reading," leading her to redefine queerness as a mode of relational care. In contrast to the idioms of "paranoid" criticism, queer experimental literature offers Sedgwick a pliable form for figuring queer relationality as a mode of agency and becoming that pertains in the face of collective mortality. Finally, in a brief conclusion, I analyze Chuck Palahniuk's controversial performance piece and short story "Guts" (2004), tracing the incipiently social relations that emerge through his figuration of reading as sex. Through this text, I contest the recent equation of affective reading with a "new modesty" in literary criticism, arguing that queer experimental literature immodestly dreams up new forms of belonging, albeit in idioms that will rarely appear critical enough to count as political imagination.

NOTES

1. See, for example, Judith Butler, *Gender Trouble: Feminism and the Subversion of Identity* (New York: Routledge, 2006); Leo Bersani, *Homos* (Cambridge: Harvard University Press, 1995); and Lee Edelman, *No Future: Queer Theory and the Death Drive* (Durham: Duke University Press, 2004).
2. For an alternative approach that embraces the queerness of positive affect, see Michael D. Snediker, *Queer Optimism: Lyric Personhood and Other Felicitous Persuasions* (Minneapolis: University of Minnesota Press, 2009).
3. See Lauren Berlant, *Cruel Optimism* (Durham: Duke University Press, 2011).
4. José Esteban Muñoz, *Cruising Utopia: The Then and There of Queer Futurity* (New York: New York University Press, 2009); Elizabeth Freeman, *Time Binds: Queer Temporalities, Queer Histories* (Durham: Duke University Press, 2010). For an overview of the debate around the "anti-social thesis" in queer theory, see Robert L. Caserio, Lee Edelman, Judith Halberstam, José Esteban Muñoz, and Tim Dean, "The Anti-Social Thesis in Queer Theory," *PMLA* 121, no. 3 (2006): 819–28. For an approach to queer relationality that shares my investment in affect and becoming, albeit from divergent methodological perspectives, see Leo Bersani and Adam Phillips, *Intimacies* (Chicago: The University of Chicago Press, 2008); and Tim Dean, *Unlimited Intimacy: Reflections on the Subculture of Barebacking* (Chicago: The University of Chicago Press, 2009).
5. Michel Foucault, *The History of Sexuality, Vol. 1: An Introduction.* (New York: Vintage, 1990).

6. For a critique of the logic of representation that posits sexuality (and homosexuality in particular) as identity, see Lee Edelman, *Homographesis: Essays in Gay Literary and Cultural Theory* (New York: Routledge, 1994).
7. See, for example, Brian Massumi, *The Parables of the Virtual* (Durham: Duke University Press, 2002).
8. See, for example, Eve Kosofsky Sedgwick, *Touching Feeling: Affect, Pedagogy, Performativity* (Durham: Duke University Press, 2003). I engage with Sedgwick and this debate at length in the introduction.
9. On relational aesthetics, see, for example, Adam Frank, *Transferential Poetics, from Poe to Warhol* (New York: Fordham University Press, 2015); Jennifer Doyle, *Hold It Against Me: Difficulty and Emotion in Contemporary Art* (Durham: Duke University Press, 2013); Jill Bennett, *Empathic Vision: Affect, Trauma, and Contemporary Art* (Stanford: Stanford University Press, 2005); and W.J.T. Mitchell, *What Do Pictures Want?: The Lives and Loves of Images* (Chicago: The University of Chicago Press, 2004). On affect as a readable form without reference to the subject, see especially Eugenie Brinkema, *The Form of the Affects* (Durham: Duke University Press, 2014).
10. Sedgwick, *Touching*, 123–51.
11. Barbara Johnson, "Philology: What is at Stake?" in *On Philology*, ed. Jan Ziolkowski (University Park: The Pennsylvania State University Press, 1999), 29.
12. My claim is that queer experimental literature contests postmodernity from within rather than positing a break or new sequence beyond its social condition. For approaches that explore the aftermath of and new horizons beyond postmodernism, see Irmtraud Huber, *Literature after Postmodernism: Reconstructive Fantasies* (New York: Palgrave Macmillan, 2014); Lee Konstantinou, *Cool Characters: Irony and American Fiction* (Cambridge: Harvard University Press, 2016); *Postmodern/Postwar and After: Rethinking American Literature*, eds. Jason Gladstone, Andrew Hoberek, and Daniel Worden (Iowa City: University of Iowa Press, 2016); and the special issue "After Postmodernism: Form and History in Contemporary American Fiction," *Twentieth Century Literature* 53, no. 3 (2007): 233–393.
13. See, for example, Carter Mathes, *Imagine the Sound: Experimental African American Literature After Civil Rights* (Minneapolis: University of Minnesota Press, 2015); Paul Grimstad, *Experience and Experimental Writing: Literary Pragmatism from Emerson to the Jameses* (Oxford: Oxford University Press, 2015); Alex Houen, *Powers of Possibility: Experimental American Writing Since the 1960s* (Oxford: Oxford University Press, 2012); *The Routledge Companion to Experimental Writing*, eds. Joe Bray, Alison Gibbons, and Brian McHale, (New York: Routledge, 2012); and Natalie Cecire, "Experimentalism by Contact," *Diacritics* 43, no. 1 (2015): 6–35.

14. Anthony Reed, *Freedom Time: The Poetics and Politics of Black Experimental Writing* (Baltimore: Johns Hopkins University Press, 2014).
15. Kathryn Hume, *Aggressive Fictions: Reading the Contemporary American Novel* (Ithaca: Cornell University Press, 2012). See Chap. 3 below for a discussion of queer approaches to the author reader contract. For a queer re-signification of the carrot-on-the-stick narrative of readerly pleasure, see the conclusion.
16. Ibid., 9.
17. Rita Felski, *The Limits of Critique* (Chicago: The University of Chicago Press, 2015), 12.

ACKNOWLEDGMENTS

Gilles Deleuze once said that "we write only at the frontiers of our knowledge, at the border which separates our knowledge from our ignorance and transforms the one into the other. Only in this manner are we resolved to write." Resolve is an important affect, to be sure, but it is unsustainable without community, without relations of support, virtual and real, that can make the thresholds of ignorance bearable, let alone pleasurable and even joyful. I am very grateful for the communities that have enabled me to learn in the transitional space of writing this book.

Queer Experimental Literature began as a dissertation in the Literatures in English department at Rutgers University. Marianne DeKoven was the ideal director, a constant source of encouragement and intellectual inspiration, and I continue to learn from her insights into the feminist and queer politics of experimental writing. My conversations with Elizabeth Grosz about affect, art, and Deleuze were the first provocations for the project, and I am indebted to her generous critical engagement throughout its many stages of development. Richard Dienst always had the right questions to ask that helped push the project forward, and I learned so much from his countless insights into critical theory. John A. McClure's conversations about politics in postmodernity were very influential for me, and I feel lucky to have had his compassionate and enthusiastic voice of support. In addition to my committee, I want to thank David L. Eng, Richard E. Miller, Harriet Davidson, Janet E. Larson, Barbara Balliet, Cheryl L. Clarke, and the Rutgers Women's and Gender Studies Department, which provided a second home for me as a doctoral student. The English department's writing seminars afforded an early forum for exploring the ideas and archives that became central to this book. I want to thank the instructors and participants for their feedback, particularly Emily Bartels, Jonathan Kramnick, John Kucich, David Kurnick, Octavio Gonzalez, Mark DiGiacomo, Sarah Balkin, and Jason Gulya. For their friendship and intellectual engagement, I also want to thank Candice Amich, Anne Keefe, Paul Benzon, Agatha Beins, Michelle Phillips, and Debapriya Sarkar.

The summer I spent at the School of Criticism and Theory at Cornell University was absolutely critical to the development of my thinking on affect and politics. Ann Laura Stoler's seminar on "The Logos and Pathos of Empire" provoked and challenged me in countless ways, and I am grateful to her and to all of the participants for their collaborative thinking. I count myself especially lucky to have met Amber Musser, whose kindness is unmatched, and Jessica Luther, whose work as a feminist, a writer, and an activist inspires me and whose care made a difference.

I am grateful to Haverford College for a postdoctoral fellowship to support the development of this manuscript. I want to thank Debora Sherman, Kristin Lindgren, Paul Farber, Gustavus Stadler, Kimberly Benston, Ken Koltun-Fromm, and Jeremiah Mercurio for their support. I also want to thank the students in my "Sexuality and Narrative" seminar for being wonderful interlocutors.

New Literary History's "Post-Critical Interpretation" seminar at the University of Virginia fundamentally reshaped this project, and I continue to reflect on the conversations and provocations that emerged during the course of our engagement. I want to thank Rita Felski for organizing the seminar and for providing such incisive feedback to the book's introduction. I also want to thank the participants, Dalglish Chew, Patrick Fassenbecker, Matt Flaherty, Nathan K. Hensley, Sarah Tindall Kareem, Kinohi Nishikawa, Julie Orlemanski, Rebekah Sheldon, and Stephen Squibb, for their feedback and collegiality. In particular, I want to thank Nathan K. Hensley for subsequently helping me to clarify the stakes and horizons of the book. Rebekah Sheldon read the manuscript in its entirety, offering countless suggestions for improvement, and I am indebted to her collaborative spirit and boundless insight.

I want to thank the broader community of scholars that have helped me think about the intersections of affective reading, contemporary fiction, and queer theory. Elizabeth Freeman's generosity and brilliance have influenced this project in more ways than I can name. Her feedback to an earlier version of Chap. 5 was essential to the development of the project as a whole, and the insightful, enabling, and generative feedback she provided to the complete manuscript improved the book in every conceivable way. I am grateful to her for modeling new ways to read the politics and erotics of queerness together. Michael D. Snediker has been a wonderful and perspicacious interlocutor on affect and queer aesthetics, and I am particularly grateful to him and Jody Greene for their thoughts on an earlier version of Chap. 5. E.L. McCallum has been a longstanding source of support, and I continue to learn from her astute thinking about queer theory. I am very grateful to the organizers, panel chairs, respondents, and audiences that engaged with various drafts of the book. In particular, I want to thank Ramzi Fawaz, Shanté Paradigm Smalls, Sean Grattan, Kevin Ferguson, Christine Varnado, Imke Meyer, Angus Brown, Charlotta Salmi, Christopher Looby, and Heather Love for their questions and provocations. I also want to thank Dawne McCance and the anonymous readers of an earlier version of Chap. 4 for their insights and suggestions for improvement. Antonio López offered enthusiastic feedback to the project's conception, and his support was absolutely essential to the manuscript finding its way to publication.

The SUNY Cortland community has been crucial to the completion of this project, and I want to thank my colleagues in the English department for their support. In particular, I want to thank the participants in our faculty writing group—Geoffrey Bender, Laura Davies, David Franke, Laura Gathagan, Andrea Harbin, and Matt Lessig—for providing a supportive and enthusiastic space to talk through all the writing blocks. Matt Lessig has been endlessly supportive of my work and of this project in particular. I am grateful to him and to Kim Stone for illuminating conversations about new methodologies in literary studies. Emmanuel S. Nelson's insights into AIDS literature enriched Chap. 2. Denise Knight has been a wonderful faculty mentor, and her kindness and insight made all the difference. Heather Bartlett's collaborations have enriched my thinking about contemporary literature and her cheerleading was essential to the final stretch. I am lucky to call Laura Davies a colleague and a friend—her wisdom, fierce intellect, and enthusiasm have been inspiring and enabling during all the tough days. I also want to thank the community of scholars in the Ithaca area, particularly Nick Salvato, Cary Howie, and Ellis Hanson, for their hospitality and engagement. Finally, I want to thank my students, particularly those in my Spring 2016 seminar on "Sexuality and Contemporary Literature," for their collaborative thinking.

I want to acknowledge the Jacob K. Javits Foundation, the Mellon Foundation, the Rutgers English Department, Haverford College, and

SUNY Cortland for the fellowships and grants that made the comple-
tion of this project possible. The librarians at Ohio State University and
Duke University provided key support to my archival research on William
S. Burroughs and Kathy Acker, respectively. I want to thank Matt Lessig,
Dean Bruce Mattingly, and the Cortland College Foundation for provid-
ing funding in support of this book's subvention.

I want to thank the editors of the *Palgrave Studies in Affect Theory and
Literary Criticism* series, Adam Frank and Joel Faflak, for their support of
boundary-crossing literary criticism. I also want to thank Ryan Jenkins,
Ben Doyle, Allie Bochicchio, and Emily Janakiram at Palgrave for shep-
herding the book along the way. My research assistant, Brooke Hughes,
has improved the manuscript in innumerable ways, and I am grateful for
her dedication, hard work, and enthusiasm. Many thanks to Marie-Pierre
Evans for producing the book's index.

Philip Longo is a wonderful intellectual ally and friend, and our email
exchanges about queer theory, sexuality, and teaching have enriched my
thinking throughout. Megan Paustian has been a source of strength and
friendship during the turbulent years of graduate school and beyond, and I
am so thankful for her warm and compassionate spirit. Dana Goode's conversations not only helped this work to flourish, but also enabled me to keep
going on many difficult days. Rodney Mader taught me so much about the
potentialities of queerness, and our countless conversations about theory,
politics, and culture (over double espressos) have molded my thinking in
more ways that I can name. Carolyn Sorisio was the first person to teach me
that I could have an intellectual life, and words cannot express how grateful
I am for her ongoing engagement and intellectual generosity as a teacher
and a friend. For his endless optimism, late-night conversations, and book-
length letters, I am thankful to Michael Jan. I owe an unpayable debt to
Joshua Crandall, who read and re-read countless drafts of this material and
who listened to my ideas with patience and care long before I understood
them. His relational care can be felt throughout this book. Emily Baroni
has been there through everything and remains the smartest, kindest, and
toughest voice of encouragement, always pointing me toward the horizon
and keeping things in perspective. Toby, Munchkin, and Frida shared naps,
long walks, and kisses every day, teaching me to take breaks and reminding
me that affect has its own languages.

I am indebted to my mother, Debbie Bradway, whose strength and
warmth and love made it possible to survive and whose unflagging support has meant everything to me.

I met Jen Lightfoot in the very early days of this project, and our ongoing conversations in the dive bars of Philadelphia about queerness, fantasy, and art were the foundation for this book. She inspires me every day as an artist and as a partner, and I am so grateful for her foul mouth, sharp wit, and passionate spirit. Throughout the years of anxiety and uncertainty that marked the writing of this book, she has been my home.

Portions of Chap. 4 originally appeared as "Queer Exuberance: The Politics of Affect in Jeanette Winterson's Visceral Fiction" in *Mosaic: A Journal for the Interdisciplinary Study of Literature* 48, no. 1 (March 2015): 183–200. An earlier version of Chap. 5 was originally published as "'Permeable We!': Affect and the Ethics of Intersubjectivity in Eve Sedgwick's *A Dialogue on Love*" in *GLQ: A Journal of Lesbian and Gay Studies*, 19, no.1 (2013): 79–110. 2013. I am grateful to the University of Manitoba and to Duke University Press, respectively, for the permission to reprint this material.

I want to thank Jen Lightfoot for the permission to publish a detail of her artwork, *She Was Her Own Experiment* (2013, Mixed Media on paper, 29" × 38.5"), on the cover.

Contents

1 Naked Lust: Obscene Relationality and the Turn to Queer Experimental Literature   1

2 Reading in Crisis: Queer Hermeneutics as Affective History   51

3 The Languages of the Body: Becoming Unreadable in Postmodernity   103

4 Queer Exuberance: Visceral Reading and the Politics of Positive Affect   145

5 "Permeable We!": Queer Theory's (Re)turn to Reading with Feeling   193

6 Conclusion: The Queerness of Aesthetic Agency   233

Index   247

LIST OF FIGURES

Fig. 1 Alison Bechdel, *Fun Home* (2006)   xlviii
Fig. 2 Alison Bechdel, *Fun Home* (2006)   xlix
Fig. 3 Alison Bechdel, *Fun Home* (2006)   l

INTRODUCTION: UNCRITICALLY QUEER—BAD READING AND THE INCIPIENTLY SOCIAL

At one time or another, everyone has been a bad reader. We have all, in countless ways, faced shame, mockery, or derision for what we read or the way that we read. Such a generalization is warranted because reading is defined through so many proscriptions. Immanently linked to context, the norms of reading idealize "good reading," permissible modes of reading that legitimate us as certain kinds of readerly subjects—cosmopolitan or provincial, juvenile or highbrow, scholarly or trashy, radical or naïve, and so on.[1] The norms of reading correlate to acceptable content: the kinds of books you can display on your coffee table and those you must tuck away under the mattress; the kinds of texts you can cite in a classroom and those you can only whisper about in bed. Although less apparent than subjectivity and content, the norms of reading also circumscribe legitimate modes of interpretation—they establish what practices of reading will get to count as *critical* and under what conditions. These norms operate constantly to condition a text's field of reception and to delimit its horizons of social engagement.[2] Even before we adjudicate an interpretation of a text, these norms precede us, demarcating disciplinary objects, generic boundaries, analytical methods, and relevant sets of data; they presuppose what style or form a text must possess to become readable and, crucially, they dictate how readers should affectively and corporeally relate to the text before them: whether it is acceptable to get lost in reverie, to identify passionately and irrationally, to read with our feet up, so to speak; or whether we must read attentively with sober precision and pencils in hand. The reader's felt relation to the text is often thought to be a subjective response or perhaps a personal choice. Yet affective relations are foundational to the norms of reading. Affect is a visceral means of entraining these norms as unconscious habit, and it is also a metadiscourse for describing the political significance of the event of reading. Indeed, readerly affect stands in for a critical or uncritical orientation to the social world more broadly. An unspoken social imaginary lies behind our felt relations to texts, charting the modes of belonging that must inhere among bodies of texts and the bodies of readers and, by extension, the body politic at large.

When we break the rules of good reading, when we become bad readers, we are labeled queer, stupid, or ill-mannered. Such moments are not individual failures of reading; they signify moments of social transgression. Indeed, these epithets constrict the field of reader relations and the social relations they imply. Allow me to provide an example. Before we descend to the academic basement, where queer experimental literature has so often been marginalized, let us look up momentarily to that canonical bad reader, Victor Frankenstein. Early in *Frankenstein* (1818), Victor arrives at university only to discover that the texts he has read with obsessive interest are hopelessly out of date. When Victor "carelessly" admits his affinity for the alchemists, his professor is shocked.[3] "The professor stared. 'Have you,' he said, 'really spent your time in studying such nonsense?'"[4] In his professor's eyes, Victor has "wasted" his time.[5] His failure to be a good reader marks him as queerly disjointed from progressive time, a nonmodern subject seduced by mysticism "in this enlightened and scientific age."[6] Thus, his professor laments, "Good God! In what desert land have you lived, where no one was kind enough to inform you that these fancies which you have so greedily imbibed are a thousand years old and as musty as they are ancient?"[7] The bad reader is stuck in a Dionysian reverie, ignorantly drunk on ancient texts, wasted in mind and body.[8] The writers in *Queer Experimental Literature* will exploit this very description of bad reading; indeed, they subversively appropriate the discourse of "fancy" to mock the sober rationalism of good reading. Not only do they encourage readers to greedily imbibe their texts, they refuse an economy of reading that discounts the value of delirium. Of course, the professor presupposes this economy to shame his student, lamenting that a "desert land" could exist without a gentle voice of critique to kindly redirect Victor to legitimate fields of knowledge. If the professor stands as a proxy for the modern social world, and a way of belonging to it as a rational subject, then Victor embodies a queer alternative. Indeed, his gluttonous attachment to dead knowledge is, famously, tied to his attachment to dead flesh.[9] In this precise sense, Victor's reader relations are a metonym for his transgressive

orientation to social relations. His unrepentant attachment to bad reading, to decayed ideas and musty texts, intimates modes of belonging that,
in the eyes of the modern subject, will appear to be uncritically queer.

As the professor's shaming attests, narratives about critical reading
derive their authority, at least in part, by legislating the appropriate affective relations that must inhere between texts and readers. Victor's reading
is not bad solely because it is out of date—he has been affectively seduced
into a solipsistic, non-utilitarian scene of fantasy. In this narrative, we can
hear the echoes of future configurations of bad reading, from pornography and pulp fiction to video games and social media. Given the recent
reconsideration of critical reading within literary studies, it is surprising
that more attention has not been paid to the vexed intersection of affect
and the proscriptive norms of reading. To be sure, many critics have pro-
posed new methodologies for reading that contest, rethink, or displace the
hermeneutics of suspicion as the *de facto* mode of cultural interpretation
within literary studies.[10] Yet these methodologies tend to overlook their
own implicit establishment of affective norms for reading, and they rarely
acknowledge their relationship to social contexts beyond the disciplinary
history of the humanities.

Eve Kosofsky Sedgwick stands alone in her path-breaking argument
that the affective relations of critical reading, as conceptualized by queer
theory, are fundamentally shaped by their relationship to sexual politics.
Indeed, Sedgwick located the emergence of paranoid reading alongside
the structures of feeling that predominated for queers and activists during the AIDS crisis. Her turn to reparative reading is inextricable from
her concerns about paranoia becoming entrenched as an affective norm
within queer theory, detached from the lived experience of a younger
generation of queer activists and scholars emerging in the aftermath of
AIDS. Sedgwick's own affirmation of reparative reading was thus attuned
to its agonistic, even dissident, relationship to academic codifications of
critical reading, and it sought to open up new relations of affective and
historical belonging among queer communities through a contextually
specific turn to positive affect. Unfortunately, Sedgwick's heuristic distinction between "paranoid reading" and "reparative reading" has since
ossified into a decontextualized binary. When we debate the relative value
of suspicion or empathy in the abstract, we miss the specific meaning that
paranoid and reparative reading had (and has) for queer communities. But
more importantly, we perpetuate a debate over good and bad modes of

reading without attending to the historical relations of power that made paranoid or reparative reading *queer* in the first place.

This book draws inspiration from Sedgwick's move to locate the affective relations of queer reading within their social and historical contexts. However, I largely put aside Sedgwick's dichotomy of paranoid and reparative reading. I do not reject paranoia and reparation so much as see them as two affective orientations for queer reading among many more that have yet to be acknowledged or explored within literary criticism. Indeed, we will discover a host of queer reading practices that have failed to count as critical within the idioms of critical theory due to their unrepentant investment in affect. To discover these modes of reading, *Queer Experimental Literature* looks beyond academic and disciplinary genealogies of critical reading, turning to the para-academic and non-academic contexts that motivate writers to reconfigure the affective relations of reading.[11] I break, then, with scholars such as Sharon Marcus and Stephen Best, who narrate the turn from symptomatic to affective reading as a largely disciplinary affair. For example, they begin their introduction to surface reading by noting that symptomatic reading enabled "exchanges between [academic] disciplines" and was particularly formative for "a relatively homogeneous group of scholars who received doctoral degrees in either English or comparative literature after 1983."[12] By focusing narrowly on the disciplinary context of literary studies, we miss a heterogeneity of aesthetic experimentations with critical and uncritical reading alike, which have developed alongside of and even in contestation with academic discourses of reading.[13] We have missed these experimentations because, as François Cusset argues, academic culture brings "harsh judgment to bear on any strange or foreign readings" of theoretical discourse.[14] To preserve our authority over "legitimate interpretations," we ignore "felicitous misreading[s]" and "creative, even performative misprision[s]" that constitute a "vast zone in which both political *and* cultural values can be discovered."[15] This book argues that the "felicitous" zones of bad reading in queer experimental literature are acutely responsive to their social contexts and that they work to redraw the parameters of what counts as a critical politics of reading in the postmodern public sphere.

As much as my methodology moves beyond the hermeneutics of suspicion, I do not reject interpretation *tout court*. I agree with Rita Felski that "We should avoid conflating suspicious interpretation with the whole of interpretation, with all the sins of the former being loaded onto the shoulders of the latter."[16] Similarly, we should resist conflating academic modes of interpretation with those fostered by aesthetic objects. Even when an aesthetic object elicits suspicion, we must attend to the specificity of its configuration of and investment in suspicion. Second, and more importantly, I worry that the turn away from interpretation obfuscates the power relations that underlie the affective relations of reading. For example, sociological turns to descriptive reading purport to approach the literary object outside of the narrow gateway of subjectivity. As Heather Love argues, the "depth" of depth hermeneutics derives "not only [from] the hidden structures or causes that suspicious critics reveal" but also from the affective "dimension that critics attempt to produce in their readings, by attributing life, richness, warmth, and voice to texts."[17] Love sees suspicion and empathy as dialectically entwined within literary hermeneutics, not opposed to one another. Taken together, these affective relations attest to what Love calls "an unacknowledged but powerful humanism— that defines literary studies."[18] Not only does this approach share Marcus and Best's privileging of academic formulations of hermeneutics, it also assumes that suspicion and empathy are the only affective relations available for interpretation. Moreover, Love attributes affect to the critic, whose interpretative acumen is either inspired by suspicion or meant to engender empathy. By contrast, *Queer Experimental Literature* asks that we suspend the institutionally sanctioned critic as the originator of the affective relations of reading. Instead, we might attend to the aesthetic object's affective agency—its capacity to foster new relational models for reading. To glimpse this agency, *Queer Experimental Literature* heeds Felski's call to "place ourselves in front of the text, reflecting on what it unfurls, calls forth, makes possible."[19] As we will see, the relations that queer experimental literature calls forth cannot, ultimately, be reduced to the dialectic of suspicion and empathy; this dichotomy fails to account for stupefaction, anxiety, masturbatory pleasure, exuberance, shameless immodesty, and so many other minor affects called forth through queer experimental literature. Rather than impose an affect theory from above, I share Adam Frank's understanding of poetic forms as offering distinct modes of affect theory. His approach enables us to see that the relays of affective and aesthetic "contact can take many forms."[20] This book seeks to be drawn into many different scenes of contact, learning new modes of relationality from the aesthetic object itself.

My other motivation for resisting the turn to description is that it assumes, as Love suggests, that the affective relations of reading are necessarily aligned with humanism. As we will see, queer experimental writers such as William S. Burroughs and Kathy Acker turn to affect to contest humanist models of subjectivity. For them, affect is an asubjective and anti-human force that reveals the irreducible animality of the human.[21] But more broadly, all queer experimental literature rejects the humanist paradigm of reading because it buttresses a heteronormative social imaginary. As Michael Warner argues, liberal humanism privileges a "hierarchy of faculties" that, particularly in the case of critical reading, "elevates rational-critical reflection as the self-image of humanity."[22] This hierarchy of faculties restricts the affective range of reader relations and, by doing so, limits the modes of social agency that are available to queers. For example, Warner observes,

All of the verbs for public agency are verbs for private reading, transposed upward to the aggregate of readers. Readers may scrutinize, ask, reject, opine, decide, judge and so on. Publics can do exactly these things. And nothing else. Publics—unlike mobs or crowds—are incapable of any activity that cannot be expressed through such a verb. Activities of reading that do not fit the ideology of reading as silent, private, replicable decoding—curling up, mumbling, fantasizing, gesticulating, ventriloquizing, writing marginalia, and so on—also find no counterparts in public agency.[23]

Note that the degraded affects of reading extend far beyond suspicion and empathy. The faculties of good reading disavow these queer textual relations and the social bodies that enact them. Reading with feeling might be disclaimed as an uncritical way of relating to culture and society, stripping us of the agency that accrues to rational–critical forms of participation in the public sphere. But, from another angle, it might provide a way to challenge the formation of that public sphere and, moreover, to elaborate alternative, embodied modes of social agency. Indeed, bad readers might purposely *amplify* their affective relations to texts, thereby contesting the hierarchy of faculties that fuses subjects into the public sphere. For Warner, such practices constitute counterpublic discourse—a counterpublic, in his view, implies an alternative social imaginary, wherein public agency is detached from the state.[24] While bad reading undoubtedly implies a non-heteronormative social imaginary, it is crucial to foreground the circuitous and heavily mediated relationship between such interpretative practices and their alternative social horizons. The distance between these affective acts of resistance and their intimations of other forms of belonging is relative. But that distance is always there, built into a text of bad reading, felt deeply and negotiated in complex ways. This distance conditions what

I will refer to as the *incipiently social* dimension of queer experimental literature. These texts actively elicit new structures of relation through the forces of affect; in this sense, the social is literally and viscerally *incipient* in these texts, not simply figured or represented. At the same time, these texts recognize the representational and political strictures that obstruct the wider flourishing of their queer relations beyond the textual encounter. The concept of the *incipiently social* thus foregrounds the conditions of power that make affect viable as a means to contest the heteronormative relations of the liberal-humanist public sphere.

Of course, the distance of bad reading from the legitimately public sphere also enables it to become a meaningful source of nourishment and self-creation for queer communities. Sedgwick hints at this affective agency long before her more famous discussions of paranoid and reparative reading. In *Tendencies*, Sedgwick variably labels her interpretative practices as "perverse" and "ardent" reading, terms that foreground the strikingly erotic investments of bad reading.[25] "[B]ecoming a perverse reader," Sedgwick explains, enabled her to locate "sites where the meanings didn't line up tidily with each other" and to "invest those sites with fascination and love."[26] Sedgwick depicts bad reading as an active means of "smuggling" texts, such as "genre movies, advertising, comic strips," and other forms of popular culture.[27] Smuggling means remaining attached, like Victor, to texts degraded as uncritically queer within the public sphere, investing them with affect and value. Arguably, one of the primary successes of queer literary criticism has been to smuggle a range of texts, including many of the ones discussed in this book, into intellectual discourse, enabling them to matter even as they are received as obscene, silly, ephemeral, or marginal.[28] At the same time, Sedgwick stresses that bad reading enables "survival" in a homophobic culture because the affective relations to a text's meaning are strangely queer. She writes,

> The need I brought to books and poems was hardly to be circumscribed, and I felt I knew I would have to struggle to wrest from them sustaining news of the world, ideas, myself, and (in various senses) my kind. The reading practices founded on such basic demands and intuitions had necessarily to run against the grain of the most patent available formulae for young people's reading and life—against the grain, often, of the most accessible voices even in the texts themselves.[29]

Sedgwick's impacted phrasing here, especially in the first sentence, points up the mediated, complex distance between bad reading and social agency.

"I felt I knew I would have to struggle to wrest" is such a bizarre grammatical construction precisely because it signals a confused relationship
between public and private, self and other, affect and knowledge, certainty
and uncertainty, present and (conditional) future. Reading has become a
"wresting" of news, and it partakes in the classical formula for the hermeneutics of suspicion, reading "against the grain." Yet, Sedgwick observes
that "becoming a perverse reader was never a matter of condescension to
texts, rather of the surplus charge of my trust in them to remain powerful,
refractory, and exemplary."[30] Even as Sedgwick herself performs a mode
of hermeneutic agency, the text possesses its own power of refraction.
Indeed, the event of reading cannot be easily circumscribed to either the
reader or the text because both are figured as permeable and plural. Here,
Sedgwick offers a figure for a mode of bad reading that places itself *in
relation* to the text, not insisting on the critic's interpretative mastery or
priority over the text.

Sedgwick does not historicize her experience of bad reading beyond
gesturing in to its general importance to her "generation" of queer critics.[31] *Queer Experimental Literature* picks up this unexplored terrain by
locating bad reading within key conflicts around the representation of
queer relationality within the postwar period. By doing so, I provide more
specificity to Sedgwick's suggestion that bad reading challenges heteronormativity. Undoubtedly, heteronormativity is a motivating cause and
critical target for all of the constructions of bad reading in this book. Yet,
heteronormativity complexly intersects with the power relations of race,
class, and gender, as well as emerging forces of biopower and homonormativity throughout the postwar period. Thus, I offer a more contextually
bound approach that locates singular formations of bad reading against
the specific configurations of power that queer experimental writers confront. Such an approach provides a sharper sense of how and why reading
has been—and continues to be—a volatile site of symbolic contestation
for queer culture. Indeed, this book demonstrates that hetero- and homonormativity naturalize themselves, at least in part, through a discourse of
reading that fuses interpretative relations into legitimate forms of erotic
contact and political collectivity. By eliciting uncritical affective responses
in readers, queer experimental literature thus strikes at the disembodied
model of critical reading and its heteronormative social imaginary. They
use experimental form to position readers and texts in a viscerally relational circuit, in which the transmission of affect engenders alternative
modes of social belonging. To lay the conceptual groundwork for this

affective politics, I will now turn to recent debates over affective reading to demonstrate why literary affect must be seen as a creative and visceral force of becoming, not merely a rhetorical trope or a psychological projection of the reader.

THE POLITICS OF LITERARY AFFECT

How does reading make us feel? For some time, literary studies has avoided this question. New Criticism famously divested itself of the problem of readerly feeling by rejecting the "affective fallacy."[32] The critique of the affective fallacy discounted the experience, feelings, and responses of readers to a text, thereby protecting literary criticism's apparent objectivity in its aesthetic evaluations. Reader-response criticism made a provocative challenge to the orthodoxies of New Criticism. As Jane Tompkins argues, reader-response directed scholarly interest back toward the reader's engagement with the text. Reader-response critics "examine[d] authors' attitudes toward their readers, the kinds of readers various texts seem to imply, the role actual readers play in the determination of literary meaning, the relation of reading conventions to textual interpretation, and the status of the reader's self."[33] Yet, as this research agenda suggests, reader-response criticism never foregrounded affect as a central facet of the reader relation. For example, Stanley Fish prioritized the way the reader's response to the text produces its meaning. Despite his use of the phrase "affective criticism," Fish conceived of the reader's response as "more than the range of feelings (what Wimsatt and Beardsley call 'the purely affective reports')," encompassing "*any and all* of the activities provoked by a string of words."[34] If the critic must "take into account all that has happened (in the reader's mind)," how can affect be distinguished from or related to the semiotic production of meaning? Insofar as affect is a force that inhabits a threshold between subjective and objective, can we conceive of the *text's* affect without attributing it solely to the reader's mind or body? Because Fish characteristically included all cognitive events within the category of response, affect remained an opaque and undertheorized aspect of reader relations.[35]

The advent of affect theory and the broader "turn" to affect in the humanities has subsequently created new opportunities for understanding literary and cultural affect.[36] Scholars such as Martha Nussbaum, Brian Massumi, Charles Altieri, Derek Attridge, and Sianne Ngai resuscitated affect as a dynamic aspect of the event of reading, and each has argued for affect's social significance, refusing to circumscribe aesthetic feeling to the realm of the merely subjective.[37] However, there remains an unacknowledged tendency among some affective critics to prioritize a specific literary form as the ideal mode for transmuting literary affect into a socially valuable force. My conception of bad reading redresses this problem by foregrounding the norms of reading as well as their implicitly heteronormative social imaginary. Yet bad reading also pluralizes the types of becomings that readerly affect can be said to elicit. As such, it presses back against the tendency to idealize a single mode of social relation or political responsibility as the endgame of affective reading. Moreover, it does not idealize a sole literary form as the objective correlative for affective reading or queer reading more generally. As such, bad reading clears a conceptual space for us to confront queer experimental literature on its own terms, attending to the becomings unleashed by its singular compositions of affect and form.

The work of Martha Nussbaum provides an apt example of the tendency to map affect onto the norms of good reading and a specific literary form. Drawing on philosophies of emotion from Adam Smith and Aristotle, Nussbaum valorizes empathy in readers because it leads us to "form bonds of identification and sympathy" with characters that express "certain hopes, fears, and general human concerns."[38] Nussbaum subsequently champions the nineteenth-century realist novel because it elicits an appropriate combination of sympathetic identification and impartial judgment that is "highly relevant to citizenship."[39] Given her investment in sympathy, Nussbaum calls for the field of affect to be "carefully circumscribed," praising the "cultivation of *appropriate emotions*" to form an engaged citizenry.[40] Here Nussbaum discounts the possibility that inappropriate emotions and ugly feelings might, in some contexts, have visceral, subjective, and social value.[41] But more importantly, she does not account for how literature stimulates affects outside of subjective identification. Only narratives that represent concrete worlds with realistically individuated characters signify, in her model, a productive fusion of literary affect with social imagination. This claim results from Nussbaum's privileging literary forms that can be mapped onto the ideology of liberal humanism. For example, while Nussbaum admits that music possesses an "emotional expressiveness" akin to the novel, she claims that it is "dreamlike and indeterminate in a way that limits its role in public deliberation."[42] By discarding non-representational, experimental, and postmodern aesthetics (those that are "dreamlike and indeterminate"), Nussbaum concomitantly ignores how writers might elicit queerer modes of relation that counter liberalism and its self-image of public deliberation.[43]

To combat the liberal model of readerly sympathy, one might argue that the event of literature is properly understood as a deconstructive event that undoes codified categories of political meaning.[44] This is precisely the model championed by critics such as Attridge. While following in the footsteps of reader-response's vision of reading as an event, he instead conceives of this event in terms of Levinasian and Derridean ethics.[45] For example, Attridge argues that

> the formally innovative work, the one that most estranges itself from the reader, makes the most sharply challenging (which is not to say the most profound) ethical demand. ... To respond to the demand of the literary work as the demand of the other is to attend to it as a unique event whose happening is a call, a challenge, an obligation: understand how little you understand me, translate my untranslatability, learn me by heart and thus learn the otherness that inhabits the heart.[46]

Estrangement, disorientation, and surprise—these are the affective jolts that otherness engenders, thereby breaking open the codified structures of identity and relationality that are presupposed by liberal humanism. The reader does not imaginatively empathize and thereby understand; instead, readers are overtaken by the other and must respond by confronting the limits of their understanding. Note that Attridge maps the untranslatable demand of the other onto the "formally innovative" literary object, which similarly challenges "all those carefully applied codes and conventions" that readers typically bring to a work.[47] As much as I share Attridge's investment in the immanence of reading, I am concerned about the correlation of estrangement with a privileged set of aesthetic protocols. Not only does this move limit the field of affect to one tone (estrangement), it enshrines modernist aesthetics as the most ethically demanding of literary forms.[48] But more problematically, the emphasis on deconstructive estrangement leads Attridge to assert a binary between so-called "literary instrumentalism" and the singularity of literature's ethical demand. Critiquing feminist and Marxist criticism, among other politically-oriented methodologies, Attridge claims that literary instrumentalism approaches a text "with the hope or the assumption that it [a text] can be instrumental in furthering an existing project, and responding to it in such a way as to test, or even produce, that usefulness."[49] Putting aside his reduction of these modes of criticism and their own considerations of these issues, Attridge does not provide a way of thinking about literary texts that might actually desire to provoke so-called instrumental political effects—how, in other words, such texts might utilize affect to elaborate the politics of feminism or queerness.

Despite their attentiveness to the dynamic imbrication of reading and affect, then, these approaches define themselves as good reading in opposition to a degraded mode of bad reading. They subordinate the queerness of the reader's body, particularly its perverse openness to becoming in the event of reading, and they circumscribe the event of reading to appropriate affects—only certain compositions of feeling and aesthetic form signify as critical. Is there, then, a theoretical precedent for bad reading that would enable us to explore the possibilities enabled by less respectable affects, including those that touch on the abject pleasures of queer eroticism? Psychoanalysis would seem to provide an affirmative answer. After all, Freud famously theorized that culture sublimates unconscious desire, and contemporary queer and feminist critics, in particular, have turned to Freud to theorize the queerness of desire.[50] Despite my respect for these approaches, I part with Freudian psychoanalysis precisely because it tends to collapse the qualitative specificity of affects into the instinctual drives. As Jean Laplanche and Jean-Bertrand Pontalis note, Freud conceives of affect as the "qualitative expression of the quantity of instinctual energy and of its fluctuations."[51] Indeed, Freud insists that the "instincts are *all qualitatively alike* and owe the effect they produce only to the quantities of excitation accompanying them."[52] In other words, an affect is simply the "subjective transposition" of a certain amount of physiological energy.[53] This conceit necessarily draws attention away from the qualitative specificity of an affect—whether happiness, sadness, annoyance, or anger—because the feeling is a surface effect of a more fundamental (and apparently more interesting) libidinal conflict. In Sedgwick's words, "The nature or quality of the affect itself, seemingly, is not of much more consequence than the color of the airplane used to speed a person to a destination."[54] Following Sedgwick and Frank's work on Silvan Tomkins, I similarly disarticulate affect from the drives to foreground the qualitative singularity of affects.[55] Rather than reducing affect into a symptom that must be decoded, we can encounter the affective relations composed through an aesthetic object on their own terms.[56]

At the same time, my approach to bad reading does not solely draw on phenomenological descriptions of affect because phenomenology misses the dynamic, asubjective becoming fomented through reader relations.[57] Because it presumes an intentional perceiving subject, phenomenology misses the unconscious and non-conscious forces of affect. For this reason, my primary theoretical reference points in *Queer Experimental Literature* are the work of Gilles Deleuze and Félix Guattari and philosophers, such as Elizabeth Grosz, that have fostered an encounter between Deleuze and Guattari's concepts and feminist and queer theory,[58] This constellation of thinkers enables us to reframe reader relations as affective events or becomings. As Grosz argues, art unleashes a "pure intensity, a direct impact on the body's nerves and organs."[59] In Deleuze and Guattari's words, art is "a being of sensation and nothing else."[60] Like many post-structural thinkers, Deleuze and Guattari disarticulate art from subjectivity. Yet they are unique in conceiving the work as an autonomous field of sensation that is neither an expression of an authorial subject nor the projection of a perceiving reader.[61] These sensations exist autonomously in the materiality of aesthetic composition, and they cannot be reduced to the human subject. Indeed, Deleuze and Guattari see art as a means to "wrest the percept from perceptions of objects and the states of a perceiving subject, to wrest the affect from affections as the transition from one state to another: to extract a bloc of sensations."[62] This bloc of sensations subsequently "undoes the triple organization of perceptions, affections, and opinions," which constitute a perceiving subject as a unified entity.[63] In art, then, "Affects are no longer feelings or affections; they go beyond the strength of those who undergo them."[64] Here Deleuze and Guattari echo their more famous concept of the body without organs insofar as aesthetic affect points toward a non-centralized and non-hierarchical body, a body at the threshold of becoming. In Deleuze's words, art intimates this "more profound and almost unlivable" power—namely, the chaotic affective forces that underlie, constitute, and dissipate the "lived body" that phenomenology assumes as its center.[65] Literary affect thus pre-exists the reader's organization into a formalized subject, and it composes (and recomposes) the reader's body in a dynamic becoming.[66]

This conception of affective becoming enables us to redress two problems of reader-response criticism. First, we can now prioritize affect as a unique force in the event of reading, irreducible to the signifier. As Brian Massumi notes, "Reading, however cerebral it may be, does not entirely think out sensation."[67] He argues that reading enfolds "muscular, tactile, and visceral sensations of attention [which] are incipient perceptions. ... In the experience of reading, conscious thought, sensation, and all the modalities of perception fold into and out of each other."[68] Here reading becomes synesthetic contact, cross-hatched by visual, auditory, and tactile sensations that are not simply attributable to a representation within the text.[69] In Grosz's words, "Artworks are not so much to be read, interpreted, deciphered as responded to, touched, engaged, intensified. Artworks don't signify (or, if they signify, they signify only themselves); instead, they make sensation real."[70] Now we can also radically expand the affects catalyzed by the literary object as well as the range of legitimate "responses" that readers might have to them. Indeed, we cannot privilege empathy or estrangement or suspicion because the artwork foments its own bloc of sensations, which demand to be engaged as forces in their own right. In fact, as Grosz suggests, the artwork's sensations may not even exist yet, except as virtual or incipient possibilities to be materialized and made sensible. Thus, we cannot circumscribe, in advance, which affects will be the most "critical" or even the most "queer" because the radical potentiality of aesthetic affect is always immanent. Second, we can dispense with the presumption that the reader precedes the text. Indeed, many queer experimental writers imagine the text and reader as inhabiting a pre-formalized relational field—a plane of immanence—where neither has fixed boundary, transcendental identity, or hierarchical priority. The plane of immanence offers a view of reader relations that cannot presume an ideal telos for becoming, particularly a telos that culminates in a good reader. On the contrary, as Deleuze writes, "To become is not to attain a form (identification, imitation, Mimesis) but to find the zone of proximity, indiscernibility, or indifferentiation where one can no longer be distinguished from *a* woman, *an* animal, or *a* molecule—neither imprecise nor general, but unforeseen and nonpreexistent, singularized out of a population rather than determined in a form."[71] Note here that becoming is *specific* insofar as it implies a singular convergences of forces within the zone of proximity. To grasp the interventions and relational potentialities fostered within queer experimental literature, then, we must trace the specific zones of proximity that each text elaborates through its own composition of the affective relations of reading.

I must make an important caveat, however, about this conceptual tradition because it is a recurrent site of confrontation throughout the subsequent chapters. In my view, some interpretations of Deleuze and Guattari lay too much stress on affect as a necessarily radical force of deterritorialization. Deleuze himself declares, referencing D. H. Lawrence, that the "highest aim of literature" is "to escape … the wall of dominant significations" that "[w]e are always pinned against."[72] For Deleuze, the most problematic of these strictures is the subject: "[W]e are always sunk in the hole of our subjectivity, the black hole of our Ego."[73] The consequence of this view is often that any association of affect with subjectivity—particularly terms such as feeling and emotion—is perceived as an obstacle, rather than a potential contributor, to becoming. The subjective/non-subjective binary is particularly striking in Massumi's work when he argues, for example, that

> emotion is a subjective content, the sociolinguistic fixing of the quality of an experience which is from that point onward defined as personal. Emotion is qualified intensity, the conventional, consensual point of insertion of intensity into semantically and semiotically formed progressions, into narrativizable action-reaction circuits, into function and meaning. It is intensity owned and recognized.[74]

In Massumi's narrative, emotion is the qualitative glue that affixes us to convention whereas affect escapes subjectivity and, by extension, its social inscription. Although emotion "*capture[s]*" affect, the latter "has always and again escaped."[75] The rhetoric of "capture," "escape," and "[re]confinement" establishes a sharp dichotomy between emotion and affect, placing them in a kind of Gothic plot, and it returns us to a view of affect as an unqualified disruptive force, akin to the Freudian instincts. Indeed, to discuss actual(ized) affects such as enjoyment, interest, or rage seems to sap the radical challenge the affect poses to subjective codification. But more importantly, Massumi's language implies that affect lies outside of signification rather than relationally enfolded with it. Affect undoubtedly puts pressure on the orders of grammar and syntax—but not simply to destroy them. Rather, queer experimental writers seek a range of new idioms for affect to be spoken, and these affective idioms feed forward into new relations between words, bodies, and the social field. Therefore, I foreground the permeable and non-dualistic thresholds that modulate between affect and signification.[76]

For this reason, I also part with Deleuze's emphasis on subjective "escape" as the aim of literature. As much as queer experimental literature contests the category of the subject, its investments lie elsewhere. In particular, it turns to affect to stimulate new relations of queerness, relations that might ultimately become inhabitable or realizable as a future. As Grosz suggests, "Unlike politics, sensation does not promise or enact a future different than the present, it en-forces, impacts, a premonition of what might be directly on the body's nerves, organs, muscles. The body is opened up now to other forces and becomings that it might also affirm in and as the future."[77] In other words, the affects of art do not represent or signify the future so much as open the body to a number of potential and incipient futures.[78] José Esteban Muñoz similarly touches on the conjunction of queer relationality and futurity when he affirms "Taking ecstasy with one another, in as many ways as possible, can perhaps be our best way of enacting a queer time that is not yet here but nonetheless potentially dawning. Taking ecstasy with one another is an invitation, a call, to a then-and-there, a not-yet-here."[79] Recalling the intoxicating delirium of bad reading that leaves Victor Frankenstein "wasted," Muñoz's call to take ecstasy stresses the intrinsic relationality of queer affect—the joy of taking ecstasy *together* and becoming taken with one another (and another, and another) in an endless social horizon. While I share the Deleuzian conception of affect as a force, I tend to use the phrase *affective relation* instead because it captures the queer relationality of affect—its perverse tendency to spread beyond the subject's calculation or control—that Muñoz so evocatively highlights.[80] At the same time, I intend for *affective relation* to highlight the complex imbrication of affective and social relations. After all, as Antonio Damasio observes, "There is growing evidence that feelings, along with the appetites and emotions that most often cause them, play a decisive role in social behavior."[81] I do not offer a master theory to define this decisive role. Rather, I track how and why queer experimental writers see affect and sociality as related and how they hope to relate these forces otherwise.

I will now explain why queer experimental literature is an apt archive for us to launch this inquiry into the affective relations of reading. I argue for a queerer and more historically located conception of experimental writing. This approach will enable us to see how the fantastical aesthetics of queer experimental literature intimate incipiently social modes of queer belonging against hetero- and homonormative reductions of sexuality to the sphere of the subject.

THE QUEERNESS OF EXPERIMENTAL LITERATURE: FANTASY AND ADHESIVE EROTICISM

More than any other domain of criticism, French feminism has been attentive to experimental writing as an archive that expresses and dynamizes the affects of the sexed body. Theorists such as Hélène Cixous, Luce Irigaray, Julia Kristeva, and Monique Wittig famously articulated and debated the concept of *écriture féminine* to signify how, in Nancy K. Miller's words, "the female *body*, with its peculiar drives and rhythms, inscribes itself as text."[82] As Miller's word "peculiar" suggests, *écriture féminine* sought to define the sexual difference of women's writing—to understand how, precisely, women's writing inscribes the corporeal specificity of the female body and how, in so doing, this writing breaks apart phallogocentric models of signification. As French feminism was challenged by poststructural feminist and queer theory, *écriture féminine* came under increasing scrutiny for its essentialist presumption of a biological foundation for sexual difference, which many rightly saw as ignoring the historically and politically constructed category of "woman." It was also subsequently critiqued, as Miller notes, for "privileg[ing] a textuality of the avant-garde" as the primary signifier for women's writing.[83] This privileging obscures the plurality of women's aesthetic traditions across time, but it also betrays an elitist bias toward *difficulty* as the basis of a radical feminist aesthetics.[84] *Queer Experimental Literature* undoubtedly follows in these critiques: I hope to expand the range of bodies and sexualities that experimental aesthetics can be said to "express"; I stress the historical and political construction of queerness and affect alike; and I insist that, in the postmodern era, experimental writing cannot be reduced to the aesthetics of the avant-garde. However, I want to acknowledge my debt to the philosophical ground that French feminism charted in its effort to conceive of signification in anti-patriarchal and affective terms. Not only has this tradition been a forerunner in theorizing the volatile forces of corporeality, it has also been a source of abiding interest and explicit reference—however ambivalent—for many of the writers I discuss below.

Given that experimental writing has been read as a paradigmatic mode of *écriture féminine*, permit me to qualify how this book reframes experimentalism in relationship to the politics of queer aesthetics. First, I do not presume that the affects "expressed" by experimental writing are necessarily anti-patriarchal. For Kristeva, the semiotic temporarily liberates the sensuous pre-Oedipal body from its suturing into the phallocentric symbolic order.[85] While William S. Burroughs's delirious stylistics could be read as a pre-Oedipal language, for example, his fictions are avowedly patriarchal; indeed, Burroughs hopes to activate a homoerotic libido untethered from sexual difference, and he does so through a misogynistic narrative that eliminates woman and femininity altogether. We will discover a queerer politics of form in Burroughs's work that operates in tension with this ideology, but it is important to acknowledge that experimental stylistics are not inherently anti-patriarchal, even if they unleash anti-Oedipal affects. Second, I break the linkage of experimental writing with the avant-garde.

In my view, the concept of the avant-garde should not be conflated with a style but reserved for signifying a community of writers and artists operating within specific historical circumstances. To be sure, some of the writers in *Queer Experimental Literature* are in conversation with one another, such as Burroughs and Acker, Acker and Winterson, and Delany and Acker.[86] But taken together, queer experimental literature does not constitute an avant-garde in any traditional sense. In fact, we will see writers, particularly Acker, distressed at the *absence* of a queer avant-garde, which has been gentrified by the forces of commodification and homonormativity in the neoliberal era. Finally, I resist the equation of experimental writing with a specific set of stylistic moves that can be identified transhistorically.[87] Rather than define "experimental" in formalist terms, then, I use the term as a heuristic to construct a genealogy of writers that share a common conception of form—namely, that deformations of narrative prose can expose reading as a social construction and an affective discipline.[88] The obstructions to sense making in these texts thus call for a contextual approach that locates a writer's turn to experimentation against the social norms that legislate the protocols for representing and interpreting sexuality in a given context.[89]

This historical approach helps us to suspend the narrative that experimental writing primarily offers a politics of anarchism.[90] Exemplifying this view, Kathryn Hume criticizes Acker for expressing "anguish over patterns of oppression" while offering "few suggestions for changing them, other than letting our impulses rip and refusing to obey social rules. ... Revolution may be an ultimate goal, but she offers no blueprint."[91] While queer experimental literature refuses or cannot represent blueprints, this does not mean that it fails to offer any intimation of new social relations. Indeed, as Elizabeth Freeman argues, queer experimental aesthetics engender "glimpses of an otherwise-being that is unrealizable as street activism or as blueprint for the future."[92] In this sense, the affective relations forged through experimental aesthetics are not directly or mimetically realizable as politics. Yet they nonetheless create what Anthony Reed calls a "hiatus of unrecognizability [that] can spur new thought and new imaginings, especially the (re)imagining of collectivities and intellectual practices."[93] In queer experimental literature, this hiatus is paired with a thoroughgoing commitment to the most degraded of affects. Thus, these texts will often appear to be insufficiently concerned with the social world. Their flights into fantasy may read as a debased narcissism or a solipsistic withdrawal into the personal. However, as Jennifer Doyle argues, "The rhetorical deployment of the personal and the emotional should not be assumed

to be a retreat into an ahistorical, apolitical self; such explicit turns to emotion may in fact signal the politicization, the historicization of that self and
of the feelings through which that self takes shape in relation to others."[94]
At the very moments, then, when queer experimental literature appears
to retreat from the legibly social world, its ineffable relations of bad reading might also be advancing outward, in a newly politicized threading
together of affective and social relations.

As a corollary to expanding the politics of experimental literature
beyond anarchism, I also wish to broaden the aesthetic politics of queerness itself.[95] Scholars such as Teresa de Lauretis, Leo Bersani, Lee Edelman,
Tim Dean, and Kevin Ohi argue that the force of queerness can be most
palpably felt through its disruption of representation.[96] For example, Ohi
identifies the queerness of Henry James's style in terms of a "radical anti-
sociality that seeks to unyoke sexuality from the communities and identities—gay or straight—that would tame it, a disruption that thwarts efforts
to determine political goals according to a model of representation."[97]
Echoing the imagery of Edelman, Ohi describes this disruptive force as
the "*corrosive* effect of queerness ... on received forms of meaning, representation, and identity."[98] I share the resistance to thinking of queerness as identity, and my approach to aesthetic becoming converges with
Ohi's Deleuzian-inspired critique of mimetic conceptions of literary form.
However, I part with the emphasis on anti-social *corrosion* as the primary
or most critical force of queerness. In addition to corrosion, queerness
also offers an *adhesive* modality.[99] In the next chapter, for example, we will
see the queer adhesion of bodies as they become dispersed, recombined,
and stuck together in ecstatically spectral blobs. In the final chapter, we
will explore what Sedgwick calls the "dissolvent relationality of [Buddhist]
pedagogy," which unglues the fixed identities of master and student and
diffuses them into newly permeable relations of bodies, affects, and surfaces.[100] Given queer experimental literature's adhesive compositions, I
prefer to stress its investment in the queerness of *eroticism* rather than
the queerness of *desire*, which has been so influential for queer theory.
Elaborating the distinction between these terms, Freeman explains that

> desire is a form of belief in the referential object that the subject feels s/he
> lacks and that would make him or her whole. ... Erotics, on the other hand,
> traffics less in belief than in encounter, less in damaged wholes than in intersec-
> tions of body parts, less in loss than in novel possibility (will this part fit into
> that one? what's my gender if I do this or that to my body?)[101]

Note the *experimental* nature of queer eroticism—its suspension of the subject's grasping for meaning to open up an event of corporeal contact and transformation. In queer becoming, as Freeman depicts it, the body is more a collection of bodies and body parts whose connective possibilities can be played with and curiously reimagined. Likewise, this assemblage of bodies is not subordinated to a dialectic of subject and object or self and other. This speculative dialectic gives way to a different kind of speculation—a playful imagination or fabulation of non-exclusive potentialities. As Freeman insists, "*artifice is part of the pleasure*: the fetishistic belief in the lost object is less important than the titillation of 'but all the same...'"[102] Here the aesthetic is irreducibly enmeshed in the scene of queer eroticism—the aesthetic is not only an agency for figuring and coordinating eroticism; it is also available to be erotically invested and drawn into surface contact with the assemblage of bodies. The titillation of "but all the same" is a visceral registration of the pull of queer relationality, of a body's potential to become differently stuck together with other bodies, body parts, and body politics.

Throughout *Queer Experimental Literature*, I conceive of "fantasy" as an aesthetic idiom for the "but all the same" of adhesive becoming. In this respect, I break with the predominately Lacanian understanding of fantasy within queer theory.[103] This tradition tends to model fantasy on the paradigm of the subject, and it critiques fantasy for mystifying the subject's incoherence, thereby preserving a normative social order. For example, Edelman argues that fantasy is "[t]he *central prop and underlying agency of futurism, fantasy alone* endows reality with fictional coherence and stability, which seems to guarantee that such reality, the social world in which we take our place, will still survive when we do not."[104] Here fantasy is invariably a fantasy of the future, a single and monolithic future, which is, in fact, an image of an "Imaginary past" that promises to satisfy the subject's narcissistic desire.[105] In Edelman's narrative, fantasy is the *sole* agency of social reproduction, and it offers no resistant or queer possibilities; indeed, queerness is radically opposed to fantasy, a force that rends apart the figural coherence of the subject and its concomitant desire for reproductive futurity. By contrast, queer experimental literature does not model fantasy on the subject and it does not offer its fantastical figurations as promissory notes of desire. In Deleuze's words, "[F]abulation—the fabulating function—does not consist in imagining or projecting an ego. Rather, it attains these visions, it raises itself to these becomings and powers."[106] For these texts, fantasy functions more as a figural scene to experiment with

and usher in new relations of the possible and the impossible.[107] To borrow Deleuze and Guattari's phrase, these texts use the idiom of fantasy to
"express another possible community and to forge the means for another
consciousness and another sensibility."[108] As they note in their analysis of
Franz Kafka, a minor literature is often "affected with a high coefficient of
deterritorialization," which for Kafka "marks the impasse that bars access
to writing for the Jews of Prague and turns their literature into something
impossible—the impossibility of not writing, the impossibility of writing in
German, the impossibility of writing otherwise."[109] In this sense, the use of
fantasy within queer experimental literature is neither a means to salve the
wounds of subjective incoherence nor a license to imagine desire liberated
from any censure, law, or social order. On the contrary, fantasy is an idiom
to grapple with the relations of power that demarcate the social possibilities
of queerness—that, in some contexts, make queerness altogether impossible. These texts do not arrest the relations between fantasy and reality,
between the virtual and the actual, because to do so would falsely close the
gap between what exists, and what could exist, and what is not allowed to
exist, let alone be collectively desired. The oscillation between these temporal states—or, more precisely, the aesthetic performance of that oscillation
and our affective contact with it—expresses a fidelity to a becoming that
queer experimental literature hopes to engender in readings yet to come.

Of course, fantasy is easy to dismiss as narcissism. Many of the texts that
I consider have been labeled as uncritical precisely because of their unrepentant investment in staging queer reading as an encounter with solipsistic fantasy. Therefore, it is important to recall that, as Valerie Rohy explains,
queer reading is "always ambivalent: what can appear as narcissistic mir-
roring or self-affirmation in fact contributes to the production of queer
subjectivity, and the queer subjectivity that may seem self-invented is never
free."[110] Here the readerly subject operates in a productive relation to
power, but, as Rohy notes, queer reading also branches out beyond the
subject into a perverse circuit of relation. In her words, "[T]he solitary
business of queer research touches circuits of seduction and exchange. ...
The scene of reading helps one know oneself in part, it seems, through
knowing others."[111] This horizon of virtual contact broaches the incipiently social dimension of bad reading that queer experimental literature
hopes to materialize. In the final section, I underscore how the literary
imagination of queer sexuality in the postwar period emerges through
these affective intimations of relationality.

THE LITERACY OF SEXUALITY

This introduction began with an exemplary bad reader who enters the university and meets shame for his readerly attachments. It seems appropriate, then, to conclude with a reader who also attends the university but, unlike Victor Frankenstein, discovers incipiently social attachments, which are intimated through the affective relations of her bad reading. In Alison Bechdel's graphic memoir *Fun Home* (2006), Alison attends literature courses that permit the analysis of sexuality in canonical works such as *Heart of Darkness*.[112] Yet the professors insist that a good reading is a psychoanalytic reading, modeled on the Freudian interpretations of symbols (see Fig. 1). Of course, this interpretative method restricts reading to a strictly heteronormative model of sexuality. But more importantly, Alison finds it boring—good reading, in this context, is reading for correspondence, in which only one type of reference is acknowledged as legitimate. Regarding her professor's similar interpretation of Joyce, Alison wonders, "Once you grasped that *Ulysses* was based on *The Odyssey*, was it really necessary to enumerate every last point of correspondence?"[113] Reading for past correspondence obstructs reading for future connections; it arrests the generative indeterminacy of the text, leaving no room for readers to encounter the text immanently on its own terms or to practice reading as a creative or even an irreverent activity.[114] As an act of resistance, and in search of an alternative archive of eroticism, Alison becomes an increasingly bad reader. Indeed, she procrastinates reading *Ulysses* and trolls the library

Fig. 1   Alison Bechdel, *Fun Home* (2006)

Fig. 2   Alison Bechdel, *Fun Home* (2006)

for texts on homosexuality, lesbianism, and feminism. When her father, Bruce, asks if she is reading anything "good," she demurs (see Fig. 2).[115] Retrospectively, Alison jokes, "If only I'd had the foresight to call this an independent reading. 'Contemporary and Historical Perspectives on Homosexuality' would have had quite a legitimate ring."[116] Here Bechdel underlines the historically contextual distinction between good and bad reading, which is defined by its relationship to institutions of power and their codification of hermeneutic legitimacy. Now, these books would count as good reading, particularly in an academic context of gender and sexuality studies. But then, these texts were shameful and inadmissible within the scene of the classroom.

Yet through her contact with bad reading, Alison's relation to the university shifts, and she begins to experience queerness as a mode of relationality. In this respect, *Fun Home* restages the coming-out narrative as a literacy narrative, in which the affects of reading provoke new possibilities for belonging. Initially, Alison notes, "My realization at nineteen that I was a lesbian came about in a manner consistent with my bookish upbringing. A revelation not of the flesh, but of the mind."[117] Here the acquisition of a sexual identity derives from a putatively rational and disembodied practice of reading. But *Fun Home* immediately undermines the distinction between revelations of flesh and mind. For example, we see a number of images of Alison masturbating while reading, which suggests that the textual and sexual are not merely entwined through discourse but also through the experience of pleasure. Alison qualifies her masturbatory reading, joking that "My researches were stimulating but solitary. It became clear I was going to have to leave the academic plane and enter the human fray."[118] Note that the academic has been radically redefined as an erotic ("stimulating")—but not yet social ("solitary")—experience. In this respect, the image of masturbatory reading must be understood as a capacious affective relation—to the text, to the self, to the body, to a collective past, to a possible future. Yet this relation is incipiently social, an intimation of potentiality that is emergent (but by no means guaranteed) in the event of reading. This is why, in the very next frame after the image of her masturbatory reading, we see Alison attend her university's Gay Union (see Fig. 3). Although she sits in "petrified silence," Alison has found the courage to materialize her yearning for a community where the

Fig. 3   Alison Bechdel, *Fun Home* (2006)

intimations of queer belonging could be realized.[119] Of course, the realization of queer belonging means *both* sexual and political contact; indeed, the memoir refuses to disarticulate these two and, instead, fuses them in the incipiently social relations of Alison's bad reading.

Part of the tragedy of *Fun Home* is that Alison's father cannot submit himself to a similarly queer becoming. Indeed, Alison wonders, "How could he admire Joyce's lengthy, libidinal 'Yes' so fervently and end up saying 'No' to his own life."[120] The answer lies, at least in part, in the absence of a social world that would say "Yes" back to Bruce's yes, that would provide a double affirmation of his queer desires and thereby give him opportunities to experiment with alternative modes of belonging. After all, Alison's bad reading leads her toward a social collective because there is a culture available to her, a set of material relations enabled by second-wave feminism, gay liberation, and the postwar university. These conditions make possible the realization of her desires for relation and, crucially, mark queerness as a mode of belonging to a political collectivity. Bruce does not have access to these material conditions. *Fun Home* thus underscores that bad reading is always an historical affair. Whatever possibilities it intimates cannot be annexed from the relations of power that either enable or obstruct their realization. This is why it is so significant that when Bruce reads Kate Millet, he *does* experience the affective jolts of queer potentiality. "I'm flying high on Kate Millet," he writes after Alison shares this text with him.[121] He admits, "I really prefer Millett's philosophy to the one I'm slave to. But I try to keep one foot in the door. Actually I am in limbo. I ... oh, hell. I don't know what I mean."[122] Bruce's "flying high" recalls Muñoz's taking ecstasy and Frankenstein's imbibing of fancy—the delirious encounter with the text opens a door to another mode of relationality. Yet Bruce cannot let his feet off the ground, keeping one stuck in the door and feeling uncertain about what he "mean[s]." From Alison's perspective, it is precisely Bruce's sense of himself as a "slave" to textual meaning that prevents him from reading himself into an alternative economy of relation. Earlier in the memoir, she jokes that Bruce misreads Camus's claim that "suicide is a solution to the absurd," taking the phrase far too literally.[123] "If he'd read carefully," Alison states, "he would have gotten to Camus' conclusion that suicide is illogical. But I suspect my father of being a haphazard scholar."[124]

But perhaps the problem is not that Bruce is a careless and "haphazard" reader. Perhaps *he cannot read haphazardly enough* so that he can detach from what he experiences as fixed truth—to put aside the question of meaning altogether in favor of relational contact. After all, in Alison's hands, the queer scholar reads herself into a new network of queer belonging, and once she is affectively immersed in this world, reading badly becomes a radically addictive proliferation. Normative culture, read by the queer scholar, becomes erotically and politically palpable in surprising ways. When Alison begins a sexual relationship with a fellow student, for example, it is

> strewn with books, however, in what was for me a novel fusion of word and deed. I lost my bearings. The dictionary had become erotic. Some of our favorite childhood stories were revealed as propaganda ... others as pornography. In the harsh light of my dawning feminism, everything looked different.[125]

Even *the dictionary* has become erotically invested—a book of correspondence and apparently objective reference has become an affective vector of seduction and relational creation. Thus, bad reading affords an agency—however partial—to redefine the hierarchy of faculties that underpin reading in queer terms. By doing so, bad reading not only opens up new modes of interpretation; it also contests the economy of relation that fuses reading and heteronormativity together, forestalling a queerer panoply of erotic and social relations. To be sure, *Fun Home* underscores the historical conditions that can bridge—or fail to bridge—the affective relations of reading and their intimations of queerer futurity. Yet the memoir nonetheless affirms bad reading as a meaningful site of symbolic contestation, subjective nourishment, and collective agency in the queer literary imagination. Bad reading can provoke us to make contact with radical social possibilities that seem to exist merely as flickerings of feeling.

Insofar as the works we will now encounter are "experimental," then, they are experiments in the most rigorous sense of the word—tests to see what might emerge; tests whose very purpose is to redefine the meaning of the known and unknown; tests based on gut feelings, with hypotheses rooted in vague sensations of the possible. A bad reader might, on the basis of this definition, be tempted to call all such experiments "queer." In the following pages, we will explore the perverse horizons that may yet emerge through such an embrace of queer experimentation.

NOTES

1. See especially, Michael Warner, "Uncritical Reading," in *Polemic: Critical or Uncritical*, ed. Jane Gallop (New York: Taylor and Francis Books, 2004), 13–38, whose work deeply inspires my approach. For a historical analysis of good and bad reading, see Michael Millner, *Fever Reading: Affect and Reading Badly in the Early American Public Sphere* (Durham: University of New Hampshire Press, 2012). For a history of reading that also privileges the discourses of affect and corporeality, see Karin Littau, *Theories of Reading: Books, Bodies, and Bibliomania* (Malden: Polity Press, 2006).
2. As François Cusset argues, "The mission of the scholarly institution is to produce readers that meet certain standards, and, in the name of professorial competence, to impose not only a list of required texts but also the various modes of reading appropriate to them" (223). See François Cusset, *French Theory: How Foucault, Derrida, Deleuze, & Co. Transformed the Intellectual Life of the United States*, trans. Jeff Fort (Minneapolis: University of Minnesota Press, 2008).
3. Mary Shelley, *Frankenstein* (London: Penguin Books, 2003), 47.
4. Ibid.
5. Ibid.
6. Ibid.
7. Ibid.
8. I take the metaphors of Dionysian intoxication from Gilles Deleuzes's discussion of minor literature that produces an undecidable hesitation between dream and reality. This fantastical state is one way that minor literature eludes systems of Apollonian judgment. See *Essays Clinical and Critical*, trans. Daniel W. Smith and Michael A. Greco (Minneapolis: University of Minnesota Press, 1997), 126–35.
9. On Victor's carnally queer relationship to knowledge, see Elizabeth Freeman, *Time Binds: Queer Temporalities, Queer Histories* (Durham: Duke University Press, 2010), 95–135.
10. See, for example, Eve Kosofsky Sedgwick, *Touching Feeling: Affect, Pedagogy, Performativity* (Durham: Duke University Press, 2002), 123–51; Sharon Marcus and Stephen Best, "Surface Reading: An Introduction," *Representations* 108, no. 1 (2009): 1–21; Rita Felski, *The Limits of Critique* (Chicago: The University of Chicago Press, 2015); Donald E. Hall, *Reading Sexualities: Hermeneutic Theory and the Future of Queer Studies* (London: Routledge, 2009); Heather Love, "Close but not Deep: Literary Ethics and the Descriptive Turn," *New Literary History* 41, no. 2 (2010): 371–91; Franco Moretti, *Distant Reading* (London: Verso, 2013); Jonathan Culler, "Critical Paradigms," *PMLA* 125, no. 4 (2010): 905–15; Derek Attridge, *The Singularity of Literature* (New York: Routledge,

2004); and Warner, "Uncritical." For the classic text in this debate, see Susan Sontag, *Against Interpretation and Other Essays* (New York: Dell Publishing, 1969), especially 13–23; also relevant, but less often cited as a touchstone in the debate, is Roland Barthes, *The Pleasure of the Text*, trans. Richard Miller (New York: Hill and Wang, 1975).

11. For convergent approaches to the conception of the para-academic, see Cusset, *French Theory*; Judith Halberstam's conception of "low theory" in *The Queer Art of Failure* (Durham: Duke University Press, 2011); and Michael Warner and Lauren Berlant, "What Does Queer Theory Teach Us About X," *PMLA* 110, no. 3 (1995): 343–49, which critiques the "panicky defensiveness that many queer and non-queer-identified humanists express [which] has to do with the multiple localities of queer theory and practice" (344–45). I agree with their insistence that "no particular project is metonymic of queer commentary. Part of the point of using *queer* in the first place was the wrenching sense of recontextualization it gave, and queer commentary has tried hard to sustain its awareness of diverse context boundaries" (345, original emphasis). For incisive analyses of the subsequent institutionalization of academic knowledge, including queer theory, see Robyn Wiegman, *Object Lessons* (Durham: Duke University Press, 2012); and Roderick A. Ferguson, *The Reorder of Things: The University and its Pedagogies of Minority Difference* (Minneapolis: University of Minnesota Press, 2012).

12. Marcus and Best, "Surface," 1.

13. To be clear, I do not accept the monolithic equation of critical reading with symptomatic reading (and vice versa) because it collapses divergent academic definitions of critical reading into one common rubric, flattening the distinct methodologies and histories of academic, para-academic, and non-academic reading. I also do not equate critical reading solely to deconstruction, psychoanalysis, or Marxism, nor do I conflate all of these modes with "good reading." Rather, my concept of good and bad reading beckons for a contextually specific genealogy of the relations of power that pertain to any mode of reading marked by an institution as "critical." On this problem, see especially Chap. 2.

14. Cusset, *French*, 338.

15. Ibid., 338, 337, original emphasis.

16. Felski, *Limits*, 10.

17. Love, "Close," 388.

18. Ibid.

19. Felski, *Limits*, 12. For a wonderful exemplification of this critical practice, see Jennifer Doyle, *Hold It Against Me: Difficulty and Emotion in Contemporary Art* (Durham: Duke University Press, 2013).

20. Adam Frank, *Transferential Poetics, from Poe to Warhol* (New York: Fordham University Press, 2015), 3.

21. For a convergent approach to the non-exclusivity of human and animal emotion, see Antonio Damasio, *Looking for Spinoza: Joy, Sorrow, and the Feeling Brain* (Orlando: Harcourt Books, 2003).

22. Michael Warner, *Publics and Counterpublics* (New York: Zone Books, 2002), 123.
23. Ibid.
24. Warner argues that public agency in liberalism is specifically tied to the state form (Ibid., 124).
25. Eve Kosofsky Sedgwick, *Tendencies* (Durham: Duke University Press, 1993), 4.
26. Ibid., 4, 3. Note that Sedgwick stresses the affective nature of this mode of queer reading: "The demands on both the text and the reader from so intent an attachment can be multiple, even paradoxical. For me, a kind of formalism, a *visceral* near-identification with the writing I cared for, at the level of sentence structure, metrical pattern, rhyme, was one way of trying to appropriate what seemed the numinous and resistant power of the chosen objects" (Ibid., 3, my emphasis).
27. Ibid., 3, 4.
28. As Berlant and Warner write, "Queer commentary has also distinguished itself through experiments in critical voice and in the genre of the critical essay. Along with queer experiments in pedagogy and classroom practice, it marks a transformation of both the object and the practice of criticism" ("What" 349). For a path-breaking exemplification of such a transformation within queer theory, see José Esteban Muñoz, *Disidentifications: Queers of Color and the Performance of Politics* (Minneapolis: University of Minnesota Press, 1999).
29. Sedgwick, *Tendencies*, 4.
30. Ibid.
31. For a historical view of bad reading that moves beyond the twentieth century, see Millner, *Fever*.
32. See W.K. Wimsatt and Monroe Beardsley, "The Affective Fallacy," *Sewanee Review* 57, no. 1 (1949): 31–55.
33. Jane P. Tompkins *Reader-Response Criticism: From Formalism to Post-Structuralism* (Baltimore: Johns Hopkins University Press, 1980), ix.
34. Stanley Fish, *Is There A Text in This Class? The Authority of Interpretive Communities.* (Cambridge: Harvard University Press 1980), 27, my emphasis.
35. As reader-response criticism waned in popularity, its questions migrated to other fields, particularly history of the book criticism and interdisciplinary approaches to literature based in cognitive science.
36. See *The Affective Turn: Theorizing the Social,* eds. Patricia Ticineto Clough and Jean Halley (Durham: Duke University Press, 2007). Within queer studies, see Sara Ahmed, *The Cultural Politics of Emotion* (New York:

Routledge, 2004); Ann Cvetcovich, *An Archive of Feelings: Trauma, Sexuality, and Lesbian Public Culture* (Durham: Duke University Press, 2003); Heather Love, *Feeling Backward: Loss and the Politics of Queer History* (Cambridge: Harvard University Press, 2007); David L. Eng, *The Feeling of Kinship: Queer Liberalism and the Racialization of Intimacy* (Durham: Duke University Press, 2010); Amber Musser, *Sensational Flesh: Race, Power, and Masochism* (New York: New York University Press, 2014); Mel Y. Chen, *Animacies: Biopolitics, Racial Mattering, and Queer Affect* (Durham: Duke University Press, 2012); and Nick Salvato, *Obstruction* (Durham: Duke University Press, 2016). For a critique of the affective turn, see Ruth Leys, "The Turn to Affect: A Critique," *Critical Inquiry* 37 (2011): 434–72; and "Facts and Moods: A Response to My Critics," *Critical Inquiry* 38 (2012): 882–91.

37. See Martha Nussbaum, *Love's Knowledge: Essays on Philosophy and Literature* (Oxford: Oxford University Press, 1992); and *Poetic Justice: The Literary Imagination and Public Life* (Boston: Beacon Press, 1997); Brian Massumi, *Parables of the Virtual: Movement, Affect, Sensation* (Durham: Duke University Press, 2002); Charles Altieri, *The Particulars of Rapture: An Aesthetics of the Affects* (Ithaca: Cornell University Press, 2003); Attridge, *Singularity*; Sianne Ngai, *Ugly Feelings* (Cambridge: Harvard University Press, 2005); and *Our Aesthetic Categories: Zany, Cute, Interesting* (Cambridge: Harvard University Press, 2015).

38. Nussbaum, *Poetic*, 7. On her Aristotelian ethics, see Nussbaum *Love's*, especially 3–53; on the influence of Adam Smith on her thinking, see *Poetic*, 74–75. For an incisive critique of Nussbaum, see Charles Altieri, "Lyrical Ethics and Literary Experience" in *Mapping the Ethical Turn*, eds. Todd F. Davis and Kenneth Womack (Charlottesville: University Press of Virginia, 2001), 30–58. For a relevant critique of Adam Smith's conception of impartial spectatorship, see Ian Baucom, *Specters of the Atlantic: Finance Capital, Slavery, and the Philosophy of History* (Durham: Duke University Press, 2005).

39. Nussbaum, *Poetic*, 10. For an incisive critique of the "affective hypothesis" and its convergence with neoliberal ideologies of personal property, see Rachel Greenwald Smith, *Affect and American Literature in the Age of Neoliberalism* (New York: Cambridge University Press, 2015).

40. Ibid., xvi, 74, my emphasis.

41. See especially Ngai, *Ugly*.

42. Nussbaum, *Poetic*, 6. Hence, Nussbaum values Walt Whitman's poetry only to the extent that it provides a "concrete depiction of different ways of life" (*Poetic* 7). "Dreamlike and indeterminate" is also an apt descriptor for the "waning of affect" that characterizes the postmodern structure of feeling. See Fredric Jameson, *Postmodernism, or the Cultural Logic of Late Capitalism* (Durham: Duke UP, 1990), 15. Jameson argues that

postmodernity dissolves the "bourgeois ego, or monad" dispersing affect
into free-floating intensities, "since there is no longer a self to do the feeling" (*Postmodernism* 16). On the potentially ethical and political value of
this dispersal, see Chap. 4. For two differing approaches to the value of
impersonality, see Smith, *Affect* and Bersani and Phillips, *Intimacies*. On
the specific affective economies of postmodernity, see Steven Shaviro's
"The Life, After Death, of Postmodern Emotions," *Criticism* 46, no. 1
(2004): 124–41.

43. As Loren Glass notes, many postwar and postmodern experimental writers are "not invested in making us better people, and there should be
ways to teach and read them that recognize and respect this basic fact"
(203). See "Contemporary Fiction and the Limits of the Liberal
Imagination," *Contemporary Literature*, 54, no. 1 (2013): 197–203.

44. For keen and relevant surveys of the ethical turn, see Dorothy J. Hale,
"Fiction as Restriction: Self-Binding in New Ethical Theories of the
Novel," *Narrative* 15, no. 2 (2007): 187–206; and Michael Eskin,
"Introduction: The Double 'Turn' to Ethics and Literature?" *Poetics
Today* 25, no. 4 (2004): 557–72. For a highly illuminating account of the
"event of literature" from a number of different post-structural view-
points, see Asja Szafraniec, *Beckett, Derrida, and the Event of Literature*
(Stanford: Stanford University Press, 2007).

45. Attridge makes clear that this attachment to absolute otherness is the
locus of his divergence from Fish. See *Singularity*, 144.

46. Ibid., 130–31.

47. Ibid, 131.

48. On his understanding of modernism and the ethics of reading, see Derek
Attridge, *J.M. Coetzee and the Ethics of Reading: Literature in the Event*
(Chicago: The University of Chicago Press, 2004). While I part with his
tendency to characterize postmodern form as lacking an engagement
with otherness and the aesthetic (6, 69), I share Attridge's concern about
allegorical reading as potentially overlooking the literal or material solici-
tousness of literary form (38, 48).

49. Attridge, *Singularity*, 7.

50. See, for example, Teresa de Lauretis, *Freud's Drive: Psychoanalysis,
Literature and Film* (New York: Palgrave Macmillan, 2008); Leo Bersani,
The Freudian Body: Psychoanalysis and Art (New York: Columbia
University Press, 1986); Tim Dean, *Beyond Sexuality* (Chicago: The
University of Chicago Press, 2000); Judith Butler, *The Psychic Life of
Power: Theories in Subjection* (Stanford: Stanford University Press, 1997);
Homosexuality and Psychoanalysis, eds. Tim Dean and Christopher Lane
(Chicago: The University of Chicago Press, 2001); and David L. Eng,
Racial Castration: Managing Masculinity in Asian America (Durham:
Duke University Press, 2001). For a relevant analysis of the relationship

between affect and language, see Shoshana Felman, *The Scandal of the Speaking Body: Don Juan with J.L. Austin, or Seduction in Two Languages*, trans. Catherine Porter (Stanford: Stanford University Press, 2002). For insightful accounts of psychoanalytic reading that contest the hermeneutics of suspicion, see Adam Phillips, *Promises, Promises: Essays on Psychoanalysis and Literature* (New York: Basic Books, 2001); and Anne A. Cheng, "Psychoanalysis without Symptoms," *differences* 20, no. 1 (2009): 87–101.

51. Jean Laplanche and Jean-Bertrand Pontalis, *The Language of Psychoanalysis*, trans. Donald Nicholson-Smith (New York: W.W. Norton & Company, 1973), 13. What Freud calls "affect," Massumi labels "emotion" and Damasio names a "feeling." Despite their terminological differences, their common point is the same—the mind perceives and interprets bodily and physiological sensations, and these perceptions are experienced as subjective emotions, which we label in qualitative terms.

52. Sigmund Freud, "Instincts and Their Vicissitudes," in *General Psychological Theory* (New York: Touchstone, 1963), 88, my emphasis.

53. Laplance and Pontalis, *Language*, 14.

54. Sedgwick, *Touching*, 18.

55. Ibid., 18–20. For Sedgwick, the problem is that the psychoanalytic reduction of affect to desire excludes the ways that affect is relatively autonomous from the drives (hunger, thirst, sexual desire, etc.) and thus possess more freedom with respect to object, aim, motivation, and temporality. Also see Eve Kosofsky Sedgwick and Adam Frank, "Shame in the Cybernetic Fold: Reading Silvan Tomkins," in *Shame and Its Sisters: A Silvan Tomkins Reader*, ed. Eve Kosofsky Sedgwick and Adam Frank (Durham: Duke University Press, 1995), 1–28.

56. The autonomy of affect from the drives also enables key possibilities for agency. See Chap. 5.

57. For a queer theory of phenomenology, see Sara Ahmed, *Queer Phenomenology: Orientations, Objects, Others* (Durham: Duke University Press, 2006).

58. This tradition has been particularly attentive to possibilities and limitations of Deleuze's and Deleuze and Guattari's concepts for minority subjects, such as the meaning of "becoming-women" for subjects that are already culturally marked as "women." See, for example, Elizabeth Grosz, *Volatile Bodies: Toward a Corporeal Feminism* (Bloomington: Indiana UP, 1994); *Space, Time, and Perversion* (New York: Routledge, 1995); "A Thousand Tiny Sexes: Feminism and Rhizomatics," in *Gilles Deleuze and the Theatre of Philosophy*, eds. Constantin V. Bondas and Dorothea Olkowski (New York: Routledge, 1994), 187–212; Dorothea Olkowski, *Gilles Deleuze and the Ruin of Representation* (Berkeley: University of California Press, 1999); Rosi Braidotti, *Nomadic Subjects: Embodiment and Sexual Difference in*

Contemporary Feminist Theory (New York: Columbia University Press, 2011); *Deleuze and Queer Theory*, eds. Chrysanthi Nigianni and Mel Storr (Edinburgh: Edinburgh University Press, 2009); *Deleuze and Feminist Theory*, eds. Ian Buchanan and Claire Colebrook (Edinburgh: Edinburgh University Press, 2000); and Claire Colebrook, "Queer Aesthetics," in *Queer Times, Queer Becomings*, eds. E.L. McCallum and Mikko Tuhkanen (Albany: State University of New York, 2011).

59. Elizabeth Grosz, *Chaos, Territory, Art: Deleuze and the Framing of the Earth* (New York: Columbia University Press, 2008), 22.

60. Gilles Deleuze and Félix Guattari, *What Is Philosophy?*, trans. Hugh Tomlinson and Graham Burchell (New York: Columbia University Press, 1994), 164.

61. Here Deleuze and Guattari exemplify the challenge to what Rei Terada calls the "expressive hypothesis," or the conceit that "emotion requires a subject" to express it, *Feeling in Theory: Emotion after the "Death of the Subject"* (Cambridge: Harvard University Press, 2001), 11.

62. Deleuze and Guattari, *What*, 167.

63. Ibid., 176.

64. Ibid., 164.

65. Gilles Deleuze, *Francis Bacon: The Logic of Sensation*, trans. Daniel W. Smith (Minneapolis: University of Minnesota Press, 2003), 39.

66. On the partitioning of the senses as a political act, see especially Davide Panagia, *The Political Life of Sensation* (Durham: Duke University Press, 2009). On the "distribution of the sensible," see Jacques Rancière, *The Politics of Aesthetics*, trans. Gabriel Rockhill (London: Continuum, 2004).

67. Massumi, *Parables*, 139.

68. Ibid.

69. For an accessible elaboration of this point, see Bruce Baugh, "How Deleuze Can Help Us Make Literature Work," in *Deleuze and Literature*, eds. Ian Buchanan and John Marks (Edinburgh: Edinburgh University Press, 2000), 34–56. For an overview of Deleuze's theory of literature, see Ronald Bogue, *Deleuze on Literature* (New York: Routledge, 2003).

70. Grosz, *Chaos*, 79.

71. Deleuze, *Essays*, 1.

72. Gilles Deleuze and Claire Parnet, *Dialogues II*, trans. Hugh Tomlinson and Barbara Habberjam (New York: Columbia University Press, 2002), 36, 45. While Deleuze and Guattari often turn to classically male-modernist figures such as Joyce and Lawrence, it is important to note, as Ronald Bogue argues, that they do not rely on a notion of modernism as apolitical or anti-political (*Deleuze* 113). Moreover, they share a fondness for non-modernist writers such as Herman Melville and William S. Burroughs, and Deleuze, in particular, cites a wide array of popular cultural texts in his books on cinema, from Charlie Chaplin to Howard Hawks.

73. Ibid., 45.
74. Massumi, *Parables*, 28. Also see Brian Massumi, *Politics of Affect* (Malden: Polity Press, 2015), which qualifies that affect is not "prelinguistic" and that there is no "antinomy between affect and language. There is accompaniment and becoming, always involving the full spectrum of the graded continuum of experience. The nonverbal grades on the continuum of experience are not in opposition to the verbal registers, any more than infrared is opposed to red. They companion them" (212). My critique here is that the rhetorical figures that affect theory often uses to describe this companionship sometimes fail to capture the non-dialectical relationality of affect and language, particularly when it comes to narrating becomings stimulated *by* and *through* language.
75. Massumi, *Parables*, 35, original emphasis.
76. Sedgwick articulates a similar desire in *Touching Feeling*, 1–25.
77. Grosz, *Chaos*, 80. For a critique of Deleuzian becoming as an asocial transcendence of the world, a position with which I clearly disagree, see Peter Hallward, *Out of This World: Deleuze and the Philosophy of Creation* (London: Verso, 2006).
78. Note, too, Massumi's point that, in reading, "sensation is a turning in on itself of the body's activity, so that the action is not extended toward an object but knots at its point of emergence: rises and subsides into its own incipiency, in the same movement. *The acts of attention performed during reading are forms of incipient action*" (*Parables* 139, my emphasis). For a different approach that influences my conception of the incipiently social, see Warner, *Publics*, 125–58, which recovers an "orientation to futurity" in counterpublic discourse (such as, in his example, academic writing) and thereby affords "a way of imagining speech for which there is yet no scene, and a scene for which there is no speech" (158). The question that Warner poses is central to every work examined in *Queer Experimental Literature*: "It may well be that extant forms and venues will accommodate many political aims. But what if they do not? *What if one hopes to transform the possible contexts of speech?*" (128, my emphasis). To understand this problem, I contend, requires not only an attentiveness to the torsions between the form, aim, and venue for speech but also to the *hope, the affective relation*, that inspires such efforts at queer world-building.
79. José Esteban Muñoz, *Cruising Utopia: The Then and There of Queer Futurity* (New York: New York University Press, 2009), 187.
80. On affect as relation, see Teresa Brennan, *The Transmission of Affect* (Ithaca: Cornell University Press, 2004). I diverge from Brennan's view that affect points toward a natural, organic unity to the human body, which she describes in avowedly mystical terms, such as "the union of spirit and sensuality that was lost with the fall into a divided mind and body" (159).

81. Damasio, *Looking*, 140. For the philosophy of affect as action and affection, see Benedict de Spinoza, *The Ethics*, trans. Edwin Curley (New York: Penguin Books, 1996); and Gilles Deleuze, *Spinoza: Practical Philosophy*, trans. Robert Hurley (San Francisco: City Lights Books, 1988).

82. Nancy K. Miller, "Emphasis Added: Plots and Plausibilities in Womens Fiction," in *The New Feminist Criticism: Essays on Women, Literature, Theory*, ed. Elaine Showalter (New York: Pantheon Books, 1985), 341, original emphasis. For a relevant analysis of lesbian experimental writing, see Elizabeth A. Meese, *(Sem)erotics: Theorizing Lesbian: Writing* (New York: New York University Press, 1992).

83. Ibid. On the skepticism toward *écriture féminine* as utopian, see DeKoven, "*Jouissance*, Cyborgs, and Companion Species: Feminist Experiment," *PMLA* 121, no. 5 (2006): 1690–96.

84. On this issue, see Doyle, *Hold*.

85. For a helpful overview, see Elizabeth Grosz, *Sexual Subversions: Three French Feminists.* (Crows News: Allen & Unwin, 1989).

86. Note Acker's significance as a vector here. While she remains a marginal figure in contemporary literary criticism, largely consigned to the rubrics of postmodern fiction, Acker had a profound and enduring influence on many of the major figures in contemporary American and British literature that has yet to be fully recognized.

87. For an overview of differing approaches to form and context in analyses of experimental writing, see the important collection, *Breaking the Sequence: Women's Experimental Writing*, eds. Ellen G. Friedman and Miriam Fuchs (Princeton: Princeton University Press, 1989), especially 3–51; and Marianne DeKoven, *A Different Language: Gertrude Stein's Experimental Writing* (Madison: University of Wisconsin Press, 1983).

88. For a convergent approach, see Alex Houen's notion of literary "potentialism" in *Powers of Possibility: Experimental American Writing Since the 1960s* (Oxford: Oxford University Press, 2012), 241. For a relevant inquiry into the relationship between experimental form and the affective relations of reading, see Leo Bersani and Ulysse Dutoit, *Arts of Impoverishment* (Cambridge: Harvard University Press, 1993).

89. As Berlant and Warner note, "Queer culture comes into being unevenly, in obliquely cross-referencing publics, and no one scene of importance accounts for its politics—neither hyperabstracted contexts, like 'the Symbolic,' nor hyperconcrete ones, like civil disobedience" ("What" 346).

90. See DeKoven, *Different*, 16.

91. Kathryn Hume, *Aggressive Fictions: Reading the Contemporary American Novel* (Ithaca: Cornell University Press, 2012), 55.

92. Freeman, *Time*, xix.

93. Anthony Reed, *Freedom Time: The Poetics and Politics of Black Experimental Writing* (Baltimore: Johns Hopkins University Press, 2014), 1.
94. Doyle, *Hold*, 72.
95. This expansion of queer aesthetics is also necessary because, in Berlant and Warner's words, queer commentary emerges *"[t]hrough a wide range of mongrelized genres and media"* (344, my emphasis).
96. de Lauretis, *Freud's Drive*; Bersani, *Freudian*; Lee Edelman, *No Future: Queer Theory and the Death Drive* (Durham: Duke University Press, 2004); Dean, *Beyond;* Kevin Ohi, *Henry James and The Queerness of Style* (Minneapolis: University of Minnesota Press, 2011).
97. Ohi, *Henry*, 1.
98. Ibid., my emphasis.
99. On the queerness of stickiness, see Ahmed, *Cultural*, 89–92. For a relevant analysis of postmodern stickiness, see Ngai, *Ugly*, 285–97.
100. Sedgwick, *Touching*, 160.
101. Freeman, *Time*, 13–14.
102. Ibid., 14, my emphasis.
103. See Edelman, *No Future*. On the Lacanian conception of fantasy, see Slajov Žižek, *The Plague of Fantasies* (London: Verso, 2008). Despite her provocative approach to fantasy in *The Practice of Love: Lesbian Sexuality and Perverse Desire* (Bloomington: Indiana University Press, 1996), Teresa de Lauretis's more recent definition of queer writing follows the Lacanian subordination of the imaginary in favor of the drives. See Teresa de Lauretis, "Queer Texts, Bad Habits, and the Issue of a Future," *GLQ* 17, nos. 2–3 (2011): 243–63. Lauren Berlant permits more agency within the scene of fantasy. As she notes in *Sex, or the Unbearable* (Durham: Duke University Press, 2014), "without allowing for ambivalence, there is no flourishing" (12), and in *Cruel Optimism* (Durham: Duke University Press, 2011), she locates fantasy as the means by which a subject "parses ambivalence in such a way that [she] is not defeated by it" (122). Yet Berlant tends to privilege the conservative function of fantasy, the way that it "make[s] the subject appear intelligible to herself and to others throughout the career of desire's unruly attentiveness" (Ibid). For Berlant's dialogue with Edelman on fantasy, desire, and queer negativity, see Lauren Berlant and Lee Edelman, *Sex, or the Unbearable*.
104. Edelman, *No Future*, 33–34.
105. Ibid., 24.
106. Deleuze, *Essays*, 3. Stressing the incipiently social nature of fabulation, Deleuze adds, "Literature is delirium, but delirium is not a father-mother affair: there is no delirium that does not pass through peoples, races, and tribes, and that does not haunt universal history. *All delirium is world-historical*" (4, my emphasis). For a relevant analysis of literary eroticism and the aesthetics of sexual fantasy, see Gilles Deleuze, *Coldness and Cruelty*, trans. Jean McNeil (New York: Zone Books, 1989).

107. On the literary representation of fantasy, see Rosemary Jackson, *Fantasy: The Literature of Subversion* (London: Methuen, 1981); and Tzvetan Todorov, *The Fantastic*, trans. Richard Howard (Ithaca: Cornell UP, 1975).
108. Gilles Deleuze and Félix Guattari, *Kafka: Toward a Minor Literature*, trans. Dana Polan (Minneapolis: University of Minnesota Press, 1986), 17.
109. Ibid., 16.
110. Valerie Rohy, *Lost Causes: Narrative, Etiology, and Queer Theory* (Oxford: Oxford University Press, 2015), 110.
111. Ibid., 118.
112. Alison Bechdel, *Fun Home: A Family Tragicomic* (Boston: Mariner, 2006).
113. Ibid., 206.
114. Similar to the professor's reading for correspondence, Alison's father dictates a mode of good reading that restricts Alison's contact with the text. When he enjoins her, "you damn well better identify with every page" of *Portrait of the Artist*, Alison feels that his "suffocating" "excitement began to leave little room for my own" (201). Here Bruce can experience an affective relationship to the texts of male modernism, but his aggressive enthusiasm saps Alison of her ability to enter these texts on her own, and it also narrows the event of reading to subjective identification.
115. Ibid., 76.
116. Ibid., 205.
117. Ibid., 74.
118. Ibid., 76.
119. Ibid.
120. Ibid., 228.
121. Ibid., 224.
122. Ibid, original ellipsis.
123. Ibid., 47.
124. Ibid.
125. Ibid., 80–81, original ellipsis.

CHAPTER 1

Naked Lust: Obscene Relationality and the Turn to Queer Experimental Literature

"Lest anyone take this seriously, of course, obviously [Naked Lunch] *is fantasy."*

—Massachusetts Supreme Court

"I'm not queer," he thought. "I'm disembodied."

—William S. Burroughs, *Queer*

The final literary obscenity trial in the United States centered on the queerness of fantasy—and the fantasies of queerness—in William S. Burroughs's experimental novel, *Naked Lunch* (1959).[1] The decision, rendered by the Massachusetts Supreme Court, hinged on whether or not *Naked Lunch* possessed "social value" despite the Court's consensus that the novel "appeals to a prurient interest in sex" and "affronts contemporary community standards."[2] The *Naked Lunch* trial was a testing ground for a historically new definition of obscenity, which separated the social value of literature from its manifestly offensive content. Previously, obscenity had been defined through the affective charge a text had on the reader.[3] If the content seemed likely to illicit lust or depravity, then the text would be censored as obscene. Yet in 1957, the US Supreme Court determined that "sex and obscenity are not synonymous," and in 1966, the Court went further, declaring that even "prurient appeal or patent offensiveness" cannot justify censorship.[4] Indeed, as Justice Brennan argued, "A book cannot be

© The Author(s) 2017
T. Bradway, *Queer Experimental Literature*,
Palgrave Studies in Affect Theory and Literary Criticism,
DOI 10.1057/978-1-137-59543-0_1

proscribed unless it is found to be *utterly* without redeeming social value."[5] In effect, the interpretation of obscenity drifted from the text's manifest content to the community of readers that find or fail to find social value in the text and the corollary "use" that the text might be said to have for its publics.[6] Responding to this shifting hermeneutic ground, Burroughs's lawyers sought to defend *Naked Lunch*'s social value by proving its literary merit. Drawing on star testimony from Allen Ginsberg and Norman Mailer, the defense lawyer, Edward de Grazia, located Burroughs's fiction within a prestigious pantheon stretching from St. Augustine to James Joyce. de Grazia concluded with quotations from Sigmund Freud and John Dewey defending the artist's imaginative labor as a necessary contribution to "civilization's knowledge and learning."[7] Yet literary bona fides, aesthetic rigor, and authorial ingenuity did not convince the Court. On the contrary, it was their reading of *Naked Lunch* as representing the fantastical "hallucinations of a drug addict" that ultimately led the Court to accept the opinion of a "substantial and intelligent group in the community [that] believes the book to be of some literary significance."[8]

Why did reading *Naked Lunch* as hallucination rather than imagination redeem the text's obscenity as socially valuable? The answer, I argue, illuminates the contradictions that shape the politics of queer experimental literature as a whole and speaks to the prohibitions on representing queerness as a mode of relationality within postwar literature more broadly. By positioning Burroughs as a submissive witness to the external control of drugs, the Court brackets the text's homoerotic fantasies. As hallucinations, these fantasies are merely one part of Burroughs's "subconscious going through all the various trials and ordeals of addiction."[9] Moreover, the writer does not actively desire these fantasies; they are forced into the mind by the horrors of drugs. Indeed, the difference between imagination and hallucination is that the former implies some measure of desire, whereas the latter suggests radical passivity and an unwillingness to witness the images that persecute one's mind. If Burroughs is merely succumbing to an external force, then the text cannot be affirming the pleasures of queer eroticism or affectively implicating readers in its perverse fantasies. Above all, the text cannot be an intentional political critique written by a homosexual that conjures a broader community of queer desiring subjects.

This anxiety fuels the Court's concern about the presence of political allegory in *Naked Lunch*. For example, the Court is concerned when de Grazia suggests that *Naked Lunch* is "projecting a kind of futuristic party, a political party" inspired by "groups today, social groups today that are involved in political struggles in the United States."[10] In response, the

Court asks Ginsberg, "What political struggles are homosexuals involved in?"; and when they are unsatisfied by his response that this is a "matter of opinion," they push further:

> Do you think he [Burroughs] is seriously suggesting that some time in the future that a political party will be in some way concerned with sex? ... When I say, "Concerned with sex," I don't mean in an attempt to reform perversion. I am not talking about any crusade to make the world a better world in which to live, as you and I understand it today; but I am suggesting that from your answer, what he is trying to portray here, is that some time in the future there will be a political party, for instance, made up of homosexuals.[11]

At stake in these questions are the homophobic undercurrents that prohibit the representation of homosexuals as an incipient political collectivity in pre-Stonewall America, prior to the emergence of a gay liberation movement.[12] While homosexuals are legible in pluralized terms, their collectivity is homophobically codified as a shared perversion. A "political party" of homosexuals therefore represents a contradiction for the Court. If homosexuals are sexual perverts, how can they possibly represent the body politic? Indeed, how can they "better" the nation if homosexuality metonymically signifies a social malady that must be "reform[ed]"? The concept that homosexuals have political desires—and that *Naked Lunch* imagines a future collectivity to realize those desires—was therefore obscene in the exact terms established by the law, opposed to any acceptable criteria of "social value."

The queer text is thus not pornographically filled with depraved sex acts. It is a text that is itself expressive of the collective agency and social imagination of queers. The Court renders this reading of *Naked Lunch* moot when they conclude that "there is absolutely no connection [in the text] with any political party in the United States as you and I understand."[13] In fact, the Court asserts—in a caveat that reads as a both instruction and threat—"Lest anyone take this seriously, of course, obviously it [*Naked Lunch*] is fantasy."[14] The redundancy of this phrase captures the vexed and overdetermined status of fantasy in queer experimental literature: fantasy is, of course, obviously, *only fantasy*, not to be taken seriously as social content; and yet fantasy offers a narrative mode for expressing desires that cannot be attributed so simply or reductively to an individuated subject. With their caveat, however, the Court rewrites *Naked Lunch*'s threatening social fantasies as subjective delusions. In doing so, they sever the referential relationship between *Naked Lunch*'s fantasies and any existing social groups, and they equally defuse the incipient and anticipatory dimension of the text—its creation of the desire for a queer collective-to-come. The Court nonetheless permits the publication of the novel, however, because of its putative "social value" as a case study of the addict's pathology.[15]

The irony is that this is precisely the reader relation that Burroughs sought to defuse by turning to experimental literature in *Naked Lunch*. His two previous novels, *Junky* (1953) and *Queer* (1985), do not utilize the famously disjunctive style that Burroughs innovates in *Naked Lunch* and carries forward into his subsequent "cut-up fold-in" trilogy, composed of *The Soft Machine* (1961), *The Ticket That Exploded* (1962), and *Nova Express* (1964).[16] Documenting drug communities and expatriate homosexuals respectively, *Junky* and *Queer* employ a relatively realist prose surface that only rarely blurs the lines of reality and fantasy and never explodes narrative structure into the intensely hallucinatory poetics that distinguishes Burroughs's experimental writing. The strict demarcation of reality and fantasy increasingly concerns Burroughs because it allows his readers to keep a critical distance from the text—they can be judgmental voyeurs of addicts and perverts, sneaking a glimpse at the seedy underbelly of postwar America, but their own affective relations are never implicated within the scene of reading. By contrast, Burroughs's experimental style collapses critical distance and viscerally folds readers into the text's fantastical eroticism. Indeed, *Naked Lunch* foregrounds the reader's newly embodied relation to the text through a series of direct addresses, proclaiming, for example: "Gentle reader, we see God through our assholes in the flash bulb of orgasm... Through these orifices transmute your body... The way OUT is the way IN."[17] No longer does Burroughs let his reader peer "in" to the psyche of the marginalized subject (the junkie or the queer) at a safe remove. Readers must now enter the porous orifices of the text itself and find their own bodies transmuted in the encounter. Meaning will not arrive through the mind or the soul—it is grasped through the asshole, and the asshole of the text swallows the reader in an orgasmic enfolding that forestalls the sovereign distance that abets a homophobic and pathologizing reading. Burroughs's turn to experimental literature thus enables him to reconfigure the hermeneutic relations to his texts as affective relations that immerse readers within their queer eroticism. As we will see, these reader relations afford an incipiently social imagination of queer relationality.

By narrating Burroughs's turn to queer experimental literature as expressing a mode of social desire, this chapter presses back against the prevailing critical narrative that Burroughs's cut-up novels nihilistically lack an affirmative representation of political collectivity.[18] This critical narrative misses the homophobic prohibitions on representing queerness as relationality, which condition the emergence of queer experimental literature and make it susceptible to being dismissed as insufficiently radical.[19] For example, Ihab Hassan laments that "we are never certain what [Burroughs] affirms," and Katherine Hayles observes that these novels emphasize "subversion and disruption rather than creative rearticulation."[20] Even Gilles Deleuze and Félix Guattari, who are elsewhere attuned to the ways that a "minor literature" can "express another possible community," contend that Burroughs's experimental style is not rhizomatic enough.[21] In particular, they critique the method that Burroughs uses to produce his experimental novels, the "cut-up fold-in" technique, which splices diverse textual bodies, from newspaper clippings to pulp fiction and high literature, in a random collage.[22] Despite the schizophrenic effects it produces, Deleuze and Guattari believe that Burroughs's method nonetheless implies a possible reunification of an originary textual whole, insisting that "[n]o typographical, lexical, or even syntactical cleverness is enough to make [the multiple] heard."[23] Their reading ignores the juridical and political codification of queer collectivity as obscenity. Consequently, they miss how form itself—even Burroughs's a-signifying affective form—can prefigure a queer social imaginary in this historical moment. After all, Burroughs conceived of his cut-up method as "produc[ing] a strong *erotic* reaction" on the reader regardless of the content it represents.[24] "In fact," Burroughs writes, "the same sexual effect can be produced by splicing in street recordings recorded by two subjects separately."[25] Here the cut-up threads a queer relationality, even when the participants are physically absent and have merely mixed together meaningless ambient noises; in other words, *form*—not its manifest content—foments an erotic and social relationality in the encounter between readers and text. Therefore, as this chapter will show, queer experimental form enables Burroughs to circumvent the censors on representing homosexuality as a social relation while simultaneously redefining the disembodied social imaginary of reading as an affective relation of queer contact.

By foregrounding the political relationship between Burroughs's aesthetic form and the postwar history of sexuality, this chapter resists the tendency to subsume queer experimental literature within a more general modernist or postmodernist tradition. Depending on one's viewpoint, Burroughs's fiction culminates, exemplifies, or anticipates both modernism and postmodernism.[26] Rather than adjudicate this long-standing debate, my purpose is to demonstrate the specific conditions of possibility that make experimental literature viable as a mode of a queer aesthetic politics. Indeed, I begin with Burroughs not only because his style has a direct influence on later queer experimental writers, such as Kathy Acker and Chuck Palahniuk. More importantly, Burroughs's use of form to subvert the hermeneutic codification of queer affect emblematizes a recurring trope throughout the subsequent chapters—namely, an author experimenting with narrative form to engender a mode of bad reading that agonistically contests the interpretative protocols that condition the reception of their work. Beginning with Burroughs—prior to the emergence of queer theory—also enables us to see that the recent literary critical entwinement of queerness and affect is, in part, a contingent byproduct of the overlapping histories of sexuality and reading in the postwar era. Moreover, we can see that the turn to affective reading in queer theory is unknowingly informed by a longer, non-disciplinary history of queer reading, one that emerges outside of and, as we will see in subsequent chapters, often in opposition to academic codifications of critical reading. We do not simply need to acknowledge this history. Instead, we need to understand that the aesthetic politics of queer experimental literature are uniquely bound up with the affective relations it forges with readers. This aesthetic politics has been ignored precisely because queer experimental literature, like Burroughs's fiction, often appears to crave bad readings, degraded, solipsistic, prurient, or simply trashy textual encounters. Yet it is precisely through its solicitations of bad reading that queer experimental literature reimagines the politics of sexuality and the social relations of queerness alike. My attention to the formal surfaces of queer experimental literature is thus not opposed to its political content—aesthetic form *is* the locus of queer experimental literature's affective politics.

To trace the development of Burroughs's politics of form, then, this chapter begins with his long-unpublished novel *Queer* focusing in particular on the novel's demarcated moments of spectral fantasy. These fantastical digressions anticipate the explosive destabilization of fantasy and reality that Burroughs's later novels will correlate with a queer possession of the reader. *Queer* stabilizes fantasy by focalizing it within the tortured psyche of its gay protagonist. As such, the novel perpetuates long-standing homophobic discourses that negatively associate homosexuals with spectrality: the homosexual is figured as a death-driven, vampiric predator that is simultaneously pathetic, ineffectual, and melancholic; homosexuals, more broadly, are defined as a pervasive collectivity that is hauntingly invisible, isolated, and standing outside of normative social and historical temporalities. Yet, as I show, spectrality also enables Burroughs to narrate homoerotic "contact" between men in ways that elude the repressively critical gaze of heteronormative judgment. These scenes thus provide a blueprint to the queer experimental form that Burroughs subsequently innovates in *Naked Lunch* and intensifies in its sequels. In his experimental literature, Burroughs transposes spectrality to the scene of reading itself, so that all readers—regardless of their sexuality or identity—become queerly possessed by the affective forces of language. This complex transposition of spectrality from the homosexual subject to the queer forces of language undoes the pathologizing position that *Queer* permits readers to inhabit. While Burroughs's politics of form has often been seen as an aggressive assault on his readers, I demonstrate that it also expresses a desire for queer relationality, which is condensed through its ecstatic dispersal of subjects into spectral litanies of body parts, fluids, and words.[27] The aesthetics of spectrality enable an incipiently social imagination of queerness, then, precisely because they can be dismissed as the solipsistic hallucinations of an anti-social junkie.

QUEER SPECTRALITY AND THE IMPOSSIBILITY OF "RECIPROCAL RELATION"

In *The Problem of Homosexuality* (1930), Alfred Adler invokes the homophobic discourse that associates homosexuals with spectrality.[28] "The problem of homosexuality," Adler writes, "hovers over society like a ghost or a scarecrow. In spite of all the condemnation, the number of perverts seems to be on the increase."[29] Homosexuality horrifies not only because of its spectral persistence but also its capacity to proliferate as a mode of desire, despite the forces of moral judgment. As Guy Hocquenghem argues in *Homosexual Desire* (1972), "Homosexuality haunts the 'normal world'" precisely because it is produced by the very homophobic repressions that seek to eradicate it.[30] For Hocquenghem, the idiom of queer spectrality affirmatively condenses the paradoxical way that "[h]omosexuality exists and does not exist, at one and the same time; indeed, its very mode of existence questions again and again the certainty of existence."[31]

Recently, queer theory has followed Hocquenghem's deconstructive resignification of queer spectrality. In one of the most incisive approaches, Carla Freccero conceives of "queer spectrality" in opposition to the normative structures of temporality, affect, and ethics that undergird historicist approaches to the history of sexuality. Queer spectrality, in Freccero's hands, resists the "urge to identify, and thus stabilize, the meaning of an event and a person."[32] By bearing witness to the spectrality of the event, the queer historian opens herself to the hauntings of the past as well as the future; indeed, the queerness of spectrality partly resides in its attentiveness to the immanence of past and future. This queer temporality operates aslant of heteronormative plots of reproductive continuity, enabling affective relations to resonate across time. As Freccero makes clear, these affective relations are not solely defined by loss; queer spectrality also affords relations of pleasure and desire because "[b]eing haunted" is experienced as "profoundly erotic."[33] At stake in this historical relationality, Freccero concludes, is a mode of political responsibility that refuses to efface the alterity of racial and sexual difference but attends to their significance by allowing oneself to be possessed or inhabited by the other in a way that keeps open the undecidable relations of sameness and difference, subjective and social, past and present.

By turning to Burroughs's approach to spectrality, I do not seek to counter Freccero's methodology so much as to shift its focus away from the historical critic to place greater emphasis on the aesthetic object. Consequently, I am less invested in the problem of the past—of how spectrality condenses a repressed or traumatic history—than in the present. Indeed, I ask: What social and erotic relations does queer spectrality enable Burroughs to figure within the representational strictures of his historical present? At the same time, I will increasingly turn from the figuration of spectrality—from ghosts, phantoms, and hauntings—to the way that figuring queer spectrality troubles narrative form. After all, as Derrida writes, "The subject that haunts is not identifiable, one cannot see, localize, fix any form, one cannot decide between hallucination and perception, there are only displacements; one feels looked at by what one cannot see."[34] Derrida aptly describes the affective effect of Burroughs's experimental novels, particularly as his figuration of queer spectrality loses its focal grounding in the subject and becomes dispersed across the entirety of the diegesis. Increasingly, readers cannot "fix any form" and thereby stabilize what is hallucination or perception, fantasy or reality. As a consequence, the reader "feels looked at" because the readerly gaze is reversed and the text develops a ghostly mode of agency, affectively "possessing" the body of the reader. One might object that Burroughs's destabilization of reality and fantasy is simply a means for him to disavow the queerness of his fantasies, to purposefully shroud them with ambiguity. Yet, as we will see, Burroughs's experimental novels are far more sexually explicit and explicitly homoerotic than his early work. Thus, queer spectrality does not repress sex; it detaches its representation from the narrowly psychological framework that isolates queer desire within the subject, opening up an erotic scene for queer relationality among incalculable participants across space and time.

Because I stress the figural relationship between queer spectrality and dissident eroticism, I am not as concerned, in this context, with the problematic of ethical responsibility that Freccero and Derrida so powerfully theorize. On the contrary, I focus on how, *pace* Adler and Hocquenghem, queer spectrality evades judgment—indeed, how its narrative of apparently cannibalistic possession, which horrifically consumes the other, enables the narration of queer relationality within the context of its being codified as obscene. Thus, I trace how Burroughs initially upholds the tentative demarcation of dream and reality but, increasingly, contests this line because it stabilizes the juridical and moral hermeneutics that censure homosexual desire. Echoing Derrida's description of spectrality's undecidable form, Gilles Deleuze notes, "[T]he question of judgment is first of all knowing whether one is dreaming or not. Moreover, Apollo is both the god of judgment and the god of dreams: it is Apollo who judges, who imposes limits and emprisons us in an organic form, it is the dream that emprisons life within these forms in whose name life is judged."[35] To be done with judgment, in Deleuze's view, is to unleash oneself from the imprisoning binary of dream and reality and to withhold an answer to the question—indeed, to not even pose the question—of whether one is dreaming or not. *Queer* is not yet able to leave the "shores of judgment" for the Dionysian intoxication of the body without organs that Burroughs's later work affirms.[36] Yet the novel illuminates the tension between queer desire and social judgment that will inspire Burroughs's turn to an experimental form that can resist the reader's interpretative stabilization of the text and foster a queerer relation to its eroticism.[37]

Of course, the irony of *Queer*'s publication difficulties is that the novel does not actually represent sex. On the contrary, it excises all sexual acts, akin to a Hollywood film that cuts from foreplay to afterglow. Compared to Burroughs's exhaustive delineation of orgies, orgasms, anal sex, masturbation, and erotic asphyxiation in the cut-up novels, *Queer* is tame. The novel primarily narrates a sentimental desire for a romantic and erotic relationship that readers rarely associate with Burroughs's work. One reason, among many, that the novel went unpublished for so long is that Burroughs himself felt that *Queer* no longer exemplified his writing. In 1959, Burroughs wrote to Ginsburg, "I really *do not* want *Queer* published at this time. It is not representative of what I do now, and [has] no interest except like an artist's poor art school sketches—and as such, I protest."[38] In a sense, Burroughs was right. *Queer* is not disorienting, obscene, satirical, crude, funny, horrifying, or difficult to read; it does not possess the anthropological scope of *Junky*; and it does not, like *Naked Lunch*, proliferate narratives in a disjunctive blur of voices, perspectives, and contexts. Through a relatively stable third-person narration, *Queer* follows the protagonist, Lee, as he attempts and fails to establish a relationship with a male lover, Allerton, in Mexico. Although Lee and Allerton begin a sexual relationship, Allerton is indifferent to Lee—he does not express any of the emotional turmoil that Lee feels, and Lee is constantly disappointed that Allerton is "not queer enough to make a reciprocal relation possible."[39] Ultimately, Lee persuades Allerton to accompany him on a trip to Ecuador by drafting a contract for sex between them. Upon returning to Mexico, Allerton disappears and Lee searches for him while he is plagued by dreams of his former lover. It is this failure of reciprocal relationality between men that leads *Queer* toward the spectral figurations that prefigure Burroughs's experimental writing.[40]

Queer establishes the association between frustrated homosexual relationality and the psyche's becoming-spectral in its opening scene. The narration explains, "What Lee looked for in any relationship was the feel of contact. He felt some contact with Carl [Steinberg, a cipher for Allen Ginsberg]."[41] Rebuffed by Carl, however, Lee feels "lonely and defeated," and he slips into a depressive fantasy.[42]

> He saw a shadowy line of boys. As each boy came to the front of the line, he said 'Best of luck,' and ran for a streetcar.
> 'Sorry … wrong number … try again … somewhere else … someplace else … not here … not me … can't use it, don't need it, don't want it. Why pick on me?' The last face was so real and so ugly, Lee said aloud, 'Who asked you, you ugly son of a bitch?'
> Lee opened his eyes and looked around.[43]

This passage is characteristic of *Queer*'s focalization of spectral imagery, which stabilizes its hallucinatory imagery by locating it clearly within Lee's mind. Demarcated by the closing and opening of his eyes, the fantastic elements of this passage (the shadowy boys, real and ugly faces) do not ultimately threaten to break the line between the real and the imagined. The sharpness of the line between reality and fantasy underscores the novel's point that the frustration of homosexual "contact" plunges Lee into solipsism, where distressing melancholic fantasies plague him. Indeed, the shadowy procession of boys performs a grotesque re-enactment of Lee's broken connection with Carl, and they give voice to Lee's paranoia that others perceive his desire as predatory.[44] Although the boys initially view the phone call as accidental ("Sorry ... wrong number"), they soon interpret Lee's contact as an unwarranted persecution ("Why pick on me?"). Lee's fear that others see him as predatory is indicative of the homophobia he suffers in both the United States and Mexico. For example, Moor interprets Lee's otherwise banal conversation as a seduction, and he portrays Lee to the bartender as a "detestably insistent queer, too stupid and too insensitive to realize that his attentions were not wanted, forcing Moor to the distasteful necessity of drawing a diagram."[45] Thus, the spectral imagery of broken connections emblematizes *Queer*'s focalization of impossible reciprocal "contact" while also establishing Lee's earnest desire for someone to pick up the phone that wishes to receive his call.

In the absence of reception, Lee turns depressive, directing his rage at himself, and *Queer*'s narrative form likewise turns spectral. As Burroughs explains in a letter to Ginsberg, the formal structure of his verbal and narrative "routines" becomes altered when they are ignored. It is important to note that the routine is the narrative unit that becomes the basis for *Naked Lunch*'s composition—it is a typically short surrealist narrative that tends to have a comical, erotic, or grotesque payoff. Lee also performs short routines throughout *Queer* as a method of seduction. Yet "[i]f there is no one there to receive it," Burroughs explains, the "routine turns back on me l̶i̶k̶e̶ ̶h̶o̶m̶e̶l̶e̶s̶s̶ ̶c̶u̶r̶s̶e̶ and tears me apart, grows more and more insane (literal growth like cancer) and impossible, and fragmentary like berserk pin-ball machine and I am screaming: 'Stop it! Stop it!'"[46] Not only does Burroughs become a passive victim of his own desire, torn apart by the frustration of contact, the routine itself becomes increasingly spectral—its schizophrenia is, at once, literal yet impossible, fragmentary yet pervasive, randomly berserk yet clearly directed at its author. The spectral hesitation between literal and figurative is therefore indicative of the refusal of erotic and narrative relationality. Both Burroughs and Lee wish to escape their mind, to experience a reciprocal desire, because such a relation might rescue them from the "homeless curse" of solipsism. In this sense, the spectral face, "so real and so ugly," that haunts Lee at the outset of the novel figures the alienated desire that persecutes him and intensifies his self-enclosed melancholia. In choosing how to narrate the problem of homosexual relationality, Burroughs thus faces a representational crossroads. He could force the reader to experience the berserk pinball machine of frustrated contact, dislodging narrative grounding and literalizing the cancer of disconnection that Lee suffers. By putting the phrase "~~like homeless curse~~" under erasure, Burroughs begins to move in this direction, rejecting analogy in favor of queer spectrality's restless and undecidable movement between literal and figurative. Alternately, Burroughs could contextualize the problem of homosexual relationality within a broader social and historical milieu, demonstrating how a repressive culture of homophobia creates and sustains the obstructions to the reciprocation of Lee's desire. *Queer* makes tentative gestures in this direction when it foregrounds Lee's hatred of moral judgment and societal persecution. Yet the novel largely settles on a modernist compromise by focalizing spectrality within the melancholic psyche of the homosexual man. As a consequence, *Queer* often reads as if it is unintentionally perpetuating the pathological narratives that infuse the discourse of moral judgment—namely, the homophobic depiction of the gay man as a tragic and predatory pervert.

Take, for example, Lee's initial introduction to Allerton where the narration transfigures Lee into a spectral creature:

> As Lee stood aside to bow in his dignified old-world greeting, there emerged instead a leer of naked lust, wrenched in the pain and hate of his deprived body and, in simultaneous double exposure, a sweet child's smile of liking and trust, shockingly out of time and out of place, mutilated and hopeless.[47]

This perception floats between Lee, Allerton, and the omniscient gaze of the narration. As such, the passage hesitates in its representation of Lee: Is he a child or an old man; is he a mutilated, passive victim or an aggressive, desiring subject? Who is it that thinks so? This "simultaneous double exposure" expresses the contradictions inherent in the homophobic narratives that delimit Lee's self-perception as well as the interpretation of his desire, his "naked lust" which is painfully obvious to the social gaze. It is important to pause here and note that this phrase is encoded as a reference in the title of *Naked Lunch*. This moment thus points up that the queer gaze, leering at its object of desire, remains a focus of concern for Burroughs even as he appears to move away from the problem of representing homosexual relationality in his experimental novels.[48] As we will see, *Naked Lunch* critically redirects the power dynamic of this lusting gaze. The title of *Naked Lunch*, as Burroughs explains, "means exactly what the words say: *NAKED* Lunch, a frozen moment when everyone sees what is on the end of every fork."[49] There, the exposure is directed to readers who suddenly realize that their gaze is spectrally reciprocal—on the end of the fork, they see their own abject subjection to the affective control mechanisms of language and society. In *Queer*, however, the revelation brought into naked view is the contradictory symbolic status of gay male desire—a "double exposure" of aggression and frustration, at once menacing and pathetic.

While homophobic vestiges of spectrality undoubtedly infuse *Queer*, the novel also deconstructs spectrality, utilizing ghostly figures to narrate queer desire as a strangely active and bodily force. Note, for example, how Lee's imaginary reverie—articulated while he listens to Allerton's routine—engenders a representation of contact between them that is far more explicit than any sexual encounter the two ultimately share.

An imaginary hand projected with such force it seemed Allerton must feel the touch of ectoplasmic fingers caressing his ear, phantom thumbs smoothing his eyebrows, pushing the hair back from his face. Now Lee's hands were running down over the ribs, the stomach. Lee felt the aching pain of desire in his lungs. His mouth was a little open, showing his teeth in the half-snarl of a baffled animal. He licked his lips.[50]

Here queer spectrality allows for the figuration of homosexual eroticism as an affectively tactile encounter. To be sure, Lee's cannibalistic mouth and his transformation into an animal perpetuate the predatory narrative about gay desire. Yet *Queer* also makes clear that Lee is made into an animal by the "invisible bars" that constrain his "unyielding" desire: "[H]is eyes looked out through the invisible bars, watchful, alert, waiting for the keeper to forget the door, for the frayed collar, the loosened bar ... suffering without despair and without consent."[51] Queer spectrality thus underscores the social prohibitions on desire and agency that are its own necessary conditions of possibility. At the same time, this figuration offers a temporary escape from these prohibitions by softly blurring the agency of Lee's and Allerton's "contact." At first, it might appear that Lee is the sole agent of desire due to the forceful phantom limb transforming into Lee's hands. Yet Allerton also reciprocally possesses Lee. Allerton speaks in a "high, thin voice, the eerie, disembodied voice of a young child. Lee had never heard Allerton talk like this before. The effect was like the possession voice of a medium."[52] Framed as a "medium," Allerton therefore possesses and is possessed by the same out-of-time and out-of-place spectrality that Lee exemplifies in his naked lust. Indeed, his voice possesses its listeners like a medium. Their mutual spectrality thus enables a permeable relation of reciprocal contact between Lee and Allerton precisely because it cannot be stabilized into the sharp distinctions of self and other, lover and beloved, possessor and possessed.

This blurring of hierarchical distinctions—and queer spectrality's disjointedness from place and time—must be understood against the racial and national contexts in which *Queer* takes place. In his retrospective description of Mexico, Burroughs fondly recalls being labeled "El Hombre Invisible" by the locals.[53] In his analysis, Timothy Murphy echoes Burroughs's affirmation of this spectral appellation, claiming that Burroughs's "invisibility stems primarily from the same circumstances that render [Ralph] Ellison's narrator [in *Invisible Man*] and [Gilles] Deleuze invisible as well: he does not fit into a tidy category that is already subordinated to the larger scheme of capitalism."[54] Murphy's equation of Ellison's, Deleuze's, and Burroughs's marginality obscures a number of significant differences between them. First, it tends to collapse the distinct circumstances of racism and homophobia, which Burroughs also obscures by offering Orientalist fantasy as the solution to homophobia. Second, it ignores that Burroughs's invisibility in Mexico largely derives from his privilege as a white, male US citizen with money; this invisibility purchases his ability to be "out" as a homosexual—visible yet invisible, expressing his desires in public without notice or comment. In his preface to *Queer*, Burroughs acknowledges this material context when he praises Mexico's supposed lack of a distinction between public and private.

> The City appealed to me. The slum areas compared favorably with anything in Asia for sheer filth and poverty. People would shit all over the street, then lie down and sleep in it with the flies crawling in and out of their mouths. ... It seemed to me that everyone in Mexico had mastered the art of minding his own business. If a man wanted to wear a monocle or carry a cane, he did not hesitate to do it, and no one gave him a second glance. Boys and young men walked down the street arm in arm and no one paid them any mind.

> It wasn't that people didn't care what others thought; it simply wouldn't occur to a Mexican to expect criticism from a stranger, nor to criticize the behavior of others.[55]

Burroughs wants to imagine Mexico as a space of radical disinterest and disregard, where no one has any knowledge of anyone else, where excrement can fall from anuses and flies can enter into mouths and no one passes a second glance.[56] Here Burroughs transposes bodily abjection into the evasion of social judgment, and his transposition is predicated on a deep-rooted Orientalism in which the erotic desires of the Western subject can be expressed through the body of the racial Other. While Burroughs fetishizes the image of boys walking arm in arm without concern, for example, he also depicts Mexico as a space of fraternal betrayal. Indeed, in a patently racist contradiction, Burroughs claims, "No Mexican really knew any other Mexican, and when a Mexican killed someone (which happened often), it was usually his best friend."[57] Narrated against the backdrop of this racist fantasy, the brief contact between Lee and Allerton becomes reframed as nothing short of a miracle, a glimmer of queer relationality that exists spectrally outside the temporality and geography of a violently anti-social world.

Intriguingly, the narrative of *Queer* contradicts Burroughs's retrospective framing in a number of ways. In particular, Mexico does not offer transcendent invisibility for the white homosexual man to evade social critique. In addition to the homophobic American expatriates, Lee confronts Mexicans who also criticize him. When Lee and Allerton drunkenly flirt in the street, for example, a Mexican walks past and utters "*Cabrones*," and Lee is incensed about being "Insulted inna public street," despite being an American citizen with money.[58] In fact, *Queer*'s narrative builds toward Lee's feeling a "killing hate for the stupid, ordinary, disapproving people who kept him from doing what he wanted to do. 'Someday I am going to have things just like I want,' he said to himself. 'And if any moralizing son of a bitch gives me any static, they will fish him out of the river.'"[59] Only the disembodiment of queer spectrality—and not the social space of Mexico—enables Lee to temporarily escape this societal disapproval and to narratively realize his desires. For example, Lee passes a group of "[s]ix or seven boys, aged twelve to fourteen," who are playing on a rubbish heap and urinating in public.[60] Upon seeing Lee, their "play [becomes] overtly sexual, with an undercurrent of mockery. They looked at Lee and whispered and laughed."[61] Lee looks back "openly, [with] a cold, hard stare of naked lust."[62] As he focuses on one boy, Lee suddenly possesses the boy's body, and the prose presses toward the spectral litany that will characterize Burroughs's experimental novels: "He could feel himself in the body of the boy. Fragmentary memories ... the smell of cocoa beans drying in the sun, bamboo tenements, the warm dirty river, the swamps and rubbish heaps on the outskirts of the town."[63] First, Lee and the boys engage in an orgy, culminating in an image of embodied intimacy: "Another boy rested his head on his stomach. Lee could feel the warmth of the other's head, itching a little where the hair touched Lee's stomach."[64] Then, Lee transports to a "bamboo tenement" where he "feel[s] desire for the woman [in the room] through the other's body. 'I'm not queer,' he thought. 'I'm disembodied.'"[65] This moment captures the complex way that queer spectrality—underwritten here by a literalization of Orientalist fantasy—enables the narration of homosexual eroticism while simultaneously deflecting its obscene implications. Not only does the novel contain the eroticism by stressing its status as a fantasy borne of frustrated desire, it also underscores the heterosexual desire that emerges within Lee as he possesses the boy. According to Lee, disembodiment and queerness are distinct, yet the former is the condition for figuring the affective and erotic relations of the latter while also negating its realization.[66]

Note, however, that Lee *can* realize his desire with these young boys: "What can I do? Take them back to my hotel? They are willing enough. For a few Sucres."[67] The problem is that he wants a *reciprocal* relation of desire. This is arguably the limit of queer spectrality for Lee, which broaches onto an image of complete control of the other, not the shared experience of masochistic submission to desire he craves. In fact, Lee attempts to materialize his possession of Allerton through drugs and through a financial contract. Lee seeks the drug Yage because it would allow him to have "thought control" over Allerton, effectively turning him into a slave.[68] At the same time, Lee pays Allerton to travel with him to Ecuador in search of the drug, contracting him to have sex twice a week. Yet both of these attempts at possession fail. They never find Yage, and Lee's desires constantly outstrip the terms of the contract: "Lee said he was sorry he asked so soon [for sex] after the last time, which was a breach of contract."[69] *Queer* thus underscores the futility of attempting to secure reciprocal queer contact through sadistic possession or economic contract.

After Allerton disappears, the novel ends with a brief dream in which Lee appears as the "Skip Tracer" from "Friendly Finance," who is "a finder of missing persons."[70] In Murphy's interpretation, the Skip Tracer is a figure of "the potential for real subversion and new community grounded in the proliferation of ghetto subcultures."[71] Yet I see the Skip Tracer as a figure for the impossibility of using material coercion to establish queer communion. The Skip Tracer tells Allerton, "We've been lonely for you in the office. We don't like to say 'Pay up or else.' It's not a friendly thing to say. I wonder if you have ever read the contract *all the way through*?"[72] Despite these threats, the Skip Tracer's "face went blank and dreamy. His mouth fell open, showing teeth hard and yellow as old ivory," and he drops hundreds of dollars on the ground for Allerton to take.[73] Here the Skip Tracer surrenders the attempt to possess Allerton through money, letting him go without settling his account. Hence, the Skip Tracer's mouth shifts from possessive incorporation to ecstatic surrender. At stake in this turn away from incorporative desire is the novel's ultimate critique of the racist and heteronormative implications of possession. In the epilogue of the novel, Lee takes pictures of people of color, stalking them and photographing them when they look away. He realizes that "[t]here is in fact something obscene and sinister about photography, a desire to imprison, to incorporate, a sexual intensity of pursuit."[74] Soon after this acknowledgment, Lee looks through a magazine entitled *Balls: For Real Men*, which displays a photograph of "a Negro hanging from a tree" with the caption "I Saw Them Swing Sonny Goons."[75] Here Lee's sinister, incorporative drive to photograph becomes correlated to hyperbolic and racist white masculinity. This magazine for "real men," a subject position that queers in *Queer* cannot inhabit as queers, secures its power through the act of witnessing the sexualized and racist violence of lynching. *Queer* ultimately turns from the possessive drive to control the other because it converges with the hyperbolic masculine violence of mainstream American culture.

By foregrounding the loneliness of the Skip Tracer, *Queer* does yearn for a specifically queer sociality that is both absent and unimaginable within the novel's present. Indeed, as we will see in his subsequent novels, Burroughs's desire for queer sociality intensifies and, in turn, the aesthetics of spectrality take on a new function—no longer figuring the subject's fantasy of unrealizable homosexual contact but actively conjuring it through an expansion of the affective conditions that were previously only attributed to the homosexual. *Queer* anticipates this transposition when Lee observes illustrations of male sodomy on Chimu pottery in Ecuador. He wonders, "What happens when there is no limit? What is the fate of The Land Where Anything Goes? Men changing into huge centipedes ... centipedes besieging the houses ... a man tied to a couch and a centipede ten feet long rearing up over him. Is this literal? Did some hideous metamorphosis occur? What is the meaning of the centipede symbol?"[76] Here *Queer* teeters on the precipice of a figurative space where "Anything Goes," where queerness can be unleashed and radically untethered from the pathological perceiving subject. Indeed, the linkage between queer eroticism and spectral aesthetics could not be clearer, as the former gives way to the latter. The consequence of that linkage is the destruction of hermeneutic grounding. In Burroughs's experimental literature, the rhetorical question that goes unanswered here, "Is this literal?" will become the question asked again and again by Burroughs's readers, not a focalizing character. As such, the texts defuse the stability of judgment that buttresses the homophobic pathology and moral judgment that so powerfully constrains Lee in *Queer*. To understand why Burroughs locates affect as the agency of this aesthetic politics we must now turn to his experimental novels and their universalization of queer spectrality into a human condition.

Giving You the Horrors: The Affective Politics of Returning it to the "White Reader"

The most succinct encapsulation of the formal break between Burroughs's early narrative fiction and his experimental writing lies in a shift in object pronouns, a transition from "me" to "you." In *Junky*, Lee is constantly "getting the horrors," typically, but not exclusively, as a result of his junk-inspired hallucinations. Upon walking into a "queer bar" in New Orleans, for example, Lee notes:

> A room full of fags gives me the horrors. They jerk around like puppets on invisible strings, galvanized into hideous activity that is the negation of everything living and spontaneous. The live human being has moved out of these bodies long ago. But something moved in when the original tenant moved out. Fags are ventriloquists' dummies who have moved in and taken over the ventriloquist. The dummy sits in a queer bar nursing his beer, and uncontrollably yapping out of a rigid doll face.[77]

Perhaps one of the most controversial passages in Burroughs's corpus, this moment exemplifies both his misogyny and homophobia.[78] Yet critics often fail to note that *Junky* is written for a mainstream audience; its title, like *Queer*, promises a voyeuristic glimpse at the titillating underbelly of postwar American life. It is notable that, after these texts, Burroughs generalizes this very same discourse of "fag" horror to humanity at large. In *Naked Lunch*, *The Soft Machine*, *The Ticket That Exploded*, and *Nova Express*, all of humanity becomes depicted as a creatural puppet in nearly the same terms Burroughs uses to figure the horror of "fags." The bureaucratic state becomes, in Doctor Benway's words, a "turning away from the human evolutionary direction of infinite potentials and differentiation and independent spontaneous action, to the complete parasitism of a virus."[79] At first glance, this contrast between spontaneous diversity and bureaucratic homogeneity seems derivative of postwar lamentations of all forms of institutional control.[80] Yet note how Burroughs transposes the specific qualities he attributed to homosexuals onto citizens of the state, effectively rendering everyone as puppet of and prey to the non-spontaneous parasite of bureaucratic control. Whereas the desiring homosexual male was the predatory, possessive figure in *Queer*, now the bureaucratic state is the "true parasitic organism."[81] Whereas Lee was the one "getting the horrors" throughout Burroughs's early narrative fiction, it is now "you," the Gentle Reader, that gets the horrors.

This expansion of the horrors marks the subversive shift in Burroughs's construction of reading. Readers become the primary figures of non-spontaneous puppetry, and they must be liberated from the ventriloquist through the agency of the cut-up, which frees them from the language that controls their minds and bodies. In Burroughs's theory, humanity is controlled by "word locks" that "enable those who manipulate words to control thought on a mass scale."[82] In Robin Lydenberg's phrasing, these word locks "dictate our ways of thinking and feeling, stifling spontaneous life and change."[83] If language rather than the homosexual is now the spectral predator, then words likewise adopt the qualities of possession as they affectively and viscerally seduce the body. Moreover, Burroughs explicitly rejects the desire for spectral control that tempts Lee in *Queer*, and he imagines the work of his writing as the means of liberation from possession. Only the cut-up can produce reflexivity by helping readers to "see who you are" as well as "who programs you."[84] To do so, Burroughs's experimental writing extends the project of exposure associated with "getting the horrors." When Lee gets the horrors during a hallucination in *Junky*, for example, he sees an "Oriental face ... eaten away by disease," which gives way to "[a] series of faces, hieroglyphs, [which] distorted and leading to the final place where the human road ends, where the human form can no longer contain the crustacean horror that has grown inside it. I watched curiously. 'I got the horrors,' I thought matter of factly."[85] Here "getting the horrors" correlates with the exposure of the inhuman Other that lurks within and parasitically controls the human subject.

This revelation is noted in passing in *Junky* and is clearly attributed to the effect of alcohol. By contrast, the project of Burroughs's experimental novels is to infuse the revelation of crustacean inhumanity throughout every sentence of the text. The cut-ups "give" readers the horrors by making form itself become-spectral—by making the prose surface become so distorted that it explodes human scales of interpretation, like the face that gives way to a crustacean horror that "human form can no longer contain."[86] The novels do so by proliferating random, spontaneous associations, which are partly the result of the cut-up method. At their most disjunctive, the novels break away from narrative sequence into an incantatory litany of short phrases. The repetitions occur in vastly different contexts, and they often have little or no logical relation with one another. Put simply, there is very little hermeneutic ground on which to build an interpretation of the cut-up texts because each signifier points, prospectively and retrospectively, to an infinite number of contexts. Equating the cut-up novels to a marijuana dream, Burroughs insists that he "do[es] not see [their] organization as a *problem*."[87] Organization is not a problem because his aim is to encourage—or rather force—the reader to surrender the desire for logical, narrative, or conceptual forms of order. By rendering every word spectral—predatory and yet also hauntingly permeable—Burroughs hopes to enable his readers to shed their word locks. Linear temporality is sundered; epistemological grounds break away; and the texts flower in and out of one another as their language pushes toward the spontaneous contingency that Burroughs idealizes as the opposite of control. This stylistic manifestation of linguistic simultaneity and horizontality—which produces spectral fluctuations between figural and literal meaning—buttresses Burroughs's attack on control.[88] Hence, his most famous pronouncement, *"Nothing Is True—Everything Is Permitted,"* delights in the conceit that there will be no limitations to either social or sexual permission.[89]

Note how far we have traveled from Lee's hesitation about unrestricted desire. Now, *everything* is permitted because no one truth or law pertains. This is why queer experimental form itself permits and encourages all possible readings—none is more permissible than another. In this respect, Burroughs's style approaches the affect produced by Gertrude Stein's experimental writing, which Sianne Ngai aptly describes as "stuplimity."[90] This affect, according to Ngai, results from a "strain on the observer's capacities for conceptually synthesizing or metabolizing information."[91] Stein's writing, like Burroughs's, engenders this combination of stupidity and sublimity because it constructs a "relationship to language founded on a not-yet-qualified or -conceptualized difference."[92] This is why, when reading Burroughs and Stein, one can feel the intense pressure of attending to every single word, because each addition reorients the immanent semantic chain. Yet, at the same time, one can feel utterly bored, exhausted, and lost by the overwhelming amount of (often redundant) data to track. The reader feels drained of memory and is, concomitantly, obstructed from other epistemological protocols that typically guide the reading of a novel.[93]

While Burroughs's form foments the affective relations of spectrality, its purpose is not to "represent" queerness. Rather, it disrupts the heteronormative social relations of reading by rewriting language itself as a corporeal force that stimulates the body viscerally—touching readers in ways we cannot control and may not desire. In this respect, Burroughs's experimental texts do not engender "critical" readers that can expose the text's control mechanisms, even if this is their stated purpose. On the contrary, at the affective and performative levels of language, Burroughs's experimental writing collapses critical distance and enfolds the reader within a spectral mystification. In this precise sense, Burroughs re-positions readers as "queer." He forces readers to become spectral, to literally inhabit the ghostly relationality that they previously experienced at a voyeuristic remove.[94] As the narration of *Naked Lunch* explains:

Gentle Reader, The Word will leap on you with leopard man iron claws, it will cut off fingers and toes like an opportunist land crab, it will hang you and catch your jissom like a scrutable dog, it will coil round your thighs like a bushmaster and inject a shot glass of rancid ectoplasm.[95]

Here the "Word" does not simply represent the queer sexuality that society has repressed. The word itself possesses a queerly affective agency: the language of the text violently tears readers apart, rendering them passive subjects of control, soliciting orgasms against their will, and injecting them with "rancid ectoplasm." As much as Burroughs claims that his writing liberates readers from control, it is key that the reader is positioned as an uncritical subject of verbal and erotic violence. The word cuts and reshapes the body; it is animalistic and mercurial in its analogical instability—becoming, at once, a leopard, crab, dog, and snake. By having "rancid ectoplasm" shot into their bodies, readers not only experience the haunted status of the junky but are now subject to the ghostliness that renders homosexual subjects spectral. This moment exemplifies Burroughs's approach to bad reading, because it appeals to apparently degraded affective relations to contest the disembodied and bloodless social imaginary of the heteronormative public sphere. The text forcefully embodies its readers—expelling jissom from their bodies—while also disembodying them through the spectral injection of ectoplasm. The text does not represent or focalize the psyche of a subject but plunges directly into the body of the reader, radically transposing the homosexual's solipsistic fantasia to the public at large.

That the ectoplasm has become "rancid" points up the discursive shift in spectrality from *Queer* to *Naked Lunch*. Although Burroughs will continue to draw on this figural idiom, he marks spectrality itself as an undesirable, even disgusting, position to inhabit. Yet it is no longer the homosexual that inhabits the ectoplasmic position alone. It is the "white reader" who, particularly in *The Soft Machine*, receives these images of abjection. Commenting on this recurrent phrase in the novel, Lydenberg claims that this "randomly generated nonsense" phrase ("Return it to the white reader") "actually stumbles on significance. It captures the ultimate direction in which Burroughs is always moving: the return back to the reader, to the reading of the word, to language as both the origin and dead end of our experience."[96] While Burroughs's fiction certainly draws reflexive attention to the limitations of language, I suggest that there is additional significance in the conjunction of *white* and *reader* in this phrase. In his essay "The Name is Burroughs," Burroughs invokes this phrase in a scene that takes place in the Interzone, the setting of *Naked Lunch*. The narrator meets a young boy, the Guide, who asks what he wants. Burroughs replies, "Well uh, I would like to write a bestseller that would be a good book, a book about real people and places."[97] The Guide replies, "That's enough Mister. I don't want to read your stinking book. That's a job for the White Reader."[98] Suddenly appearing on the Guide's face screen, the White Reader offers to connect the writer with the "best continuity man in the industry" to purchase his novel.[99] Recall Burroughs's reminder that authors should "never expect a general public to experience anything they don't want to experience" because there are some things "the general public just doesn't want to see or hear."[100]

Hence, returning "it" to the white reader translates into a challenge to the publishing industry that prioritizes safe, bourgeois comforts for a primarily white middle-class reading public. The text not only assaults the white reader through representations of sexuality, violence, and cross-racial desire but also breaks apart the "continuity" that is central to the texts preferred by white readers—a "*good* book" that purports to merely represent "real people and places."[101] Here we should recall the ending of *Queer*, where the gaze of the "white reader" is encapsulated by the hyperbolically racist fetishizing of lynching photographs in a magazine for so-called "real men."[102] By rejecting the representational function of the "continuity man," Burroughs's form contests the voyeuristic and hierarchical relation that enables the "white reader" to perceive himself as disembodied, transcendent of the corporeality he attributes to others.

In *The Soft Machine*, the white reader receives this assault within a scene that highlights how experimental form undoes the relations of critique that obstruct the realization of specifically queer eroticism.

> Pants down to the ankle, a barefoot Indian stood there watching and feeling his friend—Others had shot their load too over a broken chair through the tool heap—Tasty spurts of jissom across the dusty floor—Sunrise and I said here we go again with the knife—My cock pulsed right with it and trousers fell in the dust and dead leaves—Return it to the white reader in the stink of sewage looking at open shirt flapping and comes maybe five times his ass fluttering like—.[103]

This passage exemplifies the experimental form of Burroughs's cut-up novels in which the continuity of subjects and objects is sundered. This ass may flutter like a flapping shirt, but the broken sentence does not structurally clarify the object of analogy. Instead, the prose flows on beyond the em-dash. In this sense, Burroughs's style might be said to radically proliferate continuity rather than simply disrupt it. Any number of possible conjunctions, associations, or completions could be chosen, thereby extending the temporal continuity of the writing into infinity. We cannot, finally, decide what the ass flutters like, what precisely the cock pulses with, or which "it" is returned to the reader. Yet the juxtaposition of these elements and their disruption of representational continuity buttresses Burroughs's project to defuse the white reader's critique of queer eroticism. In *Queer*, the frustration of narrative reception was linked to the impossible realization of queer contact. Here reception is guaranteed because the white reader is bottomed by the text. After all, the passage culminates in a body having an orgasm "maybe five times his ass fluttering like." Even if that subject is indeterminate, the white reader is one possible subject or object of this ecstasy, one receiver to whom this pleasure has been "returned." At the same time, the text rezones the male body into a series of porous orifices, equating the experience of ejaculation with an anal orgasm or "ass fluttering." The text withholds a clear focalization of this body's pleasure to force the reader's direct immersion in it, unmediated by voyeuristic distance.

While Burroughs's solicitation of bad reading refuses *all* social prohibitions and permits *everything*, I want to underscore the prominence that homophobic prohibitions have in his experimental novels. By doing so, we can see that Burroughs's contestation of the "white reader" is specifically tied to a queer aesthetic politics. Let us turn, then, to *The Soft Machine*'s iteration of the "hanging routine," which has a particular prominence in the experimental novels. The hanging routine typically involves one character surrendering to, or being forced into, erotic asphyxiation that culminates in orgasm and death. The scene often entails questionable agency, cross-racial sex, transmutation of one body into another, and, above all, the eroticization of death as ecstasy. In *The Soft Machine*, for example, Lee is hanged and his neck snaps. Then:

> [S]ilver light popped in my eyes like a flash bulb—I got a whiff of ozone and penny arcades and then I felt it start way down in my toes these bone wrenching spasms emptied me and everything spilled out shit running down the back of my thighs and no control in my body paralyzed, twisting up in these spasms the jissom just siphoned me right into Xolotl's cock and next thing I was in his ass and balls flopping around spurting all over the floor and that evil old fuck crooning and running his hands over me so nasty— But then who am I to be critical?[104]

Lee's question expresses a meta-textual awareness that readers will demand an explicit critique of the violence, sexual perversity, and immorality displayed here. We can re-transcribe Lee's question in a number of ways: Who am I to be critical of Xolotl's perversion, given my pleasure in being fondled by him? Who am I to be critical, given my passivity and lack of agency in this moment? After all, Lee is "paralyzed by the medicine any case" and thus has no choice to participate or not.[105] And finally: Who am I to be critical, anyway, since I am *inside* Xolotl's genitals? The two may have switched bodies; Lee may be fondling his own body, and Xolotl has become the passive host to Lee's possession; Lee may be a mere voyeur; or Lee is a complicit participant with Xolotl. Since there is no manifest distance between Lee and Xolotl, the presumed object of critique, there is no space between their desires. Thus, there is no logic that can permit Lee to be critical. Note that Lee has no anxiety about this utterly confused situation. Indeed, the tone of Lee's question reveals the divergence of Burroughs's cut-up fiction from *Queer*. In the latter, Lee worried whether his visions of sexual violence were "literal." Here, Lee dismisses such concerns and enjoins the reader to simply enjoy the "fun and games what?" with bemusement and casual indifference.[106] Indeed, *The Soft Machine* does not explain or resolve Lee's temporary lack of a body. Right after this experience, Lee wakes up and heads south for more sex with young boys and more adventures. By refusing to stabilize the line between fantasy and reality, *The Soft Machine* denies readers a narrative framework to criticize— and thereby contain—the spectral proliferation of queer eroticism.

By utilizing experimental form to engender spectral affects in his readers, Burroughs highlights the body as a locus of political control and contestation. In fact, the affective control of homosexuals becomes the primary exemplar of all of humanity's subjugation, thereby totally inverting the postwar discourse of homophobic spectrality. The "examination" routine in *Naked Lunch* offers the clearest exemplification of this inversion. This scene introduces Carl Peterson, who becomes subject to Doctor Benway's "biocontrol" mechanisms. Benway, a "manipulator and coordinator of symbol systems," expresses the ideology of control throughout the experimental novels, underscoring the importance of instilling subjugation through affect rather than direct violence.[107] Not only does this process make resistance more difficult, since "the subject cannot contact his enemy direct" behind the "arbitrary and intricate bureaucracy" that instills these affects, the subject also believes his subjugation is appropriate: "He must be made to feel that he deserves *any* treatment because there is something (never specified) horribly wrong with him."[108] Explaining the examination to Carl, Benway claims that his function is to gather knowledge so that "the state—simply a tool" can "adjust … to the needs of each individual citizen."[109] Benway explains that the state has a "prophylactic" obligation to relieve the individual of "*any* illness."[110] Note, however, Benway's example: "For example … *for example* … take the matter of uh *sexual deviation*. […] We regard it as a misfortune … a sickness … certainly nothing to be censored or uh sanctioned any more than say … tuberculosis."[111]

Benway claims that homosexuality is merely a specific example of a general condition, yet the repetition and emphasis on its exemplarity suggests that homosexuality *is* of specific and unique interest to the affective gaze of the state—and, by extension, of singular importance to *Naked Lunch.* Indeed, despite his apparent disinterestedness as a representative of state power, Benway leers at Carl with eyes that are "at once cold and intense, predatory and impersonal. Carl suddenly felt trapped in this silent underwater cave of a room, cut off from all sources of warmth and certainty. His picture of himself sitting there, calm, alert with a trace of well mannered contempt went dim, as if vitality were draining out of him to mix with the milky grey medium of the room."[112] After Carl masturbates into a jar, he feels watched with a critical loathing: "Something was watching his every thought and movement with cold, sneering hate, the shifting of his testes, the contractions of his rectum."[113] These moments recall Lee's leer of "naked lust," but note that the gaze now clearly exemplifies the forces of social control—it does not focalize the tragic homosexual and his frustrated desire; it "focalizes" the impersonal and collective mechanisms of biopower that control sexuality itself. Note, too, the emergence of the spectral "grey medium" of the examination room and the ghostly possession of Carl's body occur at the very moment that the putatively straight character becomes subject to the state's power.

Of course, Carl may not be as straight as he claims. Despite protesting that he is attracted to women, and despite passing Benway's attraction tests, Carl succumbs to the examination and recalls repressed memories of sexual intercourse with men from his time in the military. There were no "economic factors involved" in these encounters, implying his active and specific desire for homosexual contact.[114] At this moment, "A green flare exploded in Carl's brain. He saw Hans' lean brown body—twisting towards him, quick breath on his shoulder. The flare went out. Some huge insect was squirming in his hand. His whole being jerked away in an electric spasm of revulsion."[115] Based on Benway's predatory interrogation, the scene reads as a control trap, in which the system desires him to be a homosexual, thereby confirming its necessity as an institution of social control. At the same time, Carl does indeed recall homosexual experiences (or at least appears to), and this is key to the novel's returning to the "white reader" desires he or she might otherwise disavow. Rather than firmly focalizing these desires within Carl's subjective perspective, however, the entire scene becomes spectral. When Carl attempts to escape, he observes, "the *whole thing* is unreal" and, as in a dream, a "creeping numbness dragged his legs. The door seemed to recede. ... The whole room was exploding out into space."[116] The horror here, given unto Carl and the reader, is precisely the horror of biopower, exemplified by the suffering of someone positioned as a homosexual. The horror of the situation is *not* homosexual desire but the state's predatory investment in sexuality, its attempt to control and manipulate the body of its citizens. The squirming insect recalls *Queer*'s transposition of sodomy into a creatural nightmare of inhumanity, a world that is excitingly and disturbingly without limits. Yet here the insect evokes the revulsion the putatively heteronormative subject feels when he is subjected to the desiring technologies of the seemingly innocuous "Ministry of Mental Hygiene and Prophylaxis."[117] While homosexuality has a singular and exemplary role in this narrative, the ultimate focus rests on the control of sexuality as such. After all, as Burroughs notes, "Recent experiments in electric brain stimulation indicate that sexual excitement and orgasm can be produced at push-button control or push-button *choice*, depending on who is pushing the buttons."[118] Thus, Burroughs speculates that

> a homosexual can be conditioned to react sexually to a woman, or to an old boot for that matter. ... In the same way, heterosexual males can be conditioned to react sexually to other men. Who is to say that one is more desirable than the other? Who is competent to lay down sexual dogmas and impose them on others?[119]

If sexuality, as such, is contingent and open to affective manipulation, then sexuality is a matter of power, not morality. Here heterosexuality has no privilege or priority over homosexuality or fetishism—it is equally subject to the conditions of biopower.

By positing queer spectrality as an aesthetic analogue for and a manifestation of the politics of affect, Burroughs is able to complexly elude the representational prohibitions on figuring queer eroticism. Indeed, he can directly present these images while locating the agency of desire within the mechanisms of control, not the queer subject. Indeed, the faceless Controllers of *Nova Express* denounce Hassan i Sabbah's liberatory appeal to "cold windy bodiless rock" in favor of "all pleasures of the body," which they offer through orgasmic delights and love.[120] Invariably, these pleasures turn their subjects into "[m]uttering addicts of the orgasm drug, boneless in the sun, gurgling throat gristle, heart pulsing slowly in transparent flesh eaten alive by the crab men."[121] At the same time, Burroughs can affirm

the affective relationality of his writing—its capacity to viscerally enfold
the reader within its spectral scene—as a means of engendering liberation
from control. As he contends, "All political organizations tend to function like a machine, to eliminate the unpredictable factor of AFFECT—
emotion. Any machine tends to absorb, eliminate Affect."[122] Throughout
the experimental novels, the junkie exemplifies the complete elimination
of affect because junk produces "permanent backbrain depression and a
state much like terminal schizophrenia: complete lack of affect, autism,
virtual absence of cerebral event."[123] As Benway theorizes, "The orgasm
has no function in the junky," and indeed, Lee notes that he is "forgetting sex and all sharp pleasures of the body—a grey, junk-bound ghost.
The Spanish boys call me El Hombre Invisible—the Invisible Man."[124]
Thus, queer experimental literature's capacity to affectively *stimulate* the
reader rematerializes the spectral reading public, whose invisibility is no
longer an index of sovereign transcendence but of subjugation to control
mechanisms.

　　Naked Lunch's most famous scene—Dr. Benway's "talking asshole"
routine—provides a final clue to the intersection of spectrality and the affective politics of Burroughs's queer experimental literature. In this scene, a
carnival performer teaches his anus to speak on command. However, the
anus takes on a life of its own: it talks, grows teeth, eats, drinks, demands
"equal rights," and yearns for a lover to kiss it the "same as any other
mouth."[125] Yet the performer refuses to recognize this mouth, and once
his asshole demands "equal rights," he does everything he can to silence
it. In response, the anus consumes the performer, sealing his face behind
undifferentiated tissue, causing him to become brain-dead. Although critics frequently debate the allegorical meaning of this narrative, I want to
stress the statement that Benway makes immediately after his routine.
Benway explains:

> That's the sex that passes the censor, squeezes through between bureaus,
> because there's always a space *between*, in popular songs and Grade B mov-
> ies, giving away the basic American rottenness, spurting out like breaking
> boils, throwing out globs of that un-D.T. to fall anywhere and grow into
> some degenerate cancerous life-form, reproducing a hideous random image.
> Some would be entirely made of penis-like erectile tissue, others viscera
> barely covered over with skin, clusters of 3 and 4 eyes together, criss-cross
> of mouth and assholes, human parts shaken around and poured out any way
> they fell.[126]

The "talking asshole" routine constitutes "sex that passes the censor" precisely because it does not read as *sex* but as *spectrality*. Indeed, Benway's description of un-D.T. globs spurting over humanity maps a sexual image (ejaculation) onto a horrifying image (hideous mutations). Similarly, the routine substitutes an asshole for the desirous homosexual subject. Akin to Lee, the asshole yearns to become a subject of reciprocal desire, and its queer desire refashions the asshole into active agent of possession. This moment thus condenses the political stakes for Burroughs's deconstruction of queer spectrality. Like the anus, the spectral text secretes un-D.T. that transmogrifies readers into monstrously queer beings. Mouths and assholes become crossed; genitals morph or atrophy. Readers are consumed by the text's spectrality, and the reading public is rewritten as a queer concoction of bodily parts freed from organic form. The D.T., like Burroughs's cut-up technique, produces "hideous random image," and it is their common spectrality—pitched between reality and fantasy, satire and horror—that enables both the cut-up and queerness to seep through the "space between" the censors and thereby expose the "basic American rottenness."

Perhaps most importantly, queer spectrality remakes the aesthetic into a force of queer becoming. It reproduces a "hideous random image," but this reproduction is neither mimetic nor heteronormative. Rather, the fecundity of queer experimental literature is akin to an inhuman cancer that cannot be predicted or controlled by a subject. Prior to Burroughs's turn to queer experimental literature, the cancerous prose surface indicated the non-reception of a routine by a lover or listener; its spectral elements focalized the performer's frustrated desire as it ricocheted against the walls of his mind. Now, the spectral aesthetic signifies a social critique of control and an affective assault on the "white reader." The more cancerous the text is—the more boils spurting through it—the more critical that text becomes of "the basic American rottenness." These cancerous figures evoke the horrors of social control, rewriting the white reader in the terms that have solely been written onto the bodies of queers.[127] By viscerally implicating the reader's body within the scene of reading, the spectral aesthetic reconceives of reading as a kind of queer contact in which the text has a uniquely forceful affective agency.

Based on its visceral assault on the reader, it may seem as if Burroughs only engenders an antagonistic relationship with readers. If this were the case, then critics would be correct that his experimental novels lack an affirmative horizon for the imagination of collectivity. By looking more closely at the litanies that characterize Burroughs's spectral aesthetic, I will demonstrate how queer collectivity becomes figured through the text's fusing together of words and bodies into an ectoplasmic blob.

"ONE GWEAT BIG BLOB": THE PHANTOMS OF QUEER SOCIABILITY

Flirting with Allerton in *Queer*, just before they have sex, Lee speaks to him in "baby talk" and says, "Wouldn't it be booful if we should juth run together into one gweat big blob. ... Am I giving you the horrors?'"[128] This iteration of "giving the horrors" anticipates the incipiently social imagination that Burroughs's queer experimental literature condenses through the aesthetics of queer spectrality. This is not an antagonistic or assaultive iteration of the horrors but a playful and seductive one that expresses a desire for relational contact.[129] To be sure, this seduction remains veiled in irony; the dialect of baby talk pretends that the desire for merging into a "blob" is an infantile joke. Yet that desire is expressed nonetheless. After all, flirtation often relies on an ironized surface discourse of denial. Taking that irony at face value, however, has led critics to miss the way that Burroughs's queer spectrality condenses a seductive appeal to erotic communion. For example, Murphy argues that the cut-ups are marked by "cynicism" that denies a "commitment to social change" and the production of "new social groups."[130] These texts "negate the given social order but refuse to offer new forms of social organization."[131] The language of "refusal" implies that these novels are denying something that they can actually offer.[132] Indeed, as we saw at the outset of this chapter, Burroughs's figuration of queer sociality must instead be assessed in relationship to the constraints on its representation within pre-Stonewall America. Burroughs's queer experimental literature not only desires a form of queer sociality; his experimentations seek a queerer *form* for figuring collectivity. As we will see, it is the "gweat big blob," with its dissolution of individuals into a spectrally permeable erotic communion, that affords a form for figuring queer collectivity in Burroughs's experimental novels.

To be sure, Burroughs is justifiably understood as an anti-social writer. Burroughs insists, "There are no good relationships."[133] All apparent relationality in his fiction becomes subject to the "symbiosis con," in which a parasite infiltrates its host and no possible compromise or reciprocity is possible between them. Hence, scholars often see Burroughs as, in Alfred

Kazin's words, a "victim of solitude" who possesses a lamentable "infatuation with the storeroom of his own mind."[134] Yet we have seen that Burroughs's experimental writing reconfigures the politics of solipsism, enfolding the reader into its orbit. Moreover, we should recall Michael Warner's point that counterpublic texts that seek to rewrite the existing divisions of public and private often read as "debased narcissism," precisely because publicness "requires filtering or repressing something that is seen as private."[135] Burroughs's refusal to repress queer eroticism leads his text to ironize the liberal discourses of social inclusion that predominate in his historical moment. In his coming out routine, for example, Lee tells Allerton about Bobo, the "wise old queen," who instructed him to "bear my burden proudly for all to see, to conquer prejudice and ignorance and hate with knowledge and sincerity and love."[136] Tragically, Bobo dies in a car accident, and Lee claims:

> Then I knew the meaning of loneliness. But Bobo's words came back to me from the tomb, the sibilants cracking gently. 'No one is ever really alone. You are part of everything alive.' The difficulty is to convince someone else he is really part of you, so what the hell? Us parts ought to work together. Reet?[137]

Often read as a parody of coming out stories and platitudes about human community, this passage points up the way Lee rhetorically ironizes discourses of sociality to subversively express queer desire. After all, Lee is flirting with Allerton, attempting to convince him to have sex by claiming that "we are all parts of a tremendous whole. No use fighting it."[138] There is no "use" in fighting one's desire here because homosexuality is already included within the "tremendous whole" of the social world. What might appear to be a universalizing discourse of liberal inclusion, then, becomes an ironic figure to express and provoke the desire for sexual contact. Rather than rejecting relationality, it is more apt to say that Burroughs refuses any figure of sociality that disavows queer eroticism from its body politic.

Thus, the ambivalence about sociality in Burroughs's fiction stems from the homophobic restrictions that limit the possibility of manifesting queer relationality within and against a rigidly heteronormative society.[139] This ambivalence is expressed at the outset of Burroughs's first novel, *Junky*. Lee begins the novel by narrating his failure to maintain a long-term relation with other queers. For example, he hopes his "romantic attachment" with a boy will provide an escape from the "dullness of a Midwest suburb where all contact with life was shut out."[140] Yet they are arrested for vandalism and theft, and Lee's lover "'packed [him] in' because the relationship was endangering his standing with the group. I saw there was no compromise possible with the group, the others, and I found myself a good deal alone."[141] This relationship endangers the lover not simply because Lee is a criminal but because the relationship itself is literally criminal; this is, after all, a historical moment in which homosexuality, encoded in Lee's desire for "contact with life," is illegal. Hence, homosexual relations are opposed to "compromise" with the social group—Lee and the lover experience the two as mutually exclusive. Still, Lee desires a viable queer community. After suffering exclusion at his Ivy League college, Lee meets a group of wealthy, cosmopolitan homosexuals. In them, he recalls, "I saw a way of life, a vocabulary, references, a whole symbol system, as the sociologists say. But these people were jerks for the most part and, after an initial period of fascination, I cooled off on the set-up."[142] Crucially, *Junky* contrasts the homosexual "way of life" to junk, which is similarly defined as "not a kick. It is a way of life."[143] The difference between these two ways of life derives from their approach to sociality. Junk teaches the user that "no one can help anyone else," and it simultaneously "short-circuits sex. *The drive to non-sexual sociability comes from the same place sex comes from*, so when I have an H or M shooting habit I am non-sociable."[144] Here junk provides a relief from social desire, which is reciprocally constituted by sexual desire. Although Lee desires both sexual and social relationality, we have seen how painful their frustration can be. Consequently, he seeks an asexual transcendence of the body in junk, hoping for "momentary freedom from the claims of the aging, cautious, nagging, frightened flesh."[145] At the very same time, the novel concludes with his wish for an "uncut kick that *opens out* instead of narrowing down like junk."[146] Lee thinks that Yage may be the mechanism of this kick, and as we saw in *Queer*, he will be disappointed. Yet it is significant that Burroughs ends the novel by foregrounding a desire for an *opening out* that opposes junk's asociality and uncommunicative individualism and the existing formations of homosexual community from which Lee feels alienated. This yearning for queer sociality—for an affective kick that opens the body out into a mode of relationality *without sacrificing its queerness*—will continue to echo through Burroughs's experimental novels and beyond.

How, then, do the aesthetics of queer spectrality enable the cut-up novels to figure this sociality? Spectrality fosters an erotically permeable blending of bodies while also signifying the impossibility of these relations emerging within the present. In *The Ticket That Exploded*, for example, two lovers meet in a "ruined warehouse swept by winds of time," surrounded by "ectoplasmic flakes of old newspapers," and they lie on a "mattress twisted and molded by absent tenants—ghost rectums, spectral masturbating afternoons reflected in the tarnished mirror—."[117] Here queer erotics linger outside of time, melancholically persisting in abandoned spaces.[148] The tone implies that these spaces were not always absent; at one time, the mirror reflected untarnished encounters of masturbating afternoons. Thus, queer spectrality evokes a desire for a pastoral, almost Edenic, space of queer belonging. Even if that space never existed in reality, the scenes savor and preserve the potentiality for such sociability to materialize. Of course, the realization of queer relationality is highly tentative, and its emergence is only possible if the codifications of the human body are dissolved into ghostly permeability. For example, we see the two lovers as they

> twisted free of human coordinates rectums merging in a rusty swamp smell—spurts of semen fell through the blue twilight of the room like opal chips—The air was full of flicker ghosts who move with the speed of light through orgasms of the world—tentative beings taking form for a few seconds in copulations of light—Mineral silence through the two bodies stuck together in a smell of KY and rectal mucus fell apart in time currents swept back into human form—[149]

The spectral dissolution of codified human form here enables the emergence of a new figure for queer relationality—the merging of rectums, which meet like kissing lips. At this moment, two distinct subjects blur into an indefinite plentitude of "flicker ghosts" that literally possess the entire world, moving through bodies on a chain of orgasms. For one "tentative" moment, queer desire is radically globalized, and the world coheres through queer eroticism rather than in strict opposition to it. Of course, these pleasures are destroyed by the return to organic form. The time currents become re-coordinated to the rhythm of humanity, returning the hierarchical priority of the subject over the body, of being over becoming. Yet the *becoming-sticky* of these bodies without organs, affixed here by the fluids of KY, rectal mucus, and semen, offers a momentary tactile materialization of queer contact.

Queer spectrality's transcendence from human form also temporarily evades the parasitic hierarchical relations of the symbiosis con.[150] Take, for example, Bradley's entrance into a sensory withdrawal tank with nine other men. They float in the tank

a few feet apart in darkness with no sound but feedback from the two halves
of ten bodies permutated to heartbeat body music vibrating through the
tank—Body outlines extend and break here—The stretching membrane of
skin dissolves—Sudden taste of blood in his throat as gristle vaporizes and
the words wash away and the halves of his body separated like a mold—Fish
sperm drifted through the tank in silent explosions—Skeletons floated and
the crab parasites of the nervous system and the grey cerebral dwarf made
their last attempt to hold prisoners in spine and brain coordinates—screaming "You can't—You can't—You can't"—Screaming without a throat without speech centers as the brain split down the middle and the feed-back
sound shut off in a blast of silence.[151]

Although the parasites scream and die, the doctors lament "other parasites
will invade sooner or later."[152] Thus, the ecstatic permutation of bodies does
not lead to a complete utopian space beyond control. Yet it nonetheless
identifies a path toward tentative freedom *through* the homoerotic dissolution of human subjects into corporeal blobs that become permeably recombined in the medium of sperm. Human form splits open, thereby denying
the spectral parasites throats and bodies to control the subject, yet the queer
eroticism of this passage relies on the persistence of bodily affects—the taste
of blood, the rhythmic pulse of heartbeats—even as the spectral communion
of inhuman, indistinct non-subjects verges on pure silence. Burroughs's
intimation of freedom from the codifications of social control therefore proceeds through the erotic body politic of queer relationality.

Notably, this relationality is incipient in the event of reading, precisely at the moment that "body outlines extend and break *here*."[153] Here
Burroughs stresses the affective force of his spectral aesthetic as it per-
mutates words and bodies and fluids in the endlessly potential present of
reading. Thus, queer spectrality does not solely rely on a melancholic temporality of retrospection that preserves the lost, obstructed, or destroyed
relationality of queerness. It also fosters a ghostly virtuality that outstrips
the limits of temporal and spatial boundaries, reaching out to readers like
a protoplasmic arm that beckons us to succumb to its sensory depriva-
tions and affective recombination of the human form into a communal,
corporeal blob. Therefore, the formal surface of Burroughs's experimental
writing does not so much "mirror" queer spectrality as *literally* embody it.
Its agglutination of words into spectral litanies of abjection and eroticism
are the incipient event of an affective kick that "opens out" into a mode
of queer sociality that does not permit the repression of certain bodies or

desires to stabilize itself.[154] In these spectral litanies, *Queer*'s irony about "merging" into one great blob disappears, and in its place, the prose becomes deliriously—and, I would argue, earnestly—adhesive. Although critics consistently emphasize the disjunctive *cut* of Burroughs's cut-up fold-in method, we cannot forget the *fold* as fostering new lines of association where none existed before. Recall Deleuze and Guattari's concern that the fold-in implies a spiritual reunification of the text. I would argue that the fold points up the word's *becoming-relational*—its queer stickiness, its capacity to reattach bodies and words into unrecognizable forms of collectivity. Take, for example, the famous "Hassan's Rumpus Room" routine in *Naked Lunch*. Although not evidently produced through the cut-up method, this moment prefigures the queer association engendered through the spectral litany. The narration of the orgy gives way to thumbnail sketches of various, surreal moments of queer eroticism, which become increasingly compressed—from two or three sentences to mere phrases. Then, the scene culminates in

> Pictures of men and women, boys and girls, animals, fish, birds, the copulating rhythm of the universe flows through the room, a great blue tide of life. Vibrating, soundless hum of deep forest—sudden quiet of cities when the junky copes. A moment of stillness and wonder.[155]

The entire universe opens out onto an orgy, and at its most ecstatic, the spectral litany pushes subjects and objects to the threshold of indistinction. Now, we see mere "men and women," not the figures of Aztec priests, naked lifeguards, homosexuals, and other highly specified bodies that precede this moment. In a rush of affect, the world becomes an abstract blur of relationality bound together by a "copulating rhythm" that, in its vibratory intensity, contrasts the "sudden quiet" of the junky's isolated struggle with the anti-social forces of addiction.

One might object that spectral indistinction moves away from the social world. Unlike Walt Whitman, for example, Burroughs's spectral litany does not map classes and types in an existing social milieu. Rather, it is aggressively anti-historical, refusing to represent the social as it is. While its refusal of mimesis negates the existent representational structures of the heteronormative world, the spectral litany manifests its becoming-relational through the affective forces of language itself. This is clear in *Naked Lunch*'s provocative meta-figure for the eroticism of its own words:

> The Word is divided into units which be all in one piece and should be so taken, but the pieces can be had in any order being tied up back and forth, in and out fore and aft like an innaresting sex arrangement. This book spill off the page in all directions, kaleidoscope of vistas, medley of tunes and street noises, farts and riot yipes and the slamming steel shutters of commerce, screams of pain and pathos and screams plain pathic, copulating cats and outraged squawk of the displaced bull head, prophetic mutterings of brujo in nutmeg trances, snapping necks and screaming mandrakes, sigh of orgasm, heroin silent as dawn in the thirsty cells.[156]

Here language is marked by the fragmentary disjunction that characterizes Burroughs's experimental novels as a whole. Divided into individual units, the prose surface has no sequential order grounded in linearity or continuity. Yet in the absence of sequential logic, language proliferates, spilling off the page, and as it does, the word becomes increasingly adhesive; it agglutinates percepts and affects—sights, sounds, smells, tastes, and other tactile sensations—while also becoming an affective force of expression. Crucially, this agglutinating proliferation branches out onto a "kaleidoscope of vistas," and conversely, these horizons are mapped directly back onto the geography of the body. If, as Warner argues, "the modern hierarchy of faculties and its imagination of the social are mutually implying," then Burroughs's realignment of the faculties here points toward a new imagination of the social that is predicated on queer erotics as a driving force of an embodied sociality.[157] Indeed, Burroughs's narrator elsewhere enjoins readers to literally fuse themselves into the agglutinating litany: "[E]verybody splice himself in with everybody else yes boys that's me there by the cement mixer."[158] This splicing only produces, like Burroughs's experimental aesthetics, a spectral blob—a proliferation of mixed-up body parts and words. Yet this communalism must stay indistinct—the cement mixer cannot pour this queer concoction out and allow it to solidify, because Burroughs knows all too well the censors and forces of judgment that he faces if he represents queer collectivity in a realized form. Queer collectivity cannot be cemented then, only intimated through the restless churnings of a spliced tongue.

BETWEEN SOLIPSISM AND SOCIALITY

To understand why the desire for queer collectivity must be figured through the aesthetics of spectrality, we need only recall the Court's concern over *Naked Lunch*'s anticipation of homosexuals as a political group. Ironically, queer experimental literature becomes viable as an aesthetic politics precisely in response to the discourse that seeks to censor the direct representation of queer belonging. When the Court insists that "obviously [*Naked Lunch*] is fantasy," they codify the novel in the very terms that inspire Burroughs's turn to experimental literature.[159] While Burroughs also depicts his writing as a mechanism of spectral fantasy, their sovereign interpretation attempts to reestablish the hermeneutic grounding that queer experimental form destabilizes. Indeed, the Court can interpret the text's fantasies as socially valuable only insofar as they re-focalize them within the solipsistic mind of the junkie subject. The legacy of this hermeneutic move is, as I have suggested, long standing, leading many readers to overlook the entwined desires for *queerness* and *collectivity* expressed through the aesthetics of spectrality. My goal has been to resuscitate both of these referents and to prioritize them as conditions of possibility for Burroughs's turn to queer experimental literature. The predominance of homophobic and pathologizing readerly relations leads Burroughs to confront an aesthetic paradox that *Naked Lunch* so aptly identifies in its conclusion:

> I don't know how to return it to the white reader.
> You can write or yell or croon about it ... paint about it ... act about it ... shit it out in mobiles. ... *So long as you don't go and do it.*
> Senators leap up and bray for the Death Penalty with inflexible authority of virus yen. ... Death for dope fiends, death for sex queens (I mean fiends) death for the psychopath who offends the cowed and graceless flesh with broken animal innocence of lithe movement.[160]

How can queer experimental literature give readers the horrors if the law saps the text's provocation by codifying it as a scene of compensatory fantasy—a scene for writing about desires so long as you do not actualize them in reality? What aesthetic form can "return it to the white reader" in a way that, at once, passes between the inflexible authority of the law and foments the becoming of queerness as a social reality? Burroughs's formal solution stresses the becoming-relational of the text itself, its enfolding readers within an affective scene of queer contact. As the narration proclaims, "*Naked Lunch* is a blueprint, a How-To Book. ... Black insect lusts open into vast, other planet landscapes. ... Abstract concepts, bare as algebra, narrow down to a black turd or a pair of aging cajones. ... *Naked Lunch* demands Silence from The Reader. Otherwise he is taking his own pulse."[161] I want to underline the scalar oscillation between solipsism and sociality that emerges here, as queer lust opens out onto vast planetary horizons while concepts narrow down into the corporeal materiality of excrement and genitalia. Readerly solipsism—hearing only our own pulse—is overcome by affective contact with queerness. Yet this incipient sociality is irreducibly marked by the restless figural oscillation between the brute materiality of eroticism and the permeable amorphousness of spectrality.

Queer experimental literature will always appear, then, to merely elicit bad reading—it will always narrow down into the obscenity of turds and testicles. To argue, as I have, that this narrowing is combined with an incipiently social imagination does not "redeem" the degraded queerness of Burroughs's eroticism. On the contrary, it is to underscore the mutually constituting nature of queer affect and queer collectivity. In a historical moment that perpetually permits the representation of the former at the expense of the latter, queer experimental literature uses the aesthetics of spectrality to insist on the irreducible and untranscendable entwinement of queerness and relationality. Burroughs contests the very division between them by exploding the circumscription of fantasy within the subject. This movement not only subverts the homophobic attribution of spectrality to gay men, but it also undoes the pathologizing of homosexuality that relies on a psychological narrative of the individuated desiring subject. This narrative re-merges in the defense of *Naked Lunch* when Burroughs's lawyer demands that the public perceive the novel as scientific. He notes, "A doctor is not criticized for describing the manifestations and symptoms of an illness, even though the symptoms may be disgusting."[162] Indeed, de Gazia contends that "medieval superstition and fear" is obstructing the use of "objective methods that have been applied to natural science [which] should now be applied to sexual phenomena with a view to understand and control these manifestations."[163] Note how homophobia combines with a narrative of medical secularization that ironically echoes Doctor Benway's logic of control. This framework re-contains the author's and readers' investments in queer experimentation as a strictly scholarly affair. Yet, as we have seen, the aesthetics of queer spectrality operate in direct opposition to this sovereign transcendence of the text. In fact, as Burroughs explains in the preface to *Queer*, "My concept of possession is closer to the medieval model than to modern psychological explanations, with their dogmatic insistence that such manifestations must come from within and never, never, never from without. (As if there were some clear-cut difference between inner and outer.)"[164] Simultaneously liberating and possessing the reader, Burroughs's queer experimental literature foregrounds the affective susceptibility of the reader's body—and by extension, the body politic—to become imbricated in the externality of queer possession.

As the subsequent chapters will show, queer experimental literature will follow Burroughs's provocation of affective reading, and its affective politics will similarly appear as solipsistic mystifications. Yet it is important to recall Deleuze's point that the rejection of judgment in favor of affect does not succumb to "subjectivism, since to pose the problem in terms of force, and not in other terms, already surpasses all subjectivity."[165] My goal is to demonstrate that the affective forces of queer reading foster new modes of relationality by defusing the hermeneutic grounds of judgment. As Deleuze argues, "Judgment prevents the emergence of any new mode of existence. For the latter creates itself through its own forces, that is, through the forces it is able to harness, and is valid in and of itself inasmuch as it brings the new combination into existence."[166] Queer experimental literature both affirms and attempts to create new relations of erotic and political belonging. Yet it also, as we will see, unleashes new practices of reading that contest hegemonic and institutionally sanctioned modes of interpretation. Thus, the history of queer reading cannot simply be collapsed into the disciplinary genealogies of critical reading elaborated within the academy. The next chapter elaborates this point by charting Samuel R. Delany's turn to experimental literature, which enables him to configure a mode of queer reading that fosters an affective relation to the felt history of the AIDS crisis. As we will see, the hermeneutics of suspicion do not encapsulate the plurality of affective relations that emerge in response to AIDS or the ways that queer reading grapples with the historical legacy of the crisis. Following our engagement with Burroughs, we will have to look closely at the granular movements of Delany's experimentations with form to trace the affective forces that they harness, combine, and unleash to foster new relations to queer history.

NOTES

1. William S. Burroughs, *Naked Lunch* (New York: Grove Press, 1959). I refer to the trial transcripts included in this edition of the text. For a history of the *Naked Lunch* obscenity trial, which includes lengthy summaries and excerpts of the trial transcript, see Michael Barry Goodman, *Contemporary Literary Censorship: The Case History of Burroughs' Naked Lunch* (Metuchen: The Scarecrow Press, 1981). Also see Frederick Whiting,

"Monstrosity on Trial: The Case of *Naked Lunch*," *Twentieth Century Literature* 52, no. 2 (2006), 145–74, whose views on Burroughs's intentionally subversive use of form converges with my argument below.

2. Burroughs, *Naked*, x. Judge Eugene A. Hudson presided over the trial, with Justices Spalding, Whittemore, Cutter, Kirk, Spiegel, and Reardon present. Kirk and Reardon formed the minority dissent. For the full text of the decision, see "Attorney General vs. A Book Named 'Naked Lunch,'" 351 Mass 298, October 8, 1965–July 7, 1966," accessed August 10, 2016, http://masscases.com/cases/sjc/351/351mass298.html.

3. See John D'Emilio and Estelle B. Freedman, *Intimate Matters: A History of Sexuality in America* (Chicago: The University of Chicago Press, 1988), especially 275–300. For a broader historical analysis of literary obscenity and censorship, see *Obscenity and the Limits of Liberalism*, eds. Loren Glass and Charles Francis Williams (Columbus: The Ohio State University Press, 2011); Rachel Potter, *Obscene Modernism: Literary Censorship and Experiment, 1900–1940* (Oxford: Oxford University Press, 2013); Elisabeth Ladenson, *Dirt for Art's Sake: Books on Trial from 'Madame Bovary' to 'Lolita'* (Ithaca: Cornell University Press, 2012).

4. Quoted in D'Emilio and Freedman, *Intimate*, 287.

5. Ibid., original emphasis.

6. Arguably, this concept is reversing in the age of trigger warnings, which privilege the affective effect of a text over its historical or cultural relevance to the public sphere. At the very same time, the trigger warning contests the undifferentiated and disembodied subject of the liberal-humanist public sphere, thereby re-evaluating the "value" of a text in terms of a specific minoritarian counterpublic.

7. Burroughs, *Naked*, xxxiii.

8. Ibid., x. Notably, Justice Kirk's dissent targets the invalidity of witness testimony, suggesting that the Court's deference to their opinion about the text's social value exemplifies a "surrender of the judicial function to absolutism" ("Attorney General").

9. Ibid., xvi.

10. Ibid., xxvii.

11. Ibid., xxvii–xxviii. Throughout his responses, Ginsburg strategically frames Burroughs's representation of homosexual desire as an unwanted addiction that must be exorcized through the writing of *Naked Lunch*, "an examination of the authors' sexual fantasies many of which are repellant to himself, and an exorcism of them by repetition, scrambling of them, & parody" (Goodman, *Contemporary*, 221).

12. See D'Emilio and Freedman, *Intimate*.

13. Burroughs, *Naked*, xxvi.

14. Ibid. It is notable that Judge Hudson was aware of the possibility that "under the guise of portraying the hallucinations of a drug addict, the author [Burroughs] has ingeniously satisfied his own whim or fancy, and inserted in this book hard-core pornography" (quoted in Goodman, *Contemporary*, 225).

15. For Burroughs's own contribution to this reading, see "Deposition: Testimony Concerning a Sickness," in *Naked* xxxv–xlv.

16. Although *Queer* wasn't published until 1985, it was completed around 1953. For an insightful publication history of Burroughs's works, see Oliver Harris, *William Burroughs and The Secret of Fascination* (Carbondale: Southern Illinois University Press, 2003).

17. Burroughs, *Naked*, 208, original ellipsis.

18. This narrative predominates in the popular press's representation of Burroughs, which emphasizes his anarchistic and libertarian ethos and eclipses or ignores any of his desires for communalism. See, for example, Peter Schjeldahl, "The Outlaw," *The New Yorker*, February 3, 2014, accessed August 9, 2016, http://www.newyorker.com/magazine/2014/02/03/the-outlaw-2. Critics tend to look to Burroughs's later works for his radical and anarchistic figuration of a queer political collectivity, particularly *The Wild Boys* (1971) and the Red Night Trilogy, composed of *Cities of the Red Night* (1981), *The Place of Dead Roads* (1982), and *The Western Lands* (1987). See, for example, Timothy S. Murphy, *Wising Up the Marks: The Amodern William Burrough* (Berkeley: University of California Press, 1997). For an insightful explication of homosexuality in Burroughs's fiction, see Jamie Russell, *Queer Burroughs* (New York: Palgrave Macmillan, 2001). My approach to queerness diverges from Russell's insofar as I disagree that Burroughs's understanding of queerness is solely equivalent to hyperbolic and essentialist gay male masculinity. I also disagree with Russell's conclusion that Burroughs's work does not have relevance to contemporary queer theory due to his problematic and putatively essentialist fantasies about gender identity. In fact, this chapter contends that Burroughs anticipates another mode of queer politics, one that is not predicated on linguistic demystification but on fostering affective relations. Nonetheless, Russell makes clear how profoundly misogyny and essentialism inspire Burroughs's cosmology of sexuality, and he convincingly demonstrates how these ideologies operate against the predominant homophobic narratives about gay effeminacy in postwar America.

19. For an historical analysis of Burroughs's development experimental writing that emphasizes its complex relationship to the politics of the Cold War, see Alex Houen, *Powers of Possibility: Experimental American Writing Since the 1960s* (Oxford: Oxford University Press, 2012), 103–44.

20. Ihab Hassan, "The Subtracting Machine: The Work of William Burroughs," in *William S. Burroughs At the Front: Critical Reception,*

1959–1989, eds. Jennie Skerl and Robin Lydenberg (Carbondale: Southern Illinois University Press, 1991), 66; N. Katherine Hayles, *How We Became Posthuman: Virtual Bodies in Cybernetics, Literature, and Informatics* (Chicago: The University of Chicago Press, 1999), 220.

21. Gilles Deleuze and Félix Guattari, *Kafka: Toward a Minor Literature*, trans. Dana Polan (Minneapolis: University of Minnesota Press, 1986), 17.

22. On the development of the cut-up fold-in method, see Harris, *William Burroughs*. Also see the work of Brion Gysin, who is the primary influence on Burroughs's use of the cut-up. Also see Daniel Odier, *The Job: Interviews with William S. Burroughs* (New York: Penguin Books, 1989).

23. Gilles Deleuze and Félix Guattari, *A Thousand Plateaus: Capitalism and Schizophrenia*, trans. Brian Massumi (Minneapolis: University of Minneapolis, 1987), 6.

24. William S. Burroughs, *The Ticket That Exploded* (New York: Grove Press, 1962), 18, my emphasis.

25. Ibid.

26. See Marianne DeKoven, *Utopia Limited: The Sixties and the Emergence of the Postmodern* (Durham: Duke University Press, 2004); and Murphy, *Wising*.

27. See, for example, Kathryn Hume, *Aggressive Fictions: Reading the Contemporary American Novel* (Ithaca: Cornell University Press, 2012).

28. On the association of queerness and ghostliness, see, for example, Kathryn Bond Stockton, *The Queer Child: On Growing Sideways in the Twentieth Century* (Durham: Duke University Press, 2009), especially 1–57; Carla Freccero, *Queer/Early/Modern* (Durham: Duke University Press, 2006), especially 69–104; José Esteban Muñoz, *Cruising Utopia: The Then and There of Queer Futurity* (New York: New York University Press, 2009), 33–48; Ellis Hanson, "The Undead," *Inside/Out: Lesbian Theories, Gay Theories*, ed. Diana Fuss (New York: Routledge, 1991), 324–40; Terry Castle, *The Apparitional Lesbian: Female Homosexuality and Modern Culture* (New York: Columbia University Press, 1993). On the intersections of queerness and the gothic, see George E. Haggerty, *Queer Gothic* (Urbana: University of Illinois Press, 2006); Sue-Ellen Case, "Tracking the Vampire," *differences: A Journal of Feminist Cultural Studies* 3, no. 2 (1991): 1–19; *Queering the Gothic*, eds. William Hughes and Andrew Smith (Manchester: Manchester University Press, 2009).

29. Quoted in Guy Hocquenghem, *Homosexual Desire*, trans. Daniella Dangoor (London: Allison & Busby, 1978), 36.

30. Ibid.

31. Ibid., 39.

32. Freccero, *Queer*, 74.

33. Ibid., 91.
34. Jacques Derrida, *Specters of Marx: The State of the Debt, the Work of Mourning and the New International*, trans. Peggy Kamuf (New York: Routledge, 1994), 169–70.
35. Gilles Deleuze, *Essays Critical and Clinical*, trans. Daniel W. Smith and Michael A. Greco (Minneapolis: University of Minnesota Press, 1997), 129.
36. Ibid., 130.
37. For a different approach to queer visibility and invisibility in *Queer*, see Elisa Glick, *Materializing Queer Desire: Oscar Wilde to Andy Warhol* (Albany: State University of New York Press, 2009), 107–32.
38. William S. Burroughs, *The Letters of William S. Burroughs, 1945–59*, ed. Oliver Harris (New York: Penguin Books, 1993), 430, original emphasis.
39. William S. Burroughs, *Queer* (New York: Penguin Books, 1985), 60.
40. On the cultural associations of homosexuality and melancholia, see "Unhappy Queers" in Sara Ahmed, *The Promise of Happiness* (Durham: Duke University Press, 2010), 88–120.
41. Burroughs, *Queer*, 2.
42. Ibid., 3.
43. Ibid., ellipsis in original.
44. In this moment, Lee's fantasies give voice to, and do not displace or re-inscribe, the social law. This conforms to the psychoanalytic account of fantasy, which critiques the conceit of fantasy as an agency of transgression. See, for example, Slavoj Žižek, *The Plague of Fantasies* (London: Verso, 2008). For a differing account of fantasy, see Rosemary Jackson, *Fantasy: The Literature of Subversion* (London: Methuen, 1981).
45. Burroughs, *Queer*, 9.
46. Burroughs, *Letters*, 201.
47. Burroughs, *Queer*, 18.
48. This is the phrase is that Ginsberg misreads and Jack Kerouac later remembers when he suggests the title "Naked Lunch" for Burroughs's novel. See David L. Ulin, "Afterword," in *Naked Lunch: The Restored Text*, eds. James Grauerholz and Barry Miles (New York: Grove Press, 2009), 235.
49. Burroughs, *Naked*, xxxv, original emphasis.
50. Burroughs, *Queer*, 25.
51. Ibid., ellipsis in original.
52. Ibid., 24.
53. Ibid., xii.
54. Murphy, *Wising*, 4.
55. Burroughs, *Queer*, vi.

56. Given the ambivalent tension between racism and racialized fetishism in Burroughs's work, a tension that is at play in many of the figurations of homosexual sex in his writing, it is notable that Allerton is depicted as inhabiting a racially hybrid position. In Lee's perception, Allerton has an "equivocal face, very young, clean-cut and boyish, at the same time conveying an impression of makeup, delicate and exotic and Oriental" (Ibid., 16).
57. Ibid., vii.
58. Ibid., 52–53.
59. Ibid., 97. Burroughs makes evident that so-called moralists are themselves centrally concerned with homosexuality. Hence, he expresses disgust at Donald Webster Cory's suggestion in *The Homosexual in America* (1951) that "a queer learns humility, learns to turn the other cheek, and returns love for hate. ... I never swallowed the other cheek routine, and I hate the stupid bastards who won't mind their own business. They can die in agony for all I care" (*Letters*, 105–06).
60. Burroughs, *Queer*, 95.
61. Ibid., 96.
62. Ibid.
63. Ibid.
64. Ibid., 97.
65. Ibid.
66. I do not intend to oppose homosexuality and heterosexuality here or to arrest the queer mobility of Lee's desire, only to stress that, in this moment, Burroughs figures these identifications as exclusive.
67. Ibid.
68. Ibid., 89. Also see William S. Burroughs, *Junky*, ed. Oliver Harris (New York: Penguin Books, 2003). There, Burroughs writes, "What I look for in any relationship is contact on the nonverbal level of intuition and feeling, that is, telepathic contact," and he wants *yage* because it is purported to "increase telepathic sensitivity" (127). However, he notes that the Russians are using the drug in the hopes of "induc[ing] states of automatic obedience and literal thought control. The basic con. No build-up, no routine, just move in on someone's psyche and give orders. The deal is certain to backfire because telepathy is not of its nature a one-way set-up, or a set-up of sender and receiver at all." Again, note the tension between Burroughs's yearning for queer contact and his cynicism about modes of control that obstruct this flourishing of such affective contact.
69. Burroughs, *Queer*, 103. For an insightful reading of the sadomasochistic tensions in *Queer* that diverges from my approach, see Harris, *Secret*, 78–132.
70. Burroughs, *Queer*, 132–33.
71. Murphy, *Wising*, 66.

72. Burroughs, *Queer*, 132, original emphasis.
73. Ibid., 133.
74. Ibid., 124.
75. Ibid., 130.
76. Ibid., 95, ellipsis in original.
77. Burroughs, *Junky*, 60.
78. Here Burroughs's homophobia is buttressed by misogyny, insofar as the "fags" represents the disgust and inhumanity of the feminine. As Russell points out, that distinction between "fags" and "queers" relies on their respective femininity and masculinity, and the former bears the brunt of Burroughs disgust. See Russell, *Queer*, 2.
79. Burroughs, *Naked*, 122.
80. From Ken Kesey's representation of mental institutions to Jack Kerouac's representation of domesticity, postwar American literature by white men often excoriates any regimentation of life as emasculating. (Hence, Kesey's Nurse Ratchet and Kerouac's Camille, like many women in Beat fiction, represent castrating limitations on masculine freedom). Without a doubt, Burroughs echoes the contradiction between spontaneity and social control, and he also reproduces the sexist structure of that division. For a relevant discussion of the discourse of spontaneity in postwar America, see Daniel Belgrad, *The Culture of Spontaneity: Improvisation and the Arts in Postwar America* (Chicago: The University of Chicago Press, 1998). On Burroughs's approach to spontaneity and control, Marianne DeKoven, *Utopia Limited*, 161–82; and Michael W. Clune, *American Literature and the Free Market, 1945–2000* (New York: Cambridge University Press, 2010), 77–102.
81. Burroughs, *Naked*, 121.
82. Odier, *Job*, 49, 59.
83. Robin Lydenberg, *Word Cultures: Radical Theory and Practice in William S. Burroughs's Fiction* (Urbana: University of Illinois Press, 1987), 5. Lydenberg offers the most comprehensive and incisive analysis of the relationship between Burroughs's fiction and critical theory. While she focuses on sexuality, Lydenberg tends to subordinate its significance to Western Culture's binaristic division of mind and body. By contrast, I focus more specifically on how Burroughs's style operates in relationship to hegemonic discourses on queerness and its cultural representation.
84. Burroughs, *Ticket*, 213.
85. Burroughs, *Junky*, 111.
86. Ibid.
87. Burroughs, *Letters*, 367, original emphasis.
88. In Lydenberg's words, Burroughs's style "displace[s] metaphorical habits of assimilation and vertical transcendence with metonymic patterns of

collage and horizontal juxtaposition" (x). Her phrase, "metonymic dis-
memberment," aptly captures the way that this prose style seems to inevitably draw bodily analogies (xi).

89. William S. Burroughs, *Nova Express* (New York: Grove Press, 1964),
149, original emphasis.

90. Sianne Ngai, *Ugly Feelings* (Cambridge: Harvard University Press, 2005),
248–98.

91. Ibid., 263.

92. Ibid., 252.

93. This feeling is produced by the prose's overwhelming set of possible associations. Recall Eve Sedgwick's point that readers begin novels in a "space
of high anxiety and dependence" because they must "plunge into worlds
that strip them, however temporarily, of the painfully acquired cognitive
maps of their ordinary lives … on condition of an invisibility that promises cognitive exemption and eventual privilege," *Epistemology of the
Closet* (Berkeley: University of California Press, 1990), 97. Burroughs's
fiction never relents the intensity of anxiety, and it never provides the
relief of knowledge that Sedgwick describes. For a relevant discussion of
how Burroughs's prose refuses the "relief" of knowledge, see Steven
Shaviro, "Burroughs's Theater of Illusion: *Cities of the Red Night*," in
William S. Burroughs At the Front: Critical Reception, 1959–1989, eds.
Jennie Skerl and Robin Lydenberg (Carbondale: Southern Illinois
University Press, 1991), 197–208.

94. Burroughs insists that the psyche must be tethered to the body's affect.
He writes, "Ego, Super Ego and Id, floating about in a vacuum without
any reference to the human nervous system, strike me as highly dubious
metaphysical concepts," *The Adding Machine: Selected Essays* (New York:
Arcade Publishing, 1985), 91. Burroughs also criticizes Freudian sublimation and the notion of repression because he claims Freud believes
that "we cannot enjoy the advantages of so-called civilization without
crippling conflicts. Freud uncovered the extent of marginal, unconscious
thinking, but failed to realize that such thinking may be highly useful and
advantageous" (90).

95. Burroughs, *Naked*, 208.

96. Lydenberg, *Word*, 69.

97. Burroughs, *Adding*, 1.

98. Ibid.

99. Ibid.

100. Ibid., 22.

101. Ibid., 1, my emphasis.

102. Burroughs, *Queer*, 130.

103. William S. Burroughs, *The Soft Machine* (New York: Grove 1961), 25.

104. Ibid., 17.
105. Ibid., 16.
106. Ibid., 25.
107. Burroughs, *Naked*, 20.
108. Ibid., 21, original emphasis.
109. Ibid., 170.
110. Ibid., original emphasis.
111. Ibid., original emphasis.
112. Ibid., 171.
113. Ibid., 174.
114. Ibid., 178.
115. Ibid., 178.
116. Ibid., 179, original emphasis.
117. Ibid., 168.
118. Burroughs, *Adding*, 88, original emphasis.
119. Ibid., 87.
120. Burroughs, *Nova*, 5.
121. Burroughs, *Soft*, 107–08.
122. *Conversations with William S. Burroughs*, ed. Allen Hibbard (Jackson: University Press of Mississippi, 1999), 3.
123. Burroughs, *Naked*, 33.
124. Ibid., 33, 61.
125. Ibid., 120.
126. Ibid., 121, original emphasis.
127. Cancer is also Benway's central metaphor for political control: "Democracy is cancerous, and bureaus are its cancer," because a bureau is "always reproducing more of its own kind, until it chokes the host if not controlled or excised" (Ibid.).
128. Burroughs, *Queer*, 100.
129. Ginsberg suggests reading Burroughs's routines as veiled seductions. He calls them "an exquisite black-humorous fantasy ... and a parody of his [Burroughs's] feelings, lest his desire be considered offensive. ... The reader will thus recognize many of the 'routines,' that later became *Naked Lunch*, as conscious projections of Burroughs's love-fantasies— further explanations and parodies and models of our ideal love schlupp together" (quoted in Murphy, *Wising*, 144). On the signification of the "schlupp" in Burroughs's fiction, see Douglas Kahn, "Three Receivers," in *Experimental Sound and Radio*, ed. Allen S. Weiss (Cambridge: The MIT Press, 2001), 73–80.
130. Murphy, *Wising*, 5. Jennie Skerl argues "Burroughs' utopian fantasies are always placed in the past or in the future as alternative realities that can prompt change in the present, but they are never portrayed as existing in

present time. ... They are utopian as a *force*, not as literal images of the ideal community," in *William S. Burroughs At the Front: Critical Reception, 1959–1989*, eds. Jennie Skerl and Robin Lydenberg (Carbondale: Southern Illinois University Press, 1991), 192–93, original emphasis. On Burroughs's relationship to dystopia, see Lee Konstantinou, *Cool Characters: Irony and American Fiction* (Cambridge: Harvard University Press, 2016), 103–59.

131. Murphy, *Wising*, 5.
132. I find Murphy's analysis of "radical fantasy" in *The Wild Boys* very persuasive and illuminating, and our accounts of fantasy converge in key ways. My primary disagreement is historical—I see the roots of the spectral much earlier in Burroughs's work, and I see its emergence as tied to social prohibitions on figuring queer relationality. For this reason, I break with Murphy's identification of an encompassing Deleuzian desire in Burroughs in favor of stressing how such a figure encodes critical possibilities for queer eroticism and political collectivity.
133. Burroughs, *Ticket*, 85.
134. Alfred Kazin, "He's Just Wild About Writing," in *William S. Burroughs At the Front: Critical Reception, 1959–1989*, eds. Jennie Skerl and Robin Lydenberg (Carbondale: Southern Illinois University Press, 1991), 118, 117.
135. Michael Warner, *Publics and Counterpublics* (New York: Zone Books, 2002), 62, 23.
136. Burroughs, *Queer*, 39–40.
137. Ibid., 40.
138. Ibid.
139. As D'Emilio and Freedman observe, "[T]he discourse on sexuality expanded enormously [in the culture of the postwar period], blurring the distinction between private and public that characterized middle-class life in the previous century. ... On the other hand, even as the erotic seemed to permeate American life, white middle-class America struggled to maintain sexual boundaries" (*Intimate* 276–77).
140. Burroughs, *Junky*, xxxviii.
141. Ibid.
142. Ibid., xxxix.
143. Ibid., xli.
144. Ibid., xli, 104, my emphasis.
145. Ibid., 128.
146. Ibid., my emphasis.
147. Burroughs, *Ticket*, 6–7.
148. The cut-up undoes temporality via its associative gravity, pulling the reader in retrospective and prospective directions at once. Burroughs's

representation of melancholic eroticism and ectoplasmic ecstasy are the figural corollaries of this formally produced temporality.
149. Ibid., 7.
150. Non-organized permeability allows for a kind of social indistinction that enables Burroughs to figure queerly erotic communalism. This conceit is reflected in the novels' representation of the Nova Police, who are similarly defined in paradoxically a-social terms. As the District Supervisor explains, "In this organization, Mr. Lee, we do not encourage togetherness, *esprit de corps*. We do not give our agents the impression of belonging" (*Ticket* 9, original emphasis). Not wanting him to follow orders, he insists, "This is in point of fact a *non-organization* the aim of which is to immunize our agents against fear despair and death" (10, original emphasis). Non-organization resists the bureaucratic control mechanisms of Benway and the Nova Mob. Indeed, the Nova Police frequently claim that they will disperse upon the dissolution of social control, refusing to perpetuate any hierarchy in the Mob's absence.
151. Ibid., 82–83.
152. Ibid., 85.
153. Ibid., 83, my emphasis.
154. I draw the concept of linguistic agglutination from Ngai, who describes it as "the mass adhesion or coagulation of data particles or signifying units" (263). See *Ugly*, 248–97.
155. Burroughs, *Naked*, 74. This spectral collectivity is not a utopian fantasy of universal community; it is explicitly underwritten by a homoerotic fantasy of gay male collectivity, as I have stressed throughout. At the same time, the text's queer permutation of bodies outstrips its attempt to delimit this relationality to men. This tension is negotiated through the paradoxical corporeal abstraction and concrete linguistic materiality of Burroughs's experimental form.
156. Ibid., 207.
157. Warner, *Publics*, 116.
158. Burroughs, *Ticket*, 212.
159. Burroughs, *Naked*, xxvi.
160. Ibid., 202, original emphasis and ellipsis.
161. Ibid., 203.
162. Ibid., xxxiii.
163. Ibid.
164. Burroughs, *Queer*, xix.
165. Deleuze, *Essays*, 135.
166. Ibid.

CHAPTER 2

Reading in Crisis: Queer Hermeneutics as Affective History

At the 1994 OutWrite Convention, an audience member asked a panel of young LGBTQ authors, "What do you think of experimental writing for gay writers?"[1] The fiction writer, Norman Wong, responded with disdain. "No experimentation!" Wong declared, "Experimental writing is just bad writing … It mutes and muddies your ideas, makes for dull reading, and loses you your audience. So don't do it."[2] Another panelist criticized experimental writing as being either "subjective gushing in the present tense… [or] a cascade of unrelated sentences and sentence fragments. It seems to me," the panelist concluded, "that's the last thing that gay writers—or any writer with something to say—would want to get involved in."[3] These statements aptly capture the popular aesthetic critiques of queer experimental literature—it is boring, insular, and incoherent; it is bad writing that only elicits bad (affectively "dull") reading. Moreover, experimental writing is seen as having little to say on its own terms through its manipulations of form; indeed, its resistance to the conventions of mainstream fiction is perceived as an obstruction to communicating the social messages of politically engaged gay writers, writers who have "something to say." The audience responded to the panel's assessment with enthusiastic applause, with one notable exception. Samuel R. Delany, who was also in attendance, was distressed. After all, Delany noted that many of the attendees share "just the sense of crisis that, a decade and a half ago I had (when I decided to write a novel about AIDS)."[4] However, "[they] no

© The Author(s) 2017
T. Bradway, *Queer Experimental Literature*,
Palgrave Studies in Affect Theory and Literary Criticism,
DOI 10.1057/978-1-137-59543-0_2

longer see experimental writing as a way to deal with it aesthetically."[5] In his view, the panel and the audience reveal more than a preference for narrative realism. Their reaction speaks to an internalized "publishing mentality" among queer authors, a mind-set that prioritizes marketability over intellectual or formal concerns.[6] As such, they no longer look to experimental writing, a marginal paraliterary genre, as a medium for exploring queer social concerns. Indeed, Wong does not directly address the crux of the audience member's question—namely, what are the possibilities of experimental writing for gay writers and their readers? Putting aside, for the moment, the complex question of what defines a "gay writer," Wong's judgment obscures the historical contexts in which experimental writing has been, and may continue to be, meaningful for the development of a queer politics of aesthetics, particularly in the context of the AIDS crisis.[7]

Reflecting on the aesthetic and political devaluation of queer experimental literature, Delany speculates that "the codification of it in textbooks on how to write experimental fiction and poetry and academic considerations, even such as this one, have something to do with that, however indirectly."[8] Note that Delany includes his own interview as a potentially codifying force that circumscribes experimental literature to a narrow academic audience. The academic codification of queer experimental literature creates a sovereign aesthetic judgment for how its aesthetics must appear. In Delany's eyes, this cuts against the immanent work of experimental writing. For him, experimental writing "retards readability" and forces readers to "virtually learn *how* to read" anew.[9] Indeed, as this chapter argues, experimental writing provides Delany a *para-academic mode* to critically contest the practices of reading codified within academic discourse, particularly as they circumscribe the role of affect in reader relations. Through his para-academic experimentation, Delany engenders new protocols for reading that are keyed to the unfolding and unprecedented historical crisis of AIDS.

As I define it, the para-academic mode encompasses experimental writing that is explicitly engaged with, responsive to, and invested in institutionally produced academic knowledge—but is not, itself, primarily derived from the academy nor legible to it as knowledge because it disrupts the authorized genres of academic discourse.[10] Undoubtedly, queer literary criticism often looks to Delany's work for inspiration, particularly his influential anthropological essay on sex publics, *Times Square Red, Times Square Blue*, and his memoir, *The Motion of Light on Water*.[11] Yet, it has tended to overlook Delany's agonistic relationship to academic discourse itself, particularly as it functions as a regime of legitimation that excludes degraded forms of writing such as science fiction and pornography. Delany's AIDS novels offer a new perspective on the vexed power relationships at play in para-academic experimentation precisely because they critically engage a wide range of academic discourses, from statistical analyses of HIV seroconversion to canonical works of post-structural literary theory. Yet, his novels fold these discourses into a dizzying mixture of minor literary forms. For example, Delany's first AIDS novel, *The Tale of Plagues and Carnivals* (1984), blends fantasy ("sword-and-sorcery"), postmodern metafiction, personal memoir, and an intertextual commentary on Walter Benjamin's *Arcades Project* and Mikhail Bakhtin's *The Dialogic Imagination*.[12] Similarly, Delany's second AIDS novel, *The Mad Man* (1994), cross-pollinates gay erotica (which he calls "pornotopic fantasy"), academic novel, mystery fiction, and Greek and Romantic philosophy (especially Diogenes, Nietzsche, and Hegel).[13] This chapter will show that it is precisely through his promiscuous and experimental folding of these divergent discourses that Delany engenders queer hermeneutic relations to the crisis that embrace—rather than disavow—its felt history.

Delany's queer experimental literature thus exemplifies a tension between queer and academic cultures—a tension that has been paradoxically obscured by the partial legitimation of queer theory within the academy. After all, para-academic writing has been—and continues to be—central to queer culture, precisely because queer culture refutes strict divisions between institutionally authorized and non-authorized knowledge.[14] However, in queer experimental literature, the para-academic text does not simply produce different objects of knowledge. Rather, its para-academic modes provide a form to experiment with the creation of new hermeneutic practices—indeed, these texts labor to bring new hermeneutic methods into being and, in the process, to define their social purview and political significance in response to the urgencies of sexual politics. In short, the struggle to define reading—what it is, what it can do, who practices it, and how it is practiced—underlies the para-academic text's experimentation with form. Therefore, para-academic texts not only suspend the question of what "counts" as knowledge; they also elicit new relations with their readers, implicitly drawing a new circuit of social belonging among texts, readers, and their social worlds. As Elizabeth Freeman argues in her analysis of queer aesthetics, "[H]ermeneutics, the property of art as well as criticism, indirectly feeds the making of new social forms across space and time."[15] I share Freeman's view that hermeneutics are a perversely common property of queer aesthetics and criticism; however, this chapter will tend to stress the tensions that pertain between queer art and criticism to illuminate how para-academic experimentation elicits hermeneutic modes that contest those elaborated within and employed by certain genres of academic knowledge.[16] (In Delany's case, this tension is fundamentally linked to the violence produced by interpretations of AIDS offered as scientific fact and moral truth that were, in fact, infused with homophobic bias.) As Freeman argues, queer hermeneutic practices are themselves condensations of affective history; they are "practices of knowing, physical as well as mental, erotic as well as loving 'grasps' of detail that do not accede to existing theories and lexicons but come into unpredictable contact with them."[17] To grasp the lineaments of affective history obscured by progressive historiography, Freeman utilizes a richly embodied method of intensely close reading that "grasps" (and is grasped by) figural detail. Rather than attend to the detail, I focus instead on the affective relations configured through Delany's queer hermeneutics. By doing so, I demonstrate how queer hermeneutic relations are also sedimentations of affective history, conditioned by the AIDS crisis and bequeathed to future generations as an unconscious cultural inheritance lived in the body as affect. Put simply, I show that queer modes of reading not only enable us to perceive affective history, but that they *are* affective history.

If queer theory wishes to maintain an active historical relationship to the AIDS era, then it must recover the plurality of hermeneutic relations that the crisis elicited. This requires that we suspend the monolithic narrative of "paranoid reading" as exhausting the range of hermeneutic responses to AIDS. In the following section, I pluralize the critical narrative that conflates the hermeneutics of suspicion with queer reading in the midst of the crisis. To do so, I trace Delany's increasing attention to the problem of hermeneutics in his writing, particularly his desire to elicit a "radical reader" through experimental form. I connect these hermeneutic concerns to Delany's anxiety about producing an aesthetic response to the AIDS crisis in its earliest moments, when its historical, political, medical, and personal meanings could not be stably codified. Delany turns to academic discourses of deconstruction to elaborate a queer hermeneutic for AIDS that does not seek paranoid mastery but, instead, grapples with the epidemic of unstable signification that defines the discourse of the crisis. In his para-academic revision of deconstruction, however, Delany pushes critics to attend to the affective relations implied by this mode of reading, to consider, in particular, how they uncritically perpetuate or politically engage the "epidemic of signification" in AIDS. I look, in particular, to *The Tale of Plagues and Carnivals* to show how Delany's revision of deconstructive hermeneutics illuminates the affective history of AIDS as a structure of feeling. I then turn to *The Mad Man*, published a decade later, to show how Delany's hermeneutics evolve in response to the traumatic expansion of the crisis. The academy remains a site of contestation, yet *The Mad Man* turns away from deconstruction to offer a hermeneutics of pleasure, one that the para-academic text is uniquely poised to elicit through its use of pornography as a narrative mode of queer eroticism. I conclude that *The Mad Man* recuperates the queer eroticism disavowed by gay literature and post-AIDS safe-sex discourses alike. Ultimately, Delany's para-academic experimentation demonstrates the paradoxical centrality and marginality of queer experimental literature to the AIDS crisis. Although he writes to a minor queer counterpublic, through a range of genres that barely register as socially relevant, Delany's work offers a vital archive of queer hermeneutic responses to the crisis. This archive cannot be properly accounted for by methodologies that eschew the affective relations of reading because that is precisely where the history of queer hermeneutics is inherited.

BESIDE PARANOID READING

Critics have long recognized that the AIDS crisis elicited a crisis of reading. In Paula Treichler's words, AIDS wrought an "epidemic of signification," which demanded vigilant attention to the discursive framing of the crisis.[18] For this reason, AIDS activists employed practices of reading that could contest a broad range of discourses. These discourses included the moralizing rhetoric of religious and political figures, the figural language that framed AIDS in militaristic terms, and the rarefied, seemingly "objective," languages of science, statistics, and public health. Despite the naturalized appearance of these discourses, activists had to, in Michael Warner's words, "insist over and over on the cultural construction of the discourses about AIDS."[19] Warner does not indicate the multifarious cultural forms in which this insistence took place, nor does he elaborate whether terms such as "cultural construction" and "discourse" meant the same thing for non-academics as they do for academics. Rather, he posits a homology between queer and academic cultures, insisting "Queers do a kind of practical social reflection just in finding ways of being queer."[20] This homology grants desperately needed legitimacy to queer practices of knowledge, especially in 1993 when Warner published *Fear of a Queer Planet*. Yet, the equivalence fails to qualify the singularity of the "practical social reflection" conducted by non-academic and para-academic queers; it does not capture, in other words, how their hermeneutic practices respond to or break with those legitimated by institutions such as the academy.

The legacy of this critical blind spot is evident in contemporary accounts of queer hermeneutics. In her paradigmatic essay on reading practices in queer theory, Eve Sedgwick equates the "hermeneutics of suspicion" in queer and critical theory with non-academic and activist responses to AIDS. For Sedgwick, the "hermeneutics of suspicion" encompasses the academic and non-academic range of queer responses to AIDS because this strategy of interpretation demystifies signs, denaturalizes narratives, exposes hidden causes, identifies conspiratorial connections, and dispels false consciousness. The hermeneutics of suspicion, or what Sedgwick calls "paranoid reading," thus names the field of queer hermeneutic responses to AIDS.[21] After all, Sedgwick recalls, "This was at a time when speculation was ubiquitous about whether the virus had been deliberately engineered or spread, whether HIV represented a plot or experiment by the U.S. military that had gotten out of control, or perhaps that was behaving exactly as it was meant to."[22] By privileging paranoia as the primary affective relation of queer hermeneutics, Sedgwick obscures other interpretative modes, equally engaged with the politics of the crisis, that do not share the drive to demystify. Implicitly, Sedgwick points to an alternative affective history, which she does not pursue. The essay begins with a brief anecdote about the "activist scholar" Cindy Patton, who was skeptical of the paranoid hermeneutics of AIDS activism. Patton questions the legitimacy of suspicious narratives, wondering, "[W]hat would we know then [about the crisis] that we don't already know?"[23] Patton's disinterest in paranoid reading symbolizes, for Sedgwick, an alternative affective, epistemic, and political relation to the crisis. Yet, Sedgwick positions Patton as a proleptic critic of contemporary queer theory, missing an opportunity to explore the other queer hermeneutic relations that were elaborated *concurrently* with the AIDS crisis and positioned ambivalently or agonistically against paranoid reading.

Delany elaborates such an alternative hermeneutic, and he does so in direct response to the crisis. However, Delany's hermeneutics have been obscured by the overwhelming focus on semiotics in his fiction. To be sure, Delany produces lengthy semiotic analyses of science fiction in *Starboard Wine* and *The Jewel-Hinged Jaw*, and as Jeffrey Allen Tucker writes of the *Nevèrÿon* series (which includes *The Tale of Plagues and Carnivals*),

Delany "demonstrates the influence of Saussure and Peirce, often to the point where the books read as textbooks for a graduate seminar in critical theory as much as sword-and-sorcery."[24] Delany himself declares the *Nevèrÿon* series to be a "child's garden of semiotics," and throughout the series he offers a critical metacommentary on how the novels correlate to certain problems of the sign.[25] Thus, the temptation to take Delany at his word regarding the centrality of semiotics to his work is understandable, and it has been difficult to read his work outside of this frame. Yet, Delany never simply dramatizes theoretical concepts, nor does he explicate them in any faithful way, as Tucker's analogy to a "textbook" implies. On the contrary, Delany's engagement with critical theory is dynamic and revisionary—he seeks to influence conversations in these fields as much as they influence him. This is no doubt why Delany includes lengthy citations of academic works by critics such as Barbara Johnson, Teresa de Lauretis, Michael Ryan, and Gayatri Spivak, as well as lesser-known literary scholars. His fiction offers a kind of "works cited" that makes evident to academic publics, including the critics named in his work, that he is conversing with them, albeit in a different idiom. Undoubtedly, Delany also wants to give non-academic publics a context for understanding his citations to theory and to give these readers an entrance point to theoretical discourses they might otherwise find daunting, boring, or irrelevant.[26]

Yet, a critical shift takes place in Delany's AIDS writing, a shift that complicates his previous investment in semiotics. This shift exemplifies an increasing concern with hermeneutic questions—questions pertaining to reading, reference, and truth. To be clear: Delany neither recuperates an ontological foundation for truth nor suddenly locates the grounds for transcendental meaning. Yet, the "epidemic of signification" wrought by AIDS provokes Delany's increasing attention to, and complication of, hermeneutic practices by readers. This anxiety is evidenced in an admission that Delany makes in a metafictional aside in *The Tale of Plagues and Carnivals*:

By now I'm willing to admit that perhaps narrative fiction, in neither its literary nor its paraliterary mode, can propose the *radically* successful metaphor. At best, what both modes can do is break up, analyze, dialogize the conservative, the historically sedimented, letting the fragments argue with one another, letting each display its own obsolescence, suggesting (not stating) where still another retains the possibility of vivid, radical development. But responding to those suggestions is, of course, the job of the radical reader. (The "radical metaphor" is, after all, only an interpretation of preextant words.)[27]

Here, Delany indicates the importance of historical context to his hermeneutic turn. By beginning this passage with the phrase "By now," he underscores how the contemporary moment underwrites his new willingness
to concede the ineffectiveness of narrative fiction's semiotic play. Delany
retains his belief in the potential effectiveness of the aesthetic object, yet
he displaces that potentiality from the radical signifier to a radical reader,
whose "job" is to develop a response to the text's figural language. Both
conventional and paraliterary fiction continue to perform a critical semiotics—freeing signs from their historical sedimentation and deconstructing
their apparent solidity. Yet, fiction's dialogic forms can merely "*invite* a
certain richness of reading ... they cannot *assure* such a reading. That is
something that can only be supplied by the radical reader."[28] In short, the
literary text cannot make promises about its effects in the world. If any
effects are to be successful, then they will emerge from the labor of the
reader who now has an ethical and political responsibility to bring a radical
reading into being.

The epidemic of signification wrought by AIDS is the root of Delany's
increased anxiety about the limitations of semiotics and the urgency of
radical reading. Indeed, at its outset, *The Tale of Plagues and Carnivals*
performatively foregrounds the radical instability of signifiers that conditions its own paradoxical attempt to respond to AIDS within figural language. Delany writes:

> "Dis-ease." Non-easiness. Difficulty.
> "Health." Via the Old English "haelp," from the Old High German, "hei-
> lida": *whole*, or *complete*.
> Metaphors fight each other. They also adjust one another.
> Can a person who is "whole" also be "dis-eased"?
> The answer, "Yes," would seem to be what modern medicine is all about.
> But consider a variant of the same question: "Can a whole person be
> diseased?"
> To answer, "Yes," is to give *one* answer to *two* questions with nearly diametric
> meanings. That the common form of the question can be deconstructed
> in this manner is the sign of our dis-ease before anything that might bear
> "disease" as its proper designation.[29]

This passage indicates the truly fraught—if not traumatic—status of unstable and excessive signifiers in Delany's AIDS writing, and it explains why
Delany shifts his attention from the work of metaphor to the work of
the reader of metaphor. Referencing Susan Sontag's *Illness as Metaphor*,

Delany insists, "Diseases should not become social metaphors."[30] Yet, the novel shows that even the seemingly objective descriptor "disease" implies a range of homophobic metaphors pertaining to health and personhood that imply that homosexuals "are" diseased in their whole being and also, paradoxically, "incomplete" people, illegible as persons to a heteronormative world. These metaphors "fight" and "adjust" one another on the discursive battlefield of the crisis.[31] Indeed, the novel subsequently deconstructs a wide range of other dominant metaphors for AIDS, including those used by activists (AIDS as "an opportunity for consciousness raising") and religious conservatives (AIDS as "a Scourge of Satan, the Wrath of Khan").[32] The point of doing so, the novel hopes, is to find a "*better* metaphor," one that can "stabilize those thoughts, images, or patterns that, *in the long run*, are useful—useful to those with the disease, to those who care for them, or even to those who only know about them."[33] Yet, the conclusion that Delany reaches is that "metaphors by themselves are, finally, neither radical nor conservative. They gain their ideological slant only as they are read. And any attempt to pose a radical metaphor is only a more or less conscientious call for some hard work at a more or less radical reading."[34]

This is an aching conclusion for a writer to make, particularly a queer writer seeking to articulate a meaningful and *useful* response to an emergent medical and social trauma from within the realm of the aesthetic. What else can literary fiction do, after all, if not construct metaphors? As Delany makes clear, he writes *The Tale of Plagues and Carnivals* as an effort to foreground AIDS "in [the reader's] attention as something important, so that when new information arrived, it could and would be dealt with—rather than sloughed off and ignored."[35] Yet, the novel indicates how problematic that project is in literary terms, because any representation of AIDS (even the use of the term "AIDS") risks becoming complicit with metaphors that could be—or will become—disabling for queer people in the long run. Hence, the novel insists, "What is most useful in the long run is what destabilizes short-run strategies, the quick glyphs, the clichés, the easy responses history has sedimented."[36] The desire to elicit a radical reader—capable of thinking differently about the relation between signifiers and the sedimentations of history in the AIDS era—is therefore no mere supplement to *The Tale of Plagues and Carnivals*. This is the novel's central formal project and the underlying political motivation of Delany's investment in developing a theory of reading. As we will see, Delany turns to experimental literature to "invite" the interpretative relations that will recuperate the social usefulness of queer writing. However, before heeding this invitation, we must first attend to Delany's theorization of radical reading and take note of how he perversely rewrites academic discourses of deconstruction to attend to the epidemic of signification as a specifically *felt* crisis for queer publics.

THE AFFECTIVE RELATIONS OF DECONSTRUCTION

Deconstruction is often aligned with the hermeneutics of suspicion and seen as an exemplary mode of paranoid reading.[37] Yet, Delany finds inspiration in deconstruction for his theorization of queer hermeneutics precisely because, on his reading, deconstruction undermines an omnipotent, masterful, or heroic critical position over the textual object and, indeed, over language itself. Delany looks to deconstruction to challenge the figure of the "idealized and ultimately nonextant and masterful reader," the one who arrives at the complete truth of a text in a pointedly "transcendental experience of understanding."[38] "[T]he fine points of reading," Delany claims instead, "lie in the margins of a mastery never ours."[39] These fine points are not points of insight but the ways in which our insight fails to be complete. Reading, he describes, is "always a tangle of glitches, inattentions, momentary snags, occasional snoozes, chance oversights, and habitual snarls."[40] As much as deconstruction is not a phenomenological method, Delany frequently describes the felt relations of deconstructive reading—the body's experience of finding itself snoozing or snarling, snagged or tangled, becoming aware of its lack of mastery over the text through an affective relation to its semiotic excess. When detailing experimental writing's capacity to produce readerly undecidability, he portrays the experience as an "undecidability [that] registers as an uncertainty *in the body*."[41] At stake in Delany's engagement with deconstruction, then, is a revisionary account of queer hermeneutics—one that not only attends to the uncertainty of the AIDS crisis as a moment of linguistic undecidability but also supplements deconstruction with an attentiveness to the affective relations of its historical context. Delany thus exemplifies how some queer hermeneutics might be deconstructive, but not necessarily paranoid, and conversely how para-academic experimental writing pushes academic critics to contend with the affective implications of their discourses for queer counterpublics.

In the place of the masterful reader, Delany substitutes a new figure—the "vigilant" reader. "Even if blindness is inevitable," he writes, "it is readerly vigilance that frees us."[42] The rhetoric of "readerly vigilance" might seem to evoke the hermeneutics of suspicion and its critical subject—the ever-attentive, watchful reader that holds a lookout over the battlements of discourse.[43] Yet, for Delany, vigilance condenses an attentiveness to one's proximate relation to the text: "Only through the vigilance needed to keep close to the text can the careful reader know just how distant (and idiosyncratic that distance is for each one) they are, text and reader, one from the other."[44] This paradoxical sentence points up just how radically Delany's hermeneutics complicate the notion of so-called "close" or "distant" reading. Delany displaces any transcendental reference point for closeness or distance, implying that textual relations (especially those described in spatial and embodied terms) must be conceived as relative and subject to contextual redefinition. To be sure, this undoes any formalist or idealist definition of hermeneutics as "close reading," rendering that phrase radically undecidable because closeness and distance fold into one another as inextricably entwined dynamics of reading. Not only does Delany's notion of readerly vigilance emphasize the affective torsions of the readerly process, it also suggests that all readerly relations—insofar as they are relations of proximity—are idiosyncratic. Yet, interestingly, this idiosyncrasy is not only a function of the subjective or personal nature of the reader; it is also a consequence of the text's forces, particularly its use of form to slant and even undo the codified protocols of reading that a reader brings to the text. In short, the vigilant reader does not recuperate a mastery over the text but, instead, becomes attentive to the ever-shifting affective and epistemic relations that emerge in the encounter with a text, seeing this relation as vital and immanent. In Delany's hands, deconstructive reading not only attends, then, to the slippages of meaning but also to the body's affective implication in and response to them.

Clearly, Delany's interpretation of deconstruction as a theory for reading is influenced by its reception and adaptation in the United States.[45] Yet, Delany presses back on the very critics that inspire his appropriation of deconstruction, urging them and his own readers to reflect on the implication of deconstruction's structure of feeling for those grappling with the historical crisis of AIDS. For example, Delany places an epigraph from Michael Ryan's *Marxism and Deconstruction* (1982) at the outset of *Flight from Nevèrÿon* (the collection that includes *The Tale of Plagues and Carnivals*). The epigraph quotes Ryan's claim: "There is no such thing as an absolutely proper meaning of a word, which is not made possible by the very impropriety of metaphorical displacement it seeks to exclude."[46]

We have already noted Delany's ambivalence about "metaphorical displacement," particularly the impropriety of "disease" and other metaphors associated with AIDS. Even if Delany agrees that signs are inherently iterable, he expresses uncertainty about Ryan's affirmative political corollary to this linguistic condition. Ryan contends, "The impropriety of displaceability of meaning and of infinite openness of syntactic reference beyond that circumscribed by proper meaning is a material force."[47] The result of this deconstructive force, Ryan concludes, is "the continuous revolutionary displacement of power toward radical egalitarianism and the plural defusion [sic] of all forms of macro- and microdomination."[48] In other words, the instability of signification is not merely a metaphor for political revolution; it *is* a revolutionary political force that outstrips despotic power and engenders excessively egalitarian possibilities.

By contrast, and in para-academic conversation with Ryan, Delany hesitates about the impropriety of language—not because of its conceptual weakness as a political theory but because of its affective implications. He addresses Ryan's epigraph in the second appendix to *Flight from Nevèrÿon*, asking,

> *Do* I believe, then, Michael Ryan's assertion with which I opened this volume, i.e., that the impossibility of individuating meanings at the level of the word ... is a *material* force?
> Frankly, I don't know.
> But I think the possibility must be seriously considered by anyone interested in either language or power, not to mention their frighteningly elusive, always allusive, and often illusive relations.[49]

Delany suspends the question of belief regarding deconstruction, although he acknowledges its import and calls for a future hearing of its validity. But, in a seemingly minor descriptive caveat, Delany emphasizes the *frightening* nature of the "elusive" relations between language and power. Even if linguistic displaceability provides opportunities for subversion, here Delany underlines the concomitant anxiety it stimulates. Of course, *différance* cannot be "experienced" by the subject directly, but its effects can be registered in feeling, however retrospectively, and as we will see, *The Tale of Plagues and Carnivals* does not represent the "impropriety of displaceability" of AIDS—its epidemic of signification—as an inherently positive, egalitarian revolution. If the ethos of American deconstruction affirmatively lauds iterability in abstract terms, Delany offers a crucial counterpoint. Not only does he suggest that the affective suffering wrought by linguistic displaceability matters, it must also be part of the analysis of the contextual, historically constituted relationship between language and power.

In particular, Delany's attention to the affective relations of deconstruction constitutes an important supplement to critics that highlight abstract, decontextualized anxiety or ecstasy as the primary emotional responses to the instability of language (and then implicitly privilege the latter).[50] Paul de Man, for example, claims that the "resulting pathos" one feels in response to the "suspended ignorance" of deconstruction is either "an anxiety (or bliss, depending on one's momentary mood or individual temperament.)"[51] As much as Delany finds inspiration in deconstruction's suspension of hermeneutic mastery, he locates that condition as historically and traumatically implicated in—and intensified by—the undecidability engendered by AIDS. As Delany notes, "[W]hat is *known* about AIDS ... has been changing month to month for more than a year and will no doubt continue to change until after a vaccine is developed."[52] While *The Tale of Plagues and Carnivals* strives to be a historical document, Delany therefore concedes

largely what it documents is *misinformation, rumor,* and *wholly untested guesses* at play through a limited social section of New York City during 1982 and 1983, mostly before the April 23, 1984 announcement of the discovery of a virus (human t-cell lymphotropic virus [HTLV-3]) as the overwhelmingly probable cause of AIDS.[53]

Here, the undecidability of AIDS is marked with dates, locations, and context—Delany imprints de Man's "suspended ignorance" with historical markers and links it directly to the social experience of queers. Yet, this markedly historical experience is itself undecidable because of the radical uncertainty of the cause of or cure for AIDS. Rumor, fear, and gossip spread in the absence of certainty, making the experience of language and narrative untrustworthy and wrought with anxiety. Ultimately, *The Tale of Plagues and Carnivals* attempts to communicate the affective dimension of this linguistic displacement through its reader relations; indeed, it is through a hermeneutic relation to uncertainty that Delany is able to "represent" the affective history of the crisis. As he suggests, "History begins only when we do *not* know what happened—when there is disagreement over what happened. When everyone "knows" what happened (and

I know you can detect the irony in that epistemological dictum), there is only mythology. And nothing is forgotten faster."[54] Epistemological mastery produces monolithic and mythological agreement. By contrast, Delany seeks a readerly relation to the uncertainty and disagreement over "what is happening" in the unfolding event of AIDS. His project is not to affirm the suspension of ignorance as an ontological condition of language—nor is it to falsely restabilize of history as foundational truth. Rather, by writing the felt experience of a historically conditioned queer ignorance, Delany resists the *forgetting* perpetuated by narratives predicated on the myth of historical objectivity. Paradoxically, the hermeneutic relation to embodied uncertainty keeps open the possibility for dialogic history to emerge. Thus, he turns to queer experimental literature not "to allegorize a political situation" but rather to "allegorize a feeling" that structures the collective and incipiently historical experience of AIDS—namely, the feeling of a radical and unprecedented displacement from one's words, body, and being.[55]

By drawing on and revising academic discourse, the para-academic text faces a unique concern about whether or not it will be read on its own terms. Will academic readers, who may not recognize or may simply reject the reconfiguration of their discourse, receive the text? Will non-academic readers, who may not understand the idioms in play, patiently work with the text? In Delany's AIDS writing, the stakes for these questions are high. The texts desperately want to be *useful* for their counterpublics, to make a difference in the interpretative relation to the crisis. But if their experimental form is the locus of that incipiently social usefulness, it is also the potential barrier to their reception. As we will see, *The Tale of Plagues and Carnivals* addresses this conflict through its metafictive meditation on activist and academic readers. But Delany also addresses this problem in his conception of queer hermeneutics, which emerges perhaps most clearly in his lengthy para-academic essay on Donna Haraway, "Reading at Work, and Other Activities Frowned on By Authority."[56] Delany responds directly to Haraway's "A Cyborg Manifesto," which points to Delany's fiction for an example of radical cyborg imagery. By responding to Haraway's response to his fiction, Delany reverses the power dynamic of literary criticism, where the fictional text often serves as (mute) example and model for the writer's analytic claims (as, no doubt, Delany's work serves in my own). Building on Delany's complication of semiotics, the essay hinges on his concern about the kind of reading practices that can produce social effects. In Delany's view, "[C]yborg imagery will not *do* the work, will not promote the necessary analytic vigilance, *for* us."[57] He stresses, "Critique—critical work—is created and constituted by people, by individuals, by individuals speaking and writing to others, by people who are always in specific situations that are tensional as well as technological."[58] Here, Delany imagines the incipiently social relations that emerge between people and texts through critical reading. Yet, there is no ideal here of an egalitarian dialogue. Indeed, Delany correlates hermeneutic violence with the conditions of possibility for an encounter with a text that is not arrested by the codified positions of political ideology: "Frankly, I do not see how reading can be other than a violent process .... For without violence, all ideology—radical or conservative—is incomplete and blind to itself."[59] A reading will invariably rewrite, exclude, appropriate, or miss something, but the question at stake is whether or not that violence enables the text to circulate in its ambivalence or whether it obstructs any possible encounter with the text. This is why Delany confesses that he has "*cut ... compressed, paraphrased, brought together dispersed bits, constrained and contorted* [Haraway's] *argument*" and asks "*to what ends?*"[60] We are left to consider whether his reading of Haraway, which he calls "*a simulation of an interpretation,*" is merely a "*simulation of a passage*": "*By reading, do we halt it? By reading, do we move it along? Do we move along it?*"[61]

These questions exemplify the para-academic paradox, expressing anxiety about what passage can occur across the divergent idioms of academic and non- (or not-enough) academic reading. Is Delany's "reading" of Haraway *a reading* or merely a "*simulation of an interpretation*"?[62] Are we moving with the text, and is the text moving through our reading? Who is this "we" that reads, and will our hermeneutic practices enable the passage? The uncertainty of reception is why, in its final sentence, the essay hesitates on its own movements: "*But, now, we'd best let Helva have back her screw and get on with her work. Pace, and good luck, Ms. Haraway, with yours.*"[63] *Pace* signifies respectful disagreement and, appropriately, in its archaic usage, it indicates *passage*. If critique and passage are mutually constitutive, this final line expresses the hope of a reading that moves across discordant idioms and divergent relations of institutional power. It does so by indicating, and thus desiring, a future reading—by Haraway and by readers of Haraway and Delany. Delany creates a para-academic bridge for readers to begin that interpretative labor. However, the image of Helva getting "on with her work" is an ambivalent one. Certainly, it might signify readers taking up the interpretative work, as Delany hopes. But it also might signify a parting of ways between Haraway and Delany, back to the codified discursive boundaries of fiction and theory, respectively. Delany's writing ultimately undercuts such stable distinctions between theory and fiction, narrative and speculation. In fact, his experimental AIDS fiction is marked by an intensified passage between these discourses. I contend that the blurring of fiction and theory is a central part of Delany's formal production of the radical reader—his attempt to ensure (even if he cannot promise) that Helva returning to her "work" will elicit a queer hermeneutic practice that passes between academic and non-academic publics. Experimental form enables this queer hermeneutic to emerge, but this form also reflects on the tenuous status of its interpretative relations, their fragility, their political ambiguity, and their potential to fail in an historical moment of traumatic ignorance.

AN ALLEGORY OF FEELING IN THE ABSENCE OF HISTORY

Delany calls *The Tale of Plagues and Carnivals* a "novel," but a reader could be forgiven for being confused about how exactly to categorize the text. Fredric Jameson calls Delany's *Nevèrÿon* series "a major and unclassifiable achievement in contemporary American literature," and its ambiguous classification is encapsulated in *The Tale of Plagues and Carnivals*.[64] The text appears within *Flight from Nevèrÿon*, which is the third volume of the four that comprise the *Nevèrÿon* series. All of these novels share the same genre and pre-modern setting, and many of the same characters recur. Yet, there is no single, overarching narrative that unifies the series. Each "novel" also has a series of para-texts included within it. In fact, *The Tale of Plagues and Carnivals* is labeled an appendix to *Flight from Nevèrÿon*. That appellation indicates the strangely ancillary status of this novel within a novel, even though it comprises more pages than the other two tales and the second appendix. Finally, the novel's complete title—*Appendix A: The Tale of Plagues and Carnivals, or, Some Informal Remarks toward the Modular Calculus, Part Five*—weaves the text into Delany's ongoing consideration of the theoretical "modular calculus," which extends beyond the *Nevèrÿon* series itself.[65]

The "novel" thus inhabits an absent center, existing within a vast intertextual network of Delany's corpus. Given its dispersed structure, it would seem that Delany frustrates the reader's hermeneutic work before any reading has occurred. There is no final gathering together that could unify *The Tale of Plagues and Carnivals* into a complete whole. In this respect, the novel's structure echoes the discursive crisis of AIDS itself. As Delany writes, the body with AIDS "refuses to heal, will not become whole"; it is "ravenous for metaphors to stifle its unsettled shift, its insistent uneasiness, its conceptual turbulence."[66] Delany clearly forestalls any figural reparation of this trauma, but *The Tale of Plagues and Carnivals* stresses the necessity for some hermeneutic response to the "uneasiness" of incomplete understanding. To elicit this response, Delany draws on queer experimental literature to express the anguishing experience of AIDS, when historical "reality is constantly and catastrophically—with the death of thousands as both result and cause—changing."[67] At the same time, experimental form dialogically intensifies the disagreement and opacity about "what happened" in an effort to allegorize the feeling of the crisis. *The Tale of Plagues and Carnivals* thus asks the reader to interpretatively attend to the referential relationship between the cultural text of AIDS and its fictional translation of historical context. To do so, the novel juxtaposes two narrative timelines—one taking place in contemporary New York City and the other in the fantasy city of Kolhari. In the former autobiographical narrative, Delany struggles to write *The Tale of Plagues and Carnivals*, reflects on the relationship between aesthetics and politics in the midst of the AIDS crisis, and strives to document the sense of fear and confusion about the disease among urban queer communities. In the latter fantasy narrative, a series of characters from a cross-strata of social positions grapple with the confusion around an emergent sexually transmitted plague, and the narrative tracks their various responses to the city's "carnival," planned to distract the residents from the plague.

The juxtaposition of these two narratives invites comparison and analogy, but the novel stresses the irreducible gap between them. By doing so, Delany performatively underscores the difficulty of fictionally allegorizing a historical context in which so little certainty is available.[68] In this respect, the metafictive discourse in the text is part of the allegory itself, since the metacommentary performs both the anxiety of unstable reference and the desire to stabilize reference. Indeed, Delany admits that he does not know where to look for the "material" to make his fictional characters complete: "in the past? in the future? on the roaring shore where imagination swells and breaks? in the pale, hot sands of intellection? in the evanescent construct of the here and now—that reality always gone in a blink that is nevertheless forever making history?"[69] This wave of question-marked phrases erodes any basis for his allegory to reference. Past and future, imagination and reality, are swept into and out of consideration, because reality itself is already blinked away by the end of the sentence. Certainly, Delany has

mixed his metaphors. But that mixing is the point: the author yearns for a
stable referent, regardless of whether it has a fictional or historical ontology, yet none lasts long enough. That dreadful impropriety is the force
"making" and un-making history in the novel.

Of course, postmodern fiction is often characterized by a lack of foundational "truth" and a problematizing of hermeneutic work.[70] Yet, this is
not the proper framework for reading *The Tale of Plagues and Carnivals*,
because the novel's "anxiety" about reference should be understood as a
specific response to the problem of fictionalizing AIDS. In this respect,
the novel exemplifies the broader political tension of queer experimental
literature—namely, the struggle to narrate queerness *as a collectivity* in
the face of social forces that forestall such representations.[71] *The Tale of
Plagues and Carnivals* unveils this anxious tension in its very first section, where Delany describes a "contemporary Bridge of Lost Desire" on
"On—th Street, just beyond Ninth Avenue."[72] The Bridge of Lost Desire
is a central social space in Kolhari where prostitution and other forms
of sexual congress occur. By describing a "contemporary" version of this
bridge, Delany plunges us into the speculative practice of analogy, but
he troubles its historical coordinates. He constructs a bridge in the past
from elements of the present, and yet these elements are partly opaque,
given that the street in New York is unnamed. Then, he frames the analogy as an imaginative construction that must be generated by "you," the
reader: "It's the proper width. You'd have to double its length, though.
Give it the pedestrians you get a few blocks over .... Then put the market
I saw on the Italian trip to L'Aquila at one end."[73] The use of the second
person underscores that reference is not given but supplied through the
labor of a reader. Yet, even though the fictional world will be erected out
of contemporary elements, it will nonetheless remain radically undecidable—because these contemporary elements are, themselves, uncertain.
Thus, the opening section concludes with Delany noting that this is "the
bridge Joey told me he was under that sweltering night last July when,
beside the towering garbage pile beneath it, he smelled the first of the
corpses."[74] Whose corpses are these? Why are they rotting in the open
air? What have they died from? All of these questions are begged by this
early passage, but they are left unanswered by the novel. The bodies'
irreducible and affective materiality—their stench—troubles the fictional
construct as interpretatively indeterminate, and it bespeaks an incipiently
social collective of queer bodies, marked for death but incapable, as yet,
of being transposed into a historical narration. Indeed, it is their undecidable relationship to the plague that undoes any stable reading of these

bodies, and in the absence of reference, the corpses exude affective weight, filling the diegesis with an odor that cannot be escaped, forgotten, or disavowed. By the end of the novel, it will be suggested that these corpses are the bodies of the street people who have been slaughtered by a Jack-the-Ripper-style serial murderer who is preying on the homeless. It will not be determined, however, whether the killer's targets are random or motivated by the pervasive homophobic fear that prostitutes, drug users, and the homeless, like Joey, are the "cause" of AIDS. These deaths are specific yet fundamentally ambiguous, because their cause is unclear. Such deaths haunt the allegorical project of the text, undoing its referential work as the novel strives to bridge history with fiction.

Even as Delany uses fiction to "document" historical reality, then, he does not collapse the work of fiction into other discourses, such as politics or history. *The Tale of Plagues and Carnivals* holds contradictory definitions of "reference" in constant tension. By doing so, it challenges a purely formalist understanding of aesthetics while, at the same time, undermining an equivalence between art and activism. Note, for example, the novel's critical commentary on Annie Dillard's *Living By Fiction* (1982). Delany targets Dillard's insistence that "you do not read Nabokov as a document of the times."[75] For Dillard, experimentation ("formally ordered pattern") and representation ("verisimilitude") are mutually exclusive.[76] Any attempt to read Nabokov as a "document of the times," as providing historical or allegorical reflection on his social context, will betray the aesthetic singularity of his work.[77] In direct contrast, Delany insists that his Nevèrÿon series is "from first tale to last, a document of our times," and that its relationship to the historical is "[r]ich, eristic, and contestatory (as *well* as documentary)."[78] Here Delany balances aesthetic agency alongside its historical documentation, but neither of these projects is reducible to simple, unmediated "reference." At the very same time, Delany insists that he sees "art [as] a wholly formal enterprise."[79] This concurrent appeal to formalism captures Delany's uncertainty about the political effectiveness of art within the context of the crisis. Indeed, I part with Tucker, who reads Delany's writing as a "brand of AIDS activism."[80] For Tucker, Delany's performative distinction between fiction and activism is a claim made "out of modesty."[81] Yet, I see Delany's contradictory meditation on formalism and reference as expressing a concern about politically responding to AIDS through fiction in general and through experimental literature in particular; this is the primary reason, I suggest, that *The Tale of Plagues and Carnivals* articulates such an explicit and lengthy meditation on aesthetics and politics. Delany may wish to intervene in the crisis via experimental writing. However, he is cannily aware of the ruses of signification that will undermine such an "intervention." First, any such representation (especially one written in such historical uncertainty) might later turn out to be complicit with reactionary discourses, regardless of its intent. Second, Delany notes, "In terms of AIDS itself, there are all sorts of social practicalities one can endorse," and he is therefore reluctant to fictionalize demands for "better research, better information."[82] Fiction, here, might actually *obstruct* the practical social demands of queer people. Indeed, the novel represents activism as necessarily bleached of doubt. It must claim decidability. Yet, for Delany, queer experimental literature is a medium to both express and reflect on the affective relations of a historically produced undecidability. Consequently, *The Tale of Plagues and Carnivals* skates a conceptual figure eight—the aesthetic is referential and non-referential and yet referential nonetheless—and that circuitous movement traces the novel's commitment to articulating the affective and political "usefulness" of queer experimental literature during the AIDS crisis.

Delany realizes that his experiment in undecidability may elicit severe critiques from gay and academic publics alike. These readers, the novel suggests, may not read its problematizing of allegory as "responsible historical fiction."[83] This is, in fact, the assessment of one such reader within *The Tale of Plagues and Carnivals.* Two archaeologists, uncovering a city with "uncanny" similarities to Kolhari, read and debate Delany's novel. Kermit is a white gay man, who lived in New York during the AIDS crisis, and Leslie is an African-American woman, whose research was inspired by Delany's novel. Whereas Leslie finds the novel intriguing and worthy of discussion, Kermit is disdainful. In his assessment, the text fails to "document" the actual "complex political situation" of AIDS.[84] He critiques the novel's exclusions, such as "the attempts to close the gay bathhouses and the harassment of gay-owned businesses, not to mention straight-owned gay bars."[85] Moreover, Kermit rejects the novel's representation of Kolhari: "He's just playing at their lives, anachronisms all over the place."[86] Yet, it is the juxtaposition of the two narratives—and the undecidable suspension between them—that truly offends Kermit: "If he [Delany] wanted to allegorize what was actually going on, he should have had a platoon of Imperial storm troopers arrive at the bridge and just start tearing it down because of *course* it was the source of the epidemic."[87] If allegory demands the metaphorical dramatization of a historical situation, then Kermit sees the novel as irresponsible and a failure and just bad writing that does not nearly go far enough in capturing the hyperbolic and homophobic violence enacted against homosexuals in New York and San Francisco.

To interpret Kermit's reading of *The Tale of Plagues and Carnivals* as merely "reflexive" would miss the specificity of his location as both an academic and a gay reader, which is central to the novel's negotiation of its para-academic status. Through his voice, the novel articulates the interlocking interpretative expectations that these publics may bring to the text. By acknowledging those expectations, the novel forges its para-academic relay between academic, activist, and fictional discourses, yet it also critically redraws the basis for those expectations. Of course, one could argue that Kermit simply misreads the novel, or reads it poorly. After all, he admits, "I've read it—or skimmed it, at any rate. Certainly I've read as much as I need to."[88] Yet the joke about Kermit's skimming is that his reading is sufficient only to confirm his already-established expectations. His reading is not able to attend to his *proximity* to the text, to consider how his expectations and desires orient him, affectively and politically, in relation to the text. At the same time, he misses the text's own affective relation to its historical moment. Leslie offers Kermit an alternative hermeneutic relation for the novel: "[M]aybe he [Delany] wasn't *trying* to allegorize a political situation. Maybe he was trying to allegorize a feeling, a feeling probably everybody has had about it [AIDS] at one time or another, no matter what side they finally chose—politically, that is."[89] This may sound hopelessly insular, as if the writer's struggle is the most important issue in the AIDS crisis. Yet, Delany's struggle (as a character in the novel) metonymically stands in for a broader set of struggles around the ethical and political responsibilities of queer writing during AIDS. The textual stabilization of either "history" (verisimilitude) or "allegory" (hyperbole) would betray the lived experience of the historical moment itself *and* the problems entailed in representing that moment through the aesthetic. Thus, the text's allegorizing the feeling of attempting to allegorize the crisis intersects with its broader allegory of the collective feeling about the crisis. Leslie's substitution of feeling for politics does not suggest that affect is pre-political. Rather, she suggests that the affective relations of the crisis are not simply reducible to demarcated political positions. Affect is thus part of a collective structure of feeling that infuses the political (in all of its contradictory forces and desires) prior to being codified as *history*. Therefore, readers must enact a hermeneutic relation to affect itself—and they must locate affect between allegory and history, granting that the text's meta-allegory takes on the burden of "representing" (insofar as it can be represented) the *feeling* of the crisis.

The novel dramatizes this complex mediation of affect when the text's narrative disintegrates into notes. Soon after Kermit's and Leslie's debate, Delany inserts instructions for his writing, telling himself *"Expand this scene to some six/eight pp."* and *"Possibly okay. But clean and clarify: how Pheron got in, etc."*[90] These notes perform the unfinished nature of the narrative. Yet the affective referent of "unfinished" writing becomes clear when the narrative gives way completely to the notes. Delany stops writing a scene where heterosexual couple cares for a homosexual character suffering from the plague.

> *No. Can't write it out. Not now. Partly because it touches too many emotional things in me. And partly because, seven weeks beyond my forty-second year, I'm cynical enough to wonder seriously if a young, heterosexual, working couple would give up, for a gay friend (even if he were dying), what amounts, after all, to a night's sleep on the last day of carnival before returning next morning to a full work schedule: ten, twelve hours for them both. (They probably would have gotten him home, whether he wanted to go or not, and left him there, feeling vaguely put out.) They cannot bear to think about it directly anymore than can the Master. The relation of those two feelings in me is, of course, the bottom-line political question for this particular scene. Is the cynical response to protect myself from the emotions? Or: Does my knowledge of a cynical truth make the emotions as painful as they are? Or: Are the emotions and the cynicism two valid responses to the world as I've known it at painful play within me, in no particularly contingent hierarchy? Certainly this last is what I suspect.*[91]

As this passage reveals, Delany's allegory is not simply writing about writing. It documents the affectively fraught practice of writing about AIDS within the text. The writer's affect indexes the ambivalent, mediated relationship between the narrative and the social reality of AIDS. His rhetorical questions dramatize that distance to underscore the "political question[s]" of narrative representation itself. Of course, these questions also condense the pain that gives rise to the writer's cynicism. Yet, Delany's uncertainty about which responses are "valid" (captured by the "painful play" between them) stands in for the political question at stake: Will the heteronormative world care about homosexual suffering? Delany's meditation on this question, via experimental narrative, only underscores his desire for historical accuracy: *"[T]o sketch out what I hope would happen seems fair."*[92] Yet, the text cannot actually render a "fair" portrait; indeed, it puts into question how one could judge a fictional representation as "fair" or not, given the patent unfairness of hegemonic homophobia. Delany's metafictive and metaphorical deconstruction thus foregrounds a complex affective relation to AIDS as a historical crisis of representation. The writer's feelings intimate the lack of stable narrative in the midst of the crisis, even as they betray his ethical commitment to narrating the moment fairly.[93]

The writer cannot, for all of these reasons, complete the novel. Yet, as Delany notes, "Pheron's incompleteness ... is an incompleteness of the text, not of a person."[94] He suggests, "(One could make Pheron far more 'whole' by thinking in fictional terms precisely where he was among all these possibilities that night with his particular support group, what precisely had happened, and how. Go on, then, *mon semblable, —nom* [sic] *frère!*)."[95] Here Delany cites Baudelaire's "*Au Lecteur* [To the Reader]" (in *The Flowers of Evil*), which declares "*Tu le connais, lecteur, ce monstre délicat, / —Hypocrite lecteur, —mon semblable, —mon frère!* [Reader, you know this dainty monster too; / —Hypocrite reader, —fellowman, —my twin!]"[96] In Baudelaire's poem, the reader and writer are brothers in their common knowledge of the refined monster of "Ennui."[97] In the context of *The Tale of Plagues and Carnivals*, the reference thus poses the question: Will readers supply a hermeneutic "completion" of Pheron, or will their ennui leave the text unfinished? Although it is most likely an unintentional typo, Delany misspells the French in his quotation, writing "*nom*" instead of "*mon*"). The typo produces a stutter around the possessive, "my brother." That stutter echoes the text's broader uncertainty about whether a reader will heed Delany's call for hermeneutic work. Leslie appears to provide such support. She counters Kermit's reading of the allegorical form, stating, "[Y]ou have to read the textual shape as just the kind of conservative reification you do, but at the same time opposing it with a vigorous deconstruction of—."[98] But Kermit cuts her off and, in the process, expresses Delany's characteristically para-academic skepticism about the kind of readerly practice he can solicit through experimental form. Kermit states:

> I don't understand a word you're saying. What's more I don't believe you do either. And even if the kind of reading you're talking about *did* exist, somewhere or other, I don't think any ... text—[...]that goes out into the world with an initial printing of—what? A hundred-fifty thousand copies?—can really look forward to it, assuming it *is* possible.[99]

For Kermit, academic discourses (signaled by terms like "deconstruction") intensify the marginality of the queer experimental text, with its already-small audience. It has no right to expect the reading it anticipates, and it is inconceivable that the text could, on its own terms, elicit the hermeneutic relations it desires. This tension captures Delany's para-academic anxiety, and it aptly recalls the critiques of experimental writing as insular and elitist mentioned at the outset of this chapter. The fact that the text has a small print run discounts its legitimacy, even though, as Delany stresses, it is not the breadth of the readership that matters but the intensity of the text's formal effects on readers, which will linger as they continue to confront new information regarding AIDS.[100] While he complicates the academic and the activist desire for historical accuracy and allegorical stability in narrative fiction, Delany nonetheless draws on academic discourse, as we have seen, to theorize his aesthetic response to AIDS. A non-academic public may find these terms alienating, whereas academics like Leslie may find these terms to be legitimating keywords for the text. Yet, the discursive gaps among these reading publics—activist, academic, fantasy, and queer—remains a site of conflict for the para-academic text, forcing *The Tale of Plagues and Carnivals* to stutter even as it explicitly calls out to these publics for their radical reading.

The split between academic and para-academic discourse is only intensified by their hierarchical relationship to institutional power. *The Tale of Plagues and Carnivals* makes evident how the academic reception of a text can defuse, rather than preserve, its critical energies. By virtue of its institutional authority, the academic interpretation (and its protocols of interpretation) masks its own forceful rewriting of the text. The obstacle to an allegory of feeling, then, is not solely the absence of a responsive reader; it is the possibility of a reading that excludes the text's critical and contextual violence. Delany dramatizes this revision through the Master, the administrator of a prestigious school in Kolhari. The Master's former student, the Mummer, performs politically subversive skits in the marketplace, including skits that humorously mock the Master. The Master sends his current students to watch the performances and even begins to stage his own versions at the university. Yet, the Master rewrites the performances in two key ways. First, he re-frames the dialogues between Master and Mummer with "the imaginative fancy added that he had somehow *won* them all."[101] For the Mummer, their student–teacher dialogues were "a chance to exercise my own rational faculties," not an attempt to launch an argument or take a strong position.[102] The Master not only rewrites the outcome of the original dialogue, then, but also its form—he turns a mode of immanent inquiry into the achievement of an argument. Second,

the Master re-stages the Mummer's performances in "calmed and rea-
soned rhetoric," deleting "my [the Mummer's] screams and protests, my
nose thumbings, farts, and insults—and the curses and violences against
me they elicit from violent men."[103] This second layer of revision saps the
affective violence of the aesthetic performance, it leaves out the subversive
relation between the performer's corporeality, the performance, its object
of satire, and the audience, a relation that can even result in literal violence, as the Mummer notes. At the most general level, then, the Master's
interpretation rewrites and excludes affective critique to preserve his own
authority. Yet, his interpretative violence is effaced by the revision's *form*—
its inoffensive, disembodied rhetoric—which is implicitly authorized by
his institutional power. This silent rewriting of the text, which assimilates
and saps the performance's affective force and its dialogic immanence, is
at the root of Delany's anxiety about experimental writing becoming codified by academic considerations; indeed, experimental literature is *queer*
for him precisely in the sense that it affords a perversely embodied mode
of performative critique and affective relationality.

Despite receiving critical scorn from Delany's fictive readers, the
Master's narrative constitutes the longest section in *The Tale of Plagues
and Carnivals*. "Slowly and inexorably," Kermit notes, "the Discourse of
the Master displaces everyone else's, until, finally, it completely takes over.
Soon, it's even speaking *for* the little people—at least those the Master
himself wants to consider."[104] This is a fair description of the form of
The Tale of Plagues and Carnivals, yet it misses how the novel performatively reflects this displacement. Delany purposefully underscores how the
Master's reading of others—his subordinates, his students, his research
subjects—swallows them into his own hermeneutic desires, which are
sanctioned merely as a result of his hegemonic authority. This is a polemic
portrait of "the academic," to be sure, and it may seem to overestimate
the power that academic figures have, even in Delany's context. I have
already noted that this polemic portrait of academic knowledge provides
an important critique of "objectivity" in a historical moment when the
"facts" about AIDS are represented as impartial truth, rather than partial, biased, socially motivated interpretations. Here, I want to stress that
the critique of academic interpretation also targets fields more amenable
to "subjective" interpretation, such as those in the humanities.[105] In particular, Delany critiques the fashionable (at the time) critical interest in
Bakhtin's notion of the carnivalesque as a subversion of the administered

political order. Indeed, Delany explains in the autobiographical narrative that *The Tale of Plagues and Carnivals* was written as a "critical dialogue" with an academic presentation on Bahktin's notion of the carnivalesque, and the novel mentions a conference at Temple University entitled "Post Barthes/Post Bakhtin," attended by Michael Holquist, Carol Emerson, Barbara Johnson, and Samuel Weber.[106]

In response to the academic praise of the carnivalesque as subversive, Delany emphasizes its pacifying function—its role as an aestheticized political distraction from the plague. In the fantasy narrative, the government officials sanction a week of Carnival with increased time for "leisure and license" because, as the minister hopes, "that ... should get their minds off this unbearable plague!"[107] On the one hand, Delany's representation of the carnival strategically rewrites Daniel Defoe's famous narrative in *A Journal of the Plague Year*, which has become a canonical intertext for AIDS narratives.[108] In Defoe, the government suspends "plays and interludes ... gaming-tables, public dancing-rooms, and music-houses," in favor of "public prayers and days of fasting and humiliation ... public confession of sin."[109] In Delany's narrative, the government's biopolitical sanctioning of pleasure is far more effective than its suppression. However, he refuses to accept the corollary of Bakhtin's thesis that, given its suppression, the unauthorized emergence of the carnivalesque is likely to be a subversive act. As an example of this conceit, Delany quotes Artaud's famous analogy between the theatre and the plague—wherein he suggests, as Delany writes, "the birth of true and valid art/theatre/spectacle" will take the form of a plague.[110] In Artaud's words, the plague causes all "regular forms [of society to] collapse," resulting in a pure reversal of social mores: "[T]he obedient and virtuous son kills his father; the chaste man performs sodomy upon his neighbors. The lecher becomes pure."[111] In Delany's view, this subversion merely bespeaks the "politically reactionary" response of a "mindless mob."[112] He forcefully critiques the fetishistic transformation of the plague into a metaphor of aesthetic subversion. Moreover, the novel insists that the aesthetic has a fundamentally ambiguous political value in the context of a plague, precisely because it has been historically and culturally aligned with the potential for subversion. Carnivalesque pleasure is a defense, warding off suffering, confusion, anxiety, despair, and pain. Pleasure is, moreover, a collective affect, sanctioned and constituted by the state, intended to dispel the thought of *who* suffers while others enjoy—in particular, homosexuals and people of color.

By the conclusion of the novel, the academic Master is forced to confront the failure of his hermeneutic authority, experiencing a loss of control. His reputation is marred by rumor, and his research quest only reveals "contradiction, supposition, miscalculation, impossibility, and ignorance."[113] In a movement that recalls Delany's concerns about some deconstructive narratives, the Master subsequently embraces the existential "pressure toward misunderstanding that haunts all social communion."[114] It is no surprise that he attends "The Calling of Amenwor," then. This pseudo-religious performance by the Wizard is meant to counter the carnival's "political positivism," and indeed, the Wizard encapsulates the Master's new perspective on social communication: "Failure signs our beginning … Failure will sign our end."[115] The Wizard ultimately affirms this failure as the condition of salvation:

> It is the discrepancy, the contradiction, the gap between what you recall and what you can say (even as you strive for accuracy and articulation) that vouches safe our hope, that indicates the possibility of something more, just as, at this end, its total articulation (the complete knowledge that one lies) signs, again, our failure.[116]

The failure of complete, final, or total articulation is, as we have seen, the central deconstructive point of *The Tale of Plagues and Carnivals*. Its ethical appeal to the radical reader rests precisely on the conceit of the text's incompleteness. Yet, as Kermit notes in his critique, there is a dangerous possibility that, as the Master and the Wizard imply, "in our failure lies our salvation!… Well, *whose* failure, I'd like to ask. The Master's? Oh, yes. *Do* tell me another one!… Just suppose the people who isolated the virus and who're developing the vaccine took that tack?"[117] Note that Delany *does not* attend the Calling of Amenwor. The novel includes a list of those who did not attend, stressing that "Samuel Delany (Chip)" is absent.[118] As much as he might share the philosophical view articulated by the Wizard, his own absence suggests a purposeful, political distancing from its total affirmation. Kermit's critique thus underscores the reflexively precarious nature of Delany's queer hermeneutics: readers must attend to the failures of discursive relation but must also be wary of fetishizing or simply accepting that failure; instead, they must attend carefully to the question of "who" fails, and when and where. In this respect, Delany politicizes the unmasterable incomplete text. He locates this deconstructive notion within the specific affective trauma of AIDS, insisting that any abstract proclamation must be met with the necessary critical vigilance to measure its insight against the exigencies of this historical catastrophe.

By stressing the gaps between AIDS research and the Master's rhetoric, *The Tale of Plagues and Carnivals* points up the final, irreducible ambivalence that shapes its para-academic narration of AIDS as an epidemic of signification. That ambivalence must not be arrested, however, but allowed to fibrillate in its dual trajectories—a hopeful (and para-academic) desire to bridge discourse among conflicting publics and a fear that only silence will prevail. The novel attends to this ambivalence in its final scene. Delany strolls through Riverside Park and stumbles across Noyeed, one of the characters from the fantasy narrative. Noyeed's speech is stilted and somewhat incoherent, particularly when he tries to explain how he arrived in contemporary New York City. So, Delany asks him to "[t]ell me in your own language. Go on. I'll understand."[119] In a lengthy section composed in italics, Noyeed explains how he discovered a dragon and rode it across the boundaries between their worlds: "I've never been a man to believe in limits, borders, boundaries," he says.[120] This moment represents *The Tale of Plagues and Carnivals*'s utopian desire to cross its discursive thresholds—to bridge genres, historical moments, fiction, and reality—and, in so crossing, to forge a dialogue between its disparate reading publics. Yet, despite this momentary bridge between past and present, the present seems even more strange and incomprehensible, not domesticated or familiar when compared to the fantasy. Indeed, Delany asks Noyeed, "[H]ow do you find our strange and terrible land? Have you heard that we have plagues of our own?"[121] Noyeed pauses, looking at the city, and the novel concludes in Delany's voice, "And I would have sworn, on that chill spring night, he no longer understood me."[122] This line crystallizes that the point of analogue—the comparison of *plagues*—is the point of misunderstanding. Fictional worlds have folded onto one another, but a dialogue between them is still not possible, even though they seem to share a common trauma. Is there a precedent for this plague? What causes it? What transmits it? How should it be understood? Will it be cured? These questions cannot be answered yet, and so the novel ends on the lack of passage, a failure of reading between Noyeed and Delany. Or, more precisely, in leaving their knowledge in abeyance, *The Tale of Plagues and Carnivals* cleaves a space for future readings that might turn this "near-mute" moment into a critical dialogue.[123] The failure of the text to produce a dialogue is therefore the site of possibility for reading to come. That reading, the text hopes, would not, like the Master(ful) critic, silence the text; it would attend to the text's affective torsions as the imprint of a conflicting, restless, and unresolved traumatic history.

THE HERMENEUTICS OF PLEASURE

Despite its aesthetic and social marginality, we can now see that queer experimental literature offers complex hermeneutic relations to the AIDS crisis. Queer experimental literature provokes readers to reflect on the limits of historical reference in this moment, attending to its discursive exclusion of the homophobic violence of language itself, while also locating undecidability as a queer affect that infuses the crisis's historically specific structure of feeling. In this context, deconstructive form is both the locus of and obstacle to queer experimental literature's social utility: that form affords hermeneutic relations to the affective history of the "epidemic of signification," but it hesitates in producing a hyperbolic political critique of the material forces—legal, political, medical, economic—that underlie and perpetuate AIDS. Therefore, queer hermeneutics, even those that draw on and are informed by deconstruction, are not equivalent to the hermeneutics of suspicion; they rely on affects that do not lead to a masterful or paranoid relation to text or context, affects such as anxiety, fear, exhaustion, and sadness. By tracing these affective relations in Delany's work, we see the necessity for broadening the history of queer hermeneutics beyond the disciplinary itinerary of academically located critical theory. Doing so enables us to see the eristic relations of para-academic experimental writing, but it also illuminates a whole range of motivations, historical and pragmatic, behind the increasing dissatisfaction that queer experimental literature expresses about deconstruction. The next chapter engages this dissatisfaction at length; here, it is important to highlight that Delany subsequently uses queer experimental literature to again confront the affective relations of AIDS, to render their historical specificity and to configure new queer hermeneutic practices through para-academic writing. Yet, he turns away from deconstruction to condense the affective and hermeneutic relations of AIDS, because he fears that, quite against his own intentions, this aesthetic mode perpetuates a reactionary discourse about the disease. Reflecting on *The Tale of Plagues and Carnivals* over a decade later, Delany writes, "[T]he *controlling* metaphoric structure for AIDS from the very beginning was: '*What* metaphor shall we use for it?'" AIDS has been from the beginning a term-in-search-of-a-metaphor—and, in that sense, both her book [Sontag's *AIDS and its Metaphors*] and mine fall right *into* the controlling, dominant metaphoric structure."[124]

Delany's turn from deconstruction is also a turn toward a mode of experimental writing that can redress the absence of queer eroticism in his earlier writing about AIDS. Indeed, Delany regrets his advice to gay men in the postscript to *The Tale of Plagues and Carnivals*, which states, "Given the situation, total abstinence is a reasonable choice. Whatever adjustment one makes, one must bear in mind that the social path of the disease is difficult to trace."[125] If not altogether ceasing to have sex, then Delany recommends sex within "known circles, closed if possible," particularly in "monogamous relationships."[126] Not only will Delany later regret this claim, he will come to see it as complicit with other putatively "reasonable" safe-sex rhetoric. This was not "responsible caution but rather ... a discourse as murderous, pernicious, and irresponsible as the various antisemitic and racist pronouncements from Germany before and during World War II."[127] Undoubtedly, we can see why Delany is circumspect about the radical or revolutionary function of linguistic displaceability, given his own lack of mastery over the political implications of his initial pronouncement. Yet, instead of reclaiming mastery, Delany's AIDS writing moves toward a narration of gay male eroticism against the backdrop of the crisis's emergence. As we will see, the academic codification of discursive spaces for writing about queer affect, particularly pleasure, will continue to be a point of contention in Delany's para-academic work. However, he increasingly elaborates a hermeneutic of pleasure that attends to the problem of reading gay sexuality as a perversely open social economy while also soliciting an affective relation to queer eroticism through its pornographic style. One could conceive of Delany's hermeneutic of pleasure as a kind of "reparative reading" of AIDS and of his previous attempts to write about it. Yet, the salient point is to see that the choice between paranoid or reparative reading—or, more accurately, between critical and affirmative reading—is a historically located decision. Even Brian Massumi, an unequivocal advocate for affirmative reading, admits that the balance between critique and affirmation must be approached as "a question of dosage," conditioned by "timing and proportion."[128] Massumi's metaphor of dosage is apt, perhaps more than even he realizes. Delany's linkage of hermeneutics and AIDS reminds us that queer reading operates within a complex intersection of historical, political, and bodily economies; the point, then, is not for the critic to decide whether to suspect or repair the text but, rather as I intend to do now, to enter the text on its own terms and to measure its dosages of affect against their contextual exigencies for queer publics.

Published a decade after *The Tale of Plagues and Carnivals*, *The Mad Man* (1994) is a truly experimental text: it is a 500-page historical pornographic novel that begins with a disclaimer and ends by republishing the (at the time) most recent academic study of risk factors in HIV seroconversion.[129] These bookends are not incidental. Rather, they underline the significance of *The Mad Man*'s combination of historical and pornographic narrative. As Delany observes in his disclaimer, the fact that the study was published in 1987 is an "appalling, horrifying, and ultimately criminal" testament to the continuing dearth of research on AIDS.[130] Read within this context, then, Delany insists that *The Mad Man*

> is specifically a book about various sexual acts whose status as vectors of HIV contagion we have no hard-edged knowledge of because the monitored studies that would give statistical portraits between such acts and Seroconversion (from HIV- to HIV+) have not been done.[131]

Delany continues to frame AIDS within a narrative of uncertainty. Here, that uncertainty is produced by the ongoing lack of scientific research, which is a consequence of the willed cultural ignorance about the relationship between HIV transmission and a rich diversity of queer sexual acts.[132] *The Mad Man* strikes at the heart of that cultural repression. Indeed, the novel represents—in intensely specific and pornographic detail—sexual acts that fall outside of heteronormativity's gaze and have an ambiguous relationship to HIV in the moment of Delany's writing *and* in the historical moment that the novel depicts. These acts primarily include fellatio, urophagia, and coprophagia. (Notably, the novel never represents anal sex.) *The Mad Man* places these pleasures at the core of its narrative, which focuses on gay sex counterpublics in New York City from 1980 to 1994, primarily among black men and the homeless. Delany recalls, "*[A]ny* suggestion at all [in 1984] that one mode of bodily sexual behavior was safer than another was considered totally irresponsible."[133] The novel thus challenges this discursive prohibition simply by narrating a panoply of modes for queer eroticism. Yet, pornography is also a genre that titillates; it attempts to affectively stimulate the reader's hermeneutic interest, curiosity, and desire in sex. In Darieck Scott's words, *The Mad Man* "achieve[s] for readers what it represents for John Marr through a sexual or erotic practice—in this case, primarily, an erotic and sexual *reading* practice—of Marcusian exuberance."[134] Therefore, by eroticizing acts that are barely considered sexual, let alone erotic, *The Mad Man* elicits a queer hermeneutic of pleasure: it challenges the literally reductive conception of sexuality implied by "safe sex" discourses, and it condenses an interpretative relation to an unwritten affective history of queer eroticism, which is irreducibly marked by uncertainty about its own implication in the transmission of HIV.

For all of its willful rewriting of the past, *The Mad Man* is undoubtedly a historical novel, one that, like *The Tale of Plagues and Carnivals*, strives to faithfully represent certain historically specific structures of feeling that dominate during the crisis. Unlike *The Tale of Plagues and Carnivals*, however, *The Mad Man*'s hermeneutic dilemma does not center on the writing of history itself. Rather, the novel constructs a hermeneutics in which sexuality itself is the interpretative referent that must be recovered if one is to understand the historical magnitude of AIDS. The hermeneutic stakes for *The Mad Man*'s narrative therefore lie in developing an interpretative relationship to queer pleasure that charts its changing historical meaning and social value among queer communities. The novel maps these changes through the first-person narrative of the main character, John Marr, an African-American philosophy graduate student, who describes his experiences of having public and semipublic sex with homeless men.[135] Marr's doctoral research focuses on Timothy Hasler, a brilliant young Korean American philosopher of semiotics, who was mysteriously murdered in 1973 before receiving his doctorate. As Marr discovers, Hasler was gay and, much like Marr, enjoyed a number of unconventional fetishes and sought out public sex with homeless men. Despite the many similarities between them, however, Marr insists that an "incredible historical, fundamental abyss" exists between him and Hasler.[136] That abyss is not a reductive "homily like 'Hasler was a gay man before the age of AIDS.'"[137] Rather, it is the excruciating affective "experience" Marr has when he realizes that sex during AIDS means "gambling, and gambling on one's own—rather than seeking some possible certain knowledge."[138] Ironically, this realization "obliterates the terror" Marr has in having sex, because there is, as yet, no real knowledge of the statistical "chances" of contracting the disease.[139] Marr is uniquely capable of embracing this "gamble" as a Nietzschean affirmation of life.[140] Yet, he insists that this persistent structure of fear nonetheless creates the historical abyss between gay communities that exist before and after AIDS. Therefore, as Marr writes to a friend, the disease must be "reinscribe[d] over" all of the "inner drama" of his sexual experiences.[141] As he admits, "I thought about AIDS constantly and intently and obsessively .... we [gay men] move through life fully and continually oppressed by the suspicion that we must already have it!"[142]

Here, *The Mad Man* documents the collective anguish of gay men who risk queer pleasure in the midst of so much uncertainty about the consequences of their sexual acts. It also marks the hermeneutics of suspicion as an *oppressive* affective relation to one's own sexuality; it is infused by a paranoid certainty that cannot be confirmed and that, if given free reign, drains away the queer sociality enabled by the hermeneutics of pleasure. The abyss between Marr and Hasler thus stands in for the fundamental discontinuity between reading "sex" before and after the emergence of AIDS. As Marr writes, "I don't think anyone *can* really understand what AIDS means in the gay community until she or he has some understanding of the field and function—the range, the mechanics—of the sexual landscape AIDS has entered into."[143] If *The Mad Man*'s pornography traces some outlines of this sexual landscape, its historical structure underscores the shifting hermeneutic grounds for what sexuality "means in the gay community" as the crisis unfolds. Reading queerly thus remains an important task for Delany because, in the moment that he writes *The Mad Man*, AIDS seems to have become reified as "history" precisely as he feared it would in *The Tale of Plagues and Carnivals*.

The Mad Man represents academic modes of reading as a critical obstacle to Delany's historically sensitive queer hermeneutics of pleasure. To be sure, the academic characters stand in for a generalized cultural homophobia and the repression of queer sexuality. Yet, their location in the academy is, in fact, central to *The Mad Man*'s suggestion that the hermeneutics of pleasure must be undertaken in para-academic genres of discourse, which allow for experimental bridges to be built between the erotic and the intellectual. Indeed, Marr's dissertation advisor, Irving Mossman, initially intends to write a biography of Hasler. However, Mossman discards the project when he discovers that Hasler enjoyed, to Mossman's horror, "the most degrading—and depressing—sexual 'experiments.'"[144] "[R]ather than try to separate the sexual practices from the thinking," Mossman discards his research and concludes, with racist and homophobic disgust, that Hasler was "an obnoxious little chink with an unbelievably nasty sex life."[145] Mossman's disgust prevents him from reading, let alone interpreting, Hasler's journals, because they include lengthy entries that fantasize about bestiality and document his foot fetishism. When Marr picks up Mossman's project, he refuses to "separate the sexual practices from the thinking."[146] Marr is willing to relate Hasler's sexual experimentations to his writing on semiotics, and he is capable of reading Hasler's descriptions of bestiality as fantasies—not literal transcriptions of his experiences but as complex transfigurations of his erotic desire. Concomitantly, Marr refuses to separate Hasler's philosophical writing (such as his book on the rhetoric of Nietzsche, Pascal, and Peirce) and his para-academic writing. For example, Marr publishes essays on the relationship of Hasler's philosophy to his friend Almira Adler's poetry and to Hasler's own science fiction stories. Although his essays eventually find an academic audience, Marr's work must initially be published in para-academic venues such as edited collections of science fiction and *Umbilicus*, a "Canadian magazine of radical sexual politics."[147] Since Hasler never received his doctorate, and since much of his writing was "marginal to scholarly pursuits," Marr's department chair believes it is apt that Marr's own criticism "occup[ies] an identical position" to Hasler's.[148] *The Mad Man* suggests that these "marginal" venues allow for reading practices that the academy discounts. Of course, they afford a space for the discussion of degraded subjects annexed from philosophy (poetry, sex, and science fiction). Yet, they also permit Marr to bridge genres of discourse that are otherwise segregated from one another and kept in a strict hierarchy of authorized knowledge. The vexed relationship among genres serves as a metaphor for the ways that philosophers like Mossman wish to segregate the queer intimacy of mind and body, of intellect and sex.

Clearly, then, Marr's hermeneutics of pleasure is *not* a hermeneutics of suspicion because it requires affective immersion within—not critical distance from—the erotic economies from which Hasler's texts emerge. *The Mad Man* underscores the sexual and hermeneutic value of immersion by undermining the traditional mystery plot. Adler asks Marr to discover the cause of the philosopher's murder. Almost immediately, Marr discovers the answer, simply by entering the gay bar, The Pit, where Hasler was seen before his murder. There, Marr talks with a bartender who recalls the circumstances of Hasler's death. If Hasler's murder is not a "secret," then what prevents Adler, Mossman, and others from accessing the truth? As Marr explains to Mossman, "To a lot of people, it wasn't a secret at all. Only to the official forces—the police, people like that. It's a matter of getting yourself in the right system."[149] Here Marr suggests that anyone could have discovered the truth, if they were willing to immerse themselves in unofficial economies of knowledge. Of course, these systems are marked by their entwinement with queer sexuality, and this is precisely what obstructs Alder from discovering the truth. She cannot understand her friend's death because, like Mossman, she is homophobically disgusted and ashamed of Hasler's pleasures. Indeed, she admits, "[A]t that time, I felt I didn't want to know anything at *all* about Tim's death. It was part of the ugly and tragic sector of his life I had nothing to do with—and I wanted it to stay that way."[150] Sexuality is not hidden, nor is the truth metaphysically veiled. Both are willfully repressed from entering one economy of knowledge, even as they vibrantly live on as affective history in a para-academic economy that one must find a way to enter. As a para-academic figure, Marr is adept at passing between official and unofficial social and sexual systems, and his immersion in the hermeneutics of pleasure enables him to access archives of queer history that his academic mentors cannot.

While *The Mad Man* critiques the hierarchical structures that produce the gaps between these systems, it also relies on those gaps to engender subversive spaces of social belonging. In particular, the novel suggests that the unreadability of queer sexuality to dominant systems creates opportunities for heterotopian forms of intimacy. Speaking to this conceit, Marr repeats two jokes throughout the novel. First, he reminds us that, upon entering graduate school, he wished to write a thesis in the tradition of Hegel entitled "The Systems of the World." This text would be a "six hundred-page tome on psychology, history, reality, and metaphysics, putting them once and for all in their grandly ordered relation."[151] Mossman discourages Marr's project, because, as he explains, scholars do not write these kinds of grand (notably cross-disciplinary) texts anymore. Throughout the novel, Marr himself humorously recalls the project to laugh at his naïve desire to synthesize all the systems of the world into a single totality. Marr mocks that desire because he learns, through his immersion in economies of queer sex, that the blindness between systems can be productive. Thus, his second joke derives from a story that Pops tells after Marr fellates him in the park. Pops recalls a similar sexual experience, when his partner told him not to worry about having sex midday while white men played baseball nearby. In Pops's words, the man said,

> [I]t don't make no difference. They come down here and play every week. They won't see nothin' … Look, there're two kinds of people in the world: there's baseball players. And there's cocksuckers. An' the baseball players just don't never even *see* the cocksuckers … An' they wouldn't say nothin', even if they did see.[152]

Pops's story proves to be true throughout the novel, as public sex is rarely noticed, and never chastised, by the heteronormative world. (This is perhaps the most fantastical element of the novel, but it is also a convention in pornography that narrates public sex—the danger of getting caught is a condition of, not an obstacle to, the pleasure.) Thus, Marr frequently refers to "baseball players" in the world of the novel, recalling Pops's point that these people cannot see queer eroticism because they do not know to look for it. This is because the baseball players "play every week." Their system is ordered and regimented by codified interpretative expectations for how to 'read' bodies in public space. This regimented hermeneutic ironically prevents the baseball players from perceiving any divergence from their heteronormative expectations. Quite literally, they cannot see queer bodies or pleasures, despite their apparent and unabashed visibility.

Although the unreadability of queer sex creates some space for dissident sociality, *The Mad Man* is not content to quietly position queerness on the margins of society. On the contrary, the novel signifies the perverse "revelation" of sexuality as a critical challenge to the normative economies of heteronormativity and homosexuality alike. The novel points to this revelation through the term "EKPYROSIS," which is written in excrement on the walls and windows of Hasler's apartment and which Marr later writes on his own mirror.[153] As Marr explains, the word means "conflagration" or "apocalypse" in pre-Socratic philosophy and "is generally assumed to refer to the end of the universe, when everything, according to Heraclitus, would collapse into fire."[154] To be sure, the apocalyptic ethos of the novel converges with the AIDS crisis, which gives rise to an imminent and pervasive dread of death. Yet, here Delany correlates apocalypse to sexual revelation. Note, for example, that he calls the genre of *The Mad Man* "pornotopia," because this term indicates "not the 'good sexual place.' (That would be 'Upornotopia' or 'Eupornotopia.') It's simply *the* 'sexual place'—the place where all can become (apocalyptically) sexual."[155] Pornotopia signifies a place "where any relationship can become sexualized in a moment, with the proper word or look—where every relationship is potentially sexualized even before it starts."[156] At stake here is a hermeneutic revelation that does not posit sex as a hidden secret to be unveiled but a virtual potentiality that, once activated, recreates relational boundaries in their excremental excessiveness, in their lack of some ulterior motive, meaning, or truth. Simply by enabling a hermeneutic relation to the immanence of queer eroticism, pornotopia contributes to what Delany sees as "a necessary deformation of an older, pre-AIDS discourse, which privileged sexual reticence, into a discourse that foregrounds detailed sexual honesty, imagination, and articulation. AIDS makes such a discursive adjustment imperative. (Today, anything else is murder)."[157]

At the same time, *The Mad Man* makes evident that the revelation of sexuality constitutes a scandalous para-academic challenge to the discipline of philosophy itself. In one of its many epigraphs, the novel cites Michel Foucault's claim that "[t]he *bios philosophicus* is the animality of being human, renewed as a challenge, practiced as an exercise—and thrown in the face of others as a scandal."[158] Throughout his lectures, Foucault invokes the scandalous revelations made by Cynic philosophers such as Diogenes that challenge social conventions of sexuality, power, and knowledge. Indeed, both Foucault and Delany, like other queer writers, cite Diogenes as a proleptically queer philosopher.[159] Foucault recalls, for example, that Diogenes famously masturbated in public, demanding to know: "[W]hy are you scandalized, since masturbation satisfies a need, just as eating does. I eat in public, so why should I not satisfy this need also in public?"[160] The performative erotic exhibition effectively "brings to light, in their irreducible nakedness, those things which alone are indispensable to human life," and in Foucault's argument "this mode of life simply reveals what life is ... [and] what life ought to be."[161] Like Diogenes's masturbation, *The Mad Man*'s pornographic titillation poses a scandalous question to its readers, forcing them to reconsider the philosophical norms of sexual representation and public sexuality alike. By doing so, Delany's hermeneutics of pleasure contests the philosophical reticence around sexuality and AIDS—a reticence that buttresses a specifically heteronormative hermeneutic of suspicion.

The Mad Man dramatizes the ethical dimension (Foucault's "ought to be") of the hermeneutics of pleasure in its climactic orgy, which should be read as a literalization of the Delphic Oracle's injunction to Diogenes to "[c]hange the currency."[162] In this scene, Marr meets Mad Man Mike, who was Hasler's former lover. Mike teaches his lovers a sexual game, in which everyone pays a penny to "buy" sex with one another. Beforehand, Marr grapples with the disturbing evocations of slavery that come with purchasing another human being. Yet, ultimately he comes to appreciate the game. On the one hand, as Hasler explains (paraphrasing Mike), "knowing somebody wanted you enough even to pay a penny for you meant you were not in the unenviable position that most of the people he knew ... living in the parks and the streets was in: i.e., no one wanted them at all and to most people they were worth *nothing!*"[163] (In this respect, the game constitutes a literal resignification of the "currency" of homeless, black, and homosexual bodies, which are viewed by the dominant social gaze as worthless.) It constructs an economy in which these bodies have material and especially erotic value. On the other hand, Marr's actual experience in the orgy reveals the excessive nature of exchange in this economy of pleasure. "What stays with me, of course," he explains, "were those moments that seemed in excess of this endless systematic interchange."[164] For example, when Leaky possesses all the pennies, Mike "by fiat, simply redistributed the wealth, as it were, as absolutely and autocratically as any avatar of Marx might have done. Leaky didn't complain."[165] Similarly, when all the men fall asleep together, Marr recalls that as Big Buck starts to snore "his hand open[ed], and [Marr heard] the sound of a half dozen pennies falling out."[166] Here, a penny no longer signifies meager value in a capitalist exchange. Rather, the pennies falling from Buck's hand underscores that their *only* value lies in the exchange of sociality and sexuality they have enabled. (This is why Leaky does not complain—the redistribution of wealth means the production of more collective pleasure.) This is also why Buck drops the pennies to the floor and no one cares: the pennies have no value once these relations have ceased to be performed. And everyone can continue sleeping; no one needs to watchfully hoard the pennies for a future profit, because the pennies do not condense, in this context, some abstract value that makes them exchangeable. This scene is a metonym for Delany's more general view that cross-class erotic economies pose a literal challenge to the values and hierarchies of capitalist culture. In response to critics who question his eroticizing of homeless bodies, Delany claims, "The easier it is to name, survey, and pathologize the eroticization of any particular set of class relations, then the more *dangerous* that set of relations—and their eroticization—is to patriarchal *status quo* phallocentric society."[167] Therefore, he claims that the eroticization of cross-class relations "represent lines of communication, fields of interest, and exchanges of power" that pose a challenge to the dominant social economy and its structures.[168]

This incipiently social fantasy of erotic exchange infuses *The Mad Man*'s representation of queer erotic economies. Yet, the novel is not utopian in its representation of that social field. In fact, the hermeneutics of pleasure is precisely attuned to the violence that results when a subject is incapable of properly reading the power relations that underwrite a social economy. Mad Man Mike fails to enact such readerly vigilance, and this failure leads to Hasler's death. As Marr learns, Mike and Hasler went to The Pit. The bartender explains that the Pit caters to

a lot of older men who think the only way they can get anything worth having sexually is to pay for it. And the kids who come here are all kids who
want to get paid—need to get paid ... [T]he thing that makes this whole
place possible is a belief that sex—the kind of sex that gets sold here—is
scarce. Because it's scarce, it's valuable. And because it's valuable, it goes
for good prices.[169]

In direct contrast to this economy, Mike cannot conceive of sex as scarcity,
since so many people yearn for it. Indeed, as the bartender recalls, Mike did
not "think sex was scarce at all. He thought it was all over the place. He
didn't mind older guys—'cause he liked all sorts of guys, young, old, and
everybody in between."[170] Indeed, Mike does not even perceive the body's
productions as *waste*. Instead, he views these fluids as a desirable natural
resource, a kind of endless affective plenitude. Commenting on the semen
in the orgy, for example, he proclaims, "There's gonna be so much of
that shit around ... ain't nobody gonna have to *fight* for it."[171] Obviously,
Mike's worldview presents a manifest challenge to the hustlers and their
patrons. In Ronnie Apple's explanation, "*We* come to places like this, to
pursue our clean and costly pleasures ... and *they* come to soil it all, pollute
it with pain and rage and lust."[172]As Apple implies, the economy of the hustler bar perceives sexuality as inherently costly, because sex is a commodity
structured by supply and demand. Hence, Mike's disinterest in young men
upsets the economy of demand. Threatened by Mike's alternative, Apple
necessarily degrades "them" as "polluted," even though Mike and his lovers re-signify the "polluted" body as excessively, endlessly desirable. This
discursive violence becomes actualized as literal violence when a hustler
attacks Mike and accidentally murders Hasler in the process. In the exact
same manner, and for the exact same reason, Joey (another of Mike's lovers) is murdered while Marr discovers the truth about Hasler's death in the
novel's present. This historical repetition of traumatic violence underscores
that the antagonism between economies of queer eroticism is neither in
the past nor is it solely caused by AIDS. As Marr reflects, "How could you
explain to someone like Almira Adler what happened [to Hasler] when—
for certainly this was closer to the problem—*one entire system of the world
turned on another and tried to obliterate it.*"[173] The systems of the world
are not simply nested but antagonistically oriented against one another.
Therefore, the hermeneutics of pleasure demands an ongoing attention to
the conflicting economies that underlie social and erotic relations, because
an inattention to those values will engender material violence.

Ultimately, *The Mad Man* stresses that these antagonistic circuits of sexuality also condition the lack of passage between the academic world and its queer outsides. By doing so, Delany reflects on the inability of academic discourses to account for or understand the historical and political complexity of queer eroticism and its incipiently social potentialities. No matter how much Marr passes between these economies, he cannot completely shift one discursive orbit into another. For example, Marr prepares to publish Hasler's memoir, also titled "The Mad Man," yet Leaky admits that its publication may not "mean anything to him [Mad Man Mike] at all."[174] Mike, as Hasler's mad man, stands outside meaning here, because he is incapable of being assimilated to Marr's academic economies of discourse. After Joey's death, in a shocking scene, Mike rapes Marr—it is the only sexual scene that Marr does not detail and the text does not eroticize. Yet, when Marr tries to speculate on the meaning of this violence to Mike, he cannot determine whether Mike has heard him or not. Mike nods and states, "There wasn't nobody to come with no more."[175] In a moment that echoes of the final scene of *The Tale of Plagues and Carnivals*, Marr wonders:

> Now the nod may have signified just that Mike had heard what I'd said. The look may have meant only that he didn't understand it. And the comment may have had something to do with Joey that I simply didn't follow. But I choose to read from the three together that my supposition was right: he'd questioned the past and told me his reason.
> But with madmen such readings are always questionable.[176]

Marr chooses his reading, but crucially, Mike remains a figure that, maddeningly, produces "questionable" readings. To be sure, Marr's hermeneutics of pleasure enables an immersive "revelation" of Hasler and his sexual economy. Yet, Marr cannot, finally, understand how Mike feels about the violence he has caused in the past or the present. Likewise, he cannot determine whether Hasler's writing will "mean" anything to Mike. This opacity underlines the gap between Marr's practices of reading and those subjects that cannot, finally, be understood within its terms. Yet, the opacity does not altogether undermine hermeneutic labor or forsake para-academic writing. Rather, it points to the irreducible social and historical trauma felt by queer subjects like Mike who cannot make their experience legible, readable, and meaningful to themselves or to others; this affective history cannot simply be "recovered" and represented by a retrospective historiography. Instead, it must be understood as an unclosed problem of reading that Marr can only approach tangentially and proximately. Marr wonders, "'What would the world have to inflict on Leaky to transform him into such an out-of-touch, hurtful, and outraged sexual creature [like Mike]?' Picturing the specificities of the answer actually gave me chills!"[177] Mike thus represents the incalculable losses that linger between sexual and social economies and between the economies of the queer past and present.

One could read *The Mad Man* as an allegory of the academy prior to the emergence of queer theory and other academic discourses that created analytic spaces and discursive idioms to articulate the material and historical value of queer eroticism. Yet, such a reading might imply that queer theory has dispelled the historical uncertainty underscored by *The Mad Man*. Rather than read the novel as an allegory of the academy, I have argued instead that it constitutes a para-academic dialogue with authorized discourses of sexuality and knowledge. Its experimentation with narrating queer eroticism affords modes of reading that stretch beyond those traditionally sanctioned by and rewarded in academic spaces. Indeed, pornography is rarely perceived as the aesthetically rich and valuable genre that Delany believes it to be. In Freeman's words, scholars "know a lot less about how to do things with sex than we know about how to do things with words."[178] As a consequence, we lack hermeneutic tools to contend with reading sex as, at once, titillating *and* political, erotic *and* epistemological. Their immersive juncture is, of course, central to the hermeneutics of pleasure performed by *The Mad Man*. But it is also, most importantly, the basis for Delany's final response to the epidemic of signification engendered by the AIDS crisis. Rather than begging an ear, as he does in *The Tale of Plagues and Carnivals*, Delany now calls for a proliferation of voices to speak about pleasure. He asks that "all of us begin to put forward the monumental analytical effort, in whichever rhetorical mode we choose, needed not to interpret what we say, but to say what we *do* [sexually]."[179] The pornotopic fantasy of *The Mad Man* does not offer a mode of confession that reveals or documents the historical truth of queer eroticism. Even Delany demurs on its representational status and political utility. Yet, the novel expands the viable "rhetorical mode[s]" in which this "analytic effort" can begin to be articulated, and it demonstrates that, even if we suspend the pressure to "interpret what we say" about sex, the daunting historical obstacles to reading with pleasure are still very much ours.[180]

QUEER READING AS AFFECTIVE INHERITANCE

Many critics have recently urged queer theory to keep alive an active historical relationship to the AIDS crisis.[181] This is due in no small part to the repression of the AIDS era and its radically queer politics by homonormative assimilation. Scholars such as Gregory Tomso argue that the crisis is by no means "over," as mainstream narratives often suggest; indeed, he calls for critics in the humanities to construct new methodologies of interpretation, infused by the social sciences, to deal with the enduring implications of AIDS in social life.[182] My task in this chapter has been different. Rather than look ahead, we have looked backward, to the plurality of hermeneutic relations that emerged in response to the crisis of reading engendered by AIDS. My goal has been to broaden the predominant equation of queer reading with the hermeneutics of suspicion. In particular, I demonstrated that the queer reading of AIDS is not solely marked by what Massumi calls critique's "intemperate arrogance of debunking."[183] Rather, it affords a complex relationship to the affective and social relations that are redrawn by the epidemic of signification and the suspension of epistemological mastery that marks the crisis. To register this plurality of reader relations, we have had to repatriate the concept of "queer hermeneutics" from its institutional and academic lineage, locating queer reading within the para-academic fields from which it emerges. Queer experimental literature, as Delany's AIDS novels suggest, has been one mode for the creation of hermeneutic practices that are richly responsive to the urgencies of queer sexual politics. In this respect, queer hermeneutics should not be thought of as an abstract concept or a disciplinary choice decontextualized from the urgencies of the social world. Of course, the aesthetic and political marginality of Delany's novels are emblematic of queer experimental literature's ambivalent relationship to authorized genres of literature and critique. Yet, his formal experimentations enable Delany to move passionately and agonistically between codified methods and conceptions of reading. We will see this tension in the next chapter, as Kathy Acker contests academic codifications of queer experimental literature that unintentionally fuse its aesthetic politics into neoliberal economies of value. In the final chapter, we will return to the para-academic intersection of queer reading and the AIDS crisis through Eve Kosofsky Sedgwick's solicitation of reparative reading in her own experimental writing. Across these diverse contexts, the para-academic pertains as a mode for tracking the torsions between queer hermeneutics and those that are legitimated by academic discourses.

Yet, the larger stakes for the para-academic mode rest, finally, on whether or not we can learn to see bad reading as a fundamental layer of the "accreted historical meanings" that Heather Love identifies as part of queerness.[184] My claim throughout *Queer Experimental Literature* is that recent appeals to objective modes of reading, including Love's sociological method of "descriptive reading," obscure the accretion of queer hermeneutics—unsanctioned, degraded, yet vital ways of reading that have been developed in queer spaces and have been inherited as affective history.[185] The turn to objectivity misses, I fear, the complex condensation of these interpretative relations. Critics may not have registered these modes of reading as an inheritance precisely because they are so fundamentally defined by the apparently idiosyncratic idioms of affect. Yet, as Fredric Jameson once argued, "[W]e apprehend [texts] through sedimented layers of previous interpretations, or—if the text is brand-new—through the *sedimented reading habits and categories developed by those inherited interpretative traditions.*"[186] Bad reading is one name for the inherited interpretative traditions that pertain in the affective sedimentations of queerness. The limit of Jameson's claim is that it overlooks a text's solicitation of *new* interpretative relations that operate aslant of the ones it inherits or that condition its reception in the social world. "Paranoid reading" is thus too narrow to identify the dynamic, plural, and non- (and not-only) institutional hermeneutic relations solicited by queer experimental literature. At the same time, its conjunction of feeling and reading correctly recognizes that queer hermeneutics are an *affective* sedimentation, a queer habitus inherited in the body and activated within modes of relationality. In this sense, AIDS is not simply a historical event waiting to be read. It is an irreducible event in the history of queer reading itself, a hermeneutic inheritance that cannot be transcended or effaced because it is imprinted in the affective relation between queer readers and their social worlds.

NOTES

1. Samuel R. Delany, *About Writing: Seven Essays, Four Letters, and Five Interviews* (Middletown: Wesleyan University Press, 2005), 226.
2. Ibid.
3. Ibid.
4. Ibid.
5. Ibid.

6. Ibid. On the vexed relationship between queer experimental literature and the art market in the late 1980s and early 1990s, see Chap. 3.
7. For Delany's analysis of the "gay writer," see "The "Gay Writer"/"Gay Writing"...?" in *Shorter Views: Queer Thoughts & the Politics of the Paraliterary* (Hanover: University Press of New England, 1999), 111–14.
8. Delany, *About*, 226–27.
9. Ibid., 213, 234, original emphasis.
10. Delany conceives of academic writing as another paraliterary genre. See *Shorter*, vii–xii. While I agree with this definition in formalist terms, I stress the differences of institutional authority that pertain between academic and para-academic writing. The former produces and sanctions its own hermeneutic protocols, whereas the latter is often rendered illegible or discounted as bad reading by the discourse of the university. This tension is particularly evident in Delany's fiction, and thus, I use the concept of the *para-academic mode* to highlight the relations of power-knowledge that operate within Delany's narratives. At the same time, the concept foregrounds how the interpretative protocols solicited through Delany's experimental writing cut against those practiced and lauded by the academic figures within his narratives. For a queer approach to academic knowledge that converges with mine, see Judith Halberstam's conception of "low theory" in *The Queer Art of Failure* (Durham: Duke University Press, 2011), especially 1–25.
11. See, for example, José Esteban Muñoz, *Cruising Utopia: The Then and There of Queer Futurity* (New York: New York University Press, 2009); Tim Dean, *Unlimited Intimacy: Reflections on the Subculture of Barebacking* (Chicago: The University of Chicago Press, 2009); Nishant Shahani, *Queer Retrosexualities: The Politics of Reparative Return* (Lehigh: Lehigh University Press, 2012); and Judith Halberstam, *In a Queer Time and Place: Transgender Bodies, Subcultural Lives* (New York: New York University Press, 2005).
12. Samuel R. Delany, *Flight from Nevèrÿon* (Toronto: Bantam Books, 1985). While the book that contains *The Tale of Plagues and Carnivals* is published in 1985, Delany dates the completion of the novel as May 1984, hence my reference to the latter date.
13. Samuel R. Delany, *The Mad Man* (New York: Richard Kasak, 1994). Note that I refer throughout this chapter to the first hardcover edition of the book. Delany has since published revised editions of *The Mad Man*, first in 2002 and most recently as a digital e-book in 2015. For this edition, see *The Mad Man: Or, The Mysteries of Manhattan* (New York: Open Road Media, 2015). As the new subtitle suggests, the 2015 edition contains substantial revisions and additions. I do not address the later

editions in this context, focusing exclusively on the first edition of the book, because my argument hinges on Delany's historically specific return to experimental writing in 1994 to again grapple with the problem of representing the AIDS crisis, which was nearly at its height in the United States at that time. An analysis of the revised editions would have to take stock of the changed political, historical, and affective contexts for writing about AIDS in 2002 and 2015, in which many (wrongly) perceive the crisis as "over."

14. See Michael Warner and Lauren Berlant, "What Does Queer Theory Teach Us About X," *PMLA* 110, no. 3 (1995): 343–49.

15. Elizabeth Freeman, *Time Binds: Queer Temporalities, Queer Histories* (Durham: Duke University Press, 2010), xix.

16. For an approach to hermeneutics and queer theory that differs from mine, see Donald E. Hall, *Reading Sexualities: Hermeneutic Theory and the Future of Queer Studies* (London: Routledge, 2009).

17. Freeman, *Time*, xx–xxi.

18. Paula Treichler, "AIDS, Homophobia, and Biomedical Discourse: An Epidemic of Signification," *Cultural Studies* 1, no. 3 (1987): 263. For an incisive analysis of AIDS as a crisis of reading, see Jeffrey Allen Tucker, *A Sense of Wonder: Samuel R. Delany, Race, Identity, and Difference* (Middletown: Wesleyan UP, 2004), 230–76.

19. Michael Warner, "Introduction," in *Fear of a Queer Planet: Queer Politics and Social Theory*, ed. Michael Warner (Minneapolis: University of Minnesota Press, 1993), xii.

20. Ibid., xiii.

21. Eve Kosofsky Sedgwick, *Touching Feeling: Affect, Pedagogy, Performativity* (Durham: Duke University Press, 2002), 123–51. Later, Sedgwick stresses that paranoia is a secondary response to the predominant affects of abjection and "intense dread" that queers suffered in the midst of AIDS, but she never revises this correlation of the hermeneutics of suspicion with queer hermeneutic responses to AIDS. See "Melanie Klein and the Difference Affect Makes," *South Atlantic Quarterly* 106, no. 3 (2007): 639.

22. Sedgwick, *Touching*, 123.

23. Ibid.

24. Tucker, *Sense*, 118–19.

25. Delany, *Flight*, 357. For examples from Delany's earlier fiction, see especially *Babel-17* (New York: Vintage, 2002), which provides a complex allegory of semiotics via alien languages. Delany's conceit of the "modular calculus" is also central to *Trouble on Triton* (Middletown: Wesleyan University Press, 1996) and is addressed in *The Tale of Plagues and Carnivals*. For his metacommentary on the modular calculus, see Delany, *Flight*, 375–77.

26. As an example, see Samuel R. Delany, "Neither the First Word nor the Last on Deconstruction, Structuralism, Poststructuralism, and Semiotics for SF Readers," *Shorter Views: Queer Thoughts & the Politics of the Paraliterary* (Hanover: University Press of New England, 1999), 141–85.

27. Delany, *Flight*, 339, original emphasis.

28. Delany, *Shorter*, 126.

29. Delany, *Flight*, 176–77, original emphasis.

30. Ibid., 176.

31. Ibid.

32. Ibid., 179.

33. Ibid., original emphasis.

34. Samuel R. Delany, *Longer Views: Extended Essays* (Hanover: University Press of New England, 1996), 108.

35. Delany, *About*, 212.

36. Delany, *Flight*, 179.

37. See Sharon Marcus and Stephen Best, "Surface Reading: An Introduction," *Representations* 108, no. 1 (2009): 1–21. Note that Marcus and Best align "deconstruction, ideology critique, and the hermeneutics of suspicion" and do not distinguish or differentiate their "demystifying protocols" (2).

38. Samuel R. Delany, *Silent Interviews: On Language, Race, Sex, Science Fiction and Some Comics* (Hanover: University Press of New England, 1994), 4, 7.

39. Ibid., 16. For a convergent approach to deconstructive reading, see Richard Klein, "The Future of Literary Criticism," *PMLA* 125, no. 4 (2010): 920–23.

40. Delany, *Silent*, 7.

41. Delany, *About*, 243, my emphasis.

42. Delany, *Silent*, 6.

43. On the limits of the hermeneutics of suspicion, see Rita Felski, *The Limits of Critique* (Chicago: The University of Chicago Press, 2015).

44. Delany, *Silent*, 6.

45. Delany contends that his radically expansive conception of "reading" mirrors Derrida's expansion of "writing" (*Silent* 277). As François Cusset notes, critics in the United States specifically emphasized deconstruction as a theory of *reading*. See *French Theory: How Foucault, Derrida, Deleuze, & Co. Transformed the Intellectual Life of the United States*, trans. Jeff Fort (Minneapolis: University of Minnesota Press, 2008), 113. On the adaptation of deconstruction within contemporary literature, see Judith Ryan, *The Novel After Theory* (New York: Columbia University Press, 2014); *French Theory in America*, eds. Sylvère Lotringer and Sande

Cohen (New York: Routledge, 2001); and Daniel Punday, *Narrative After Deconstruction* (Albany: State University of New York Press, 2003). On deconstruction and the Nevèrÿon series, see Kathleen L. Spender's "Nevèrÿon Deconstructed" in *Ash of Stars: On the Writing of Samuel R. Delany*, ed. James Sallis (Jackson: University of Mississippi Press, 1996).

46. Quoted in Delany, *Flight*, epigraph.
47. Ibid.
48. Michael Ryan, *Marxism and Deconstruction* (Baltimore: Johns Hopkins University Press, 1982), 8.
49. Delany, *Flight*, 360, original emphasis.
50. For a nuanced analysis of affect in deconstruction, see Rei Terada, *Feeling in Theory: Emotion after the "Death of the Subject"* (Cambridge: Harvard University Press, 2001), 128–51.
51. Paul de Man, *Allegories of Reading: Figural Language in Rousseau, Nietzsche, Rilke, and Proust* (New Haven: Yale University Press, 1979), 19.
52. Delany, *Flight*, 352, original emphasis.
53. Ibid., 351, original emphasis.
54. Delany, *Silent*, 147, original emphasis.
55. Delany, *Flight*, 333.
56. Samuel R. Delany, "Reading at Work, and Other Activities Frowned on By Authority: A Reading of Donna Haraway's "Manifesto for Cyborgs: Science, Technology, and Socialist Feminism in the 1980s,"" in *Longer Views: Extended Essays* (Hanover: University Press of New England, 1996), 87–118.
57. Ibid., 117, original emphasis.
58. Ibid., 115.
59. Ibid., 98.
60. Ibid., 118, original emphasis.
61. Ibid., original emphasis.
62. Ibid., original emphasis.
63. Ibid., original emphasis. With "Helva," Delany is referencing the Anne McCaffery short story, "The Ship Who Sang" (1961), which Haraway also cites in her essay.
64. Quoted in *Ash of Stars: On the Writing of Samuel R. Delany*, ed. James Sallis (Jackson: University of Mississippi Press, 1996), ix.
65. This is a recurring motif, originating in Delany's science fiction novels (beginning with *Trouble on Triton*). Inspired by Willard Van Orman Quine's theories of grammar and description, the calculus addresses representational questions such as "[H]ow do we know when we have a model of a situation; and how do we tell what kind of model it is?" (*Flight* 377).

66. Delany, *Flight*, 178.
67. Delany, *Silent*, 157.
68. The problem of representing AIDS is central to the literary response to AIDS itself, and many critics and writers have grappled with this issue, especially in the first wave of academic criticism on AIDS literature. See, for example, *AIDS: The Literary Response*, ed. Emmanuel S. Nelson (New York: Twayne Publishers, 1992); and Lawrence Howe, "Critical Anthologies of the Plague Years: Responding to AIDS Literature," *Contemporary Literature* 35, no. 2 (1994): 395–416. On AIDS literature more broadly, see Ross Chambers, *Untimely Interventions: AIDS Writing, Testimonial, and the Rhetoric of Haunting* (Ann Arbor: The University of Michigan Press, 2004); and Tim Dean and Steven Ruszczycky, "AIDS Literatures," in *The Cambridge History of Gay and Lesbian Literature*, eds. E.L. McCallum and Mikko Tuhkanen (Cambridge: Cambridge University Press, 2014), 712–31.
69. Delany, *Flight*, 188.
70. See Brian McHale, *Postmodern Fiction* (London: Routledge, 1987).
71. On the relationship between postmodern American literature and the AIDS crisis, see Tyler Bradway, "Literature in an Age of Plague: The AIDS Epidemic," in *American Literature in Transition, 1980–1990*, ed. Quentin Miller (New York: Cambridge University Press, forthcoming).
72. Delany, *Flight*, 175.
73. Ibid.
74. Ibid.
75. Quoted in Ibid., 237.
76. Annie Dillard, *Living by Fiction* (New York: Harper Perennial, 1982), 30–31.
77. Ibid.
78. Ibid., 237, 377, original emphasis.
79. Ibid, 273.
80. Tucker, *Sense*, 233.
81. Ibid.
82. Delany, *Flight*, 339.
83. Ibid., 329.
84. Ibid., 333.
85. Ibid., 332.
86. Ibid., 326.
87. Ibid., 333, original emphasis. *The Tale of Plagues and Carnivals* also includes an epigraph from Allen Mandelbaum's introduction to Dante's *Infereno*: "Ours, too, is an age of allegoresis" (*Flight* 173). Citing Benjamin, Mandelbaum's point is that there are significant "proximities" between the medieval and the modern and that moderns possess a desire to allegorize much as Dante did (viii). See Allen Mandelbaum, "Introduction," in *The*

Divine Comedy of Dante Alighieri, trans. Allen Mandelbaum (New York: Bantam, 1980). This term "allegoresis" recurs throughout *The Tale of Plagues and Carnivals* and is an apt descriptor for Delany's metafictive, reflexive approach to reading an allegory of feeling.

88. Delany, *Flight*, 327.
89. Ibid., 333, original emphasis.
90. Ibid., 337, original emphasis.
91. Ibid., 338–39, original emphasis.
92. Ibid., 339, original emphasis.
93. Delany's representation of history resonates with Fredric Jameson's understanding of history as an "absent cause" that is "inaccessible to us except in textual form ... our approach to it and to the Real itself necessarily passes through its prior textualization, its narrativization in the political unconscious," *The Political Unconscious: Narrative as a Socially Symbolic Act* (Ithaca: Cornell University Press, 1981), 35. AIDS is very much an absent cause in *The Tale of Plagues and Carnivals*. Yet, I would qualify that, in Delany's novel, its structure of feeling inhabits an indeterminate space between the Real of history and the Symbolic of the political narrative.
94. Delany, *Flight*, 339.
95. Ibid., 340, original emphasis.
96. Charles Baudelaire, *The Flowers of Evil*, trans. James N. McGowan (Oxford: Oxford University Press, 1993), 4–6.
97. Ibid., 7.
98. Delany, *Flight*, 328.
99. Ibid., original emphasis and ellipsis in original.
100. Delany, *About*, 212.
101. Delany, *Flight*, 263, original emphasis.
102. Ibid.
103. Ibid., 267.
104. Ibid., 326, original emphasis.
105. A recurrent trope of *The Tale of Plagues and Carnivals* includes Delany's speculation on how the characters would respond to a contemporary psychoanalytic reading of them. Except for the Master, all of the characters have fables that function as their own means of interpretation and understanding, which are similar to psychoanalysis; Delany also notes each character's reaction to the hypothetical psychoanalysis by a modern reader. Not only does this trope de-prioritize and historicize psychoanalytic reading, but it also provides hermeneutic agency to characters that might otherwise be stigmatized as non-modern and therefore ignorant (184, 189).
106. Delany, *Flight*, 267–68.

107. Ibid., 216.
108. See Laurel Brodsley, "Defoe's *The* [sic] *Journal of the Plague Year:* A Model for Stories of Plagues," in *AIDS: The Literary Response,* ed. Emmanuel S. Nelson (New York: Twayne, 1992), 11–22.
109. Quoted in Delany, *Flight,* 221.
110. Ibid., 222.
111. Quoted in Ibid., 205.
112. Ibid., 206.
113. Ibid., 302.
114. Ibid., 201.
115. Ibid., 253, 320. For a reading of the Calling that differs from mine, see Jes Battis, "Delany's Queer Markets: *Nevèrÿon* and the Texture of Capital," *Science Fiction Studies* 36 (2009): 478–89.
116. Ibid., 326.
117. Ibid., 327, original emphasis.
118. Ibid., 320.
119. Ibid., 346.
120. Ibid., 349.
121. Ibid., 350.
122. Ibid.
123. Ibid., 202.
124. Delany, *Shorter,* 137, original emphasis.
125. Delany, *Flight,* 352.
126. Ibid.
127. Delany, *Silent,* 160.
128. Brian Massumi, *Parables of the Virtual: Movement, Affect, Sensation* (Durham: Duke University Press, 2002), 13.
129. On the relationship between *The Mad Man* and AIDS, see Tucker, *Sense.*
130. Delany, *Mad,* xiii–xiv.
131. Ibid., xiii.
132. For relevant critical considerations of these issues, see Delany's "On the Unspeakable," "Street Talk / Straight Talk," and "Pornography and Censorship" in *Shorter Views.* See also "Averson/Perversion/Diversion" in *Longer Views* for Delany's non-fictional articulation of this project. For Delany's queer ethnography and theory of public sex in New York City, see *Times Square Red, Times Square Blue* (New York: New York University Press, 1999). For incisive readings of *The Mad Man*'s ethics of abjection, see Mary Catherine Foltz, "The Excremental Ethics of Samuel R. Delany," *SubStance* 37, no. 2 (2008): 41–55; and Darieck Scott, *Extravagant Abjection: Blackness, Power, and Sexuality in the African American Literary Imagination* (New York: New York University Press, 2010), 204–56. Also see Ray Davis, "Delany's Dirt," in *Ash of Stars: On the*

Writing of Samuel R. Delany, ed. James Sallis (Jackson: University Press of Mississippi, 1996), 162–88. On Delany's use of pornography, see Gabriel Zinn, "Marginal Literature, Effaced Literature: *Hogg* and the Paraliterary," *Anamesa* 4, no. 1 (2006): 45–53. On queerness in Delany's early work, see Tavia Nyong'o, "Back to the Garden: Queer Ecology in Samuel Delany's *Heavenly Breakfast*," *American Literary History* 24, no. 4 (2012): 747–67.

133. Delany, *Shorter*, 50, original emphasis.
134. Scott, *Extravagant*, 30, original emphasis.
135. For Delany's thoughts on cross-class eroticism, see *Silent*, 127–63.
136. Delany, *Mad*, 177.
137. Ibid.
138. Ibid., 176.
139. Ibid.
140. Elsewhere, *The Mad Man* quotes Nietzsche's dictum, "Man needs what is most evil in him for what is best in him. The secret for harvesting from existence the greatest fruitfulness and the greatest enjoyment is—to live dangerously" (237).
141. Ibid., 172.
142. Ibid., 172–74.
143. Ibid., 179, original emphasis.
144. Ibid., 22.
145. Ibid., 46–47.
146. Ibid., 46.
147. Ibid., 493.
148. Ibid., 240.
149. Ibid., 488.
150. Ibid., 301, original emphasis.
151. Ibid., 10.
152. Ibid., 57–58, original emphasis.
153. Ibid., 480. On apocalypse in *The Mad Man*, see especially Chapter 3 of Guy Davidson, *Queer Commodities: Contemporary US Fiction, Consumer Capitalism, and Gay and Lesbian Subcultures* (New York: Palgrave Macmillan, 2012).
154. Delany, *Mad*, 307.
155. Delany, *Shorter*, 133, original emphasis.
156. Ibid.
157. Ibid, 123.
158. Quoted in Delany, *Mad*, 5.
159. Notably, Michael Warner also references the Diogenes tale in the beginning of *The Trouble with Normal* (Cambridge: Harvard University Press, 1999), 2.

160. Michel Foucault, *The Courage of Truth* (New York: Palgrave MacMillan, 2011), 171.
161. Ibid.
162. Quoted in Delany, *Mad*, 89.
163. Ibid., 456, original emphasis.
164. Ibid., 442.
165. Ibid.
166. Ibid., 445.
167. Delany, *Silent*, 136, original emphasis.
168. Ibid., 136–37. This is why the novel's disclaimer disavows historical reference, stating "Correspondences are not only coincidental but preposterous" (xiii). This is a strange declaration, given that the novel goes to such efforts to demarcate its historical contexts. Yet, as Delany notes, the novel leaves out a great deal of violence in its idealization and fantastical narration of queer, black, and cross-class sexuality. Indeed, the disclaimer admits that its representation of homelessness leaves out the winter and many other forms of violence faced by people living on the street.
169. Ibid., 353–54.
170. Ibid., 354.
171. Ibid., 434, original emphasis.
172. Ibid., 478, original emphasis.
173. Ibid., 483, my emphasis.
174. Ibid., 499.
175. Ibid., 497.
176. Ibid.
177. Ibid., 483.
178. Freeman, *Time*, 172.
179. Delany, *Shorter*, 56.
180. Ibid.
181. See, for example, Sarah Schulman, *The Gentrification of the Mind: Witness to a Lost Imagination* (Berkeley: University of California Press, 2012).
182. Gregory Tomso, "The Humanities and HIV/AIDS: Where Do We Go From Here?" *PMLA* 125, no. 2 (2010): 443–53.
183. Massumi, *Parables*, 13.
184. Heather Love, *Feeling Backward: Loss and the Politics of Queer History* (Cambridge: Harvard University Press, 2009), 30.
185. Heather Love, "Close but not Deep: Literary Ethics and the Descriptive Turn," *New Literary History* 41, no. 2 (2010): 371–91.
186. Jameson, *Political*, 9, my emphasis.

CHAPTER 3

The Languages of the Body: Becoming Unreadable in Postmodernity

Kathy Acker's fiction has often been called "unreadable" by her critics.[1] On the one hand, her novels maintain the barest level of narrative consistency, with characters shifting names, genders, and personalities as their plots ignite and fizzle out at a feverish pace. In this sense, Acker's novels are literally unreadable, if readability is defined by realist or Aristotelian narrative conventions.[2] On the other hand, a primary concern of Acker's novels is the sexually taboo. In the tradition of transgressive writers such as the Marquis de Sade, Pauline Réage, and Georges Bataille, her fiction represents rape, incest, patriarchal and sadistic violence, maternal hatred, forced prostitution, and the constant betrayals wrought by lovers and the ideology of love alike. All of these dynamics are narrated with an eroticized, detached, and bemused tone, which produces a truly discomfiting gap between form and content. For this reason, Acker's novels have been, for many readers, morally and politically repulsive and thus unreadable.

Yet it is rarely noted that Acker embraced the unreadability of her fiction. To be sure, many writers craft texts that are estranging, ambiguous, and schizophrenic. Few writers, however, rival Acker's performative claims to unreadability, which she frequently articulates in interviews and even incorporates into the marketing of her work. Take, for example, the caption placed on the back of *Hannibal Lecter, My Father* (1991), a collection of Acker's short writings published by *Semiotext(e)*: "This writing is

© The Author(s) 2017
T. Bradway, *Queer Experimental Literature*,
Palgrave Studies in Affect Theory and Literary Criticism,
DOI 10.1057/978-1-137-59543-0_3

all fake (copied from other writing) so you should go away and not read any of it."³ This assertion appears without quotations in front of a photograph of the author, so it is unclear whether this is a quote from Acker, the publisher, or someone else. With its ambiguous attribution, the caption undermines the conventions of literary consumption: there will be no seduction of the reader as consumer; there will be no advertisements of authenticity or originality, which typically grace the back-cover of books; and there will be no sanctioning of the author, via praise, by an external critical authority. Taking estrangement to its anti-social extreme, Acker's avowed unreadability defuses the conventional relationship between writers, readers, texts, and literary institutions of authority. Not only does she resist framing her writing as a commodity—one worth purchasing and consuming because of its singular novelty—she also refuses to conceive of "the reader" as a consumer-subject who is the privileged addressee implied by the normative literary object. Such a reader should simply "go away" without reading because, as we will see, Acker's work dispenses with any notion of reading that can be stabilized in the consumer terms of "subject" and "object."

Of course, one can interpret Acker's refusal of the reader as totally disingenuous, a sly hipster-cool that was a part of her self-cultivated punk aesthetic.⁴ After all, as much as the caption dismisses our reading, it has already captured our eyes, hailing the very "reader" Acker wishes to disrupt. Yet this chapter will contend that there is an earnestness and complexity to Acker's cultivation of unreadability that points to her underlying project to redefine the social relations of reading through the idiom of queer affect. As Acker suggests in her interview with Sylvère Lotringer, "I'm not writing for the reader."⁵ "[T]he primary pleasure is not for the reader, it's for me," she explains, "Probably it makes my texts a bit unreadable."⁶ Here, "unreadable" takes on a new meaning, one that diverges from the three (formal, thematic, and moral) elaborated above. Unreadability derives from the text's resistance to the economy of pleasure that typically underwrites the ideology of literature as either a commodity purchased by the reader for pleasure or an affective gift given by the author to the reader. Acker's texts are "a bit unreadable" because they complicate both the use-value and exchange-value of literary affect—the text does not serve its traditionally relational instrumentality (to educate, to please) nor does it offer aesthetic affect as a commodity that can be transposed into the terms of consumer exchange. Yet, as we will see, pleasure is *not* annexed from the event of reading; rather, by becoming-masturbatory, Acker's writing performs an erotic experiment with affective thresholds that cannot be easily circumscribed by the categories of reader, writer, or text.

Contrary to accounts of Acker's fiction as unpleasantly "aggressive," then, I will trace Acker's redefinition of reading as a stimulating encounter with what she called the sensuous and chaotic "languages of the body," which cannot be stabilized in terms of subject–object dialectics.[7] Predicating the value of her writing on the affective event of the material body-in-becoming, Acker carves out an oppositional space for queer experimental literature within the political economy of neoliberalism that commodifies and annuls aesthetic subversion.[8] This becoming is not simply directed toward the undoing of logocentric meaning and rational–critical subjectivity, although it undoubtedly extends those postmodern projects. Rather, it reinvigorates the political agency of queer aesthetics by redrawing the social relations of aesthetic consumption, forestalling the abstraction of queer experimental literature into yet another form of exchangeable capital. Acker's figuration of reading as an affective experimentation with chaotic materiality stands against a political economy that would dematerialize aesthetic affect into the idiom of abstract commensurability necessary for exchange value.

Acker's turn to the languages of the body remains an underanalyzed aspect of her politics of reading. Indeed, most critics tend to focus on Acker's earlier work with plagiaristic deconstruction. When critics do engage Acker's languages of the body, however, they tend to position it as unreflectively symptomatic of neoliberalism rather than contextually emergent alongside, and complexly opposed to, neoliberalism.[9] Walter Benn Michaels, for example, aligns Acker's work with Michael Hardt and Antonio Negri's *Empire*, arguing that she "ontologize[s] [writing] in the same way that politics is in *Empire*."[10] By conceiving of "writing as bleeding," Michaels perceives Acker as a symptom of a biopolitical "discourse of terrorism" that supplants problems of meaning and conflicting ideologies with a mystified investment in the "ontology of the subject."[11] In a highly literal reading, Michaels contends that the turn to ontology results in a "commitment to new subject positions instead of to more just societies. ... The Left must make up for its refusal of better ideas by a demand for better bodies."[12] By contrast, Michael Clune argues that Acker's languages of the body do, in fact, signify a reimagination of social order. However, he interprets Acker's fiction as yearning for a natural, organic market liberated from any political control, a "market without a society."[13] Indeed, he identifies a convergent biological and economic essentialism within

Acker's figuration of bodily writing, one that resonates with the free market ideologies of neoliberalism emerging in the late 1980s. These critiques subordinate the queerness of Acker's figuration of the affective body, particularly its resistance to heteronormative and patriarchal figurations for the body politic. But more importantly, they occlude the context in which Acker reconceptualizes her aesthetic politics aslant of the discourses available for encountering postmodern fiction, namely poststructural literary theory.[14] Indeed, the irony of Acker's proclaimed unreadability is that she was—and continues to be—manifestly readable within the now-institutionalized discourses of continental theory. Critics have found no shortage of suggestive links between Acker and thinkers such as Jean Baudrillard, Judith Butler, Gilles Deleuze and Félix Guattari, Jacques Derrida, Julia Kristeva, and Luce Irigaray, all theorists that Acker herself references and discusses.[15] Yet the emphasis on Acker's engagement with theory obscures her ultimate frustration with the way that these discourses, particularly deconstruction, made her writing too narrowly readable, rendering it ironically subordinate to and exemplary of an external master discourse.[16] To be sure, Acker herself turned to theory to make her work readable to critics and scholars. As she explains to Lotringer:

> By introducing me to the French philosophes, you gave me a way of verbalizing what I had been doing in language. I didn't really understand why I refused to use linear narrative; why my sexual genders kept changing; why basically I am the most disoriented novelist that ever existed. ... I was like a death-dumb-and-blind [sic] person for years, I just did what I did but had no way of telling anyone about it, or talking about it. And then when I read ANTI-OEDIPUS and Foucault's work, suddenly I had this whole language at my disposal. I could say, Hi! And that other people were doing the same thing. I remember thinking, Why don't they know me? I know exactly what they're talking about. And I could go farther.[17]

In Acker's narrative, theory renders her a social subject, shifting her from insularity and ignorance to social articulation ("I could say, Hi!") and potential reception ("Why don't they know me?"). Yet even as she prioritizes theory as a frame, Acker insists her work can somehow "go farther." The problem is that readers often do not agree. Take, for example, David Foster Wallace's emblematic review of Acker's novels, in which he labels her work a "theory-vector," claiming that its "entire interest for the reader lies in the theoretical justifications for its form."[18] Wallace jokes that "Acker should have to hand over 15% of every royalty-dollar to the authors of *Anti Oedipus*," and he concludes that the ideal audience for Acker's fiction is academic.[19] Although theory secures her canonization as a postmodern and experimental writer of scholarly interest, Acker finds her writing paradoxically consigned to the bourgeois elites that her novels mercilessly satirize.[20]

Acker's turn to the languages of the body thus takes place in the shadow of the disciplining of her work, and in this respect, her aesthetic turn exemplifies the paradoxical tensions faced by queer experimental literature as it becomes assimilated into the idioms of academic theory. Indeed, Acker subsequently disavows theory. Despite the clear influences of French feminism on the languages of the body, Acker tells Lotringer, "I'm at this place where I was prior to when I met you where don't [sic] have the theory anymore to talk about it."[21] Yet this disavowal of theory is not simply a marketing ploy or an attempt to recapture critical cachet; it is linked to Acker's concern that theory itself has abetted the gentrification of the avant-garde art scene in New York City, which had offered such an important community for Acker's artistic production and reception. It is not a coincidence that Sarah Schulman identifies Acker as a central literary figure in her narrative about the gentrification and repression of queer radicalism. With the rise of neoliberal homonormativity, Schulman notes that Acker's fiction fades from view. This is because "[H]er context is gone. Not that she was a gay male icon, but rather that she was a founder and product of an oppositional class of artists, those who spoke back to the system rather than replicating its vanities."[22] As we will see, a central motivation for Acker's purported break from what she variously labels "deconstruction," "conceptual art," and "postmodernism" hinges on her searching for a politics of aesthetics that is not defined by conceptualist replication or deconstructive resignification, methods that she believes have been depoliticized by the US academy and the art market alike.

In resistance, then, Acker elaborates a notion of affective aesthetics that targets what Sianne Ngai calls the "market's disarmingly friendly *tolerance* of art—a tolerance that assumes its social ineffectuality or innocuousness."[23] She does so through a broad restructuring of the affective relations that underpin the smooth assimilation of art to the dematerializing structures of neoliberal value. Acker's languages of the body clear away the disciplinary codifications of her work in the hopes of unleashing a *becoming-unreadable* among her reading publics. This becoming is not an anarchic fantasy of libertarian transcendence of the social. On the contrary, she is writing for the "people who are missing," intimating and eliciting a queer counterpublic in a context in which its conditions of possibility have been decimated.[24]

AGAINST "DECONSTRUCTION"

Roland Barthes famously argued that the "fundamental ethical problem is to recognize signs wherever they are; that is to say, not to mistake signs for natural phenomena and to proclaim them rather than conceal them."[25] Barthes's ethic effectively encapsulates the project of Kathy Acker's early fiction. Acker was primarily inspired by conceptual art and "deconstruction," a term that, as will become clear, she does not use in any orthodox way. Acker plagiarized, appropriated, and rewrote canonical fictions such as *Don Quixote, Great Expectations,* and *Huckleberry Finn,* as well as popular fiction by William Gibson and Ian Fleming. In each case, she re-contextualized these narratives to reveal their latent sexism, racism, homophobia, and exploitative class relations. The goal, in her words, was "to deconstruct, to take apart perceptual habits, to reveal the frauds on which our society's living."[26] Despite initial resistance to her work by feminists, Acker's transgressions of normative sexuality, her dissolutions of essentialist gender roles, and her expropriation of male texts has been lauded by feminist and queer critics as representative of a politically engaged postmodernism.[27]

What has received less attention, however, is Acker's movement away from the politics of resignification.[28] This movement was sparked by Acker's experience of living in England for six years, where she became disillusioned by the intense class stratification and the commodification of the art world. Before living in England, Acker felt that art could be "an angel miraculously living amid the greed and zombielike behaviors of those outside the art world, the faceless business-suits who crowded into Wall Street every morning."[29] Yet, Acker was disappointed in her search for an "art community" like the one she inhabited in New York, which was influenced by punk culture and incorporated a diverse array of class positions. Acker recalled "in England I found an art world, if not composed, then certainly defined by the upper-middle class," which made art appear to be "another game played by the upper and upper-middle classes for their own amusements."[30] This experience changed her perception of the American art world upon her return: "Art was simply stock in a certain stock market."[31] Ironically, conceptual artists that previously worked alongside Acker, including Sherri Levine, Richard Prince, and Jenny Holzer, had become marketable commodities. In Acker's view, "[T]he New York art world seemed to have closed its ranks: the old community in which an underground gradually became commercial has disintegrated into a market whose share-holders, frightened, are determined to take no more chances."[32] Acker's narrative underscores the significance of the art world as a context for understanding her own aesthetic development as a whole, and it dramatizes the emergence of new economic conditions that reduce the support for experimental political art. Despite the market's affirmation of risk, art that takes chances cannot predictably offer a return on investment. However, Acker does not simply mourn the loss of an aesthetic style; her concern focuses on the erosion of a marginal and oppositional art *community*, an avant-garde underground that supported, practiced, and valued one another in the relational process of creating experimental art.

In the face of the gentrification of conceptual art, Acker began to "question all the precepts" of her aesthetics, asking, "What were and are the political realities surrounding Conceptualism?"[33] For Acker, conceptual aesthetics are intimately tied to poststructural theory, partly because the latter enabled her to articulate the purpose of her fiction. Citing Foucault and Deleuze and Guattari, Acker explains, "I had been writing in certain ways due to certain theories about deconstruction and decentralization," and these philosophies were "working for cultural and *political* purposes," noting Deleuze and Guattari's involvement with Autonomia.[34] Yet, Acker fears:

> The Anglo-Saxon adoption and adaptation of deconstruction had depoliticized the theories. It seems not by an act of chance that Jean Baudrillard, out of all those French theorists, became the theoretical idol of the New York art world, Baudrillard whose politics, unlike Deleuze's and Guattari's, are, at best, dubious...
> Suddenly and ironically, in this Anglo-Saxon climate, deconstructive, now known as postmodernist, techniques became methods for applauding the society and social values composed by American postindustrialization. Freed of Nietzschean *sovereignty*, any value or text could be equivalent to or substitute for any other value or text.[35]

To be clear, Acker's use of "deconstruction" indicates a broad cultural practice rather than an orthodox version of Derridean deconstruction. Acker targets a postmodern mode that presupposes that "every phenomenon, every act is a text and all texts refer to all other texts. Meaning is a network, not a centralized icon."[36] Her concern is that postmodernist aesthetics—those predicated on the *equivalence* of exchangeable text—cannot combat the postindustrial depoliticization of critical theory and conceptual art alike. Their approach inadvertently "applaud[s]" rather than critiques the status quo.[37] This is precisely why Acker laments that, of all the poststructuralists, Baudrillard had the most impact on the art world.[38] For her, Baudrillard's success signals an apolitical relativism that buttresses the status quo by confirming the all-pervasive subsumption of the real into the cultural simulacrum. She fears that an aesthetic practice, inspired by the "simulacrum" and based in exchangeablity of text, cannot combat the values of postindustrial culture, let alone imagine a new field of social relations beyond it.

Consequently, Acker desires "somewhere to go, a belief, a myth. Somewhere real."[39] Clearly, the alignment of reality with myth, belief, and "somewhere" does not indicate an empirical real. Yet it expresses a desire for an affirmative art, based in Acker's sense that perhaps "society is now in a 'post-cynical' phase."[40] Here, Acker anticipates a broader shift among postmodern writers that explore what Irmtraud Huber calls "reconstructive fantasies," testing out potential aesthetic strategies that might move beyond postmodernism's deadlocks, particularly in the aftermath of its institutionalization and dissemination within popular culture.[41] For Acker, this movement begins with the materiality of the body. She writes that her novel *Empire of the Senseless* (1988) concluded with "hints of a possibility or beginning: the body, the actual flesh, almost wordless, romance, the beginning of a movement from no to yes, from nihilism to myth."[42] Rather than take all of these terms as literal equivalents, they should be read as Acker's exploration of new idioms to conceive of the political value of her aesthetic practice. Indeed, Acker's reinvestment in the body should be read as a specific challenge to the precepts of conceptual writing that previously defined her work. After all, Acker "was taught by the Conceptualists that all that matters, in art, in the making of art, is the intention, intentionality. ... That all that does not concern intention is simply prettiness; that prettiness is, above all, despicable."[43] By direct contrast, the final line of *Empire of the Senseless* declares, "And then I thought that, one day, maybe, there'ld be a human society in a world which is beautiful, a society which wasn't just disgust."[44] Rife with hesitation—"one day, maybe"—this is not a utopian declaration. But it signals Acker's increased emphasis on finding an affirmative aesthetic, one that can re-imagine the social order rather than merely expose its exploitations. This emphasis is matched by a concomitant shift in aesthetic terms. Indeed, the language of beauty cuts against Acker's previous conceptualist rejection of "prettiness." Implicitly, *Empire of the Senseless* suggests that the imagination of a "human society" organized by different values will require a different aesthetic form—a form that not only allows for aesthetic values to emerge but also relies on affect to figure relations of power that differ from the hegemonic society of "just disgust."

Of course, Acker's turn to "the body, the actual flesh" breaks with conceptualism's privileging of the concept as the organizing principle of art. But it also strikes at conceptualism's full-throated resistance to subjectivity. As the conceptual writer, Kenneth Goldsmith, explains in his "Paragraphs on Conceptual Writing," "If the author wishes to explore her idea thoroughly, then arbitrary or chance decisions would be kept to a minimum, while *caprice, taste and other whimsies* would be eliminated from the making of the text."[45] For Goldsmith, the cultural privilege of subjectivity in aesthetics is a lamentable remnant of Romanticism that is outdated in the posthuman culture of late capitalism. Hence, Goldsmith's "writing" attempts to eliminate subjectivity, challenging any "expressive" notion of writing as the subjective extension of the author's feeling. To do so, Goldsmith re-presents text with little to no alteration. In his most famous example, *Day* (2003), Goldsmith copies a complete issue of the *New York Times* (September 1, 2000), changing only the spatial layout of the text. In *The Weather* (2005), he transcribes weather reports for an entire year. These texts exemplify how conceptual writing appropriates text to challenge the very notions of writing (and rewriting) as derived from self-expression and human creativity. Indeed, Goldsmith and other conceptual writers often critique Acker's self-proclaimed alignment with the conceptual movement, given how much she revised the texts she appropriated.[46]

Therefore, the context for Acker's shift away from appropriative aesthetics is more specific than her term "deconstruction" would suggest. Whereas deconstruction problematizes the referential moorings of the signifier, exposing its internal difference and the endless play, conceptualism takes a different approach; it conceives of appropriative writing as an "allegory" that directly mirrors the culture. As Vanessa Place and Robert Fitterman write, "Allegorical writing (particularly in the form of appropriated conceptual writing) does not aim to critique the culture industry from afar, but to *mirror it directly*. To do so, it uses the materials of the culture industry directly. ... The critique is in the reframing."[47] Ultimately, Acker worries that the notion of critique as mirror cannot combat the society of disgust. The mirror cannot engender new affective or social relations, nor can it imagine writing itself as an *event*, where contingency and potentiality derive from the corporeality of language. Thus, Acker concludes that the aesthetic practice of "[d]econstruction is always a reactive thing and as long as you're dwelling in the reactive you're really reinforcing the society that you hate."[48] Acker breaks with the conceit of writing as a mirror, arguing instead, "Writing must break through the representational or fictional mirror and *be in equal force* to the horror experienced in daily life."[49] The phrase "be in equal force" appears to echo the conceptualist method of reproducing the existing social order. Yet two key shifts have occurred. Writing is now an affective event (in this case, a force of horror), and it is conceived as fully non-representational; whatever intensifications the work creates at the level of reading, its figurations will not be mimetically attached to either an appropriation of the world's existing signifiers or to a realist notion of the world as a referential index. Crucially, Acker invokes one of her mentors, William S. Burroughs, as an inspiration for her experimental aesthetics, but not, as is typically thought, because of his development of the cut-up fold-in method of textual resignification. Rather, she praises Burroughs's experimental style for creating "weapons in the fight for our own happiness," contrasting him with a hypothetical realist "novelist who writes about the poor Cambridge vicar who can't deal with his homosexuality."[50] Note that *happiness* is invoked here as an affective signifier of a queer aesthetic politics. Indeed, happiness is not mapped onto the realist character's experience of oppressive heteronormativity. Instead, happiness signifies a political struggle in which the affects elicited through experimental form play a central role. Thus, Burroughs's affective force emerges through the "discontinuity" of his form, which not only reflects the postmodern world but also "fights [its] post-bourgeois language with poetry: images, dangling clauses, all that lingers at the edges of the unsaid, that leads to and through dreams. As Burroughs has said: without dreams, our desires, especially sexual desires, we will die."[51]

Queer experimental literature, in the tradition of Burroughs, affords Acker a "dwelling within verbal sensuousness" without recuperating the concepts of author-centered expressivity that conceptual writing rightly critiqued.[52] By aligning the impersonality of queer sensation with language, Acker makes her final break with conceptualism's desire to transcend the body. This break is memorably staged in the conclusion of *Empire of the Senseless* when the main character, Abhor, repeatedly stops her motorcycle to check *The Highway Code* for the "rules of road behaviour."[53] After a series of collisions and altercations, Abhor realizes that she cannot relate the rules of the pre-determined code to her embodied situation. She tears out the pages that do not conform to her "commonsense," urinates on the book, and decides that the code "no longer mattered. I was making up the rules. This is my rule."[54] Abhor's rejection of transcendent rules, abstracted from the immanence of her body, highlights Acker's satire of a pre-determined and invariable "intention" governing textual production. Abhor's urinating opposes the rulebook because, for Acker, the body is figured through its excremental immanence. Modeling her writing on the excremental word, Acker locates affect as the basis for an aesthetic politics that is incommensurable with conceptualism and its incorporation into the market's logic of commensurability.

Sensuous Words and the Thresholds of Becoming

Although the phrase "the languages of the body" appears intermittently throughout her last three published novels, Acker addresses its aesthetic politics most extensively in a series of essays composed in the early 1990s, subsequently collected in *Bodies of Work* (1997). In these essays, Acker stages a complex rethinking of her relationship to the poststructural theories that have rendered her fiction legible to the academy and marketable within the political economy of the art world. Her goal is to create an idiom for non-mimetic affective writing, where language becomes an impersonal force of visceral intensity that merges with the body's affects. To do so, Acker draws promiscuously from a wide range of philosophical and literary archives to reimagine the relationship between materiality and signification outside of the terms of Saussarian semiotics that so dominated poststructuralism's linguistic turn. For example, in "Seeing Gender," Acker draws on Lewis Carol, Luce Irigaray, and Plato to critically engage with Judith Butler's essay "Bodies That Matter." She writes:

> [W]hat if language need not be mimetic?
> I am looking for the body, my body, which exists outside its patriarchal definitions. Of course, that is not possible. But who is any longer interested in the possible? Like Alice, I suspect that the body, as Butler argues, might not be co-equivalent with materiality, that my body might deeply be connected to, if not be, language.
> But what is this language? This language which is not constructed on hierarchical subject-object relations?[55]

Acker agrees with Butler's equivalence between bodies and language, yet she twists the implicit meaning of the "connection" between language and materiality as Butler conceives it. Rather than conceive the materiality of the body through its discursive inscription within a signifying economy, Acker begins to imagine language itself as a force of non-dialectical intensity.[56] Indeed, she wonders whether there might be *languages* of the body, "a plurality or more of such languages," including "the language that moves through me or in me or ... for I cannot separate language body and identity ... when I am moving through orgasm or orgasms."[57] Although this is not the only language of the body that Acker identifies, orgasmic writing becomes a privileged figuration of affective languages that undo hierarchical structurings of perception, expression, and sensation. Acker increasingly conceives of experimental writing as a means of working toward this masturbatory threshold of indistinction wherein identity disappears into the broader play of affective forces that subtend the subject.[58]

Undoubtedly, Acker's languages of the body draws inspiration from *écriture féminine* and the theories of Monique Wittig, Hélène Cixous, Julia Kristeva, and particularly Luce Irigaray, whom she frequently cites within her essays.[59] She similarly yearns to discover a language for women outside of the structures of phallogocentrism, which exclude the material specificity of women's bodies and reduce the plurality of sexual difference to patriarchal identity. She also shares their equation of avant-garde and experimental stylistics with this embodied writing. However, Acker rejects the pre-Oedipal maternal semiotic as the locus of the "outside" to phallocentric writing, precisely because it remains entwined with a heteronormative symbolic order. Indeed, throughout her novels, the maternal is a source of violence and trauma, a figure firmly invested in stabilizing patriarchal power relations and compulsory heterosexuality. Invoking a myth that is central to all of Acker's fiction, "Seeing Gender" represents the mother as "a woman who loves to laugh and she never has any fun. She lives in a monogamous marriage with a man who isn't mean enough to her, who yields to her every silly whim."[60] The mother's laugh is not the anarchic laughter of Medusa that Cixous invokes; it is a sneer that reproduces, and even aims to aggrandize, patriarchal power.[61] Indeed, this mother's laughter is often directed at men that do not properly inhabit their gendered position of phallic master. While Acker initially perceives the maternal as "the key to my buried treasure," she ultimately discovers that her mother prohibits becoming beyond the terms of gendered subjection.[62] "I wasn't a pirate because my mother wouldn't allow me to be one," Acker writes.[63] The pirate is Acker's prototypical figure for the queer, anti-Oedipal, and non-heteronormative dissident. Because "pirates didn't have parents," they elude the symbolic order of sexual difference that perpetually denies access to a mode of embodied queer being.[64]

Arguably, a more influential inspiration for the queerness of the languages of the body is Bataille, particularly his readings of Nietzsche and his affiliation with the Acéphale society. This tradition affords Acker with a "non-patriarchal language" that refuses heteronormative figurations of the body.[65] Fascinated by the imagery of the Acéphale society, Acker finds inspiration in their substitution of abject corporeality—excrement and the colon in particular—for the logos of reason. Acker writes, "When the colon or labyrinth is center, our center, we, human, learn how little, if anything, we know and can know. ... A colon's end is shit. Not transcendence, but waste. Beyond meaning. For the head is no longer the head; we live, perceive, and speak, in our bodies and through our bodies."[66] The overcoming of the logos results in a folding-in of perception, sensation, and expression—a threshold of indistinction that becomes a scene for aesthetic composition that cannot be conceived as separate from the forces that compose the body. Indeed, Acker sees the labyrinth of the colon as "also the labyrinth of language. It is these languages that I want to begin to find."[67] Throughout her essays, Acker positions herself as a queer Ariadne, experimenting with languages of the body to draw readers into a sensorial becoming—a becoming that is not yet achieved. It is an active event being discovered in the non-simultaneous encounter of Acker's writing and our reading. The colon figures this queer labyrinth of affective becoming, but it is not opposed to the vaginal, or the "cunt," as Acker always calls it.[68] Rather, she makes the anal and vaginal figurally equivalent—both are pulsating and invaginated surfaces of vitalistic corporeality, the body folding on itself in ways that do not conform to the phallic economy of presence and absence or to psychoanalytic plots of castration.[69] Acker locates this queer materiality as the "place of sex" and the "ground for art," but this is not a foundational grounding "in" a specific body nor is it a foundation that art can or should represent.[70] Rather, Acker contends, "Art's realm, according to this picture or god, is not transcendence, but play in the world of change, the world of limitations, radical difference and Nietzschean 'sovereignty.'"[71] Here Acker extends postmodernism's critiques of essentialism, transcendence, and reference, but she recovers a "material" outside to language that she fears the emphasis on simulacra and simulation has lost.[72] If "[f]reed of Nietzschean *sovereignty*, any value or text could be equivalent to or substitute for any other value or text," Acker has not so much recuperated moral foundationalism as positioned the aesthetic as an extension of Nietzschean sovereignty—a Dionysian experimentation with the affective forces of life itself.[73]

In this respect, Acker exemplifies experimental literature's deracination of meaning, its project to erase the logos of the word itself and to cancel its own coherence as it is brought into material expression. But she differs, for example, from Burroughs's figuration of the word as a larval parasite or Beckett's literalization of words as excremental smears on the page. Acker wants language to become a material body in its own right, a stimulating force of intensity that cannot be conceptualized as abstract thought but must be *felt* as a pluralized wave of sensation. Hence, she describes the languages of the body as "[a]bove all: the languages of intensity. Since the body's, our, end isn't transcendence but excrement, the life of the body exists as pure intensity. The sexual and emotive languages."[74] If conceptualism and deconstruction previously rendered her fiction readable to institutional publics, Acker reclaims unreadability by shifting its citational grounds.[75] But more importantly, Acker creates an idiom that moves away from the politics of conceptualist appropriation or deconstructive resignification—where meaning emerges in relation to context and remains the primary focus of hermeneutic concern, even as that meaning is exposed as contingent, constructed, and oppressively logocentric. Now, the politics of experimental literature emerge through the affective forces it fosters. For example, in "Against Ordinary Language: The Language of the Body," Acker writes, "In ordinary language, meaning is contextual. Whereas the cry of the beggar means nothing other than what it is; in the city of the beggar, the impossible (as the Wittgenstein of the *Tractatus* and Heidegger see it) occurs in that meaning and breath become one."[76] Here language is not merely performative and non-representational but *gestural*—it means "nothing other than what it is," and its ontological essence is equivalent to the body's forces of affection. In one stroke, this conceit relinks language and affect, effecting the "return to the body" for which Acker yearns after conceptualism.[77] Hence, Acker invokes crying as well as "laugher, silence, [and] screaming" as figurations for the languages of the body.[78] Of course, a cry or a scream might have any number of contextual meanings, and it is important to note that Acker describes this threshold of indistinction as the "impossible," a pure limit of expression.[79] Yet in writing toward this threshold, queer experimental literature eludes the emphasis on meaning to unleash non-referential and affective forces of language that are co-constitutive of the body.

It is tempting to dismiss the languages of the body as an increasingly mystified view of language, a retreat from a properly political understanding of language as a social discourse constituted by historical relations of class and power. Such a critique is characteristic of many appraisals of postmodern aesthetics more generally. In an influential version of this argument, Sean McCann and Michael Szalay critique postmodern fiction written after the ascendency of the New Left for its acute opposition between ordinary language and a language of irrationality.[80] A variant of late-romantic literary ideology, they contend, postmodern fiction assumes that language possesses "a magical and anti-authoritarian power only to [the] degree that it has nothing to say."[81] In deracinating the content of language—its capacity to say *something*—postmodernism rejects "mundane political efforts to work toward imperfect justice" in favor of a "deep investment in the therapeutic value of ineffable mystery."[82] As such, this fiction "concedes virtually every kind of established political institution to the realm of violence and injustice while casting any beneficial alternative as insusceptible to collective action."[83] Their contention is that narratives of this stripe obstruct collective efforts at redressing injustice within the real world by displacing the focus of social struggle onto culture itself, unduly and self-servingly inflating the prophetic powers of writers, theorists, and academics to access this ineffable power. Hence, while narratives of affective language may appear to offer a utopian dream of an anti-instrumental world, they are in fact symptomatic of late capitalism itself.

McCann and Szalay's critique resonates with those that read Acker—and experimental writers more generally—as yearning to transcend all forms of social order in favor of an anarchic or transgressive individualism. However, there are a number of problems with the critique for understanding queer experimental literature's affective politics. The conceit that aesthetic politics must lie within conventional representational forms is deeply flawed for writers seeking to contest the terms under which queer collectivities are capable of being represented as political. As I argue in the fourth chapter, this conceit grows even more problematic for queers as "LGBTQ" literature becomes assimilated to the homonormative politics of identity and liberal recognition. This is precisely why affective reading becomes a viable idiom for the politics of queer aesthetics and its attempt to foment new relations of collectivity. To be sure, Acker's languages of the body are figured through activities—masturbation and bodybuilding—

that are, at least in her depiction of them, public but non-communal.[84] Yet, Acker turns to Bataille precisely because she sees his affective writing as linked to a search for new models of political belonging. She states, "Humans have to live in a society—they can't just survive as individuals. That's not a viable condition."[85] As such, Acker concludes "We've got to find some new models—a model of what society should look like," predicated on "the joys that aren't based on economic accumulation and the workaday world, but based on giving it all up."[86]

Joy is a key concept in affect theory, particularly for the Nietzschean and Spinozan tradition. Reflecting on this tradition, Brian Massumi notes that joy is not equivalent to happiness or the good life. Rather, these thinkers understand "joy as affirmation, an assuming by the body of its potentials, its assuming of a posture that intensifies its powers of existence. The moment of joy is the co-presence of those potentials, in the context of a bodily becoming. That can be an experience that overcomes you."[87] This disruptive and intensifying notion of affect underlies Acker's model of collectivity. It also provides her with an alternative to dialectical models of aesthetic critique—particularly Hegelian narratives that presume the necessity of negation and the sad passions of *ressentiment*.[88] At the same time, as Massumi notes, the concept of joy also points toward a renewed "belief in the world."[89] This belief is not, following Deleuze, a transcendent notion of God or a sovereign morality; it is an ethical immersion in and affirmation of the relationality implied by affect. For Acker, this ethical and affective relationality must be summoned through the event of the languages of the body. Hence, she concludes "Critical Languages" with the declaration: "Let one of art criticism's languages be silence so that we can hear the sounds of the body: the winds and voices from far-off shores, the sounds of the unknown. May we write, not in order to judge, but for and in (I quote George [sic] Bataille), 'the community of those who do not have a community.'"[90] Acker's languages of the body imagine the emergence of a queer community-to-come not through judgment or critique but through the affirmation of joyful intensity felt through the body's affective relatedness.

Acker's writing for an absent community—"the voices from far-off shores"—is inextricably linked to her project to reinvigorate a politicized avant-garde. After all, Acker's exemplary form of "ordinary language" is art criticism. Such a specific—even idiosyncratic—definition suggests that the appeal to affective language must be located in relation to its aesthetic and political contexts. Postmodernism might offer a generalized discourse of the sublime, as McCann and Szalay contend. But we cannot assume in advance that all irrational words have the same putatively anti-political meaning. Indeed, Acker points to art criticism as the prime example of "ordinary language" because this discourse, in her view, abets the commodification of aesthetics. She writes:

> Any artwork which is not propagandic and perhaps artwork which is, is ambiguous with regard to deep meaning. Art criticism must deny this ambiguity, so that the buyers know what to buy. So that the culture-mongers know what culture to eat. Those who deal in commerce do not want to, cannot afford to live in chaos.[91]

Here, Acker literalizes the commodification of art as eating, which must be guided by a critical-metadiscourse of representation: "[A]rt criticism, as said, represents the pertinent work of art. The homogeneity of the criticism dissimulates the heterogeneity of the art. Often for the purposes of the art market."[92] By contrast, she hopes, "From this model [the languages of the body] will arise, hopefully, possible models of art critical languages which, being of the body, no longer reduce difference to identity, radical difference to a schematic, controllable form."[93] Acker reimagines art criticism as a mode that cannot dematerialize the aesthetic into terms of abstract exchange, thereby reducing the event of art to "pertinent work" that can be judged in terms of value. Instead, Acker's ontology of difference resists the enchroachment of abstract modes of value and reimagines the aesthetic as a *generative* force of affective potentiality.

Acker begins to experiment with the languages of the body precisely because *she* has begun to internalize these abstract economic values. In other words, she is not a prophet standing above the order of commodification but affectively immersed in it. She worries:

> I might be writing what people expect me to write, writing from that place where I might be ruled by economic considerations. ... I'm working at trying to find a kind of language where I won't be so easily modulated by expectation. I'm looking for what might be called a body language. One thing I do is stick a vibrator up my cunt and start writing—writing from the point of orgasm and losing control of the language and seeing what that's like.[94]

Here, experimental writing becomes a literal experimentation with the queerness of masturbatory pleasure. In the famous opening lines of *The Madwoman in the Attic*, Sandra M. Gilbert and Susan Gubar invoke the figural equivalence of penis and pen, wherein male sexuality "is not just analogically but actually the essence of literary power. The poet's pen is in some sense (even more than figuratively) a penis."[95] Acker queers the equation of pen, penis, and literary power by turning to the vibrator as the external stylus that "writes" inside her body while she writes; inside and outside fold into one another, like the vaginal and anal labyrinth, and writing becomes a body without organs, an affective event that cannot be read as representing, analogically or even metaphorically, "an" orgasm. Rather, writing becomes a threshold of indistinction, an event of potentiality where expectation and representation cannot arrest the forces of affective becoming. Acker's goal is not to *achieve* orgasm, to punctually *arrive* at a place of self-shattering; it is to *begin* from within this scene of queer eroticism, to move within it, exploring what emerges in the unfolding thresholds that follow from a space where writing is not codified by expectation.

Notably, Acker's other example of the language of the body is bodybuilding, which she practiced with great intensity late in her life. Much like her masturbatory writing, the point is not simply to dissolve the self but, much more importantly, to create an event of becoming. She seeks "[a]n unexpected event. For though I am only repeating certain gestures during certain time spans, my body, being material, is never the same; my body is controlled by change and chance."[96] Acker works toward "unexpected failure," and indeed, she insists "I want to fail" because this produces a Spinozan testing of the body's unpredictable thresholds of becoming: "I want to break muscle so that it can grow back larger, but I do not want to destroy muscle so that growth is prevented. ... I want to shock my body into growth; I do not want to hurt it."[97] This is, in Jack Halberstam's words, a "queer art of failure," a working with failure to open up other kinds of embodied and non-institutionally codified knowledge.[98] In failure, Acker begins to "glimpse the laws that control my body, those of change or chance, laws that are barely, if at all, knowable."[99] Ultimately, she will ask if the "equation between destruction and growth [is] also a formula for art."[100] At stake here is an experimental writing that does not represent the body but writes from and within its queer openness, a writing that draws its forces of becoming from a shared ontology because art, like the body, "being material, is never the same."[101] Its aesthetic surface, much like bodybuilding, can involve repetition, as Acker's earlier work did, but its purpose is no longer to expose ideological commitments; instead, the repetition of gestures in time creates the possibility for a failure of expectation and the emergence of new thresholds for growth.

The languages of the body are not, then, a failed form of a social critique but an incipiently social mode of affective politics, a mode that works the aesthetic toward failure to create a queer becoming in the event of reading. While Acker's languages of the body rewrite queer experimental literature as corporeally relational, then, they also alter the author–reader contract that typically conditions the reader's relation to the text. As we will see, Acker offers a queer contract that requires readers to expose themselves to the scene of affective contact to make an event of becoming possible.

QUEERING THE AUTHOR–READER CONTRACT

In *Aggressive Fictions*, Kathryn Hume argues that contemporary experimental fiction breaks the "author–reader contract" by disrupting expectations in a way that "ordinary readers" will experience as unpleasant.[102] Rather than please or instruct, as the conventional author–reader contract dictates, "Aggressive fiction tramples reader sensibilities, offends and upsets willfully and deliberately."[103] Kathy Acker has a prominent status in Hume's project. For Hume, Acker's fiction exemplifies a rhetorical mode of political "complaint" characterized by a *"relentless articulation of discontent,* usually characterized by *strong emotive elements."*[104] Her novels prominently feature a victim's self-centered raging against social oppression, which the ordinary reader will experience as "whining."[105] Hume encourages the reader to respond to the text with "the gesture of a friend or relative of listening patiently."[106] Hume's overarching goal is to guide non-academic and non-professional readers into an engagement with experimental literature. Yet, she does so primarily by assimilating these works to the norms of the liberal-humanist public sphere. Hence, she reads the aggressive text's "[u]nfriendliness towards readers" as a problem to be overcome by the reader rather than a challenge to—and an alternative configuration for—the author–reader contract itself.[107]

When Hume imagines a readerly subject that would enjoy or even partake in the transgressive pleasures of aggressive fiction, she assimilates these subjects to an existing coterie. Authors like Acker "may partly address themselves to a coterie audience of kindred spirits who revel in the subject matter and stylistic extremism. Most writers, though, also hope their novels will be read by a wider public, many of whose members will be upset by this sort of fiction."[108] Notably, Hume does not describe the coterie as a subculture, a counterpublic, or an oppositional avant-garde.

Rather, the coterie audience enjoys experimental writing because they have learned to master its interpretative codes, thereby accessing pleasure and knowledge from experimental literature by means external to the text itself. Hume's model cannot properly account for experimental writers, like Acker, that seek to queer the affective terms on which fiction is read. First, Hume's account of the author–reader contract is underwritten by a readerly pleasure principle—one that moves toward cognitive mastery of the text. Negative affects can be experienced in the reading, but they must be subordinated to a more transcendent epistemological purpose, specifically the expansion of cultural knowledge or interpretative mastery. All of Acker's fiction is oriented against this plot for reading. Moreover, as many critics note, Acker's fiction represents and engenders complex sado-masochistic relations, which do not conform to the binarized model of submission and mastery that Hume ascribes to Acker.[109] Indeed, her work explores queer models of agency that assume, at the very least, that power is a mobile and productive force. Second, the author–reader contract cannot account for becoming—for a text's active renegotiation of the terms of the contract, its attempt to bring reading publics into being that do not conform to the institutionalized models of the mass or the coterie. As we have seen, Acker's languages of the body nullify the existing contracts for reading her fiction offered by conceptual art and poststructural theory, rendering her work acutely unreadable. Yet, at the same time, she seeks to establish a new contract with readers, one that will not assimilate the text to the norms of epistemological and economic expectation. This contract is incipient in her texts, forged within the event of reading—it does not exist outside the diegesis as a sovereign order that precedes the text.

The problem Acker faces is whether or not the languages of the body can engender this incipient contract in the face of an unabated gentrification of her work and the art community that once supported it. This paradox is particularly apparent in Acker's first avowedly postconceptual novel, *In Memoriam to Identity* (1990).[110] Published after *Empire of the Senseless*, *In Memoriam to Identity* continues to display Acker's career-spanning practice of appropriating and rewriting literature. She draws primarily on Arthur Rimbaud's poetry and William Faulkner's novels as well as biographical texts on both authors. However, the context for her appropriations has dramatically changed. *In Memoriam to Identity* includes a postscript explaining to the reader that "[a]ll the preceding has been taken" from these sources. As such, the event of reading no longer centers on Acker's performative intertextuality, which beckons for a deconstructive "doubled reading" of her novels.[111] As we have seen, this shift is due in part to Acker's turn away from conceptualism. Yet, the turn from conceptualism is also conditioned by the material circumstances that informed the composition of *In Memoriam to Identity*. While writing the novel, Acker was sued by Harold Robbins's publisher for her plagiarizing portions of his novel *The Pirate* (1974) in her novel *The Adult Life of Toulouse Lautrec* (1975), which had recently been republished in the collection *Young Lust* (1989). Despite the support of Burroughs and others, Acker's publishers issued an apology on her behalf without her permission, an experience that made Acker feel utterly humiliated. This event sparked her return from England to the United States, and it compounded the sense of isolation she felt on returning to New York City.[112]

In Memoriam to Identity represents this event in largely autobiographical terms. Capitol, one of the novel's three artist-protagonists, undergoes the same betrayal by her publishers in the conclusion of the novel: "Her own dealer had signed the public apology for her without her permission and published it in a prominent art magazine. I've lost, she thought. I had already lost my body. What's going to happen to my work? Now, nothing."[113] Nothing can "happen" to Capitol's (or Acker's) work because its event has been extinguished by a sovereign discourse that controls the text. Capitol's loss of her body mirrors the loss of her work, which is a body that has become violently expropriated. If the languages of the body lack identity—and, indeed, if they render the exchange-value of Acker's aesthetics unreadable—then the public apology radically assimilates her work back into those very structures: the apology assumes the work is expressive of and coextensive with authorial subjectivity and morality; and it concedes that the aesthetic object is a form of property ultimately defined by authorial and corporate ownership.[114] In effect, the aesthetic object can be exchanged for and as capital, but it cannot be appropriated or plagiarized, and its value and effect cannot be articulated on its own terms.

Capitol's name is an irony, then, that signifies the convergence of capitalism and the law, a *différance* that is nonetheless entrapped by the economy of "Ownership. If anything. Ownership is money. Capitol learned. The lawmakers of this world (lawyers, judges, dealers) ... demanded that Capitol ... publicly apologize for using a rich famous person's work, for hating ownership, for finding postcapitalist and Newtonian identity a fraud."[115] Capitol's parenthetical aside equates lawyers, judges, and dealers as "lawmakers," but their sovereign function is less to support the state than to perpetuate capitalism's transposition of all values into economic terms. Indeed, the fundamental backdrop of *In Memoriam to Identity*—which cuts across all of its varied urban landscapes in New York, Germany, and France—is the rapacious expansion of neoliberal privatization, signified in the novel by the deindustrialization of urban spaces. As much as the protagonists try to find another space outside of gentrification, they cannot, and indeed, economic values begin to define their very being. Harry, Capitol's lover and also a struggling artist, believes they must escape New York City because "the only value in this city is fame or success, if they stayed in this city, they would never love each other."[116] Likewise, Airplane, another of the novel's protagonists, returns to New York City and discovers that "the old New York art world was dead."[117] The artists that once composed this world "had become totally desperate to be famous because, approaching middle age, it was their last chance."[118] Their collective desire for fame exemplifies the subsumption of an oppositional artistic community into neoliberalism's economy of value, which the novel depicts with bracing bitterness.

In Memoriam to Identity therefore implies that the "author–reader contract" has become an inescapably *literal* contract, a proprietary relation that is not, ultimately, negotiated between authors and readers, or between artists and their publics, but between the "lawmakers" and "dealers" that define, defend, and exchange the aesthetic commodity as a property. In its dystopian, neoliberal landscape, the *values* of this contract spread into other zones, leading the characters to perpetually lament the absence of uncorrupted values for life. The most problematic scene for this gentrification in the novel is in the erotic relations between lovers. Indeed, the three protagonists—R, Airplane, and Capitol—all embark on a quest to find what Airplane calls a *"symbiotic relationship ... when two people want to join, become a new person."*[119] Frustrated, oppressive, and sadistic relationships are central to all of Acker's novels; they are, arguably, the bedrock narrative structure for her work. Yet those relationships—typically focused on love and sex—always intersect with and metonymically stand in for societal relations more broadly. In this novel, (failed) symbiotic relationships emerge against the backdrop of an increasingly commodified world in which an artist hopes to make contact with a lover that changes them both, enabling them to become beyond the existing terms of passion and commitment. This is particularly apparent in "Rimbaud" the first and longest section (of four) in the novel. In a rewriting of the relationship between Rimbaud and Verlaine, R pursues V and they have a passionately sexual affair, but V continually returns to his wife, unwilling to forsake

bourgeois domesticity for what he perceives as the degradation of homosexuality. Even in the midst of their affair, V wants to contain the potentiality of their eroticism: "We have a pact not to interfere with each other's
lives," he claims.[120] "That's a new one," R responds, "Our first pact was
made when we were having sex and sex is sacred. Since that time when you
irrevocably bonded with me, you have been SLOWLY, IRREVOCABLY,
taking reality away from me."[121] The repetition of irrevocable underscores
R's view of relationality as *contact* rather than *contract*—a relation figured by and engendered through eroticism that cannot be undone.[122] V is
unwilling to commit to becoming otherwise through this relation because
to do so would mean leaving behind his wife and children, sacrificing his
patriarchal and heteronormative male power. As much as he constantly
appeals to a "pact" to which R never agreed, V views all relations as fungi-
ble. Indeed, his pact is premised on non-reciprocal affection—sex without
bonds, incapable of "interfering with" the social relations that underpin
one's life. When V does temporarily leave his wife, he can only understand
it as an end in itself, as pure sexual transgression rather than a movement toward an alternative relational contract. R asks, "So where're we
going?"[123] V responds, "We're leaving. Isn't that enough?"[124]

In Memoriam to Identity suggests that merely leaving is *not* "enough,"
reflecting Acker's dissatisfaction with aesthetic politics that lack an affirmative horizon. R hates that V enjoys their passionate sexual encounters but
refuses to see them as a "Going away to *affection* and a new way of communicating."[125] Indeed, R insists that "Fucking without dreaming's boring.
You [V] define yourself, your marvelous manhood, quantitatively. How
many people you've fucked. I've fucked as many fucks as you, fuckface."[126]
Too often, queer experimental literature is misread as "fucking without
dreaming," as sensuous transgression or erotic experimentation without
any affirmative social imagination. Here, Acker presses back against this
narrative by equating fucking without dreaming to phallogocentric calculation, which reduces sex to an act that can be quantitatively measured.
Capitol later echoes V's criticism of "marvelous manhood," noting that
men are proud to remember "whom they fucked: they brought out memories for display, notches cut into a belt, to name identity."[127] Fucking without dreaming only creates a mirror to aggrandize individual (patriarchal)
identity; it counts its conquests, reifying identity and reducing all erotic
encounters to exchangeable "notches." By contrast, fucking *with* dreaming is, at once, dissolvent of identity and perversely relational; it is a relation that is singular and productive of a becoming that irreducibly alters

the participants in the encounter. Notably, R's retort that he has "fucked as many fucks as you, fuckface" anticipates the shift to come in his character.[128] Later in the novel, R will resurface as R, Airplane's partner "the rapist," and Rimbaud, Capitol's brother. Both of these men wish to control women's sexuality for the purposes of economic exchange, to dematerialize the affective singularity of the body and its pleasures. Indeed, Rimbaud becomes "A dead poet," forsaking art for business.[129] Catherine Rock suggests that Rimbaud's altered perspective later in the novel, from feminist to patriarchal, demonstrates the possibility of "unethical becomings."[130] It also suggests that queerness itself can be gentrified—that it is not essentialistically tethered to R's homosexuality but that it emerges from a specifically relational intersection of the erotic and the social.

Fucking without dreaming is not only patriarchal and neoliberal—it is also "boring," which *In Memoriam to Identity* depicts as a habituated affect that capitulates to the normative social order. The most bored characters in the novel are the bourgeoisie who hate life but refuse—and are disgusted by—queer affects that upend the status quo. At the outset of the novel, R considers suicide as a means to deal with his own hatred of normative life. However, he concludes that

> the blood that dropped out of his razor-bladed wrist was no solution to boredom. For boredom comes from the lack of correspondence between the desire of the mind and body and the society outside that mind and body. From impossibility of any desire's actualization … [U]nder no circumstances did he want to die.[131]

R masochistically enjoys the razor blade's cutting because "Pain exists," but he rejects suicide as solution to the lack of correspondence between desire and the social.[132] Many of Acker's characters are tempted by suicide; indeed, Airplane's and Capitol's mothers, much like Acker's own mother, commit suicide, leading their daughters to question the value of living in an oppressive world that seeks to negate their existence as women.[133] Yet Airplane and Capitol, like R, reject suicide as a triumph of boredom's nihilistic defeat. Neither suicide nor fucking without dreaming can forge a *new* correspondence between mind, body, and society—a correspondence, like R's "new way of communicating," that could engender the social actualization of queer desire. It often frustrates Acker's critics that she offers no "blueprint," to use Hume's metaphor, to achieve the "revolution" for which her characters yearn.[134] I contend that Acker leaves this question in abeyance not because, as is commonly said of postmodern writers, she lacks the ability to imagine other social worlds beyond the present. Rather, Acker foregrounds the "lack of correspondence" between desire and the social because it is a figure for the politics of aesthetics. In a world where the aesthetic object can be so easily assimilated to norms of economic value, how can writing actualize the queer desires that it unleashes? If writing cannot actualize desire—if writing cannot overcome the lack of correspondence that makes *boredom* a hegemonic structure of feeling—then what potentiality can queer experimental literature really offer?

The novel meditates on this problem by representing a literal lack of correspondence between R and V. At each abandonment, R sends lengthy, passionate letters to V. Although V encourages his writing, telling R that "I love your writing, and telling me you love me and need me," R's letters go largely unread.[135] R nonetheless continues to write in an effort "[t]o transform absence to presence and to defeat solitude or the absence of human values."[136] In the process of this fervent composition, R discovers a language of the body in the "land of childhood," which is Acker's figure for a queerly dissident space that resists proper assimilation into Oedipal adulthood.[137] R describes this language as sensuous and affective:

> Since language and the flesh are not separate here, language being real, every vowel has a color. *A* is black; *E*, white; *I*, red; *O*, blue; *U*, green. The form and direction of each vowel is instinctive rhythm. Language is truly myth. All my senses touch words. Words touch the senses. Language isn't only translation, for the word is blood.
> At first, this is all just theoretical.
> But I wrote silences, nights, my despair at not seeing you and being in a crummy hotel next to you. I saw wrote down the inexpressible.[138]

At first glance, the languages of the body seem to evoke the metaphysics of presence. Words become sensual, and the signifiers of language are not simply denotative but objectively expressive of sense perception—sight and sound—and the instinctual rhythms of reality. To be sure, R calls this language "myth" and admits that his theory is initially speculative. But his writing does engender a convergence of senses in a threshold of becoming: "I saw wrote" makes seeing and writing interpenetrated modes of accessing the ineffable. Recall, however, that the languages of the body are merely an *attempt* to "defeat solitude or the absence of human values," an attempt that does not succeed even as R's writing accesses an affective threshold to language. Rather than a relation to presence, then, R's affective language offers a different way of relating to absence. The languages of the body emerge precisely in the context of their impossible actualization by a reading—conducted by V, in this case—that would not only engage with the writing but also submit to the impropriety of fucking *with* dreaming, of queer becoming, which is the erotic corollary for R's sensual language as it moves toward "myth."

At stake, then, in R's turn to affective writing is the paradoxical distance between the intensity offered by the languages of the body and the absence of a counterpublic or an oppositional collective that could actualize such a relation with the text's intensities and actualize these intensities as a form of social desire. The final line of "Rimbaud" would seem to accede to the inadequacy of the languages of the body for confronting this problem within its own terms. R proclaims that "*The imagination is nothing unless it is made actual.*"[139] This line evokes the critique of experimental writing that stylistically inhabits the imaginary rather than producing a realist representation of the social world. Yet *In Memoriam to Identity* complicates this critique in a lengthy scene that recalls Burroughs's aesthetics of queer spectrality.[140] Airplane performs a sex show routine that stylistically blurs the lines between actuality and the imaginary. A doctor (possibly a performer, possibly a psychiatrist) interrogates a girl (possibly Airplane, possibly Halitosis) in front of an audience. The interrogation blurs with Airplane's memories of being raped and going to a hospital, and the tone shifts between flirtation and sadism, parodic satire and earnest eroticism. Halo (short for Halitosis) tells the doctor, "If the world in which you live is sick, you have to live in the imaginary."[141] He dismisses her belief, asking "Do you think it's possible to destroy poverty or any other social ill or rejection by an act of the imagination?"[142] When the girl "bow[s] her head" and says no, "The doctor was beginning to control her. As control always works, through the imagination."[143] Here the critique of the imagination ironically operates *through* the imagination. Airplane succumbs to the doctor's control and forsakes the space that enables her to dream of a healthier, more viable social world, yet Acker makes clear that the imaginary is politically significant, both for inculcating oppression and for fomenting opposition.

As the sex show scene reveals, the force of the imaginary does *not* lie in its representational content, which then becomes mimetically actualized in reality. Instead, the imaginary is a relational scene configured through an aesthetic that makes possible certain affective effects. For example,

Airplane repeats the doctor's words: "'What is it that you want? What is it that you want?' The girl, murmuring over and over as if words no longer had meaning, fell backwards over the stage, her legs open to the audience in the manner of a temple."[144] As a consequence of her performance, Airplane is able to learn that she "love[s] fucking."[145] Indeed, she is able to access a mode of bodily knowledge and agency in the erotic despite the exploitation of her sexuality by R, the rapist. Yet she cannot articulate an answer in the text of the performance itself; rather, the repetition of the question disperses the meaning of the words, and the question—repeated like the language of bodybuilding—moves toward "failure," toward a threshold of becoming that is figured here as an ecstatic collapse. In this moment, Airplane speculates, "Maybe the audience was one huge lover," capturing the necessity of potential reception—figured as an erotic relation—for the performance to work.[146] Yet, the performance is not only a kind of sexual communion. It also engenders a satirical and self-reflexive critique of certain subjects in the audience.

> Though the audience wasn't versed enough in fine theatrical technique or interested enough in anything but their own immediate sexual gratification to appreciate the artistry of the text and acting, except for a few black couples who had perhaps also come here to laugh at whites, the girl and her acting partner were able to make the men laugh almost against themselves.[147]

The audience's narcissistic gratification recalls fucking without dreaming, an enjoyment of sex without an investment in its political or social horizons. Yet Airplane's performance makes the white, male audience members unknowingly laugh at themselves. Even if the critique is not evident or articulated in the text of the performance itself, it operates on an affective level. The author–reader (or performer–audience) contract has shifted here. It does not center on pleasing the audience but on creating a scene for pleasure to emerge as a vector of critique and agential becoming. Airplane's performance echoes Acker's claim, discussed at the beginning of this chapter, that her work is "a bit unreadable" because the pleasure is not for the reader but for herself. This apparently narcissistic or masturbatory circuit of pleasure differs from the narcissism of the sex show audience and of V—from spectators invested in their own gratification and egotistical aggrandizement and from spectators that hope to avoid an affective implication in the text. By contrast, Airplane's masturbatory performance foments a relational scene in which affect can create unpredictable and incipiently social effects on those (performers and audience members alike) immersed in the aesthetic encounter.

The final scenes of *In Memoriam to Identity* suggest that this queer author–reader contract currently lacks a reader, a spectator, or a public to become drawn into its affective relations. At the same time, it also affirms the affective dimension of queer experimental literature for offering the possibility of desire's actualization in the world. Capitol returns to New York, and she feels that "for the first time, she was being given a way to be a person. To say other than *no*. Through work or the movement of the heart or of imagination in the world. This material movement of the heart or the imagination, which is also the world, in this simultaneously angelic and rotten city, gave the worker fame (credentials) and formed a community not otherwise found in the world."[148] As we have seen, Capitol discovers, to her dismay, how much the terms for artistic community have been reduced only to their economic value. At the same time, she nonetheless is able to begin "building a new life. Not in terms of content, but form. Fiction."[149] Here, Acker links the aesthetic *form* of queer experimental literature to the creation of an incipient community "not otherwise found in the world." It offers an aesthetic politics of affect—defined by "the heart or the imagination," which moves toward affirmation, toward a saying that is "other than *no*." This articulation is not yet expressible or readable in the present, but it is incipient in the text's unfolding in and as the world. This is why Capitol rejects suicide in the final paragraph of the novel. After her breakup with Harry, she thinks, "It's time to suicide. It's time to lop off the consciousness of memory. Memory is deathless and inescapable as long as alive."[150] Yet Capitol changes her mind:

> "Fuck you," said aloud. "The waste isn't just me. It's not waste. It's as if there's a territory. The roads carved in the territory, the only known, are memories. Carved again and again into ruts like wounds that don't heal when you touch them but grow. Since all the rest is unknown, throw what is known away.
> "Sexuality," she said, "sexuality."[151]

Queer experimental literature does not map the roads that exist, nor does its content function like a blueprint, charting the territory to come by representing it as mimetically as possible. Instead, as Capitol explains, "Writing is one method of dealing with being human or wanting to suicide cause in order to write you kill yourself at the same time while remaining alive."[152] Acker's writing works toward an overcoming of the self, toward writing a "memoriam to identity," while also embracing a mode of life that offers more than a nihilistic acceptance of reality. Capitol's affirmation of sexuality, then, condenses queer experimental literature's alternative contract for its readers—a contract that anticipates new paths, pre-figuring, through its erotic contacts, a queerer territory that lies in the horizon of the unknown and can be felt as potential all the same.

STOPPING READING

In "Seeing Gender," Acker asks, "Can I escape by stopping reading? I am Alice who ran into a book in order to find herself. I have found only the reiterations, the mimesis of patriarchy, or my inability to be. No body anywhere."[153] In this chapter, I argued that Acker's entrapment by institutionalized academic and aesthetic discourses—specifically poststructural theory and conceptual writing—compel her desire to escape from "reading." On the one hand, the academy and the art market codify her deconstructive aesthetics, rendering them legible and exchangeable while sapping their affective estrangement. Hence, for Acker, deconstructive aesthetics increasingly signify a gentrified mode of aesthetic politics, a once-oppositional method that has been consumed by postmodernity's political economy. Of course, as *In Memoriam to Identity* attests, the juridical, economic, and political sanctions against Acker's plagiaristic writing, and her increasing isolation from an avant-garde community, also play an important role in her search for a new politics of aesthetics. On the other hand, Acker believes that deconstructive methods cannot relocate the "body"—the affective, erotic, and sexed corporeality that we have tracked through her subsequent turn to the languages of the body. Undoubtedly, Acker's search for the body resonates with *écriture féminine* and other avant-garde aesthetics that contest the "mimesis of patriarchy" that denies both women's bodies and queer eroticism. Yet Acker's lamentation of "No body anywhere" also intersects with her frustration about there being *nobody* anywhere—about the lack of a *body politic* somewhere, a collectivity of queer dissidents that can actualize and affirm alternatives to the interlocking social orders of patriarchy, heteronormativity, and postmodernity. Thus, Acker does "stop reading" by queering the terms on which she has been read, which are also the terms for which she has conceived of reading as a perceptual disruption, a demystification of ideological codes through the subversion of cultural signifiers. Acker's stopping reading enables an alternative mode of contact to emerge within her text—an encounter with its affective relations that may compel a queer becoming. This becoming is not solely an overcoming of subjectivity or habit but also a creative movement toward a queerer correspondence between desire and the social world.

Of course, critics have often claimed that Acker misunderstands the politics of her experimental aesthetics. Some contend that Acker not only anticipates the political economy that she resists but also actively abets its rise to social hegemony. For example, Konstantinou argues, "Acker's powerful attack on 'postcapitalist' rationalism fortified the new regime of justification that undergirded the projective city [of neoliberal deregulation]. This is why punk's anti-Utopianism, valorization of cut-up, and D.I.Y. ethic could seamlessly transition from seeming to resist capitalism to becoming a feted component of neoliberal apologetics."[154] It is notable that Konstantinou does not name the languages of the body in this list, but surely both affect and queerness have been similarly considered as a vanguard for neoliberalism's reduction of the political to the private territory of the body.[155] The problem with this narrative, I believe, is that it underestimates Acker's own awareness of the rapacious collapse of the aesthetic into the economic, of the oppositional becoming the hegemonic. Beginning with *In Memoriam to Identity*, Acker mercilessly satirizes and condemns artists for colluding with neoliberal gentrification while also bitterly acknowledging the inability for her to prevent the languages of the body from becoming assimilated to the market, just as Baudrillardian poststructuralism, in her view, became a discourse for applauding late capitalism.

The question is not whether queer experimental aesthetics were "co-opted" or whether they unwittingly abetted the transition to a new order; surely, both are true. The question itself focuses too narrowly on aesthetic content and not on the writer's contextual work to resuscitate—and, indeed, give birth to—an oppositional avant-garde that does not exist in the present. As much as her work embraces the irrational, Acker always narrates affective reading as an incipiently social movement toward a queer mode of belonging that cannot yet be articulated or interpreted from the vantage point of the present. Nonetheless, the questions we should bring to Acker's fiction are not whether her work is properly political or not, particularly if that propriety is interpreted within the terms of critical theory that Acker sought to elude. Instead, we should remember that the languages of the body were a method—not content or a telos—for experimenting with failure. If, today, the languages of the body fail to achieve the unreadability Acker desired, one can imagine that she would not mourn for dead concepts. She would, as she always did, urge us to begin again with an eye toward constructing and affirming a society made of more than just disgust. After all, failure was not an endpoint for her but a scene for becoming otherwise; it was a threshold that must be crossed again and again, with a willingness to explore the chaos that exceeds our efforts to control it. She did not want to merely give in to chaos, to end with the lack of correspondence between aesthetic affect and the material world, but to affirm a new correspondence between them that could actualize a queerer and more radical social order.

As we will see in the next two chapters, queer experimental literature continues to experiment with a politics of affirmation in the wake of the postmodern political economy. However, these writers will tend to move away from explicit figurations of sexuality and begin to experiment with idioms for positive affect such as love, care, and happiness, which have often been marked as "uncritical." Yet as sexuality becomes increasingly assimilated to biopolitical discourses of identity, affect itself becomes a viable terrain for configuring new modes and values for queer belonging. In this context, writers such as Jeanette Winterson refuse to cede the discourses of positive affect to the social order of heteronormative consumption; indeed, in exuberance, Winterson discovers an idiom to affirm relational models that contest the reduction of queerness to identity. The provocative and abject figures of queer eroticism that we have glimpsed in Burroughs, Delany, and Acker will fall away in the next two chapters, but as we will see, their notions of queer reading as an affective relation will endure as a means for reimagining the political agency of contemporary aesthetics.

Notes

1. See, for example, Stephen Schiff, "Rimbaud and Verlaine, Together Again," *The New York Times,* July 22, 1990, accessed August 7, 2016, http://www.nytimes.com/1990/07/22/books/rimbaud-and-verlaine-together-again.html.
2. For a critique of Acker's aesthetics in these terms, see David Foster Wallace, "Portrait of an Eye: Three Novels by Kathy Acker," *Harvard Review* 1 (2002): 154–56.
3. Kathy Acker, *Hannibal Lecter, My Father* (New York: Semiotext(e), 1991).

4. On Kathy Acker's relationship to punk, see Lee Konstantinou, *Cool Characters: Irony and American Fiction* (Cambridge: Harvard University Press, 2016), 103–59; and Larry McCaffery, "The Artists of Hell: Kathy Acker and 'Punk' Aesthetics," in *Breaking the Sequence: Women's Experimental Fiction*, eds. Ellen G. Friedman and Miriam Fuchs, (Princeton: Princeton UP, 1989), 215–30. For a relevant analysis of the intersections and divergences between queerness and punk cultures, with particular attention to their affective relations, see Tavia Nyong'o, "Do You Want Queer Theory (or Do You Want The Truth)? Intersections of Punk and Queer in the 1970s," *Radical History Review* 100 (2008): 103–19; and José Esteban Muñoz, *Cruising Utopia: The Then and There of Queer Futurity* (New York: New York University Press, 2009), 97–114.

5. Acker, *Hannibal*, 14. Acker articulates similar variations of this statement in a variety of her interviews.

6. Ibid., 15.

7. On Kathy Acker as aggressive fiction, see Kathryn Hume, *Aggressive Fictions: Reading the Contemporary American Novel* (Ithaca: Cornell University Press, 2012).

8. On the commodification of aesthetics in late capitalism, see Fredric Jameson, *Postmodernism, or the Cultural Logic of Late Capitalism* (Durham: Duke UP, 1990). For an analysis that links affect and aesthetics to this economic condition, see Sianne Ngai, *Ugly Feelings* (Cambridge: Harvard University Press, 2007); and *Our Aesthetic Categories: Zany, Cute, Interesting* (Cambridge: Harvard University Press, 2015). On the political economy of neoliberalism, see David Harvey, *A Brief History of Neoliberalism* (Oxford: Oxford University Press, 2005).

9. For an exception that offers a richly historicized account of the development of Acker's aesthetics alongside the emergence of biopolitics, which also captures the dissidence of Acker's fiction, see Alex Houen, *The Powers of Possibility: Experimental American Writing Since the 1960s* (Oxford: Oxford University Press, 2012), 145–92.

10. Walter Benn Michaels, *The Shape of the Signifier: 1967 to the End of History* (Princeton: Princeton University Press, 2006), 176. For a counterpoint to Benn Michaels, see Christina Milletti, "Violent Acts, Volatile Words: Kathy Acker's Terrorist Aesthetic," *Studies in the Novel* 36, no. 3 (2004): 352–73.

11. Benn Michaels, 175, 177.

12. Ibid., 177.

13. Michael W. Clune, *American Literature and the Free Market, 1945–2000* (New York: Cambridge University Press, 2010), 104.

14. For an analysis of this context that converges with mine, see Katie R. Muth, "Postmodern Fiction as Poststructuralist Theory: Kathy Acker's *Blood and Guts in High School*," *Narrative* 19, no. 1 (2011): 86–110.
15. For insightful examples, see David Brande, "Making Yourself a Body Without Organs: The Cartography of Pain in Kathy Acker's *Don Quixote*," *Genre* 24 (1991): 191–209; Douglas Shields Dix, "Kathy Acker's Don Quixote: Nomad Writing," *The Review of Contemporary Fiction* 9, no. 3 (1989): 56–62; and Carol Siegel, "The Madness Outside Gender: Travels with Don Quixote and Saint Foucault," *rhizomes* 1 (2000), accessed August 7, 2016, http://www.rhizomes.net/issue1/mad/quixote.html.
16. On the response to poststructuralism within postmodern fiction more broadly, see Judith Ryan, *The Novel After Theory* (New York: Columbia University Press, 2014).
17. Acker, *Hannibal*, 10.
18. Wallace, "Portrait," 155.
19. Ibid.
20. In Konstantinou's apt description, "What Acker wanted was reception without understanding, production and circulation without consumption" (138–39). While he reads this class paradox primarily in terms of punk culture, I stress Acker's vexed relationship to academic publics and avant-garde communities that have become increasingly commercialized.
21. Acker, *Hannibal*, 24.
22. Sarah Schulman, *The Gentrification of the Mind: Witness to a Lost Imagination* (Berkeley: University of California Press, 2012), 53.
23. Ngai, *Ugly*, 345, original emphasis.
24. On the concept of the "people who are missing," see Gilles Deleuze, "Literature and Life," in *Essays Critical and Critical*, trans. Daniel W. Smith and Michael A. Greco (Minnesota: University of Minneapolis Press, 1997), 4; Gilles Deleuze and Félix Guattari, *Kafka: Toward A Minor Literature,* trans. Dana Polan (Minneapolis: University of Minnesota Press, 1986); and Maryvonne Saison, "The People Are Missing" trans. Melissa McMahon, *Contemporary Aesthetics* 6 (2008), accessed August 7, 2016, http://www.contempaesthetics.org/newvoume/pages/article.php?articleID=509.
25. Quoted in Jonathan Culler, *Structuralist Poetics: Structuralism, Linguistics, and the Study of Literature* (London: Routledge, 1975), 308.
26. Kathy Acker, *Bodies of Work* (London: Serpent's Tail, 1997), 11.
27. See, for example, Annette Schlichter, "'I Can't Get Sexual Genders Straight': Kathy Acker's Writing of Bodies and Pleasures," *Postmodern Culture* 17, no. 2 (2007), accessed August 7, 2016, http://

www.pomoculture.org/2013/09/10/i-cant-get-sexual-genders-straight-kathy-ackers-writing-of-bodies-and-pleasures/.
28. For the definitive account of postmodern aesthetics as a practice of "complicitous critique," see Linda Hutcheon, *A Poetics of Postmodernism: History, Theory, Fiction* (London: Routledge, 1988); and *The Politics of Postmodernism* (London: Routledge, 2002).
29. Acker, *Bodies*, 84.
30. Ibid.
31. Ibid., 86.
32. Ibid.
33. Ibid., 85.
34. Ibid., original emphasis.
35. Ibid., original emphasis and ellipsis in original.
36. Ibid., 83.
37. Ibid., 85. For a different interpretation of Acker's relationship to conceptualism, see Matthew James Vechinski, "Kathy Acker as Conceptual Artist: *In Memoriam to Identity* and 'Working Past Failure,'" *Style* 47, no. 4 (2013): 525–42.
38. For a differing perspective, Ellen G. Friedman argues that Acker and Baudrillard similarly believe that those who control the "means of representation" hold ideological and political power (43). See Ellen G. Friedman, "'Now Eat Your Mind': An Introduction to the Works of Kathy Acker," *Review of Contemporary Fiction* 9, no. 3 (1989): 37–49.
39. Acker, *Bodies*, 11.
40. Ibid. For a view on Acker's postcynical turn that differs from mine, see Konstantinou, who argues that "desire for positivity is not a new concern for Acker but the fulfillment of an agenda set by her earliest writing" (144). While Acker's earlier work may express the desire for positivity, I argue that the languages of the body do not extend, in particular, the theory of reading and writing as remix, *détournement,* "appropriation or collage" shared, in different ways, by conceptualism, punk, and deconstruction (137). To be sure, the aesthetic surface of Acker's work remains largely the same, but the languages of the body mark a conceptual shift in Acker's work around affect, sexuality, and corporeality, drawing new attention to the convergence of aesthetic and sexual politics in the context of a diminishing community of queer radicalism in New York City. Similarly, I agree that Acker's queerness resonates with the "anti-social" thesis in queer theory, which Konstantinou rightly notes is inspired by punk cultures. However, this chapter argues that an affirmative mode of queer social imagination, infused by affect, emerges through the languages of the body.

41. See Irmtraud Huber, *Literature after Postmodernism: Reconstructive Fantasies* (New York: Palgrave Macmillan, 2014); as well as Daniel Punday, *Narrative After Deconstruction* (Albany: State University of New York Press, 2003); and Robert McLaughlin, "Post-Postmodernism" in *The Routledge Companion to Experimental Literature*, eds Joe Bray, Alison Gibbons, and Brian McHale (New York: Routledge, 2012), 212–23.

42. Acker, *Bodies*, 13.

43. Ibid., 83.

44. Kathy Acker, *Empire of the Senseless* (New York: Grove Press, 1988), 227.

45. Kenneth Goldsmith, "Paragraphs on Conceptual Writing," *Electronic Poetry Center*, accessed August 7, 2016, http://epc.buffalo.edu/authors/goldsmith/conceptual_paragraphs.html, my emphasis.

46. See, for example, Vanessa Place and Robert Fitterman, *Notes on Conceptualisms* (Brooklyn: Ugly Duckling Presse, 2009). Acker is best understood in Place and Fitterman's terms as a post- or impure conceptualist because she extensively revises the material she appropriates.

47. Ibid., 20, my emphasis.

48. Acker, *Hannibal*, 17.

49. Acker, *Bodies*, 68, my emphasis.

50. Ibid., 11. Note that Acker does not oppose postmodernism to realism but reclaims Burroughs's style as a different mode of realism (3).

51. Ibid., 3. On Acker's relationship to William S. Burroughs, see Konstantinou, *Cool Characters*, 103–59; and Robert A. Latham, "Collage as Critique and Intervention in the Fiction of William S. Burroughs and Kathy Acker," in *Modes of the Fantastic: Selected Essays from the Twelfth International Conference on the Fantastic in the Arts*, eds. Robert A. Latham and Robert A. Collins (London: Greenwood Press, 1995), 29–37.

52. Acker, *Bodies*, 3.

53. Acker, *Empire*, 213.

54. Ibid., 214, 222.

55. Acker, *Bodies*, 166.

56. Acker's ambivalence about Butlerian semiotics echoes Claire Colebrooke's critique: "It may not be that the body or materiality is only known or posited through difference (or the linguistic structures of difference). Corporeality might itself be *differential*" (82, original emphasis). See Claire Colebrooke, "From Radical Representations to Corporeal Becomings: The Feminist Philosophy of Lloyd, Grosz and Gatens," *Hypatia* 15 no. 2 (2000): 76–93.

57. Acker, *Bodies*, 167, original emphasis and ellipsis in original.

58. On affective thresholds, see Brian Massumi, *Parables of the Virtual: Movement, Affect, Sensation* (Durham: Duke University Press, 2002), especially 23–88.

59. Acker tends to privilege Irigaray over Kristeva. She notes, "I was disappointed in Kristeva's text, for there she indicated that she seemed unable to leave herself" ("Paragraphs" 89). See Kathy Acker, "Paragraphs," *The Journal of the Midwest Modern Language Association* 28, no. 1 (1995): 87–92. I would argue that Acker's investment in Irigaray stems from her locating sexual difference ontologically, prior to the body's entrance into the symbolic order, whereas Kristeva understands sexual difference as an inscription within the symbolic. Hence, as Elizabeth Grosz observes in *Jacques Lacan: A Feminist Introduction* (New York: Routledge, 1990), Kristeva sees feminism as "usually a negative and reactive counter-struggle against sexism. It does not provide the materials needed for developing alternatives. Its function is to say 'no' to this or that view, opposing what exists, without actively contributing to something new" (166). By contrast, Irigaray seeks to affirm "accounts of subjectivity and knowledge that acknowledge the existence of two sexes, two bodies, two forms of desire and two ways of knowing" (169). Similarly, I contend that Acker is drawn toward an ontologically based feminist and queer politics precisely because she wishes to affirm new modalities of desire, epistemology, and relationality that have been obstructed by the patriarchal symbolic order.

60. Acker, *Bodies*, 159.

61. Hélène Cixous, "The Laugh of the Medusa," trans. Keith Cohen and Paula Cohen, *Signs* 1, no. 4 (1976): 875–93.

62. Acker, *Bodies*, 159.

63. Ibid., 158. Acker's representation of piracy is sometimes read as a signifier of political economy, which I fear eclipses its irreducible relationship to queer and gender dissidence. See, for example, Clune, *American Literature*, 103–26.

64. Acker, *Bodies*, 158. Hence, Acker's feminist and queer politics are fundamentally entwined; they emerge out of a shared refusal of patriarchal and Oedipal familial structure and the attendant relations of heteronormative power that stem from this structure.

65. Ibid., 89. In addition to her discussion of Bataille throughout *Bodies of Work*, also see Acker's novel *My Mother: Demonology* (New York: Grove, 1993) for its complex revision of the relationship between Bataille and Colette Peignot. Aesthetically, Bataille shares Acker's investment in amoral aesthetics, figured through sexual and erotic transgressions of heteronormative taboos. Conceptually, Acker's understanding of Bataille appears to be greatly influenced by Allen S. Weiss, *The Aesthetics of Excess*

(Albany: State University of New York, 1989); and Steven Shaviro, *Passion & Excess: Blanchot, Bataille, and Literary Theory* (Tallahassee: The Florida State University Press, 1990). On Acker and Bataille, see Terry Engebretsen, "Re-Educating the Body: Kathy Acker, Georges Bataille, and the Postmodern Body in *My Mother: Demonology*," in *Devouring Institutions: The Life Work of Kathy Acker*, ed. Michael Hardin, (San Diego: San Diego State University Press, 2004), 69–84. In addition to Bataille, other influences on the languages of the body include Heidegger, Wittgenstein, Blanchot, and Klossowski.

66. Acker, *Bodies*, 91.
67. Ibid.
68. As she writes, "[T]he head is ruled by the cunt" (Ibid., 90).
69. An obvious influence here is the work of Luce Irigaray, particularly *This Sex Which Is Not One*, trans. Catherine Porter (Ithaca: Cornell University Press, 1985).
70. Acker, *Bodies*, 90.
71. Ibid., 91.
72. On this move, see Punday, *Narrative*; and Brande, "Making," who argues that "A book and a sexual practice have the same ontological status as machinic assemblages through which desire flows—whether desire is impeded or augmented," and thus concludes, invoking Deleuze and Guattari, that Acker's writing "maps a set of practices; it is 'oriented toward an experimentation in contact with the real'" (207). This point underscores that Acker's non-mimetic notion of affective writing refuses a notion of art as sublimated desire, a conceit that re-installs, in Acker's view, the Freudian narrative that denies desiring agency to women and other non-patriarchal subjects who signify and embody lack.
73. Acker, *Bodies*, 85, original emphasis.
74. Ibid., 92.
75. Note that Acker extends conceptualism's critique of romantic or individualistic creativity while simultaneously affirming the potential for asubjective becoming: "I have become interested in languages which I cannot *make up*, which I cannot *create* or even *create in*: I have become interested in languages which I can only come upon (as I disappear), a pirate upon buried treasure" (166, original emphasis).
76. Ibid., 148.
77. Ibid., 82.
78. Ibid., 92.
79. Ibid., 148.
80. Sean McCann and Michael Szalay, "Do You Believe in Magic? Literary Thinking after the New Left," *The Yale Journal of Criticism* 18, no. 2 (2005): 435–68.

81. Ibid., 451.

82. Ibid.

83. Sean McCann and Michael Szalay, "'Eerie Serenity': A Response to John McClure," *boundary 2* 36, no. 2 (2009): 148. It is important to note that McCann and Szalay's broader targets, beyond postmodern fiction, are the humanities and iconic figures of poststructural theory, particularly Michel Foucault. They take issue with a wide range of discourses that, in their view, position culture itself as the most significant terrain of politics, separate from other social and economic forces (441). Grouping all of these ideologies under a "libertarian" ethos, they interpret any modality of so-called magical discourse as "a cherished and ultimately comforting folklore of the late-capitalist economy" (460). For an incisive critique of their position, see John A. McClure, "Do They Believe in Magic?: Politics and Postmodern Literature," *boundary 2* 36, no. 2 (2009): 125–43; and *Partial Faiths: Postsecular Fiction in the Age of Pynchon and Morrison* (Athens: University of Georgia Press, 2007). For their response to McClure, see McCann and Szalay, "'Eerie Serenity,'" 145–53.

84. For example, Acker gets her labia pierced and rides on a motorcycle, experiencing a rush of masturbatory pleasure on the road; she also describes "walk[ing] around with a strap-on, having orgasms." See R.U. Sirius, "Where Does She Get Off?" accessed August 7, 2016, http://www.altx.com/io/acker.html. Also see her interview in *Re/Search #13: Angry Women* (San Francisco: Re/Search Publications, 1991), 177–85.

85. Sirius, "Where Does?" Notably, in her essay on Acker, Schulman concludes with a quote from *Don Quixote* (New York: Grove Press, 1986), "Language presupposes community. Therefore without you, nothing I say has any meaning" (quoted in *Witness* 77). This line underscores how important the concept of social community is to Acker's work.

86. Ibid.

87. Brian Massumi, *Politics of Affect* (Maldin: Polity Press, 2015), 44. Notably, Massumi invokes Antonin Artaud as an aesthetic exemplar of this tradition, a writer that inspires Acker and other queer experimental writers.

88. As Deleuze writes in *Nietzsche and Philosophy* (New York: Columbia University Press, 2006), "Opposition can be the law of the relation between abstract products, but difference is the only principle of genesis or production; a principle which itself produces opposition as mere appearance" (157). Not only does difference-as-dialectic buttress abstract relations of comparison, Deleuze claims that the dialectic rests primarily on sad passions, particularly passivity, suffering, and melancholy (*Nietzsche* 195–96). Indeed, Nietzsche argues that the only "creative deed" of the

dialectic is to say no; to denounce and reject but not to affirm (10). The dialectic thus produces a reactive form of self-constitution, a morality made through negation and ressentiment, a morality that does not challenge established values. Tied to what it negates, parasitic on the terms of established values, based in a struggle for recognition within these pre-established terms, it is "powerless to create new ways of thinking and feeling" (159). The qualities of *ressentiment* include a desire for and means of revenge and a "capacity for disparagement" that undermines the ability to "admire, respect, or love" and is linked to reproach, judgment, and blame (117). Passivity is coupled with "perpetual accusation," which is not aggressive (and thus active) but a reactive delineation of another's faults and responsibilities (118).

89. Massumi, *Politics*, 45.
90. Acker, *Bodies*, 92.
91. Ibid., 88.
92. Ibid.
93. Ibid., 89.
94. Sirius, "Where Does?"
95. Sandra M. Gilbert and Susan Gubar, *The Madwoman in the Attic: The Woman Writer and the Nineteenth-Century Literary Imagination* (New Haven: Yale University Press, 2000), 4.
96. Acker, *Bodies*, 149.
97. Ibid., 146.
98. Judith Halberstam, *The Queer Art of Failure* (Durham: Duke University Press, 2011).
99. Acker, *Bodies*, 150.
100. Ibid., 146.
101. Ibid., 149.
102. Hume, *Aggressive*, 2, 13.
103. Ibid., 8.
104. Ibid., 44, original emphasis.
105. Ibid.
106. Ibid., 56.
107. Ibid., xii.
108. Ibid., 8.
109. Acker's queer approach to relations of power is influenced by her affiliation with SAMOIS, the lesbian-feminist BDSM collective co-founded by Gayle Rubin, among others.
110. Kathy Acker, *In Memoriam to Identity* (New York: Grove Press, 1990).
111. On deconstruction as double reading, see Jeffrey T. Nealon, *Double Reading: Postmodernism After Deconstruction* (Ithaca: Cornell University Press, 1993).

112. For a brief biographical sketch of this time, see Chris Kraus, "Discuss Rules Beforehand," September 2014, accessed August 7, 2016, http://www.believermag.com/issues/201409/?read=article_kraus.

113. Acker, *Memoriam*, 262.

114. For an elaboration of this point, see Acker's "Dead Doll Humanity," *Postmodern Culture* 1, no. 1 (1990), accessed August 7, 2016, http://pmc.iath.virginia.edu/text-only/issue.990/acker.990. For an incisive analysis of the politics of piracy and property in Acker's late work, see Caren Irr, *Pink Pirates: Contemporary American Women Writers and Copyright* (Iowa City: University of Iowa Press, 2010), 105–32.

115. Acker, *Memoriam*, 261.

116. Ibid., 241.

117. Ibid., 244.

118. Ibid.

119. Ibid., 257.

120. Ibid., 56.

121. Ibid.

122. On this tension in Burroughs's work, see Chap. 1.

123. Acker, *Memoriam*, 61.

124. Ibid.

125. Ibid., 59, original emphasis.

126. Ibid.

127. Ibid., 203.

128. Ibid., 59.

129. Ibid., 183.

130. Catherine Rock, "Poetics of the Periphery: Literary Experimentalism in Kathy Acker's *In Memoriam to Identity*," *Lit: Literature Interpretation Theory* 12, no. 2 (2001): 220.

131. Acker, *Memoriam*, 9–10.

132. Ibid., 9.

133. As Svetlana Mintcheva argues "Entangled in the structures she is protesting against, Acker's subject can only reject them if she rejects herself: her very subjectivity is formed within these structures" (50). See "The Paralyzing Tensions of Radical Art in a Postmodern World: Kathy Acker's Last Novels as Exploratory Fictions," in *Devouring Institutions: The Life Work of Kathy Acker*, ed. Michael Hardin (San Diego: San Diego University Press, 2004), 47–66.

134. Hume, *Aggressive*, 55.

135. Acker, *Memoriam*, 37.

136. Ibid., 38.

137. Ibid., 89.

138. Ibid., 89–90.

139. Ibid., 95, original emphasis.
140. See Chap. 1.
141. Acker, *Memoriam*, 141.
142. Ibid.
143. Ibid.
144. Ibid., 139.
145. Ibid., 149.
146. Ibid., 139.
147. Ibid., 137.
148. Ibid., 228, original emphasis.
149. Ibid., 244.
150. Ibid., 264.
151. Ibid. Note that there is no quotation mark to enclose the statement or to clearly demarcate its vocalization by a subject. Syntactically, *In Memoriam to Identity* frays as its narration becomes increasingly desubjectified. Yet this syntax also performatively underscores Acker's movement away from the critical politics of quotation toward a new, "unknown" aesthetic and political territory, which is engendered through the languages of the body.
152. Ibid., 174.
153. Acker, *Bodies*, 166.
154. Konstantinou, *Cool*, 154. On the projective city, see 112.
155. For this view, see David Harvey, *The Condition of Postmodernity* (Oxford: Blackwell, 1990). For a queer critique of this reduction, see Judith Halberstam, *In A Queer Time and Place: Transgender Bodies, Subcultural Lives* (New York: New York University Press, 2005).

CHAPTER 4

Queer Exuberance: Visceral Reading and the Politics of Positive Affect

"*Love is an intervention.* Is that true? I would like it to be true. Not romance, not sentimentality, but a force of a different nature from the forces of death that dictate what will be."

—Jeanette Winterson, *The Stone Gods*

The title for Jeanette Winterson's most famous novel *Written on the Body* (1992) is drawn from a moment when the queerly opaque, unidentified narrator describes their lover's capacity to read their body.[1] The narrator states,

Written on the body is a secret code only visible in certain lights; the accumulations of a lifetime gather there. In places the palimpsest is so heavily worked that the letters feel like braille. I like to keep my body rolled up away from prying eyes. Never unfold too much, tell the whole story. I didn't know that Louise would have reading hands. She has translated me into her own book.[2]

Here Winterson draws attention to her novel's experimental conceit. The narrator is never named, gendered, racialized, or identified with any other embodied specificity. By not "tell[ing] the whole story," Winterson's readers careen through the novel with a suspicious hermeneutic, seeking to ferret out the narrator's "true" identity in the marginal details of the text. Yet the irreducible and unresolved ambiguity about the narrator's body

© The Author(s) 2017
T. Bradway, *Queer Experimental Literature*,
Palgrave Studies in Affect Theory and Literary Criticism,
DOI 10.1057/978-1-137-59543-0_4

reflexively underscores that gender and sexuality have no essential identity outside of language. The sex of the speaking subject is revealed to be an "accumulation" of signs, of cultural associations, and of discursive inscriptions that encode their body like a palimpsest. Thus, *Written on the Body* forces readers to confront their own complicity with the mechanisms of interpellation; we desire gender to stabilize the narrator's queerness, to punctuate and arrest the fluidity and groundlessness of their body and its erotic relations with others. For this reason, critics have read *Written on the Body* as a paradigmatic text of contemporary queer fiction.[3] Indeed, the novel's title echoes the canonical method of critique in queer theory—namely, the demystifying exposure of the body as a signifying surface, which reveals that gender and sexuality are fictions written by the social "on the body" rather than truths borne in the core of a self.

Yet there is another mode of queer reading intimated by *Written on the Body*, one that is predicated on the visceral transmission of affect that outstrips the subject's attempts at calculation and opens their body to relational becoming. Note, for example, that Louise's "reading hands" overcome the narrator's desire to keep their body "rolled up away" in disembodied opacity. Louise's reading the "braille" of the body does not expose the false essentialism of its signifying surface; rather, she unrolls the discursive palimpsest that the narrator uses to hide. Although the narrator is illegible in certain lights, their body becomes affectively readable as a consequence of Louise's tactile hermeneutics. Notably, this affective "translation" of the narrator's body into Louise's book does not signify a violation of their singular alterity, as it often does in poststructural ethics. On the contrary, the ethical violation lies in the narrator's desire to prevent corporeal exposure—in their stated intention to keep the materiality of the body hidden "from prying eyes." In this respect, Louise presents the narrator with an ethical choice: Can they embrace an affective openness with the other, or will they repress embodied relationality and remain hidden by the games of language? This is a fundamental problem in Winterson's novels, and it inspires the narrative trajectory for many of her main characters. Winterson's protagonists initially inhabit a solipsistic and disembodied self-enclosure, which is coded as patriarchal in its unwillingness to share the mutual exposure of affectivity. Then, these characters move toward an exuberant becoming with the other that undermines the subject's patriarchal transcendence of corporeality and embraces their body's irreducibly queer relationality.

Written on the Body's representation of affective reading points toward a conception of queer critique based in the solicitation of affect. Not merely exposing the writing "on" bodies, queer fiction can also affectively write "with" the bodies of its readers, exposing them to new relational possibilities.[4] In this sense, the exposure offered through queer writing is not a demystifying revelation but a corporeal contact that strikes the body as intensity. Indeed, as this chapter will demonstrate, Winterson conceives of queer experimental literature's political agency as an affective encounter that disrupts the subject's linguistic and perceptual habituation to sensorial norms. For Winterson, queer experimental literature transmits an affective shock that teaches readers to feel differently, detaching affect from its narrow affixation to the embodied norms of consumption and patriarchal heteronormativity. At the same time, her writing contests negative affects that underwrite a fearful, melancholic acceptance of the status quo. These affects, she suggests, forsake a more radical horizon for queer becoming, an incalculable future pitched toward social relations that embrace, rather than repress, the body's irreducible affective relatedness to others. Clearly, Winterson builds on the genealogy of bad reading charted through the previous chapters: she maps the politics of queer experimental literature onto the affective relations of reading, which stimulate an incipiently social imagination of queer belonging; and that social imagination cannot be charted through conventional forms of representation and must be provoked through experimentations with literary form. Yet Winterson innovates on bad reading in two significant ways that speak to the representational and political constraints confronted by contemporary queer experimental literature. First, Winterson emphasizes the emotional rather than the sexual as the basis for defining queer reader relations; while the body has a primary status in her narratives and in her account of visceral aesthetics, Winterson privileges "emotion"—a term that has frequently been degraded in affect theory—as the domain of social control and contestation alike. Second, Winterson resuscitates the queerness of emotions such as love, happiness, and hope, which have often been marked as uncritical within the affective idioms of queer theory.

Given its unabashed embrace of positive affects to affirm non-heteronormative relationality, Winterson's fiction would thus appear to be least transgressive of the writers in this book, the least "queer." Not only does Winterson fully embrace the idioms of sentimentality, she barely represents sex at all. Her novels offer little taboo breaking in the vein of William S. Burroughs's and Samuel R. Delany's pornographic assaults on conventional eroticism; nor does she reclaim the ugly feelings of abjection as Kathy Acker does. One might conclude, then, that Winterson is a perfect analogue for "homonormativity," the neoliberal depoliticization and privatization of radical sexual politics that defines the contemporary moment.[5] After all, neoliberalism has shifted the focus of LGBTQ politics from sex to love in the form of gay marriage and other state-sanctioned forms of relationality.[6] This context partly inspires queer theory's equation of negative affects such as shame and abjection with queer critique. Undoubtedly, these affects appear "critical" when measured against the conservative, desexualized visions of gay love, happiness, and pride affirmed within mainstream discourses of consumption.[7] Due to the current priority granted to negative affect in queer theory, it is difficult to conceive of Winterson's affirmative embrace of positive affect as anything other than an uncritical capitulation to homonormativity's dominant structure of feeling. Yet this chapter will argue that positive affect can inspire a queer social imagination that cuts against homonormativity's narrow association of queerness with privatized identity. Indeed, Winterson's fiction turns from sexuality to emotionality precisely because sexuality has become, in her view, increasingly codified as the biopolitical basis for consumer identity. Despite its rhetorical echoes of homonormative sentimentality, then, Winterson queers positive affect, contesting the relational economy that underpins the prevailing lover's discourse trumpeted by neoliberalism. Winterson's fiction thus provides a case study for how the cultural expression of positive affect inspires queer experimental literature to resist the affective politics of neoliberalism.[8] By looking to Winterson's conception of bad reading as the locus of her affective politics, this chapter unsettles the dominant relations between "critical" and "uncritical" feelings in queer theory itself, thereby expanding the affective politics that are legible to us as queer.

Winterson also diverges from other authors in this study because her work is pitched firmly between mainstream and academic publics. Unlike Delany and Acker, for example, Winterson is not enacting a para-academic critique of academic discourses that codify the affective relations of queer reading. As Sarah Schulman notes in her account of the gentrification of queer literature, Winterson is among the few lesbian writers to achieve mainstream success and to receive legitimate recognition from the wider institutions of literary authority.[9] At the same time, Winterson's fiction gained mainstream popularity alongside the institutionalization of queer theory, which is one reason why her work has so often been interpreted by academics as exemplifying the dominant methods of queer theory. Although Winterson continues to produce new fiction and remains popular among mainstream publics, her work has recently faded from academic interest, partly because scholars fear that Winterson's affirmation of positive affect bespeaks a retreat from the proper idioms of social critique. Elaine Showalter, for example, laments Winterson's focus on "[c]ities of the interior," exemplified in her representation of "love instead of money ... sex instead of power ... [and] the past instead of the future."[10] Even sympathetic critics such as Sonya Andermahr claim that Winterson's "desire ... for change" is narrowly "personal, individual change rather than the social, collective change of political utopianism."[11] For evidence of her solipsism, critics invariably point to Winterson's sentimental lover's discourse and her concomitant vision of literature as an affectively transformative love relation. To be sure, critics such as Jean-Michel Ganteau and Andrea Harris have defended Winterson's lover's discourse for its revision of patriarchal and heteronormative romance traditions.[12] Yet these approaches tend to conceptualize Winterson's queer politics primarily in terms of deconstructive resignification. As such, critics have overlooked the complex historical relationship between queer aesthetics and sexual politics in Winterson's work. Indeed, we have not sufficiently appreciated that Winterson's critique of the biopolitical codification of sexuality identity converges with the codification of her own fiction as "queer" and "lesbian" among mainstream institutions of literary authority. As I demonstrate in this chapter, Winterson turns to experimental aesthetics— a turn that many critics denounced as abstruse and solipsistic—to resist homonormative approaches that arrest the queerness of her writing by conceiving of literature as an identitarian mirror for the reader or an autobiographical extension of the author.[13]

Winterson rejects this identitarian foundation for queer literature and re-locates its queerness in the pre-subjective affective relations that emerge between readers and art objects; these visceral relations compel the emergence of what I call Winterson's *queer exuberance*: the body's incipient opening toward social forms of queer relationality that oppose the biopolitical regimentation of sexual identity. The personal is therefore not the end point of Winterson's affective politics. On the contrary, the pre-personal realm of affect is the starting point for glimpsing queer relationality in a historical moment otherwise committed to its privatization. My approach to queer exuberance breaks, in particular, with theories of political affect that emphasize the inherent "cruelness" of positive affects.

In these narratives, positive affects function as deceptively false promises that fuse subjects to hetero- and homonormative ideologies and thereby obstruct a radical queer politics. Queer exuberance acknowledges the danger of drawing on idioms of affect that have been so fruitful for homonormativity's recuperation of the social order, but it also refuses to leave those terms uncontested; to do so reproduces a binary that stigmatizes positivity as a degraded form of subjective knowledge—indeed, as only false consciousness—and it ignores that *both* positive and negative affects are complexly soldered to neoliberalism's economy of values. It is important to remember that Winterson's audience is primarily a mainstream public that is undoubtedly familiar with—and perhaps even moved by—the idioms of homonormative sentimentality. My claim is that Winterson develops a complex affective relation with these publics, speaking in the idiom of positive affect but radically queering its underlying political imaginary. To be sure, queer exuberance does not disavow or attempt to transcend negativity or trauma, as homonormativity does; it maintains an irreducible relationship to queer histories of hurt. At the same time, it worries that the affirmation of negative affects can fail to adequately combat neoliberalism's structure of feeling, in which melancholy, depression, anxiety, and fear restrict the desire for queer becoming, for an exuberant social imagination that looks beyond the constricted present.[14] In my epigraph, taken from Winterson's science fiction novel *The Stone Gods*, the narrator hesitates about the possibility of an affective idiom that can contest the forces that reproduce the future as mortifying sameness. To embrace love as an "intervention," when read literally, smacks of the privatizing sentimentality that many critics disdain. Yet the narrator desires an idiom of queer exuberance that breaks from patriarchal romance and consumer sentimentality. Such an idiom would function as more than a signifier—it would *intervene* as an affective force of becoming itself, making a future for the emergence of queer relationality possible.

THE POLITICS OF QUEER AFFECT

On the day after Barack Obama's first election as president, Judith Butler circulated a brief online essay entitled "Uncritical Exuberance."[15] As the title implies, Butler feared that progressives would succumb to the seduction of positive affects. "Very few of us are immune to the exhilaration of this time," Butler admitted.[16] Consequently, she called for a "critical politics" to inoculate intellectuals from the apparently "unambivalent love" displayed by Obama's supporters.[17] "After all," Butler wrote, "fascism relied in part on that seamless identification with the leader, and Republicans engage this same effort to organize political affect when, for instance, Elizabeth Dole looks out on her audience and says, 'I love each and every one of you.'"[18] In an astonishingly broad sweep, Butler conflates the "political affect" of Democrats, Republicans, and fascists. Their common root lies in the deployment of positive affect to suture the public into a passive identification with oppressive power.[19] Exuberance is "uncritical" because it obstructs a properly "dis-illusion[ed]" relationship to power.[20] In this respect, "Uncritical Exuberance" is the affective shadow of Butler's more famous argument in "Critically Queer." There, Butler equates "queer" and "critique" because both disrupt naturalized norms, bringing to crisis the discursive mechanisms of interpellation.[21] To dramatize her definition of queer critique, Butler invokes negative affects, such as melancholia, ambivalence, and grief. Indeed, Butler famously characterizes melancholia as an ethically queer relationship to the heteronormative symbolic order, and she endorses grief because it "furnishes a sense of political community of a complex order."[22] The use of affective idioms to narrate—and to galvanize—a queer social imagination is therefore not inherently uncritical. However, in Butler's narrative, positive affect invariably supports normativity in its concealment of power relations while only negative affects clear a path for becoming both queer and critical.[23]

Must exuberance and critique be so stridently opposed? What forms of queer community can be imagined through the idioms of positive affect? Despite recent interest in affect, queer scholars have been reluctant to explore the critical agencies of positive affect.[24] Butler's short essay exemplifies the assumption that "critical politics" demystifies deceptive relations to the social. Invariably, these deceptive relations operate through happiness, love, hope, and pleasure. Eve Kosofsky Sedgwick famously challenged this binary between positive and negative affects; she identified the epistemological limitations of defining queer critique as an act of paranoid "exposure," and she urged queer theory to reappraise the latent agencies of reparative affects within queer activism and culture.[25] Yet some of the most prominent scholars in queer theory continue to identify positive affect as the central threat to queer politics. Thus, Lee Edelman positions "compassion" at the core of his scathing critique of reproductive futurity.[26] Similarly, Sara Ahmed's *The Promise of Happiness* targets the rhetorical ruses of happiness that compel subjects toward heteronormative objects.[27] These critiques overlook contexts in which positive affects might encode critical, political, or life-sustaining possibilities for queer subjects. Queer theory has yet to answer Michael D. Snediker's urgent question in *Queer Optimism*: "[W]hat if we could ... imagine happiness as theoretically mobilizable, as conceptually difficult? Which is to ask, what if happiness weren't merely, self-reflexively happy, but interesting?"[28]

Queer theory's interest in positive affect has been obstructed because it continues to represent critical agency through negation and subversion rather than affirmation and becoming.[29] Undoubtedly, queer studies broke lasting ground by destigmatizing the discursive negativity that labels queer subjects as perverse.[30] By recovering denigrated structures of feeling such as melancholy, queer theory articulated a powerful counterdiscourse to the rhetoric of assimilation in lesbian and gay political organizations, exemplified by "gay pride," military enfranchisement, and marriage equality. For queer scholars, these goals represent homonormativity's repression of queer relationality in favor of state-sanctioned social forms.[31] I do not wish to diminish the drastic commodification of LGBTQ identities in recent years. Yet it is perhaps time to reflect on the consequences of queer theory's self-positioning as a discourse of radical negativity. What is lost when queer theory opposes a fantasmatically coherent "mainstream" as its primary enemy? Queer theory might overlook opportunities to exploit and radically reimagine the partial social recognition of LGBTQ political demands. The insistence that negativity is the sole idiom for political engagement prohibits a rigorous consideration of the "successes" of LGBTQ politics, however riven these developments are. By depicting those invested in liberal LGBTQ politics as uncritically sentimental and naive, queer critics may also miss an opportunity to speak with publics that experience positive affect as complexly related to political imagination. Most importantly, queer theory overlooks how positive affects can encode desires for queer social relations in historical moments when those relations are under attack. To be able to read this complex political imagination, queer theory must pluralize the affects that count as "critical" and the ways in which affect can ignite political imagination. By doing so, queer theory can establish a more dialogic rapport with LGBTQ movements and affirm its own relations as desirable alternatives to the structures of hetero- and homonormativity.

Some domains of queer theory have been skeptical about affect offering such possibilities for becoming, because queer critique has been defined as the performative subversion of discursive norms.[32] Butler argues, for example, that the "critical promise of drag does not have to do with the proliferation of genders ... but rather with the exposure or the failure of heterosexual regimes ever fully to legislate or contain their own ideals."[33] Here queer critique operates through a hyperbolic "allegory" that demystifies the seemingly natural connection between gender performance and biological sex. Butler cautions against imagining drag as a free field for "proliferation" because early readers interpreted her work as naively utopian in its affirmation of performative agency. Yet in the process, Butler annexes queer cultural forms whose "critical promise[s]" may not operate through subversive exposure but through creative becoming. Responding to the "foreclosure" of Deleuzian becoming in Butler's theorization of performativity, E.L. McCallum and Mikko Tuhkanen argue that

> Doing away with a stable subject is thus crucial to retooling becoming in a queer way, but it's only the first step. To imagine the new forms of relationality that queer becoming promises—or, for that matter, to fully imagine a dynamically queer becoming—calls for a reconsideration of the axes of becoming, a rethinking of the modes of temporality queers inhabit, beyond a Hegelian or even a Nietzschean or Deleuzian framework.[34]

Like McCallum and Tukhanen, I look to queer cultural production as a key locus for this reconsideration, but while they highlight the axis of temporality in queer becoming, I stress the axis of affect—the body's immanent openness to qualitative change. Affect underscores the openness of the body to becoming as well as the "new forms of relationality" that incipiently emerge through queer experimentations with affect. Yet, following Brian Massumi, affect also unsettles the presumption, central to Butlerian queer theory, that "signification or coding" precedes bodily "process."[35] By suspending the privilege granted to the performativity of signification, we can recover queer cultural forms—and their productions of relationality—that have failed to count as "critical" because of their investment in the creative agencies of affect.

However, we cannot begin to re-evaluate the critical politics of queer affect without also suspending the priority granted to ideological critiques of affect.[36] Recall, for example, Lauren Berlant's influential claim that "*psychic pain experienced by subordinated populations must be treated as ideology*, not as prelapsarian knowledge or a condensed comprehensive social theory."[37] Berlant's point is that ameliorating affect should not be substituted as the primary goal of politics; moreover, affects are underwritten by ideological attachments and fantasies that compose social relations. While I agree that "sensual experience" must not be mistaken as the endgame of politics, Berlant diminishes how affect, prior to its subjectification, has become a terrain of collective bodily struggle in the postmodern political economy.[38] As Michael Hardt and Antonio Negri argue, affect is now a primary locus of value in biopolitical production.[39] As examples, they cite health care workers, flight attendants, and sex workers (and I would add artists, teachers, and customer service workers) as examples of affective laborers. In each case, a central basis for their labor lies in intangible, non-discursive, and non-subjective structures of feeling. If feeling is now a crucial element of exchange, then we must expand the meaning of "political economy" to include this pre-ideological sensual domain. The affective field must be seen as a discursively constituted ideological regime, in Berlant's sense, as well as a field of visceral intensities: the two are mutually implicated with one another; the former threads affects, forces, and bodies with words, values, and commodities. Yet the two fields exist in constant friction, with the latter perpetually unleashing its own immanent, uncaptured, and incipiently resistant lines of flight. If contemporary biopower cultivates specific associations of feeling and value for profit, then there are political stakes in deforming and realigning these sensual relations. As much as cultural production may attack ideological constructions, it also deploys affective forces that, in certain contexts, must be thought as queer modes of aesthetic agency.

It may be that the aesthetic forms unleashed by postmodernism's "waning of affect"—forms that exuberantly embrace the subject's dispersal—can catalyze relations that counter the prevailing political economy.[40] Indeed, the often-mischaracterized notion of the "waning of affect" should be understood as a newly vexed and particularly urgent locus of political struggle. The dispersal of affect into pre-subjective intensities creates an opportunity for cultural producers, particularly those who seek to counter or defuse the structures of feeling that consumer capitalism produces and enforces. First, the waning of affect implies that feeling can no longer be mapped in the narrow terms of "the subject." Not only does affective labor point toward the pre- and non-subjective movements of affect, it also understands corporeality itself as irreducibly relational, as queerly exposed to and implicated within the becoming of intensity as it moves among the body politic. Second, the politics of aesthetics must be thought as equally embedded in and responsive to the affective relations of the postmodern cultural economy. Art does not transcend or escape the social; it is relationally implicated within their shared ontology of affect. Therefore, queer experimental literature's reformulation of the affective relations of reading must be thought as a micropolitics that utilizes the axis of affect to create new associations of power, desire, and value.[41]

If a politics of affect can enable the creation of new associations, then it is perhaps also time to rethink the affective relations that underwrite and are fostered by queer theory itself.[42] For example, Wendy Brown expresses concern about the predominance of melancholia as a structure of feeling in leftist political activism and social imagination.[43] Brown perceives progressives as "caught in a structure of melancholic attachment to a certain strain of [their] own dead past," an attachment which may inadvertently buttress conservative agendas.[44] To be sure, Brown acknowledges the crushing erosions of liberalism, the welfare state, the labor movement, and the discrediting of viable alternatives to capitalism.[45] Yet she nonetheless worries that

> the feelings and sentiments—including those of sorrow, rage, and anxiety about broken promises and lost compasses—that sustain our attachments to Left analyses and Left projects ought to be examined for what they create in the way of potentially conservative and even self-destructive undersides of putatively progressive political aims.[46]

As anyone who has ever held a political conviction knows, feelings cannot be divorced from the work of politics—we feel rage, despair, indignation, hope, or righteous anger, and these emotions can just as easily enable as disable political action. Political actions themselves can live or die by the intensity of collective passions, rather than the relative merit of the values and issues at stake. As Brown implies, this is because emotional sentiments crystallize around and adhere to specific political attachments. Concomitantly, emotional dispositions have some, however minor, capacity to incite and sustain political intervention. If melancholic sentiments have short-circuited more radical desires for social transformation, perhaps new affective relations are required. These affective relations would have to counter a Left that, in Brown's words, "has become more attached to its impossibility than to its potential fruitfulness, a Left that is most at home dwelling not in hopefulness but in its own marginality and failure."[47] The attachment to impossibility aptly captures one structure of feeling that predominates among academic idioms of queer theory, which often equates queerness itself with negativity. From within these idioms, it sometimes seems impossible to talk hopefully and joyfully about the creative *fecundity of queerness*—of the pleasures, relational horizons, and social imagination that queerness brings into being and preserves against the restriction of the present. This is why this chapter and the next focus on explorations of the queerness of affirmation—not, again, to perpetuate a reductive binary between positivity and negativity but to think freshly about how the affective relations of queer critique, reconceived as *also* a project of affirmation, can foster horizons for queer relationality against the ascendance of homonormativity.

Of course, my focus on the affective relations of social imagination may seem to miss the broader target of critique. Following Brown, Berlant contends, for example, that the attention to "traumatic identity" among leftists must be replaced "with a subjectivity articulated utopianly, via the agency of imagined demand, [which] will take from pain the energy for social transformation beyond the field of its sensual experience."[48] The call to reconstruct a located subject with agency and the capacity to represent demands may be worthwhile, although I fear that the stress falls too heavily on the need for recognition—an authority to hear the demand—than on the creation of social transformations through the medium of so-called "sensual experience." It is worth attending, in other words, to the ways that queer writers grapple with, revalue, and reconceive the proximate and mediated relationship between feeling and politics—what I have called the incipiently social dimension of queer reading. As we have seen, the incipiently social relations of affect provide queer experimental writers an agency to reconfigure queerness in ways that cannot be otherwise represented, narrated, or read in their present. I argue that this project underwrites Winterson's understanding of the aesthetic as a relational circuit of affect, which transposes the desire for queer relationality and social transformation into the seemingly solipsistic discourse of sentimentality. But to be clear: I do not claim that Winterson articulates a veiled utopian politics of the sort that Berlant intimates. The temporal horizons of the utopian, as I discussed in the introduction, do not accord with the affective relations of becoming fashioned through bad reading. Akin to Berlant's more recent conception of optimism as a social relation that structures the present as an impasse, Winterson's queer exuberance emerges incipiently from the conditions of the present.[49] Its horizons are therefore immanent to the encounter with the aesthetic object and remain necessarily open ended. Moreover, Winterson's aesthetic conceit struggles against the utopianism of neoliberalism, which projects an uncontestable and purified future of radical freedom in the form of the consumer subject unfettered from all social relations.[50] Winterson attempts to solicit new relational structures, which oppose a political economy that equates happiness with purchase power, desire with privatized subjectivity, and art with consumption. The sensual, pre-subjective affects that Winterson affirms in queer aesthetics must be treated as ideology, as Berlant suggests. But they must also be treated as *less than ideology*—as a creative deformation and reformation of the discursive, affective, and social relations that underpin contemporary regimes of biopower.

BIOPOLITICS AND JEANETTE WINTERSON'S VISCERAL AESTHETICS

In *The Stone Gods*, Winterson draws on science fiction to satirize the political codification of sexuality that inspires her transposition of queerness into the idioms of emotionality.[51] In the dystopian society of the Central Power, the government has legalized all manner of taboo desires. Pedophilia has been authorized by the state. Translucents—which are people that "When you fuck them you can watch yourself doing it"—are the consumer rage.[52] The primary struggle for sexual liberation centers on genetic Fixing, which arrests the aging process. As yet, children are not allowed to be Fixed. However, one proponent of the process, McMurphy, claims, "It's like every other Civil Rights and Equal Rights battle, OK? You had Blacks at one time. You had Semites at one time. You had mixed marriages, you had gays. All legal. No problem. We're just victims of prejudice and out-of-date laws."[53] The protagonist, Billie Crusoe, replies, "It's called paedo-philia," but McMurphy insists, "That's just a word, like 'homosexual.'"[54] Insulted, Billie counters, "No, it's not a word like 'homosexual,' it's a word like 'goat-fucker.'"[55] Winterson's satire seems to evoke conservative anxieties about the proliferation of queerness once homosexuality has become accepted and normalized by the state. Yet the real satirical target is McMurphy's libertarian equation of *sexual freedom* with *political freedom*. As we later discover, the strictures on sexual freedom are relaxed by the state to mask new forms of control. Indeed, the neoliberal state legalizes prostitution, gambling, and drinking and lowers the age of consent to "distract from" its erosion of civil liberties, militarization of civilian life, foreclosure of political dissent, and implementation of a surveillance state.[56] Moreover, patriarchal social relations ultimately underwrite the apparently permissive attitude to sexuality. Billie notes that "the future of women is uncertain," since they are no longer needed for reproduction and men prefer young girls and boys as sexual objects.[57] Consequently, women are Fixing at younger ages or desperately seeking to reverse their aging. Here Winterson critiques a specific biopolitical instrumentation of sexuality, a deployment of the technologies of pleasure that abets the expansion of state sovereignty and patriarchal oppression under the guise of expanding sexual agency.

Queer affect in Winterson's work stands against this incorporation and codification of sexuality by the state.[58] Indeed, the most prominent signifier of queerness in *The Stone Gods* is not sex but emotion. In fact, Billie appears queer to other characters not because of her lesbianism but because of her queer exuberance, succinctly expressed in her refrain throughout the novel "Love is an intervention."[59] In an intertextual citation of the final line of Acker's *Empire of the Senseless* (1988), a novel that figured prominently in the previous chapter's argument, Billie yearns for a "human society that wasn't just disgust."[60] Whereas Acker offers the "languages of the body" as an experimental method for fostering the relations for that society, Winterson characteristically privileges emotionality. Billie explains

> Since the Enlightenment we have been trying to get away from emotionalism, the mother of all isms. … For my part, I think we need more emotion, not less. But I think, too, that we need to educate people in how to feel. Emotionalism is not the same as emotion. We cannot cut out emotion—in the economy of the human body, it is the limbic, not the neural, highway that takes precedence.[61]

The Stone Gods implicitly positions itself as part of this project of "educat[ing] people in how to feel." In Billie's view, this affective pedagogy teaches that "the value of the world" does not lie in "economic potential" but in "art" and other "invisibles never counted by the GDP and the census figures. It means knowing that life has an inside as well as an outside. And I think it means love."[62] Here queer exuberance condenses a relation of non-instrumentality that stands outside the calculated measures of economic value. If read reductively—as saying that individual emotion directly solves political problems—then Winterson is surely guilty of overinflating the personal, as her critics fear. Yet the relation between the "inside" and "outside" of emotional life takes on a particularly queer configuration in Winterson's notion of the aesthetic as a visceral relation. I propose, then, to read the pedagogy of feeling intimated in *The Stone Gods* back through Winterson's earlier essays on the affective agency of visceral aesthetics.[63] By doing so, I will establish that the queer exuberance she locates in "art" works complexly against the biopolitical codification of feeling that solders subjects to neoliberalism through their affective attachments.

Winterson conceives of literary affect as anterior to codified subjectivity. In her narrative, the viscerality of art disperses the subject and expands affective relations beyond the structure of feeling that constricts the postmodern social imaginary. In her book of essays on aesthetics, *Art Objects: Essays on Ecstasy and Effrontery* (1995), Winterson claims, "[A]rt works to enlarge emotional possibility. In a dead society that inevitably puts it on the side of the rebels."[64] For Winterson, rebelliousness does not connote unqualified opposition or the aestheticized resistance of "bohemians and bad boys."[65] Rather, she insists that "[t]he rebellion of art is a daily rebellion against the state of living death routinely called real life."[66] As we will see, Winterson attacks "real life" from a series of angles—aesthetic and economic—in a manner that echoes the investment of queer experimental literature in non-realist forms of representation that draw inspiration from fantasy and the imaginary. In this context, the living death of real life that Winterson critiques is ideological, constituted by "the tragic paradigm of human life" premised on "lack, loss, finality, a primitive doomsaying that has not been repealed by technology or medical science. The arts stand in the way of this doomsaying. Art objects. The nouns become an active force not a collector's item."[67] Throughout Winterson's fiction, the tragic ideology of lack underwrites capitalist and patriarchal political economies alike, engendering "the fighting, the killing, the lack, the loss, for power, for envy, for every stupidity that man can devise."[68] In Winterson's argument, art objects to this economy of relation through its queer exuberance—its affirmation of an ontology premised on the incalculable excessiveness of affect, glimpsed through the dynamic forces of intensity catalyzed by the aesthetic. These forces counter institutions of "social and emotional training" such as "the state, the family, the way most of us are educated, [which] dampens down spontaneous feeling and makes us wary of excess."[69]

Is it not the case that contemporary capitalism promotes and, in fact, requires "spontaneous feeling" to encourage "excess"? After all, Hardt and Negri's examples of affective labor all produce pleasure. Negativity cannot be tolerated because it diminishes consumption. Yet, as Gopal Balakrishnan observes, contemporary capitalism is "seemingly powered by the pursuit of happiness—but [it is] in reality based on the mobilization of desires that are intimately wedded to the fear of failure, exclusion and loneliness."[70] In other words, the forces of negativity underwrite the consumer discourse of positive affect. It is fruitless, then, to simply oppose negative and positive affects in a decontextualized binary. Rather, we must consider how affects fuse the body into the body politic, privileging certain social attachments and relations of value in specific contexts. Thus, Winterson opposes her investment in queer exuberance to consumerism's false discourse of positivity:

> In a repressive society that pretends to be liberal, misery and breakdown can be used as subtle punishments for what we no longer dare legislate against. Inability to cope is defined as a serious weakness in a macho culture like ours, but what is inability to cope, except a spasmodic, faint and fainter protest against a closed-in drugged up life where suburban values are touted as the greatest good? A newborn child, the moment of falling in love, can cause in us seismic shocks that will, if we let them, help us to re-evaluate what things matter, what things we take for granted.[71]

Even as Winterson undermines an essential subject, she idealizes authentic feeling, which she defines through the unrepentantly sentimental images of birth and love. In her view, contemporary social "taboo[s]" are not organized around the repression of sexuality but the suppression of "complex emotion."[72] By dynamizing these taboo intensities, then, art contests the deadening structure of feeling required by patriarchal and consumer culture, enabling its audiences to "re-evaluate what things matter."

Before we explore the specificity of this social revaluation, we must note that Winterson consistently narrates visceral aesthetics through a "love parallel."[73] She writes, for example, that the denial of an artwork based on its being "boring/pointless/silly/obscure/elitist, etc." might result from a

> work [that] falls so outside of the safety of your own experience that in order to keep your own world intact, you must deny the other world of the painting. This denial of imaginative experience happens at a deeper level than our affirmation of our daily world. Every day, in countless ways, you and I convince ourselves about ourselves. True art, when it happens to us, challenges the 'I' that we are.
>
> A love-parallel would be just; falling in love challenges the reality to which we lay claim, part of the pleasure of love and part of its terror, is the world turned upside down. We want and don't want, the cutting edge, the upset, the new views. Mostly we work hard at taming our emotional environment just as we work hard at taming our aesthetic environment.[74]

Placing the "I" that art challenges in scare quotes, Winterson evokes her abiding suspicion of identity. What art reveals and elicits into becoming is a subject that strives to "convince" itself of its stability. Yet art unleashes a bit of the affective chaos that subtends our provisionally "tam[ed]" emotional and aesthetic territory, inciting a productive dispersal of the subject. Consequently, Winterson insists that the affects of art are neither a subjective projection of the reader nor expressive of the authorial self. The former supports the commodification of art as "separate, Other, self-contained," and the latter contributes to the reading of art as autobiography, wherein the work narrowly "represents" the writer's identity.[75] Undoubtedly, this is a vitalistic narrative of aesthetic affect, one that generalizes "art," leaving its content unspecified and seemingly irrelevant. Yet this narrative operates as a frame to conceptualize the incipiently social becoming provoked by Winterson's own visceral aesthetics. Hence, she contrasts the structures of feeling enabled by art to those demanded by consumer culture, which engender "bodies insinuated to desire what they do not desire and ... hearts turned to stone."[76] Not only does this conceit justify Winterson's transposition of queer dissidence from sex to emotion, it also underlies her qualification that art offers "Creation" rather than "Consolation."[77] At stake in this distinction is Winterson's critique of therapeutic models for art, where aesthetic feeling is ultimately located inside the subject and the artwork merely offers comfort to the individual who retreats or escapes from "reality" into the work. The therapeutic model ignores the incipiently social relational space afforded by the artwork, and it reifies a binary between imagination and reality that Winterson's essays radically deconstruct; indeed, Winterson critiques this model for denying the affirmative agency of the work—its capacity to provoke the collective desire for change and transformation. "I think of [art] as Creation," she writes, "I think of it as an energetic space that begets energetic space. Works of art do not reproduce themselves, they re-create themselves and have at the same time sufficient permanent power to create rooms for us, the dispossessed. In other words, art makes it possible to live in energetic space."[78] Here the queerness of art emerges in its affective relationality, which is not conceived through a heteronormative language of reproductive mimesis. Rather, the work is described through a language of becoming that affords an incipiently social vision of collectivity, of a marginalized "us" that does not pre-exist the aesthetic object but comes into being through "our" affective contact with it.

We must pause to distinguish between the affective unsettling Winterson affirms via art and its putatively political effects. Although she substitutes the pleasures of art for the pleasures of sex, Winterson's investment in pleasure nonetheless exemplifies a tendency in queer writing to, in

Elizabeth Grosz's words, praise the "radicality of its sexual practices, their social transgressiveness and ability to break social taboos."[79] Grosz urges queer theory to provisionally disarticulate politics and pleasure in the sense that "engaging in whatever sexual and other pleasures one chooses may produce political effects, but it is not primarily the political that is at stake in this relation. It is instead a relation of production or assemblage, which may have political effects at particular moments, but is primarily productive or creative rather than critical."[80] In other words, politics and pleasure are both generative affective forces and are complex assemblages that intersect with regimes of power, but they are "not the same."[81] Similarly, I would suggest that the exuberant pleasure Winterson aligns with visceral aesthetics should be understood as a relation of production that is creative but not necessarily or intrinsically political—it may become so, depending on how it is activated, elaborated, and encountered. But on an ontological plane, the artwork engenders a becoming whose subjective, relational, and social effects cannot be predicted in advance and whose ultimate value must be assessed immanently, not in terms of a transcendent political project.[82] In this respect, the politics of aesthetics that Winterson describes is queer precisely insofar as it does not represent an existing political coalition or cause that requires recognition by a subject or an institution of sovereign authority; it is an assemblage of visceral forces that work on and through the porous body directly. Grosz's recent work on art understands aesthetic affect as incipiently political. She writes, "Art is intensely political not in the sense that it is a collective or community activity (which it may be but usually is not) but in the sense that it elaborates the possibilities of new, more, different sensations than those we know. Art is where the becomings of the earth couple with the becomings of life to produce intensities and sensations that in themselves summon up a new kind of life."[83] To be sure, art does not represent or conceptualize these incipient futures directly, as a decipherable content, yet its experimentation with intensity nonetheless enables those potentialities to be "affectively and perceptually anticipated."[84] In Winterson's phrasing, "Art is for us a reality beyond now. ... The reality of art is the reality of the imagination ... not the reality of experience."[85] In other words, the work of art possesses a real, yet virtual, force of affect; it is not yet experienced by a subject, nor is it representative of a subject's experience, but the work creates a relational space for the actualization of its forces as intensity.

    At stake in this visceral conception of queer aesthetics is Winterson's insistence that critics and consumers must approach art outside of the "narrow gate of subjective experience," which she laments as becoming "fashionable" again in this historical moment.[86] Indeed, Winterson claims, "If Queer culture is now working against assumptions of identity as sexuality, art gets there first, by implicitly creating emotion around the forbidden."[87] The "complex emotions" that art manifests are defined by their relation to the forbidden and their subsequent capacity to dynamize a "clash" between feeling and expectation that results in a failure of the "logical self."[88] Emotional "effrontery" works, then, to challenge the seeming stability of the subject and to redraw social expectations that fuse the subject into the real. As much as Winterson invokes Romantic discourses here, she clearly frames art's "creativity" as a deformation of the self and its values, not an authentic expression of subjectivity. One motivating reason for this narrative is that mainstream readers frequently collapse Winterson's fiction to autobiography. Indeed, Winterson rejects the tendency to reduce her fictions to her own sexual identity, and she critiques queer culture for being implicated in this interpretative project: "The Queer world has colluded in the misreading of art as sexuality. Art is difference, but not necessarily sexual difference."[89] Hence, she claims that "[f]orcing the work back into autobiography is a way of trying to contain it."[90] In Winterson's aesthetic narrative, autobiographical reading narrows the affective becoming of art, its capacity to bring new desires into being. But her critique should also be read as part of a queer opposition to the cultural codification of sexuality as identity—the tendency to read queer writers' cultural expressions as merely "representing" their own sexualities or, more broadly, an extant subculture of which they are taken to be representatives.

Winterson's challenge to sexuality as identity, and fiction as self-expression, is intimately bound up with her investment in the non-representational aesthetics of queer experimental literature. Yet her visceral aesthetics do not simply target the representational structures of identity. Winterson positions them against "[m]oney culture [which] depends on symbolic reality."[91] Indeed, Winterson suggests that realist aesthetics buttress "notional reality where goods are worth more than time and where things are more important than ideas."[92] In her view, notional reality stands in opposition to the "reality of the imagination," which she locates as the basis for her own fiction.[93] She reclaims the tradition of eighteenth-century fiction as her inspiration, a tradition that conceives of art as "play, pose and experiment."[94] She also praises the Romantics for being "emotional, introspective, visionary and very conscious of themselves as artists."[95] Together, these traditions enable her to sidestep Victorian realism and its values, which she believes mainstream contemporary literature and popular culture perpetuate. The Victorians narrowed the question of art to representation, to how it "correspond[s] to actual life," which results in a conception of art as "rational, extrovert, didactic, [and] the writer as social worker or sage."[96] The best of the Victorians (she cites Dickens) express the tension between "the dead weight of an exaggeratedly masculine culture valuing experience over imagination and action above contemplation and the strange authority of the English poetic tradition."[97]

At issue here is not the accuracy of Winterson's literary history, which could easily be critiqued for its simplification of these aesthetic movements and their periodization.[98] The point I wish to underline is that Winterson narrates this aesthetic history to legitimate her turn to queer experimental literature and to conceptualize its affective agency against approaches to the politics of aesthetics that require a mimetic relationship between the work and the world. Winterson' s rejection of realism is ultimately less about literary history or aesthetic formalism than it is tied to a critique of the aesthetic ideologies that buttress the existing structures of consumption. Thus, Winterson narrates the "realist" and the "capitalist" as possessing the same values: The realist "thinks he deals in things and not images and ... is suspicious of the abstract. ... A lover of objects and objectivity, he is in fact caught in a world of symbols and symbolism."[99] Likewise, the "symbolic man," who exemplifies the "symbolic reality" that undergirds "Money culture," is a consumer subject who confuses "the object and what the object represents. To keep you and me buying and upgrading an overstock of meaningless things depends on those things having an acquisitional value."[100] For Winterson, consumption is predicated on the unsatisfactory nature of objects: "They are wish-fulfillment nightmares where more is piled on more to manufacture the illusion of abundance. They are lands of emptiness and want. Things do not satisfy. In part they fail to satisfy because their symbolic value changes so regularly."[101] In a crucial inversion of the discourse applied to experimental writing—as too invested in the imaginary—Winterson claims that commodities are "illusion, narcotic, hallucination," whereas art offers "energetic space."[102] In effect, Winterson's spiritualist vitalism *expands* the aesthetic of illusion, what Deleuze calls the "powers of the false," to unravel the sutures that narrowly thread desire into consumption.[103] At the same time, Winterson avoids the language of desire, emphasizing emotion because it stands against the teleological narrative of *satisfaction*. Of course, satisfaction never arrives, but its impossibility perpetuates the circuit of seeking material objects to finally slake the subject's hunger. By contrast, Winterson claims that "Art is not Capitalism" because it possesses "a different rate of exchange. … energy for energy; intensity for intensity, vision for vision," which ultimately challenges a world of "passive diversions" and enables bodies to experience an expansion in capacity.[104] She insists, "[W]hat I find in [art], I may keep."[105] In other words, art offers materially immaterial value; it communicates with "living realities with the power to move" rather than abstract "symbols."[106] Winterson's aesthetic narrative positions queer experimental literature against the dispositions of consumer capitalism; she conceives of non-representational aesthetics and the investment in affect as affording a vital connection to life, even as her writing undermines essentialist notions of the real.

If abstracted from their context, Winterson's visceral aesthetics may read as naively utopian. Yet Winterson's aesthetic concepts—and, indeed, her compulsion to write a book of essays about the value of experimental writing—must not be extricated from the context of contemporary sexual politics. As José Esteban Muñoz argues, "Turning to the aesthetic in the case of queerness is nothing like an escape from the social realm, insofar as queer aesthetics map future social relations."[107] If queerness can be seen as "that thing that lets us *feel* that this world is not enough, that indeed something is missing," then Winterson's narrative of visceral aesthetics must be read against the reduction of queerness to a consumer identity.[108] We should note, after all, that Winterson composes *Art Objects* at the height of her mainstream and academic fame—at a moment when her writing had become increasingly codified as representative of lesbian fiction and queer theory alike. This codification informs her refusal to locate sexuality as a source of social becoming, and it inspires her desire to distinguish the relation afforded by visceral aesthetics from hegemonic modes of consumption. Indeed, her essays often read as a direct plea for readers to become more than mere consumers—to teach them how to read in a way that preserves and actualizes the queer potential for becoming that art affords. Whether or not Winterson's readers heard this plea, Winterson's critics chided her movement toward experimental aesthetics in *Art and Lies* (1994), a novel composed alongside of *Art Objects*. Widely denounced at the time of its publication, many critics saw *Art and Lies* as offering a hermetic vision of the aesthetic. Winterson herself describes *Art and Lies* as her most "closed" work.[109] To be sure, *Art and Lies* moves away from Winterson's more accessible mode of historical metafiction and postmodern intertextuality, although elements of these styles appear in the novel. Instead, the novel offers a complex metacommentary on the function of art in a postmodern world, and it uses a blend of experimental styles to contest the structures of feeling that make readers, critics, and the public resistant to aesthetic experimentation. As she notes in *Art Objects*, "For an experimenter these are hard times."[110] Characteristically, Winterson identifies the emotional foundation to this resistance: "The buoyancy and exuberance of the Renaissance comes out of a confidence and curiosity that we don't have. We are insecure and cynical and this makes us hostile to experiment."[111] Turning to *Art and Lies*, we can see that Winterson imagines queer experimental literature as a means to instigate queer exuberance—a disposition toward positive affect that contests the underlying fear of becoming that conjoins the resistance to experimentation with the acceptance of postmodernity's subsumption of all social relations into consumer relations.[112] As we will see, it is *through*—not in spite of—its apparently solipsistic and abstract aesthetics that *Art and Lies* provokes this queer renewal of social imagination.

THE QUEER EXUBERANCE OF *ART AND LIES*

Given Winterson's claim in *Art Objects* that art creates "flight-maps" of possibility, it is unsurprising that the three main characters of *Art and Lies* are named after artists—Handel, Picasso, and Sappho—and that each traces a line of flight from the degraded city to the rejuvenating sea.[113] To the extent that the novel has a narrative, it entails these three characters co-habiting an abstract, ethereal train "hosed in light" in "2000 AD" as it leads them to the Aegean coast.[114] They reflect in eight individual monologues on the traumas, disappointments, and desires that led them to escape the city, and meanwhile, they unknowingly exchange a bawdy eighteenth-century pornographic satire ("The Entire and Honest Recollections of a Bawd") that occasionally overtakes the diegesis. The novel concludes with the three characters recognizing one another and engaging in a brief dialogue before Handel sings on the shore and Sappho and Picasso stand together, reunited as lovers. Then the text gives ways to nine pages of untitled German musical notation from Strauss's opera *Der Rosenkavalier*.

As this summary indicates, *Art and Lies* is among Winterson's most abstract and formally experimental novels: it lacks determinate historical context—it may be the year 2000, although Sappho's explanation that AD means "After Death" rather than Anno Domini has led some critics to argue that each of the main characters are dead and on a journey to the underworld.[115] Furthermore, the novel lacks determinate characters. Sappho, for example, may or may not be the Greek poet alive in 600 BC, a woman named Nelson visiting friends at Christmas in 1997, or somehow both of these. Picasso may be, at once, Sappho's former lover and muse Sophia as well as a woman escaping her oppressive family after her father attempts to murder her. Fredric Jameson's conception of postmodern texts as "hologram[s]" aptly describes the shimmering that Winterson effects between these characters and their historical referents.[116] Short-circuiting character individuation is one of the formal tactics the novel uses to undo fixed distinctions between the imaginary and the real in the novel. By proliferating interpretive possibilities regarding character, plot, space, and time, *Art and Lies* creates what Brian McHale calls "an ontological oscillation, a flickering effect" between the text's possible worlds.[117] The novel does not choose "between alternative states of affairs" but instead leaves them radically undecidable and affirms this indeterminacy as enabling for its characters.[118] The symbolic excess generated by doubling the characters' names unmoors them from a determined place in the symbolic order. That excess, as their names suggest, is correlated with the aesthetic, thereby foregrounding the significance of art in Handel's, Picasso's, and Sappho's queer becoming beyond the patriarchal and heteronormative structures that oppress them.

Despite its diegetic undecidability, *Art and Lies* situates its narrative arc (from city to sea, from alienation to imagination) against a postmodern structure of feeling, which compels the characters' lines of flight. This context is implied through the novel's focus on urban space. In one haunting image, Winterson describes "people [who] have begun to roam in posses, looking through the city skips for a part of their past."[119] Without "personal landmarks ... they have no means to the past except through memory. Increasingly unable to remember, they have begun to invent."[120] As we will see, *Art and Lies* invests agency in imaginative invention. But here invention is a weak bulwark against the deterritorializing forces of capital that liquidate public and historical memory and replace them with the "People's Architecture."[121] This architecture is produced by "little men who like to simulate," as Handel derisively claims, and it results in what the narration calls the "cemeteries of the Dead. The box houses in yellow brick, each fastened against its neighbour. ... Rows of scuffed couches identically angled towards the identical televisions."[122] Rather than explore the immanent possibilities that lie in a multitude "fastened" together, Handel fears that the similarity of houses, couches, and televisions produces a "homogeneous people."[123] This is because, for Handel, consumerist homogeneity poses a fundamental obstacle to the individual. He laments:

> It's awkward, in a society where the cult of the individual has never been preached with greater force, and where many of our collective ills are a result of that force, to say that it is to the Self to which one must attend. But the Self is not a random collection of stray desires striving to be satisfied, nor is it only by suppressing such desires, as women are encouraged to do, that any social cohesion is possible. Our broken society is not born out of the triumph of the individual, but out of his effacement.[124]

Here *Art and Lies* foregrounds the conflicted status of the postmodern "turn to the self"—namely, that it proceeds under the same discourse of the consumerist "cult of the individual."[125] Affirmations of the self thus risk echoing the ethics of individualism, narcissism, and self-gratification that buttress consumerism. Yet Handel yearns for an alternative conception of a "Self," one not purchased through the "satisfaction" (nor the patriarchal-inflected "suppress[ion]") of desire. Although it remains unspecified by Handel, the novel's alternative will be a *production* of desire that counters the structures of feeling that efface difference to secure social cohesion.

Handel cannot imagine this alternative because he is melancholically attached to eclipsed social orders of the past. He yearns for the "systems and hierarchies" of the medieval period that provided people with fixed position and "place."[126] He laments the loss of "self-distinguishing little shops, each with its own identity and purpose. Each with customers it knew and a responsibility towards them" that are lost to the "multinational stores, that each sell the same goods, from the same markets."[127] Looking for "identity and purpose" and "place" in the globalized postmodern market, Handel turns back to social systems that are no longer available, systems that were no less oppressive, particularly for minorities, women, and the working class. In this respect, Handel evokes a dangerously conservative structure of feeling that idealizes an older version of capitalism as more "responsible" because he finds the "systems and hierarchies" of the past comforting. As *Art and Lies* underscores, Handel's nostalgia is predicated on the erosion of his own power as a priest in an age that has turned away from the institutions of religion: "Once upon a time I would have been listened to with respect, now, I am regarded with suspicion."[128] Yet Handel is also mourning for, in Freud's words, "the loss of some abstraction ... such as fatherland, liberty, an ideal."[129] Indeed, unlike Picasso and Sappho, Handel remains cathected to past definitions of "Progress, Love, Human Nature."[130] He is incapable of redefining these terms to embody new values or of recognizing that these terms have perpetuated highly oppressive relations of power. In Winterson's discussion of the novel, this is because Handel is "afraid of the brave new world as well as being conscious of it being the logical product of men like himself."[131] Indeed, Handel cannot accept that the "new brutalism of the universe" is borne from his own values.[132] Contrary, then, to Handel's desire for a "context, a perspective" to re-ground "Progress" as "not one of those floating comparatives, so beloved of our friends in advertising," the novel demonstrates how the melancholic attachment to the past can perpetuate oppression rather than engender the imagination of a more radically egalitarian future.[133]

Handel recalls the most consistent trope in Winterson's corpus—a melancholic (usually male) subject raging against modernity. Too often, critics conflate the voice of these characters with the author herself. While these characters allow Winterson to also express a critique of modernity, Winterson simultaneously rejects the subject that is attached to an unrecoverable past. Again and again, her novels narrate the awakening of these subjects to their *ressentiment*. In doing so, Winterson dramatizes the shift from passivity to activity, from critique to creation, from mourning to exuberant affirmation. This is why *Art and Lies* articulates Handel's *ressentiment* in relationship to the discourses of emotion. On the one hand, he asks the reader, "Are you happy?" aligning the paucity of positive affect with the contemporary social condition.[134] Critiquing sentimentality ("Romance. Love's counterfeit"), Handel laments a world of "Apathy. From the Greek A Pathos. Want of feeling."[135] On the other hand, he represses his own feelings of compassion for patients and parishioners, "kill[ing] in himself the starts of feeling he feared."[136] Thus, Handel is a uniquely split patriarchal subject. He can critique the Church, telling his Bishop that the "punishable sin is not lust ... It is a failure of feeling. Not an excess of passion but a lack of compassion."[137] (For this opinion, Handel is labeled a Communist and a heretic.) Yet his definition of compassion is markedly sexist. He became a doctor, he explains, because "I like to look at women ... they undress before me with a shyness I find touching. I try to keep my hands warm. I am compassionate. I do care. If a woman is particularly young or particularly beautiful, I treat her as softly as I know how."[138] Here the discourses of compassion and care are sutured to objectification. The kind of "touching" Handel offers is the opposite of the reciprocal affection that Winterson's writing affirms. Indeed, Handel refuses the touch that would demand mutual exposure. As he recalls,

> The rallying cry of the operating theatre was [also] the jest of the brothel. We had to protect ourselves. We had to be careful of the body beneath. Protection always involves some sort of loss. Hold back, watch yourself, wrap up, look for cuts, mind the blood, don't exchange fluid, Now Wash Your Hands Please. The riskiest thing you can do is to be naked with another human being.[139]

Here Winterson critiques medicine as a distinctly objectifying patriarchal discipline, insofar as the doctors fear the "body beneath" for its capacity to "*exchange* fluid."[140] The proliferation of commands—hold back, watch yourself—expresses the intense masculine anxiety the doctors feel about maintaining bodily integrity.[141] Handel recognizes that a "loss" results from this self-protection, but he nonetheless fears the ecstatic "naked[ness]" of erotic relation. Hence, when Handel falls in love with an unidentified woman who has researched the science of "Haptics," he ultimately rejects her.[142] He is "threaten[ed]" by the affective relationality she offers, by the feeling that "*her* breasts were holding [him], safe, firm, sexed."[143] Being held, reciprocally and erotically, is too threatening for Handel because it undoes the hierarchical superiority he maintains through his patriarchal transcendence of corporeality.

Art and Lies exuberantly embraces, rather than represses, exposure as a path to imagining an alternative mode of queer relationality. *Art and Lies* transposes this relation to the reciprocal energetics of "the Word." As Sappho affirms, "Out of our risk comes our safety, not the small sad life that will cling to anything because it has nothing."[144] The novel formalizes this relation of risk in Sappho's intersubjective, libidinal monologues. "Say my name and you say sex," Sappho declares, suggesting that eroticism is not sublimated into discourse but charges it viscerally.[145] In fact, her "Sexualist" discourse is the reason why the Church of Rome "burned her poems and excommunicated her," never granting her a pardon: "The Word terrifies. The seducing word, the insinuating word, the word that leads the trembling hand to the forbidden key. ... The word that does not repent."[146] Sappho's language—reciprocal, seductive, penetrative, infective, unrepentant—is the rhetorical analogue of Winterson's queer exuberance precisely because it tethers positive affect to an affirmation of becoming. She refuses the reactive negativity that "cling[s]" to a "small sad life," perpetuating the status quo out of fear and insecurity.[147] At the same time, Sappho's language exemplifies queer experimental literature's investment in forms of writing that map the affective relations of reading onto an incipiently social imaginary. Note, for example, that Winterson critiques modernist experimentation as resulting in an elitist "private language."[148] Describing her alternative approach to experimental aesthetics, Winterson qualifies: "Lover's talk? yes. Private language? no."[149] The difference between them, Winterson claims, is that "[a]rt is intimacy, lover's talk, and yet it is a public declaration."[150] Although framed as talk between lovers, then, Sappho's language functions as an incipiently social relation—it performs intimacy as an intersubjective seduction, yet it extends this erotic relation to the reader in the hopes that a public "you" will embrace the becoming offered by the text's affective exposure.

Sappho's monologues intensify relational affection through their complex use of the grammar of the second person, which suspends readers between the intimate and the public. At one moment, Sappho demands, "Cut me. You do. You cut me down in heavy trusses, profusion, exhaustion, and soak me in a stream of love."[151] At another, she insists, "Read me. Read me now. Words in your mouth that will modify your gut. Words that will become you."[152] The push and pull enacted between these commands exemplifies the way Sappho's reciprocal discourse affects her and her addressee: the words affectively become "you," and she is likewise "soak[ed]" in love. At the level of narrative, Sappho's second-person address seems to imply that Picasso is Sophia, Sappho's former muse and lover, and that Sophia is her actual addressee. But on a formal level, the second person address interpellates the reader, hollowing out a space in the shifter "you" for the reader to inhabit as the novel's direct addressee. Sappho's repeated injunction to "Read me," for example, is a performative command that traverses the metaleptic space between the fiction and the reader's world, and it underlines this dynamism by claiming that the words "will become you." McHale argues that metaleptic discourses in postmodern fiction "seduce" readers by "reach[ing] across an ontological divide to become a force to reckon with in the reader's real world."[153] While "[m]odernist aesthetics ... all but eliminates the explicit *you*," postmodern fiction frequently exploits it, "*modeling* ... erotic relations through foregrounded violations of ontological boundaries."[154] Thus, the grammar of the second person performs love as "less an object of representation than a *meta*object, less a theme than a *meta*theme."[155] Through the discourse of seduction, Sappho's "you" crosses the divides of self and other, fiction and reality, performing a metagrammar of queer relationality.

Of course, Sappho's lover's talk exemplifies what many readers describe as the disconcerting sentimentality of Winterson's writing. In her otherwise positive review of *The Stone Gods*, for example, Ursula K. Le Guin notes that the novel is "distressingly sentimental," qualifying that "[s]entimentality, the product of a gap between the emotionality of the writing and the emotion actually roused in the reader, is very much a matter of the reader's sensibility."[156] But what if the "gap" that Le Guin critiques is a carefully constructed *effect* of Winterson's fiction? What if this feeling of emptiness is, perversely, the performative point of Winterson's affective reading? In Le Guin's view, Winterson's writing does not actually dramatize the emotionality it so desperately invokes in its breathless incantatory prose. Of course, this assessment is, as she notes, partly a matter of the reader's sensibility. Yet Winterson's writing is emotionally unsatisfying if the reader seeks emotional catharsis, or a "rous[ing]" of sensual experience, from the characters or plot. This is not simply due to Winterson's resistance to narrative realism, which results in plots that speed up into a disappointing anti-climax of irresolution. Rather, it is tied to her deeper project to detach the affective norms that suture readerly expectation to narrative desire. In disappointing these expectations, Winterson contests the demand that any aesthetic object satisfy our yearnings. Unlike a consumer object, the aesthetic object thus retains a certain irreducibility to the reader's desire, while also affirming an excessive incompleteness that stems from the aesthetic's immanent production of desire. This is why so many of Winterson's novels are addressed to a "you" that takes on many possible referents but is never, finally, stabilized. In Sappho's monologues, the "you" may be the reader, Sophia, the entirety of literary history, or any number of other possible addressees. The grammar of the second person is the correlative of Winterson's queer exuberance, then, because few words so immediately collapse the distance between reader and text without, at the same time, representing a specific subject or identity. This is due to the strange queerness that emerges in reading "you." Used with frequency, you rebounds onto the I. I and you begin to tremble and lose their distinctive referents. You becomes open to us, the incipiently social public that lover's talk conjures. But you is also abstract, empty of content, more a placeholder for a relation to come than a person that exists.

(After all, we cannot all fit into you, and you cannot possibly be meant for all of us.) Reading in the second person, if taken to such extremes, produces a grammatical solecism, where you and I begin to reveal their (or our) transgressive impropriety as pronouns, and the reader is no longer certain of where the textual bodies of you begin and I end. The generality of Winterson's second person projects these relations outwards, offering these relations to readers as affective potentiality. Of course, Winterson stacks the deck, because the text reads us into affective being before we have time to consciously decide how to respond. Recall that becoming "readable" in *Written on the Body* meant becoming affectively readable in the hands of another against the narrator's avowed desire to remain hermeneutically illegible. Similarly, Winterson's readers find that they are no longer holding a book in their hands. Instead, the book is holding them. We are, akin to Handel, held "safe, firm, sexed" by the text's "reading hands."[157] Perhaps at this moment, we discover that there is no need for us to "queer" the text because the text has already been queering us.

One could argue that the second person merely gives the appearance of false intimacy, mystifying interpellation as an erotic communion and furthering a logocentric fantasy of linguistic self-presence. Yet the purpose of Winterson's second person is to contest the apparent immediacy and self-enclosure of the subject. As Picasso claims:

> The freedom of the individual is the freedom to die without ever being moved by anything. What can pierce the thick wall of personality; your voice, your hand, a picture, a book, the sweet morning air? Myself imprisons me ... I think therefore I am. Does that mean 'I feel therefore I'm not'? But only through feeling can I get at thinking. Those things that move me challenge me. Only a seismic shock can re-order the card index of habit, prejudice and other people's thoughts that I call my own.[158]

Here the shock of affect re-orders the card index of the self, but it does not unveil a more authentic or immediate self. On the contrary, affect precedes consciousness and, in particular, the fictive enclosures of personality. As Handel insists, "None of us is Rousseau Man, that noble savage, honest and untrained. Better to acknowledge that what we are is what we have been taught, that done, at least it will be possible to choose our own teacher."[159] Anticipating the pedagogy of feeling affirmed in *The Stone Gods*, *Art and Lies* critiques the melancholic desire to return to an original self. In Jacques Derrida's words, the "lost or impossible presence of the absent origin" often results in "the saddened, *negative*, nostalgic, guilty Rousseauistic side of the thinking of play."[160] Derrida suggests that "other side [of play] would be the Nietzschean *affirmation*, that is the joyous affirmation of the play of the world and of the innocence of becoming, the affirmation of a world of signs without fault, without truth, and without origin."[161] Broaching this affirmation late in the narrative, Handel affirms: "Speak Parrot! ... I know that what I am is quite the opposite of an individual. But if the parrot is to speak, let him be taught by a singing master."[162] Here Handel begins to shake off the "nostalgic, guilty" feeling of loss for a non-existent original self, and instead, he desires to be taught to sing—to become otherwise through an economy of aesthetic affection that relies on the subject's inherent inauthenticity. This alternative economy of relation is signified by the novel's title. Rather than substituting "art" for "truth" as the binary opposite of "lies," the novel brackets truth altogether. In its place, Winterson offers *two different modes of fiction: lies*, which seek control and dominance over the other in a fruitless retrenchment of the self; and *art*, which embraces the self's inauthenticity as a condition of queer becoming.

Picasso's narrative exemplifies the political stakes that underlie this aesthetic pedagogy. Throughout her life, Picasso's family codifies her within their representations, telling her, "This is you," and "los[ing] their temper" when Picasso does not "recognize" herself in their (literal) drawings.[163] Seeking to escape their representations, Picasso yearns to step "out of the stoked-up conspiracy to lie" that encloses her family.[164] The conspiracy of lies concerns her brother, Matthew, who, until Picasso is 15, uses her "as a cesspit for his bloated adolescence," raping her "night after night."[165] Against the violence and insanity of her childhood, it is the "strange vital yellows of Van Gogh that bore out a sane place in the babble of that overbright world."[166] When Picasso's brother rapes her, she "clung to life through a patch of red" that is "on a Leonardo robe."[167] As these moments suggest, art provides a site for Picasso's self-preservation in the midst of trauma. But it also enables her to create a new relation to her self and her body. Although she has "learned to hate her body because he [Matthew] said he had loved it," Picasso also "wondered if she would ever feel the acute sensuality she saw in pictures. Things of canvas and paint, not flesh and blood, they told her of a fire she did not know. She would find it or light it in herself."[168] Here art provides a sensual intimation of a future that cannot be gleaned through the flesh and blood of her material body in the present. One way that Picasso begins to light this "acute sensuality" in her self is through her painting.[169] Picasso paints at night in her father's preservatives factory, appropriating the factory's space of production and its commodities: "Denied paints she painted in mustard ... [a]gainst the blank crates, plastic-wrapped pallets and vinegar vats."[170] Although the "factory clock ticked factory minutes," the "white disc of light" created by the inspection lamp she uses to illuminate her work wards off the "vampire dark" around her.[171] In this illuminated space, Picasso's visceral aesthetics begin to engender an incipient future, one whose temporality cannot be consigned to the restrictions of her present or the temporal order of consumption represented by the embalmed artificiality of the preservatives factory.

The aesthetic style of Picasso's painting poses a challenge to the realist aesthetics that her father adores. "My father had often encouraged me to paint likeness," Picasso recalls;[172] and like his son, who "only ever draws himself," Sir Jack's preference for (self-)representational art extends to the 55 self-portraits that he has commissioned, including the "oil portrait of [himself] in military uniform" that hangs over the family parlor as an ominous reminder of his authoritarian power.[173] Where Freud infamously aligns narcissism with homosexuality, Winterson re-maps narcissism onto heteronormativity and patriarchy, suggesting that the drive to reproduce "likeness" underlies their concomitant refusals of queer becoming.[174] Notably, *Art and Lies* suggests that queerness must also embrace a relation to sexual difference. Not only does Sappho proclaim that "language is rich when it is fed from difference," the novel critiques Cardinal Rosso's affirmation of male castration as the utopian solution to transcending sexual difference.[175] Without the knowledge or permission of his parents, Rosso persuades young Handel to be castrated as a young boy because it "[r]eturn[s] to a man his femininity and the problem of Woman disappears. The perfect man. Male and Female He created him."[176] One could argue that Winterson stigmatizes male homosexuality here and flatly positions it against a positively figured lesbianism (via the erotic relationship between Sappho and Picasso). Yet the satirical target of the Handel narrative is the castration plot that underlies Freudian notions of heterosexual differentiation. First, Handel's castration desexes him. As a result, castration does not insert him into the economy of heterosexual and phallic identification. Instead, it creates the conditions of possibility for his homoerotic love affair with Cardinal Rosso. Second, Handel's entry into the social order is purchased by the literal loss of his homosexual love object. This loss is uncannily consistent with Butler's revision of the Freudian

narrative, which underscores the ego's melancholic attachment to its foreclosed homosexual identifications.[177] Significantly, *Art and Lies* does not
resolve Handel's melancholia by re-uniting him with the woman that he
briefly loved. To do so would imply that the heterosexual economy and
nuclear family offer a reparative resolution of homosexual trauma. Such
a resolution would deny the violence that these structures of relation
themselves engender, and it would also disavow, quite simply, Handel's
love for Rosso. Thus, the moment of queer exuberance arrives for Handel
when he, much like Picasso, can again practice the art that he had once
forsaken. Singing represents Handel's embrace of his eunuch body in its
queer specificity, and it condenses the novel's earnest refusal to answer
the question: "Which cut did the harm? His [Rosso's] or theirs [Handel's
parents]?"[178] By leaving this question unanswered, *Art and Lies* tentatively
affirms the "enchanted space" of queer relationality that Handel experiences with Rosso, which teaches him to love opera and the playfulness of
art's unrepentantly false invention of life rather than its truthful representation of actuality.[179]

Ultimately, *Art and Lies* affirms the non-referentiality of Rosso's,
Sappho's, and Picasso's affective aesthetics as the means for fostering an
inventive becoming. Indeed, Sappho declares that she wants to "love the
image and not the idol."[180] Sappho suggests that the image is "stamped
upon the retina, repeated behind the eyelid, stored in the rhomenceph-
alon [sic], returned to the body in injections of emotion."[181] In other
words, an art of the image viscerally imprints the body rather than signifying the actual. Sappho distills the implications of this non-representational
aesthetic when she proclaims, "I'm no Freudian. What is remembered is
not a deed in stone but a metaphor. Meta = above. Pherein = to carry.
That which is carried above the literalness of life. A way of thinking that
avoids the problems of gravity."[182] Inspired by the transcendent lightness
of metaphor, Sappho calls for "art, that never concerns itself with the actu-
alities of life, neither depicts it as we think it is, nor expresses it as we hope
it is, and yet becomes it. Not representations, but inventions that bear in
themselves the central forces of the world, and not only the world."[183] We
should take pause at the stark rejection of actuality pronounced here. To
articulate this vision of art, Sappho troublingly opposes art to the political: "Art. The invisible city not calculated to exist. Beyond the lofty pretensions of the merely ceremonial, long after the dramatic connivings of
political life, like it or not, it remains."[184] Here Sappho transforms the
distressing social conditions depicted earlier in the novel into a metaphor
by making the "invisible" city of vanishing, abject, and impoverished

people into the city of "art" that outlives the political world. It is under-standable, then, why critics might read Winterson's vision of art as an escape from the political into the eternal. Yet Sappho's affirmation of non-representational art insists that the aesthetic's affective forces contribute to an incipiently social becoming that outstrips the existing codifications (the pretensions, ceremonies, and dramas) of the political world—it does not depict or express the world "*and yet becomes it.*"[185] It is important to remember that, as Davide Panagia argues, "the first political act is also an aesthetic one, a partitioning of sensation that divides the body and its organs of sense perception and assigns to them corresponding capacities for the making of sense."[186] Insofar as aesthetic sensations "disfigure" this political ordering of the body's perception, they shake us from the "slumber of subjectivity" and "invite occasions and actions for reconfiguring our associational lives."[187] While Sappho may reject a representational politics of aesthetics, then, her visceral aesthetics are therefore no less bound up with a commitment to reconfiguring the affective politics of the body and the body politic.

Art and Lies makes evident the political significance of the sensual reconfiguration of association in the effect that Picasso's painting has on her family. On Christmas, Picasso paints once the family has gone to sleep. As a consequence of her painting, the family, their mansion, and the land-scape become suffused with color. Her mother, for example, wakes up with dreams of a former lover, "rear[ing] up from her matrimonial sheets, infidelity colouring her cheeks."[188] Indeed, the entire family is affected: "Uncles, aunts, cousins, in-laws, all the weights and ephemera of family life, were dreaming in colour that night."[189] In the morning, the family wears "their darkest clothes, their soberest expressions, they whispered like church wardens," although the "stain" of color nonetheless clings to them.[190] "They were spotted with guilt, each could see in the other, the patterns of infection."[191] Picasso's painting unleashes the queer truths of the family, which they "colluded" in denying despite seeing one another's "infection."[192] Embodying the patriarchal fear of affective exposure, the family seeks to repress the stains of color; they go so far as to deny the liter-ally disfigured reality around them—the orange rain, the purple snow and clouds, the plum-colored tea. Picasso's painting disarticulates their modes of perception and, in the process, opens up the possibility for the family to realign their relational structures with one another, with themselves, and with their narratives—to recognize rather than repress the erotic truths to which the now crimson-stained bedding attests. With a great deal of effort, however, their collusion maintains the heteronormative and patriarchal structure of power, perception, and association. This is not the case for Picasso. "Paint[ing] herself out of the night" disjoins her, however briefly, from the strictures of the nuclear family, making possible an act of self-dislocation and creation: "Without thinking, Picasso ran into the parlour, into the newspapers, into the best clothes and the dead air. She was painted from head to foot. 'Self portrait,' she said to their astonished faces."[193]

The becoming afforded through aesthetic disarticulation is accompanied by the danger of betrayal. In part, the dangers are physical, such as the family's committing Picasso to an asylum. When she says she's "going to tell the police" about the sexual assaults committed by her brother, her father pushes her off the roof, possibly to her death.[194] Yet disarticulation also presents an ethical danger for Picasso, which arises in her response to her father's attempted murder. She decides to kill her father in turn, stabbing, shooting, gassing, melting him, and feeding him to dogs. As a result of these actions—which do not appear to have an effect on her father—Picasso experiences a new affective state:

> I breathed hate, ate hate, plumped up hate for my nightly pillow, I felt a strange numbness, new to my body. In my efforts to be rid of him, I was becoming like him, his rage, his misery, his methods, his pain circulating my veins. The more I hated him the better I pleased him. Not only would I become like him, I would become him, that is how the dead reproduce themselves.[195]

The interpretative question—Is Picasso dead or isn't she?—must not be stabilized here so as to maintain the narrative's point that Picasso's father is (emotionally) dead. "All this I did but he would not die. Impossible to murder the dead."[196] At issue, then, is the risk that the moment of aesthetic disarticulation will result in *ressentiment*, which reproduces sameness and traps the subject in a cycle of negation. Picasso begins to become like her father, adopting his affective dispositions—rage, misery, pain—which counterintuitively produce "numbness" in her body. Ultimately, Picasso realizes that to resist her father *and* to prevent becoming him, she must do "What already hurt him most of all," namely, to throw "life in his face" and to insult "his morbidissima by refusing to be of his clan. The dead thrive only among their own."[197]

By refusing the "clan" of the dead, Picasso rejects the heteronormative family's reproduction of sameness and discovers the possibility of "[m]ore life into a time without boundaries."[198] This temporality affords "[a] beginning outside of hurt. A beginning outside of fear," but it is important to underscore that this is not a utopian outside that transcends or disavows the past.[199] At stake in the novel's final sentence—"It was not too late"—is the possibility of not compulsively repeating the past or melancholically yearning for its return but of creating a new relation to the past.[200] Indeed, in the final moments of the novel, a great deal of memory is quickly revealed for the characters. Yet rather than producing a narrative epiphany for readers, the conclusion is strangely opaque and anticlimactic. For example, we see "[s]quares and circles of light that dropped through the cut clouds and made single sense of all the broken pieces of beach, cliff, man and boat. His [Handel's] past, his life, not fragments nor fragmented now, but a long curve of movement that he began to recognize."[201] Although the narration suggests that these abstract figures and their relation now make a "single sense," we do not have interpretative access to its meaning.[202] Of course, this moment recalls Sappho's coy questions: "Am I making any sense? No?"[203] By making rational sense inaccessible, Winterson holds open the possibility that *Art and Lies*'s visceral aesthetics might, like Picasso's, make new sensual associations emerge for her readers. At the same time, the novel makes clear that Handel's new relation to his past enables him to exuberantly affirm, rather than disavow, the irreducible trauma that imprints his queer body. After Handel's vision, "He began to sing. He sang *from the place that had been marked*; the book, his body, his heart. The place where grief had been hid, not once, but many times. His voice was strong and light. The sun was under his tongue. He was a man of infinite space."[204] Despite Winterson's insistence that "art is not therapy" but an "engagement with life itself," it might appear that *Art and Lies* offers a straightforward reparation of the self's trauma rather than a more substantive re-imagination of the social world.[205] But note the hesitation in the novel's concluding narration: "From the cliff-head, the two women [Picasso and Sappho] standing together, looked out. Or did they look in?"[206] Here the queer lovers face an affective Möbius strip: looking out, they look inward; looking in, they look outward to others. Of course, we cannot forget that the tentative communion among the three protagonists is enabled by their escape from the city of actuality into this fantastical scene of aesthetic invention, where they are freed from the constraints of mimesis and can finally stand together. As Sappho and Picasso listen to Handel's singing, the narration describes the scene around them: "Held in the frame of light, was *not the world, nor its likeness, but a strange equivalence*, where what was thought to be known was re-cast, and where what was unknown began to be revealed, and where what could not be known, kept its mystery but lost its terror."[207] This moment underlines the queer exuberance that emerges through Winterson's visceral aesthetics: the recasting of the known enables an unpredictable relation of becoming that is no longer experienced with terror or fear but is also not reducible to subjective calculation or conscious rationalization. The aesthetic relation of "strange equivalence" is an apt analogue for queer experimental literature more broadly, which invests in the liminal, non-representational scene of the imaginary to escape heteronormative codifications of its present. The affirmation that it is "not too late" is thus held out for readers as well as its characters, in the hopes that we might exuberantly open ourselves to a queer relation that cannot be written as likeness, only felt through waves of sensation that emerge through aesthetic disfigurations of the known.[208]

WHY BE NORMAL WHEN YOU COULD BE HAPPY?

Of course, the potential for disappointment haunts any discourse of affirmation, and the political stakes of disappointment are acute. Recall that in her critique of uncritical exuberance, Butler worries that if Obama does not satisfy the public's "nearly messianic expectation[s]" for his presidency, "we will punish him mercilessly when he fails us (or we will find ways to deny or suppress that disappointment in order to keep alive the experience of unity and unambivalent love)."[209] Butler cannot see other responses to the frustration of hope; in her narrative, disappointment only engenders manic and sadistic denial. This is partly due to the appropriation of psychoanalysis in critical theory, which largely conceives of positive affects as codifying unambivalent identifications with normative ideals.[210] This is why Edelman, for example, opposes queerness to the "seamless coherence of the Symbolic [Order]."[211] Indeed, he defines politics itself as the "struggle to effect a fantasmatic order of reality in which the subject's alienation would vanish into the seamlessness of identity."[212] In his narrative, exuberance seals us within an illusory fantasy world, chasing an impossible narcissistic unity, and the purpose of queer critique, achieved through the "corrosive force of queer irony," is to unravel the seams of the symbolic order.[213]

But what if queerness also has an affirmative mode? What if, in addition to unraveling and critiquing, queerness also weaves Ariadne-like threads for others to follow? What if it intimates potentialities for relation that have been obstructed within the collective present? Through what language would such an affirmative mode of queerness speak? What language could expose us to the relational potentialities of queerness and make possible our affirmation of this becoming? This chapter has argued that queer exuberance provides such an idiom for Winterson, enabling her to reconfigure the postmodern structure of feeling that restricts the agency of queer aesthetics to the representation of a codified and commodified identity. However, as I conclude, it is necessary to underscore that queer exuberance is neither utopian nor unambivalent in the ways that Butler and Edelman might critique. This is because queer exuberance emerges from within the conditions of homophobic repression, and its glimpses of futurity never disavow the indelible and enabling imprint of trauma. Consider, as a final example, the scene that inspires the title of Winterson's 2011 memoir, *Why Be Happy When You Could Be Normal?*[214] Horrified by her discovery of her daughter's lesbianism, Mrs. Winterson asks, "Jeanette, will you tell me why?"[215] Jeanette responds, "When I am with [my lover] I am happy. Just happy."[216] Her mother "nodded. She seemed to understand and I thought, really, for that second, that she would change her mind, that we would talk, that we would be on the same side of the glass wall. I waited. She said, 'Why be happy when you could be normal?'"[217] The subordinate clauses prolong Jeanette's hope for a relation of understanding with her mother. Yet her mother's question frustrates this anticipation of immediacy and reciprocity. In Mrs. Winterson's binary logic, queer happiness and heterosexual normality are fundamentally opposed. For her, happiness indicates social abnormality and a thoroughgoing commitment to eternal damnation. By contrast, Jeanette's idiom of happiness is queerly opaque—she does not fantasize a redemptive future where the self will be narcissistically satisfied. Rather, to borrow Muñoz's phrasing, Jeanette's feeling of "just" happiness in the present offers an "anticipatory illumination" of so many "varied potentialities"[218]: a future without the "glass wall" that reductively divides sexuality into normative and queer; a future where her love will be seen as "just"; a future where her happiness can be "just" happiness, without an immoral or suspicious underside. The visceral intimation of being "just happy" combines with the performative declaration of "just happiness," and together, they point toward incipiently social futures worth pursuing.

While queer exuberance affirms the becoming of an alternative economy of relation, its futures are not experienced unambivalently.[219] Indeed, as the memoir attests, Jeanette never forgets her traumatic past, nor does she ever imagine that she has reached the fulfillment of sexual liberation. Rather, she affirms the "wound" of homophobia, noting that "the healed wound is not the disappeared wound; there will always be a scar."[220] The affirmation of the "healed wound" is an ambivalent affirmation of queer history in its necessity and its inexorable writing on the body. Yet it is also a genuine affirmation of queer potentiality—of finding ways to re-read scars to enable their own affective becomings. Indeed, happiness tentatively unburdens Jeanette, enabling her to escape her repressive upbringing and to yearn for something more than the reproduction of normality. This is why Winterson—recalling Sappho's grammar of the second person—repeats her mother's question, extending it outward to her readers. The title asks us: "Why be happy when you could be normal?" and Winterson leaves the answer in abeyance. By doing so, she opens a relational space for us to affirm a future where queerness and happiness cannot be reactively and reductively opposed to one another, a future where queerness charts an entirely new field of affective relation.

Notes

1. Jeanette Winterson, *Written on the Body* (New York: Vintage, 1992). I use the plural pronoun here to preserve the queerness of the narrator's gender opacity and potentiality, which cannot ultimately be conceived within a binary model of sexual difference.
2. Ibid., 89.
3. See, for example, Leigh Gilmore, "Without Names: An Anatomy of Absence in Jeanette Winterson's *Written on the Body*," in *The Limits of Autobiography: Trauma and Testimony* (Ithaca: Cornell University Press, 2001), 120–42; Lisa Moore, "Teledildonics: Virtual Lesbians in the Fiction of Jeanette Winterson," in *Sexy Bodies: The Strange Carnalities of Feminism*, eds. Elizabeth Grosz and Espeth Probyn (London: Routledge, 1995), 104–27; and Laura Doan, "Jeanette Winterson's Sexing the Postmodern," in *The Lesbian Postmodern*, ed. Laura Doan (New York: Columbia University Press, 1994), 137–55. For relevant readings of lesbian sexuality and queer desire in Winterson's fiction, see Gemma Lopez, *Seductions in Narrative: Subjectivity and Desire in the Works of Angela Carter and Jeanette Winterson* (Youngstown: Cambria Press, 2007); and Madelyn Detloff, "Living in 'Energetic Space': Jeanette Winterson's Bodies and Pleasures," *English Language Notes* 45, no. 2 (2007): 149–59.
4. For approaches to Winterson's ethics that diverge from mine, see Andrew Gibson, *Postmodernity, Ethics, and the Novel: From Leavis to Levinas* (London: Routledge, 1999), 25–53; and Chloë Taylor Merleau, "Postmodern Ethics and the Expression of Differends in the Novels of Jeanette Winterson," *Journal of Modern Literature* 26, no. 3/4 (2003): 84–102.

5. On homonormativity, see Lisa Duggan, *The Twilight of Equality?: Neoliberalism, Cultural Politics, and the Attack on Democracy* (Boston: Beacon Press, 2003).

6. As an example of this discourse, see the popular #*Loveisloveproject*, accessed August 5, 2016, http://loveisloveproject.org.

7. See Sara Ahmed, *The Promise of Happiness* (Durham: Duke University Press, 2010).

8. My use of the phrase "positive affect" highlights the affective discourses through which political claims are articulated, and it challenges the assumption that affirmative discourses cannot mobilize critical forms of political imagination.

9. Sarah Schulman, *The Gentrification of the Mind: Witness to a Lost Imagination* (Berkeley: University of California Press, 2012). Compared to the United States, Schulman notes, "England seems like the promised land" for lesbian literature (151). Writing of Winterson and Sarah Waters, "They are published by the most mainstream publishers, are represented by high-rolling agents, are reviewed in regular newspapers by real critics, contextualized with other British intellectuals, given mainstream awards, have their stories broadcast on television and as a result of all this respect and consideration, they are read by a broad constituency in England and the rest of the world."

10. Elaine Showalter, "Eternal Triangles: Jeanette Winterson's *The.Powerbook* is Lost in Cyberspace," *The Guardian*, September 1, 2000, accessed August 5, 2016, https://www.theguardian.com/books/2000/sep/02/fiction.jeanettewinterson1.

11. Sonya Andermahr, "Reinventing the Romance," in *Jeanette Winterson*, ed. Sonya Andermahr (New York: Continuum, 2007), 97.

12. On Winterson's reclamation of romance as an ethics, see Jean-Michel Ganteau, "Hearts Object: Jeanette Winterson and the Ethics of Absolutist Romance," in *Refracting the Canon in Contemporary British Literature and Film*, eds. Susana Onega and Christian Gutleben (Amsterdam: Rodopi, 2004), 165–85; and Chapter 5 of Andrea L. Harris, *Other Sexes: Rewriting Difference from Woolf to Winterson* (Albany: State University of New York Press, 2000). For a sharp critique of Winterson's lover's discourse, see Lisa Moore, "Teledildonics." For a comprehensive survey of love within Winterson's corpus, see Julie Ellam, *Love in Jeanette Winterson's Novels* (Amsterdam: Rodopi, 2010).

13. For a brilliant reading of Winterson's resistance to autobiographical reading, see Gilmore, "Without Names."

14. On "gay pragmatism" and the reduction of queerness to the "here and now," see José Esteban Muñoz, *Cruising Utopia: The Then and There of Queer Futurity* (New York: New York University Press, 2009).

15. Judith Butler, "Uncritical Exuberance," *Indybay*, November 5, 2008, accessed August 5, 2016, https://www.indybay.org/newsitems/2008/11/05/18549195.php.

16. Ibid.

17. Ibid.

18. Ibid.

19. Ibid.

20. Ibid.

21. Judith Butler, "Critically Queer," in *Bodies That Matter: On the Discursive Limits of "Sex"* (New York: Routledge, 1993), 223–42.

22. Judith Butler, *Precarious Life: The Powers of Mourning and Violence* (New York: Verso, 2004), 22.

23. For her critique of affirmative approaches to affect, see Judith Butler, *Subjects of Desire: Hegelian Reflections in Twentieth-Century France* (New York: Columbia University Press, 1987): 205–17; and *Undoing Gender* (New York: Routledge, 2004), 174–203.

24. More recent queer criticism has begun to challenge this reluctance, reconsidering the epistemological, aesthetic, hermeneutic, temporal, and historiographical potentialities afforded through optimism, pleasure, empathy, happiness, and joy. See, for example, Michael D. Snediker, *Queer Optimism: Lyric Personhood and Other Felicitous Persuasions* (Minneapolis: University of Minnesota Press, 2009); José Esteban Muñoz, *Cruising Utopia: The Then and There of Queer Futurity* (New York: New York University Press, 2009); Elizabeth Freeman, *Time Binds: Queer Temporalities, Queer Histories* (Durham: Duke University Press, 2010); Eve Kosofsky Sedgwick, *Touching Feeling: Affect, Pedagogy, Performativity* (Durham: Duke University Press, 2003); and Eve Kosofksy Sedgwick, *The Weather in Proust*, ed. Jonathan Goldberg (Durham: Duke University Press, 2011).

25. Sedgwick, *Touching*, 149.

26. See Lee Edelman, "Compassion's Compulsion," *No Future: Queer Theory and the Death Drive* (Durham: Duke University Press, 2004), 67–109.

27. Sara Ahmed, *The Promise of Happiness* (Durham: Duke University Press, 2010). Also see Lauren Berlant, *Cruel Optimism* (Durham: Duke University Press, 2011), which similarly stresses the way that positive affects fuse subjects to normative attachments that obstruct queer flourishing.

28. Snediker, *Queer Optimism*, 30.

29. On the politics of affirmation, see Michael Hardt, *Gilles Deleuze: An Apprenticeship in Philosophy* (Minneapolis: University of Minnesota Press, 1993).

30. See, for example, Ann Cvetkovich, *An Archive of Feelings: Trauma, Sexuality, and Lesbian Public Cultures* (Durham: Duke University Press, 2003); Heather Love, *Feeling Backward: Loss and the Politics of Queer History* (Cambridge: Harvard University Press, 2009); *Loss*, eds. David Eng and David Kazanjian, (Berkeley: University of California Press, 2003); and Douglas Crimp, *Melancholia and Moralism: Essays on AIDS and Queer Politics* (Cambridge: MIT Press, 2002).

31. See Duggan, *Twilight*; Michael Warner, "Something Queer about the Nation-State," *Publics and Counterpublics* (New York: Zone Books, 2002), 209–24; and Jasbir Puar, *Terrorist Assemblages: Homonationalism in Queer Times* (Durham: Duke University Press, 2007).

32. For an alternative philosophy of queerness rooted in the affective volatil- ity of the body, see the work of Elizabeth Grosz, particularly *Space, Time, and Perversion: Essays on the Politics of Bodies* (New York: Routledge, 1995); and *Time Travels: Feminism, Nature, Power* (Durham: Duke University Press, 2005), which contests the Hegelian tradition that underlies much of queer theory's politics of performativity.

33. Butler, *Bodies*, 237.

34. E.L. McCallum and Mikko Tuhkanen, "Becoming Unbecoming: Untimely Meditations," in *Queer Times, Queer Becomings*, eds. E.L. McCallum and Mikko Tuhkanen, (Albany: State University of New York Press, 2011), 12.

35. Brian Massumi, *Parables of the Virtual: Movement, Affect, Sensation* (Durham: Duke University Press, 2002), 7.

36. On rethinking ideology critique after affect, see Sharon Marcus and Stephen Best, "Surface Reading: An Introduction," *Representations* 108, no. 1 (2009): 1–21.

37. Lauren Berlant, "The Subject of True Feeling: Pain, Privacy, and Politics," in *Cultural Pluralism, Identity Politics, and the Law*, eds. Austin Sarat and Thomas R. Kearns (Ann Arbor: University of Michigan Press, 1999), 77, original emphasis.

38. Ibid. Berlant's recent work in *Cruel Optimism* complicates this binary between affect and ideology, particularly in her approach to fantasy as a mode of apprehending the entwinement of the somatic, the subjective, and the social. However, the stress of Berlant's argument falls on how affect operates as a force of "structural causality" in determining subjec- tivity (15). While I agree that affect attaches subjects to oppressive ide- ologies and social structures, I also stress the pre-subjective, pre-attached dynamism of affect. By doing so, I underscore the contemporary biopo- litical investment in affect as a visceral and pre-discursive force to exploit as well as the concomitant possibilities for redirecting these forces through affect, thereby creating attachments that are not necessarily equivalent to those enforced by structures of oppression. Thus, I echo

186   T. BRADWAY

Berlant's hesitation about proclaiming which "specific experiential modes of emotional reflexivity, if any, are especially queer, cool, resistant, revolutionary, or not" (13). Yet I believe that critical theory's tendency to read positive affect as normative demands a provisional willingness to locate critical and agonistic relations that contemporary queer culture foments through the forces and idioms of positive affect.

39. Michael Hardt and Antonio Negri, *Empire* (Cambridge: Harvard University Press, 2000), 22–41, 292–94. For an approach to queerness and late capitalism that diverges from mine, see Rosemary Hennessy, *Profit and Pleasure: Sexual Identities in Late Capitalism* (New York: Routledge, 2000).

40. Fredric Jameson, *Postmodernism, or the Cultural Logic of Late Capitalism* (Durham: Duke UP, 1990), 16.

41. On the micropolitics of affect, see Elizabeth Grosz, "(Inhuman) Forces: Power, Pleasure, and Desire," in *Time Travels*, 185–96.

42. For a relevant reflection on critical theory's structure of feeling, see Bruno Latour, "Why Has Critique Run Out of Steam? From Matters of Fact to Matters of Concern," *Critical Inquiry* 30, no. 2 (2004): 225–48. See also Massumi, *Parables*, 12–21; and Jennifer Doyle, *Hold It Against Me: Difficulty and Emotion in Contemporary Art* (Durham: Duke University Press, 2013).

43. Wendy Brown, "Resisting Left Melancholia," in *Loss*, eds. David L. Eng and David Kazanjian (Berkeley: University of California Press, 2003), 458–65.

44. Ibid., 464.

45. Ibid., 460.

46. Ibid., 464.

47. Ibid.

48. Berlant, "Subject," 77.

49. On the present as an impasse, see Berlant, *Cruel*, 1–22 and 191–222.

50. See David Harvey, *A Brief History of Neoliberalism* (Oxford: Oxford University Press, 2005).

51. Jeanette Winterson, *The Stone Gods* (Boston: Mariner Books, 2007). For an extended analysis of *The Stone Gods* that addresses the tension between Billie's exuberance and her melancholia, see Tyler Bradway, "Queer Exuberance: The Politics of Affect in Jeanette Winterson's Visceral Fiction," *Mosaic* 48, no. 1 (2015): 183–200.

52. Winterson, *Stone*, 19.

53. Ibid., 21.

54. Ibid.

55. Ibid.

56. Ibid., 130.

57. Ibid., 22.

58. Winterson's positive and indeed queer representation of sexuality appears among the collective of dissidents who have established a pluralistic, semi-anarchistic heterotopia (temporarily) outside of the government's control. There, we see positive representations of gay, lesbian, bisexual, and other specifically sexual relations among human and posthuman bodies, which do not mask patriarchal desires but affirm the queerness of the body's incalculable and irreducible becoming, including its becoming older.

59. Ibid., 205.

60. Ibid., 182. For an analysis of this line within the context of Acker's *Empire of the Senseless*, see Chap. 3.

61. Ibid., 141–42.

62. Ibid., 167.

63. Regarding the concept of an affective pedagogy, it is important to recall Eve Sedgwick's point in *The Weather in Proust* that pedagogy need not refer "to the academic institution so much as to a mode of relationality" (139). Sedgwick admits that the affective pedagogy of Buddhism may signify "evasion, as the notion of the Aesthetic is now commonly seen as functioning" (142). I suggest here that Winterson's pedagogy of feeling and her understanding of the aesthetic must be read together to see how they afford a thinking of queer relationality that is ultimately imbricated with the social, not in flight from it.

64. Jeanette Winterson, *Art Objects* (New York: Vintage, 1995), 108.

65. Ibid.

66. Ibid.

67. Ibid., 19.

68. Winterson, *Stone*, 203.

69. Winterson, *Objects*, 97.

70. Gopal Balakrishnan, "Hardt and Negri's *Empire*," *New Left Review* 5 (2000), accessed August 5, 2016, https://newleftreview.org/II/5/gopal-balakrishnan-hardt-and-negri-s-empire.

71. Winterson, *Objects*, 113–14.

72. Ibid., 113. In some moments, Winterson expresses postmodernism's egalitarianism. At other moments, and against her stated intentions, Winterson reiterates a more modernist elitism, affirming what Marianne DeKoven, in *Utopia Limited: The Sixties and the Emergence of the Postmodern* (Durham: Duke University Press, 2004), calls the "priestlike power of the modernist artist, the transcendent greatness of imagination and highly evolved artistry" (175).

73. Winterson, *Objects*, 15.

74. Ibid, 14–15.

75. Ibid., 31.

76. Ibid., 115.

77. Ibid., 114.
78. Ibid.
79. Grosz, *Time Travels*, 194.
80. Ibid.
81. Ibid., 195.
82. On the politics of artistic sensation, see Elizabeth Grosz, *Chaos, Territory, Art: Deleuze and the Framing of the Earth* (New York: Columbia University Press, 2008). On the relationship between politics and the ontology of immanence, see Elizabeth Grosz, *The Nick of Time: Politics, Evolution, and the Untimely* (Durham: Duke University Press, 2004), especially 244–61.
83. Grosz, *Chaos*, 79.
84. Ibid.
85. Winterson, *Objects*, 148.
86. Ibid., 133.
87. Ibid., 106.
88. Ibid., 113.
89. Ibid., 104.
90. Ibid., 106.
91. Ibid., 144. On Winterson's ambivalent relationship to class, see her interviews with Libby Brooks, "Power Surge," *The Guardian*, September 2, 2000, accessed August 5, 2016, https://www.theguardian.com/books/2000/sep/02/fiction.jeanettewinterson; and Angela Lambert, "Jeanette Winterson," *Prospect Magazine*, February 20, 1998, accessed August 5, 2016, http://www.prospectmagazine.co.uk/1998/02/jeanettewinterson/.
92. Winterson, *Objects*, 138.
93. Ibid., 150.
94. Ibid., 29.
95. Ibid.
96. Ibid., 28, 29.
97. Ibid., 31.
98. Indeed, Winterson exemplifies a reductive approach to "realist" aesthetics that is characteristic of postmodernism and some strains of post-structural theory. This reduction implies, as Michael McKeon argues in *Theory of the Novel: An Historical Approach* (Baltimore: The Johns Hopkins University Press, 2000), that realist aesthetics repress literary "production *in the same way* that the mechanism of the market, of general exchangeability, represses production in capitalist society" (588, my emphasis).
99. Ibid., 143.
100. Ibid., 144.
101. Ibid., 145. Here Winterson echoes queer theory's critique of the imaginary that I discuss in the introduction.

102. Ibid., 145, 114.
103. On the powers of the false, see Chapter 6 of Gilles Deleuze, *Cinema 2: The Time-Image*, trans. Hugh Tomlinson and Robert Galeta (Minneapolis: University of Minnesota Press, 1989). For an affirmation of postmodern simulation that converges with Winterson's, see Brian Massumi, "Realer than Real: The Simulacrum According to Deleuze and Guattari," *Copyright* 1 (1987): 90–97. Rather than mourn the loss of the real in postmodernism, Winterson similarly advocates non-representational aesthetics to counter the territorializing resemblance (what Winterson calls the "actual") that capitalism exploits.
104. Winterson, *Objects*, 112, 139.
105. Ibid., 112.
106. Ibid., 145.
107. Muñoz, *Cruising*, 1.
108. Ibid., my emphasis.
109. Jeanette Winterson, "Art & Lies," *Jeanette Winterson*, May 25, 1995, accessed August 8, 2016, http://www.jeanettewinterson.com/book/art-lies/.
110. Winterson, *Objects*, 191.
111. Ibid., 190.
112. Jeanette Winterson, *Art and Lies* (New York: Vintage, 1994).
113. Winterson, *Objects*, 117.
114. Winterson, *Lies*, 33.
115. See Sonya Andermahr, *Jeanette Winterson* (New York: Palgrave, 2008), 95.
116. Jameson, *Postmodernism*, 23.
117. Brian McHale, *Postmodern Fiction* (London: Routledge, 1987), 32.
118. Ibid.
119. Winterson, *Lies*, 44.
120. Ibid.
121. Ibid., 68.
122. Ibid., 12, 83.
123. Ibid., 25.
124. Ibid., 24.
125. On the politics of turning to the subject in postmodernity, see DeKoven, *Utopia Limited*, 189–287.
126. Winterson, *Lies*, 23.
127. Ibid., 24–25.
128. Ibid., 184.
129. Sigmund Freud, "Mourning and Melancholia," in *General Psychological Theory* (New York: Touchstone, 1963), 164.
130. Winterson, *Lies*, 106.

131. This statement originally appeared in an interview about the novel published on Winterson's website, which has since been deleted. An excerpt of the interview has been preserved in *Winterson Narrating Space and Time*, eds. Margaret J-M Sönmez and Mine Özyurt Kılıç, (Tyne: Cambridge Scholars Publishing, 2009), 122.
132. Winterson, *Lies*, 144.
133. Ibid., 109.
134. Ibid.
135. Ibid., 14.
136. Ibid., 178.
137. Ibid., 120.
138. Ibid., 9.
139. Ibid.
140. Ibid., my emphasis.
141. On the patriarchal anxiety of corporeal volatility, see Elizabeth Grosz, "Sexed Bodies," in *Volatile Bodies: Toward a Corporeal Feminism* (Bloomington: Indiana University Press, 1994), 187–210.
142. Winterson, *Lies*, 111.
143. Ibid., my emphasis.
144. Ibid., 147.
145. Ibid., 66.
146. Ibid., 54–55.
147. Ibid., 147.
148. Winterson, *Objects*, 93.
149. Ibid.
150. Ibid., 71.
151. Winterson, *Lies*, 61.
152. Ibid., 144.
153. McHale, *Postmodern*, 222.
154. Ibid., 223, 227, original emphasis.
155. Ibid., 227, original emphasis.
156. Ursula K. Le Guin, "Head Cases," *The Guardian*, September 22, 2007, accessed August 5, 2016, https://www.theguardian.com/books/2007/sep/22/sciencefictionfantasyandhorror.fiction.
157. Winterson, *Lies*, 111; Winterson, *Written*, 89.
158. Winterson, *Lies*, 87–89.
159. Ibid., 184.
160. Jacques Derrida, *Writing and Difference*, trans. Alan Bass (Chicago: The University of Chicago Press, 1978), 292, original emphasis.
161. Ibid., original emphasis.
162. Winterson, *Lies*, 184.
163. Ibid., 161, 43.

164. Ibid., 43.
165. Ibid., 42.
166. Ibid., 155.
167. Ibid., 154.
168. Ibid., 82.
169. Ibid.
170. Ibid., 38.
171. Ibid., 38–39.
172. Ibid., 161.
173. Ibid., 162, 41.
174. See Sigmund Freud, "On Narcissism," in *General Psychological Theory* (New York: Touchstone, 1963), 56–82.
175. Winterson, *Lies*, 64.
176. Ibid., 196.
177. Judith Butler, "Melancholy Gender/Refused Identification," in *The Psychic Life of Power: Theories in Subjection* (Stanford: Stanford University Press, 1997), 132–50.
178. Winterson, *Lies*, 201.
179. Ibid., 200.
180. Ibid., 131.
181. Ibid., 132.
182. Ibid., 136–37.
183. Ibid., 137–38.
184. Ibid., 137, my emphasis.
185. Ibid., my emphasis.
186. Davide Panagia, *The Political Life of Sensation* (Durham: Duke University Press, 2009), 9.
187. Ibid., 3–4.
188. Winterson, *Lies*, 46.
189. Ibid.
190. Ibid., 46–47.
191. Ibid., 46.
192. Ibid.
193. Ibid., 47–48.
194. Ibid., 157.
195. Ibid., 163.
196. Ibid.
197. Ibid., 163–64.
198. Ibid., 163, 164.
199. Ibid., 164.
200. Ibid., 206.
201. Ibid.
202. Ibid.

203. Ibid., 51.
204. Ibid., 206, my emphasis.
205. Jeanette Winterson, "Introduction to *Midsummer Nights*," *Jeanette Winterson*, April 2, 2009, accessed August 5, 2016, http://www.jeanettewinterson.com/book/midsummer-nights/introduction-mn/.
206. Winterson, *Lies*, 206.
207. Ibid., my emphasis.
208. Ibid.
209. Butler, "Uncritical."
210. See, for example, Jane Elliot and John David Rhodes, "The Value of Frustration: An Interview with Adam Phillips," *World Picture* 3 (2009), accessed August 5, 2016, http://www.worldpicturejournal.com/WP_3/Phillips.html. Queer theory critiques reparation when it appears to converge with heteronormative teleologies. Hence, Berlant rejects "projects of queer optimism that try to repair the subject's negativity into a grounding experiential positivity" (5). See Lauren Berlant and Lee Edelman, *Sex, or The Unbearable* (Durham: Duke University Press, 2014). For queer approaches to reparation and optimism that turn to object relations, particularly Melanie Klein and D.W. Winnicott, see Sedgwick, *Weather in Proust*; and Snediker, *Queer Optimism*. Until recently, object relations has had little purchase within critical or queer theory compared to the predominance of Lacan.
211. Edelman, *No Future*, 26.
212. Ibid., 8.
213. Ibid., 26. On corrosive versus adhesive modes of queerness, see the introduction.
214. Jeanette Winterson, *Why Be Happy When You Could Be Normal* (New York: Grove, 2011).
215. Ibid., 113.
216. Ibid., 114.
217. Ibid.
218. Muñoz, *Cruising*, 18.
219. On the ambivalence of the incipiently social and its distinction from utopianism, see the introduction.
220. Winterson, Why, 223. The necessary endurance of the traumatic wound is underlined when Winterson states, "All my life I have worked from the wound. To heal it would mean an end to one identity—the defining identity" (ibid.). Note, too, that Winterson's work—her affective and aesthetic labor—emerges through working from and with the wound.

CHAPTER 5

"Permeable We!": Queer Theory's (Re)turn to Reading with Feeling

Queer Experimental Literature began by stepping to the side of queer theory to uncover a broader genealogy of queer reading that pre-exists, develops alongside of, and complexly engages with the emergence of queer theory as an academic discourse, particularly as it has been shaped by the hermeneutics of suspicion and poststructural theory. By doing so, we have seen that experimental literature critically responds to the convergence of the politics of sexuality and the politics of queer aesthetics throughout the postwar period by contesting institutionally sanctioned conceptions of reading that underlie them both—from the legal codification of queer collectivity as obscenity, to the disavowal of affective histories that infuse the hermeneutics of AIDS, to the neoliberal gentrification of the queer avant-garde and the homonormative privatization of queerness. In each context, queer writers use experimental form to configure and solicit modes of bad reading; these modes of reading often appear degraded because they are infused by and predicated on affect, or because they invest in affects such as love, pleasure, or exuberance that simply fail to count as critical within the idioms of critical theory. Yet I have attempted to show that bad reading has an affective politics, glimpsed through its reorientation of the relations of reading. This reorientation occurs through finely textured experimentations with form that redraw the relationship between affect, language, and the social. The configurations and conceptions of this relationship shift, depending on the urgencies of the political moment

© The Author(s) 2017
T. Bradway, *Queer Experimental Literature*,
Palgrave Studies in Affect Theory and Literary Criticism,
DOI 10.1057/978-1-137-59543-0_5

in question, but each modality of bad reading figures an incipiently social imagination, thereby demonstrating that the queer turn to affect is by no means a simple concession to or symptom of the privatizing forces of the postwar era. On the contrary, bad reading can, in certain instances, press back against these forces, particularly by configuring queerness as an experiment in collective becoming that resists the reduction of sexuality to an identity that requires institutional recognition.

While queer theory has inhabited the margins of each chapter, I have argued that queer experimental literature proleptically speaks to queer theory's recent reconsideration of its own reading practices, particularly as these methods draw on the hermeneutics of suspicion and equate paranoid demystification with queer critique. The goal has been to displace queer theory as the governing context for thinking about queer modes of affective reading. My purpose was not to delegitimize reparative reading or other affective methods elaborated by queer theorists themselves. It was important to temporarily suspend the authority granted to academic definitions of queer reading so as to pluralize the formations that queer reading can be said to take and the politics it can be said to enact. We have been able to meet these modes and politics on their own terms, as it were, to glimpse their motivating contexts and their self-articulated horizons of possibility without pre-emptively judging their critical worth in terms of existing disciplinary formations for critical reading. By no means does *Queer Experimental Literature* exhaust this genealogical work, but at the very least, it has revealed that affective reading does not solely fall within the purview of the literary critic and that it is far more socially attuned than academic narratives about its emergence would suggest.

This chapter culminates the project of rethinking queer reading through practices elicited by queer experimental literature. However, it does so by now turning directly to queer theory and, in particular, to one of the most important founders of queer theory as an academic discourse, Eve Kosofsky Sedgwick. A great deal of attention has been paid to Sedgwick's work on reading in light of her field-changing essay, "Paranoid Reading and Reparative Reading, or, You're So Paranoid You Probably Think This Essay is About You."[1] Yet Sedgwick's theory of reparative reading—and her turn to affect more broadly—has tended to be understood in the relatively narrow context of the academy's exhaustion of critique.[2] This focus obscures that Sedgwick's investment in affective reading was motivated, in large part, by the politics of the AIDS crisis and the inheritance of para-academic and activist hermeneutics that we examined in Chap. 2.

As I argue below, reparative reading emerges out of a number of concerns around the social exigencies of queer politics in the post-AIDS era, particularly the need to imagine and configure forms of relational belonging in the midst of death. At the same time, we have tended to forget that Sedgwick's investment in the reading of queer culture was also bound up with her own creation of queer aesthetic objects, which included textiles, poetry, and experimental writing. Placed alongside the previous chapters, Sedgwick's mutual turns to affect and to experimental writing can now be read as part of a broader queer literary history that Sedgwick inherits and to which she contributes in turn. By concluding with Sedgwick, I do not intend to place reparative reading as the telos of bad reading or of queer reading practices more broadly. Rather, I want to reveal how queer experimental literature enables Sedgwick to reconfigure reading as a queerly permeable scene of relation in which affect has a dynamic link to queer agency and social imagination. In this respect, Sedgwick's reparative reading, as developed through her experimental writing, extends the history of bad reading and keeps alive its horizons of potentiality.

QUEER THEORY'S AFFECTIVE RELATIONS

In one of her last published essays, Sedgwick registers a concern about the affective relations that animate contemporary LGBTQ movements. Echoing the sentiments of many queer theorists, Sedgwick fears that "mainstream gay and lesbian culture and politics" has enacted a "programmatic disavowal" of the formative traumas of the AIDS crisis.[3] What has resulted from this disavowal, she suggests, are cultural and political "venues [that] have become affectively hollowed out, brittle and banalized."[4] At the same time, Sedgwick worries that subsequent generations of queer theorists have not provided a sufficient methodological alternative to combat the mainstream's collective forgetting. Instead, queer theory has retained the projective affects of paranoia with less and less grounding in the context from which these feelings emerged and were necessary as motivators of activism and community formation. Indeed, Sedgwick laments that queer theory perpetuates these affects in excess of a "palpable purchase on daily reality" and suggests that paranoia has perhaps, for the moment, outlived its usefulness as an organizer of queer relationality.[5]

Why do the affective undercurrents of these cultural and political projects matter to Sedgwick's critique? At stake, I argue, is an assumption central to Sedgwick's late-career turn to theories of affect that she never made explicit—namely, that specific affective states contribute to qualitatively unique intersubjective, ethical, and political relations. It is for this reason that Sedgwick urges queer theory and culture to access and offer a broader palette of affects beyond paranoia, and that she is compelled to search for ways to connect our affective dispositions and relations to the exigencies of the contemporary moment. In this search, Sedgwick is unique among her contemporaries. While other queer critics share Sedgwick's analytic investment in affect, few urge the cultivation of positive affect as she does.[6] Despite their methodological divergences, Sara Ahmed, Lauren Berlant, Judith Butler, Ann Cvetkovich, Douglas Crimp, Lee Edelman, Jack Halberstam, and Heather Love each consider positive affects with suspicion. Their work strives to depathologize the negative affects of unhappiness, melancholia, trauma, self-shattering, or shame and to define these feelings as constitutive of queerness. Consequently, they suggest that the counternormative force of queerness lies in its capacity to contest the redemptive futures mainstream gay liberalism affirms in the discourses of positive affect.[7] By "clinging to ruined identities and to histories of injury," Love suggests, queers defy "the call of gay normalization" and thereby "refus[e] to write off the most vulnerable, the least presentable, and all the dead."[8]

Without a doubt, Sedgwick also insists on the psychic and social significance of negative affects to queer communities. Yet she ultimately questions the conflation of counternormative critique with negative affect and, conversely, of mainstream assimilation with positive affect. In the process, Sedgwick seeks out an alternative relational model, distinct from those underwritten by self-consolidating paranoia or self-shattering jouissance.[9] I argue that Sedgwick's turn to positive affect is motivated by an attempt to envision a relational ethics premised on permeable intersubjectivity, based in the non-foundational selves of poststructuralism and Buddhism— Sedgwick's "Permeable We!" To map Sedgwick's ethics, I focus on her experimental memoir, *A Dialogue on Love* (1999), as it represents a significant effort on Sedgwick's part to cultivate the affective relations that she values for queer theory and culture.[10] It also offers a privileged site from which to glimpse the lexical, formal, and conceptual models that she uses to articulate the ethical values of affect in her critical writing. To be sure, a fine line cannot be drawn between Sedgwick's critical and creative writing. Each displays her singular blend of lyricism, metaphor, speculative discourse, and narrative condensation. We should thus resist subordinating Sedgwick's aesthetic work to her theoretical discourse as adjunct or mere example. To do so would enact a paranoid disarticulation of queer aesthetics from queer critique, which Sedgwick's late work so powerfully forestalls. It would also assume that we know everything there is to know about queer reading from Sedgwick's critical writing. I hope to show that we cannot appreciate the social urgency of reparative reading or properly understand its conceptual richness without attending closely to Sedgwick's own use of experimental aesthetics to redraw the relations of queer reading. Indeed, *Dialogue* hybridizes a range of experimental forms to model its conceptions of affect, intersubjectivity, and reparation. These forms locate readers within a network of contingent and reciprocal affective relations. In doing so, *Dialogue* provides us with an ethical model of intersubjectivity based in a set of feelings more capacious than paranoia and more welcoming to possibilities for relations of mutual nourishment.

If the tradition of queer experimental literature informs Sedgwick's pluralization of queer reading beyond suspicion, it also enables her to use form to reconfigure queerness itself as a method of affective negotiation and impersonal relational care. The memoir's use of *haibun* and its construction of typographic space manifest reparative affects without relying solely on a first-person narrative to express these feelings.[11] *Dialogue*'s manifestation of pedagogical permeability through these forms is central to its structuring an ethical relation between self and other. Never naive about pedagogy's political connotations, Sedgwick admits that it may signal "evasion, as the notion of the Aesthetic is now commonly seen as functioning."[12] Yet Sedgwick's conception of the pedagogical does not imply a retreat from the social. On the contrary, pedagogical permeability models an intersubjective dynamic of "holding" that affirms the inextricability of the self from a field of impersonal others. As a specific "mode of relationality," pedagogy aims to mitigate projective affects and, alternately, to cultivate reparative care for the other.[13] The pedagogical is thus an inhabited, intersubjective relation, as well as an ethical practice that endeavors to "*offer*" a "radically, ever newly unpreempted space" for the attenuation of negative affect.[14] Since Sedgwick represents the pedagogical as a queer relation one can choose to inhabit, *Dialogue* carves out a space for agency within permeable intersubjectivity. Sedgwick's conception of agency is premised on embodied negotiations and seeks to sidestep Michel Foucault's "repressive hypothesis," which has been foundational to queer theories of agency. Sedgwick's "middle ranges of agency" are defined by the ability to engender change for a self through affective exchanges that do not conform to the polarities of liberation or repression.[15] Such affective negotiations underwrite *Dialogue*'s exhibition of Sedgwick's sadomasochistic masturbation fantasies and contribute to her representation of sexual confession as a performative solicitation rather than a technology of repression.

Ultimately, Sedgwick casts the contingency and necessity of intersubjective reparation in the discourse of positive affect, specifically an idiom of queer happiness. Locating happiness within the temporal horizon of mortality, Sedgwick expands queer theory's affective modalities to include durable and impersonal relations of holding that extend beyond any one individual life. *Dialogue*'s reformulation of queer relationality thus condenses an incipient form of social imagination, one that aims to hold readers within the vanishing of our shared present.

WRITING FEELING WITHOUT A FIRST PERSON

"What kind of a narrative … are we trying to construct—or do we think we need to construct—about Eve's history?"[16] When Sedgwick poses this question to her therapist, Shannon Van Wey, she foregrounds the conflicted status of self-narrative in *Dialogue*. Van Wey wants to construct a narrative that enables Sedgwick to "*turn out* different."[17] Though his goal is for her to see herself as "more continuous," Sedgwick qualifies that this self will not be "identical" but "just floating onward."[18] What kind of narrative form can produce this alternative mode of being? *Dialogue* suggests that the answer might not lie in narrative at all; indeed, the text shares Sedgwick's own "non-narrative" view of people, weakening the drive to plot in favor of "a kind of cubist three-dimensionality" that recursively accumulates perspectives of an object rather than its changes over time.[19] Despite its diminution of plot, *Dialogue* nonetheless depicts a series of legible events within a clear context: it begins in 1992 after Sedgwick has been diagnosed with breast cancer and has undergone chemotherapy and a double mastectomy; she is forty-two and suffering from a resurgence of the depression she experienced in her youth. Throughout the treatment, Sedgwick confronts her fraught familial relations, her difficulty with emotions and sexuality, and her mortality. By *Dialogue*'s end, substantive change has occurred for Sedgwick: her anxiety abates, her poetry returns, and she discovers a nourishing interest in textile crafts and Buddhism.

Yet the conceptual content of *Dialogue* lies less in its narrative than in the formal means by which it destabilizes conventional structures of memoir. These forms include the discursive moves Sedgwick outlines in

"Teaching 'Experimental Critical Writing.'"[20] Above all, *Dialogue* relies on the interpenetration of haiku and prose and the alternation of voice, which it effects by integrating Van Wey's session notes in different fonts.[21] Because of Sedgwick's and Van Wey's constant ventriloquizing of one another, the reader is confronted by a subtle vertigo when trying to distinguish between their uses of "I." Sedgwick describes this focal oscillation as creating a "permeable first person" such that "[t]here are times when even I can't tell whose first person it is."[22] *Dialogue*'s sometimes-indeterminate "I" counters the "bumptious narcissism" that subtends autobiography's "primordial first person singular."[23] Moreover, this polyvocal "I" is central to Sedgwick's creation of a pedagogical form that has the capacity "to aerate, expose, and ideally to disable or 'burn out' the potency of certain violent defenses."[24] Sedgwick's understanding of these defenses is based on Melanie Klein's conception of the psyche's paranoid/schizoid position. In this position, the ego sadistically projects its own negative, persecutory affects onto the other as a way to manage its own anxiety. It is precisely these defenses that Sedgwick sees motivating political memoirs by Alberto Gonzalez, John Edwards, Condoleezza Rice, and Clarence Thomas, and that she seeks to counter with a pedagogical form of life writing.

However, Sedgwick does not explicate the alternate ethical and political utility that adheres to memoir crafted with pedagogical motives. We lack the critical tools to answer her reticence because our notions of the ethical and political value of narrative continue to discount the force of affect. If not consigned to the "affective fallacy," then the affective relations of reading are cast as inadequate to narrative's representational powers for social intervention.[25] In her analysis of *Dialogue*'s value for disability studies, Cynthia G. Franklin invokes this critical bias against experimental writing. Though she affirms its depiction of "complexly structured moments of empathy and identification," Franklin laments that the memoir does not represent a "full exploration of how institutions and individuals interact."[26]

Rather than critique the indeterminacies of *Dialogue* as a solipsistic denial of social context, I argue that Sedgwick's memoir effects its intervention by reimagining the relation between self and other in ways that mitigate the intersubjective violence of paranoid defenses, which it does through—not in spite of—its opaque, non-figural affective spaces. *Dialogue* accomplishes this project by manifesting affect through formal means that are more capacious than plotted conflict or first-person narration. When Sedgwick considers what genre can represent her encounter with Van Wey, she becomes intrigued by the seventeenth-century

Japanese *haibun*, particularly its combination of haiku and travel narrative. "It comes to me as a possible form for writing of Shannon and me," she writes, because it challenges "bathetic" forms of "complaint" as well as the teleological plot of psychoanalysis that "fixate[s]" on "truths uncovered, the excavated past."[27] These revelatory plots tend to recuperate "the Western//heroic thrust for/individuation" that Sedgwick rejects in favor of Buddhism's insistence on interconnectedness.[28] Not only does individuation consolidate an ideology of autonomous selfhood that *Dialogue*'s permeable first-person critiques, such individuation is typically realized through narratives of cathartic resolution underwritten by the triumph of normative values—values that look suspiciously akin to heteronormativity. For example, when Sedgwick's estranged sister, Nina, reconnects with the Kosofsky family, Sedgwick resists Van Wey's hope for the family's happy reunification, because the fantasy is premised on the values of "blood and law" that privilege the biological and nuclear family as the only family that matters.[29]

As alternatives to the psychoanalytic plot, Sedgwick considers "Platonic dialogues" and "novels."[30] The value of the novel in particular, she writes, is its epistemic opacity:

> [Y]ou needn't know in advance what the subject *is*: a love? A failure? A mess? A bliss?
> But that's—prose.
>
> To notate our strange
> melody, I have some use
> for all the white space.[31]

On the one hand, the *haibun* shares the novel's immanence—not knowing the subject at the outset—and as a form of travel narrative, *haibun* expresses the movements between Sedgwick and Van Wey that lead both to altered senses of their selves. On the other hand, the *haibun* is not "—prose." Sedgwick's strident punctuation of "prose," dashed aside and stopped short by a period, underscores the novel's insufficiency to "notate our strange/melody" because it risks sapping the estrangement of an experience that cannot be solely rendered through language. Thus, the *haibun* does not dispense with affect; it enables a more capacious expression of feeling—it "[s]weep[s] into and through the arias, silent impasses, the fat, buttery condensations and inky dribbles of the mind's laden brush."[32] Here form becomes, at once, aural, savory, tactile, and visual. To disregard this synesthetic interpenetration of the sensory and the textual as simply metaphorical would miss the significance of the translation that the haiku effects in this passage. Converting the kinetic energy of their "strange/ melody" into the potential energy of "all the white space," the haiku underscores the capacity of form—even empty space—to express affect without a subject to channel its feelings. In short, Sedgwick employs the haibun to express the "inky dribbles of the mind's laden brush" because it does not require a first person to possess that mind.[33]

But why is the first person an obstacle to be overcome in aesthetic form, and what significance does the haibun's affective texture have for Sedgwick's vision of relationality? According to Van Wey's notes, writing in "the first person is both labor intensive and felt to be constraining... there were emotional registers that weren't available while generating first person."[34] We should appreciate the ambiguity in Van Wey's paraphrasing here. Are these emotions unavailable because they are unconscious to the "I," such that it cannot recognize these emotions as its own? Or are these feelings unavailable because the "I" is too narrow to render emotional registers that are not solely its own? Although both dynamics are at play in Dialogue, the latter helps us understand why Sedgwick comes to engage in "the nonlinguistic work of textile art" over the course of Dialogue.[35] In Van Wey's words, "A texture book wouldn't need to have a first person at all, any more than weaving itself does."[36] The focus on texture de-emphasizes the constraints of personhood and concurrently expands the possibility for expressing "emotional registers" unavailable to an "I." It is in the "indiscriminate realm [of textiles], that conscience has no foothold," and Sedgwick can savor "materials in my hands; seeing, at an instant of pause and speculation, whether there's something satisfying, something surprising to me, that they almost are."[37]

Following Renu Bora's suggestion that "how one feels matter seems to invite comparisons with how one's own or someone else's matter can be shaped," Sedgwick's relief in textiles provides a clue to the affective transformation enabled through her perception of Dialogue as textural.[38] Flowing between prose and poetry, and between Sedgwick's and Van Wey's words, the haibun provides a correlative subjective orientation to the textiles' ontological immanence, one that contrasts her previous poetic genre, the lyric. The lyric provided Sedgwick a potent combination of discipline and authority through the rhythms of enjambment.[39] Rather than a sensual "Kristevan semiotic" that outstrips the regulation of patriarchal syntax, lyric's enjambment corresponded to what was "most abstract and cognitively under control in the poem."[40] In *Dialogue*, by contrast, the transitions from prose to poetry signal, in Katy Hawkins's words, a "relaxing [of] the beat of intellectual and emotional working through" such that the "'plot' is slowed to set in motion the play of ideas."[41] These dislodged moments of cognition are not necessarily revelatory; they merely offer moments of "pause and speculation" for meditative consideration.[42] In this respect, the *haibun* and textiles equally provide access to what Sedgwick calls "the sky-like nature of mind, where clouds can scoot across it, but it still remains just the sky. When your mind is occupied in conversations among bits of you, *where* is the conversation happening?"[43] The *haibun* figures both these "bits" of the dialogic self as well as the underlying "emptiness that isn't constituted by any of the parties to the conversation."[44]

This figure of spaciousness leads Sedgwick to represent affect and subjectivity as inherently relational. Van Wey inspires this conception when he suggests to Sedgwick that timidity is not "a trait that lives inside a person, but instead, something relational."[45] Sedgwick relishes this insight as "just plain true! /Like going to a party/where no one knows you—// excruciating/by yourself, effortless when/a friend will come too—."[46] Counterposing "excruciating" estrangement to "effortless" friendship, Sedgwick suggests that affects are contingent on our relational circumstances—their weight may suddenly become light with the presence of another. This is a significant realization for Sedgwick because, as Van Wey explains, it was difficult for her "to have emotions [as a child], a sense of their claims or weight," because her parents "preemptively discredited" the "emotional field."[47] Part of the process of therapy, then, involves their accessing positive affects because, as Sedgwick explains, "if anything can bring me through to real change, it may be only some kind of pleasure."[48] Rather than a "grim process" of "masochistic" self-surrender, the relational cultivation of positive affect with Van Wey becomes central to Sedgwick's alleviation of depression.[49]

Dialogue itself is a material expression of the "pleasure" Sedgwick feels in therapy and in constructing a "record" of the experience.[50] As such, the memoir indicates the complex relationship between affect, texture, and language that defines Sedgwick's late-career resistance to what she calls deconstruction's "analyzing apparently nonlinguistic phenomena in rigorously linguistic terms."[51] Beyond the "vast pleasure" Sedgwick feels in creating haiku and crafts, she describes the experience as "floating downstream with a current that's so resolutely wordless. As though in all its modesty, its refusal to generate propositions, selves, ideas, this might be a cataclysmic change disguised as an unassuming indulgence."[52] I would argue that here Sedgwick articulates a proleptic critique of the "new modesty" in literary criticism that I discuss in the conclusion. Here modesty does not signal withdrawal from the social or political, nor does it mark an attenuation of the transformative possibilities for aesthetic or cultural work. Rather, modesty's "unassuming indulgence" "disguise[s]" a more profound potentiality for change. The force of modest pleasure does not need to be critically exposed as a symptom of structural oppression. On the contrary—and characteristic of bad reading more broadly—the guise of indulgence affords a relation to a plane of immanence that does not demarcate the boundaries of self and other, word and texture. In fact, the unassuming nature of this affective indulgence is key to its transformative potentiality. By adopting this queerly modest affect, *Dialogue* beckons its readers into the currents of becoming.

If words are a dialogue's condition of possibility, its matter of exchange, how can *Dialogue* express this wordless current? Here "current" echoes an excerpt from James Merrill quoted earlier in *Dialogue*: "Our state is exciting as we move with the current & emotion becomes an element of its own force."[53] If emotion is a central element in the current, how should we conceive the relationship between wordlessness and emotion? Affect theories that insist on a strict demarcation between affect and emotion would suggest that a worded affective wordlessness is a paradox. Brian Massumi famously disarticulates emotion from affect by reading the latter as the pre-signified and pre-subjective modulation of a body's constantly varying sensation.[54] Emotion, by contrast, is a "qualified intensity" that is "owned and recognized" by a self in language—in "semantically and semiotically formed progressions, into narrativizable action-reaction circuits, into function and meaning."[55] To specify *an* affect in language is to have already depleted its virtual challenge to subjectivity by freezing intensity into "subject-object relations."[56] From this perspective, Sedgwick's wordless current cannot have an emotional *quality* as such, and it fosters a current of becoming only insofar as it remains unarticulated.

Yet Sedgwick suggests that language and affect need not be opposed to one another on the axis of subjectivity; instead, language might contribute to, rather than obstruct, the becoming of both affective and emotional intensities.[57] The critical readings in Sedgwick's late work are thus premised on the assumption that "the line between words and things or between linguistic and nonlinguistic phenomena is endlessly changing, permeable, and entirely unsusceptible to any definitive articulation."[58] Sedgwick presents this claim as a counter to "deconstructive" analyses of "nonverbal aspects of reality [as if they were] firmly under the aegis of the linguistic."[59] One might object that deconstructing the dichotomy of matter and signification need not inflate the purview of the latter over the former—it grasps precisely the permeable tension between the two that Sedgwick affirms. Yet Sedgwick is nonetheless concerned that certain forms of deconstruction prioritize the signifier's non-referentiality to "the world" and thereby obscure the relation that language has "to its own reference."[60] Casting this relation in affective terms—as "torsion" between reference and performativity—Sedgwick suggests that the reflexive twists of utterances to their contexts and toward other performatives provide one way to grasp the "textures and effects of particular bits of language."[61] Note that language here, like the dialogic self, becomes disarticulated into "bits" so that its phenomenological specificity and efficacy can be digested. Because she also values the affective motivations that underlie these utterances, Sedgwick rejects Freudian sublimation for interpreting affect's relation to its means of conveyance. In Sedgwick's polemical phrasing, "The nature or quality of the affect itself, seemingly, is [for Sigmund Freud] not of much more consequence than the color of the airplane used to speed a person to a destination."[62] The drawback of conceiving affect as autonomous from a homogenous libidinal drive is that it does not allow queer critics to expand the field of sexuality—to see culture, at large, as underwritten by sexual desire. However, it encourages us to account for how affects "saturat[e]" aesthetic objects beyond their sublimation into linguistic content and to evaluate the qualitative force of specific affects on their own terms.[63]

The benefit of affect's autonomy for Sedgwick is primarily ethical; it enables her to valorize the affective qualities of distinct intersubjective relations, and it enables her to craft—and offer—these non-sublimated affects to others in writing. Take, for example, *Dialogue*'s configuration of typographic space. Though the text's graphic aspects are not linguistic, they contribute to the memoir's manifestation of the affective relationality underlying Sedgwick's and Van Wey's interaction. For this reason, I depart from Jason Edwards's metaphorical reading of the text's white space, because it subordinates Sedgwick's investment in demonstrating how non-subjectified, yet qualified, affects can be expressed through texture. For Edwards, *Dialogue*'s white spaces evoke "the cancer working its way through Sedgwick's oeuvre"; concomitantly, he reads the eight blank pages that follow the memoir as representing Sedgwick's dissipation into death.[64]

Read more literally, the blank pages foreground the materiality of the text itself. After all, the space of the page is the texture holding together Sedgwick's and Van Wey's words. We see each page's negative space anew as the haikus linguistically reference and graphically redraw the emptiness around them. In the absence of words, the page's materiality is highlighted as the condition of possibility for the preceding print and for its (re)emergence in the form of the reader's notes. There is no guarantee the reader will respond, but the space creates the possibility for readerly participation in a temporality akin to *Dialogue*'s non-simultaneous post-session written dialogue. It is no coincidence that a recurring word in Sedgwick's lexicon is "interleaving." To "interleave" denotes the process of *Dialogue*'s production—the collation of two different perspectives, the literal binding together of and oscillating between Sedgwick's and Van Wey's words.[65] This is why *Dialogue*'s cover image presents two white spaces separated by a gray line that bleeds into each space, reminiscent of a photocopied book with the spine in the center. It indicates the binding that holds these pages together, enabling a textual relation between Sedgwick and Van Wey.

Dialogue's foregrounding of binding has significant implications for its ethics of intersubjectivity. As noted above, it becomes difficult to determine when one writer is paraphrasing the other or expressing her or his own feelings. What makes this indeterminacy so disorienting is that Sedgwick interleaves the notes in different fonts: her narrative sections are in center-justified Times; her haikus are in Arial; and Van Wey's notes are in a capitalized font set non-justified and ragged right. It *should* be clear who is speaking because of the obvious graphic distinction between their words. But it is not. *Dialogue* thus visually crystallizes the affect of "besides." Being besides, Sedgwick explains, is an experience of "noncontradiction"—hence *Dialogue*'s permeability of perspectival relation.[66] Yet "besides" does not succumb to a "fantasy of metonymically egalitarian or even pacific relations."[67] To understand how *Dialogue* balances these two polarities—non-dualistic relation and individuated conflict—we must first understand Sedgwick's permeable intersubjectivity.

THE PEDAGOGY OF PERMEABILITY

Sedgwick's conceptions of affect and pedagogy intersect in their intersubjectivity, which is an ethical relation she inflects as specifically queer. Critics have long recognized the relationality of Sedgwick's definition of queerness. Stephen M. Barber and David L. Clark suggest that, for Sedgwick, queer denotes "a force, specifically a *relational* force."[68] Nancy K. Miller notes, "The surprises of kinship ... lie at the core of Sedgwick's body of writing and shape her role as a cultural critic."[69] However, Berlant worries that Sedgwick's work emblematizes queer theory's problematic "orientation toward interiority."[70] In elaborating Sedgwick's queer permeability, then, I address the broader problem Berlant identifies when she asks, "Must the project of queerness start 'inside' of the subject and spread out from there?"[71]

Berlant's interpretation of Sedgwick's "interiority" rests partly on a reading of *Dialogue* that perceives Sedgwick as surrounded by "a crowded world of loving family and friends in which she thrives partly by living in the fold of her internal counternarrative."[72] Not only does *Dialogue* depict the non-loving ambivalences that underlie Sedgwick's familial relations, it reveals the fraught nature of the crowd that surrounds Sedgwick and the difficulty of her producing any narrative within it, both normative and queer. At stake here is not merely contesting Berlant's reading of *Dialogue* but, rather, the ideology she perceives in Sedgwick's self-narratives and in "reparative reading" more generally. Berlant concludes that Sedgwick recuperates a "mode of virtuously intentional, self-reflective personhood" symptomatic of liberalism, capitalism, certain strains of psychoanalysis, and "cultural and national modernity."[73] The keystone of Berlant's critique is that Sedgwick lacks a conception of "impersonality" that would more adequately contest "the march of individualities toward liberal freedoms."[74]

Based on Buddhist conceptions of pedagogy, *Dialogue*'s impersonal intersubjectivity is premised on a relation between self and other quite contrary to liberal individualism. Liberal individualism requires a clear demarcation of the cogito, enabling self-determination and the pursuit of one's own, typically economic, interests in competition with the social collective. The pedagogical values that Sedgwick draws out of various Buddhist traditions, by contrast, undermine these premises. First, Sedgwick values the Bodhisattva's "pedagogical imperative": subordinating her attainment of enlightenment to enabling others', thereby inverting the liberal value of individualistic self-fulfillment.[75] Second, Sedgwick valorizes both the Mahayana Buddhist "refus[al] to differentiate at the level of identity between teacher and learner" and the Tibetan Buddhist "mobility of teacher-student positioning."[76] Although the latter "thrives on personality and intimate emotional relation," Sedgwick notes that its pedagogical scene also "functions as a mysteriously powerful solvent of individual identity."[77] What persists despite loosening the self, however, is the "dissolvent relationality of pedagogy itself," which leads Sedgwick to conclude that "it is as though relation [in Tibetan Buddhism] *could only be* pedagogical—and for *that* reason, radically transindividual."[78] In short, Sedgwick's pedagogy of Buddhism relies on the singular qualities of personality while also deindividuating self and other to reveal the intersubjective nature of relationality. The dispositions that derive from such relatedness are "tenderness and gratitude (not Oedipal-style envy, lack, violence)."[79] These affects are symptoms of perceiving the other relationally, but they are also ethical orientations that mitigate violent affects central to liberal individualism's aggressive self-interest.[80]

Dialogue entwines these two modes of relationality in its representation of intersubjectivity as a network subtended by positive affect. The "tension" of this model, Van Wey notes, is that it is "intersubjective (e.g., teacher/student) but nondual."[81] Yet Sedgwick merges both relations in her "favorite pronoun: the dear/first person plural," which *Dialogue* announces in one of its most significant haikus: "Promiscuous we! /Me, plus anybody else. /Permeable we!"[82] How does permeability replace promiscuity by the last line, and what significance do these terms have for Sedgwick's queer relationality? Promiscuity implies the movement of an object among other objects, hence Sedgwick's affirmation of additive relation ("Me, plus anybody else"). Permeability goes farther—the object itself, the "me," is riven and open to movements within and through it. The redefinition of love in *Dialogue* is thus premised on an expansive network of relations that precede and exceed the self without a definable limit. This network comes into relief when Sedgwick contrasts the "narrow sexual triangle" of "adulterous romance" with "post-Proustian" love.[83] The former has a

circuit small enough
that its allure was, you would
eventually

get back all of the
erotic energy you'd
sent around it (so

that the point of this
fantasy was *nothing is
ever really lost*)—

in post-Proustian
love, on the other hand, the
circuit could be big.

Imagine it big
enough that you could never
even *know* whether

the system was closed,
finally, or open. So
the point could only

lie in valuing
all the transformations and
transitivities

in all directions
for their difference, trans-i-ness,
and their skilled nature.[84]

This decentralized network of love represents a "vastly more spacious and inviting field of queerness" for Sedgwick because it explodes the Oedipal triangulation of desire.[85] While imagining this "circuitry was a vital *self-protective* step" for her, this is only a defensive spur toward participating in queer relationality as an open system.[86] Therefore, Sedgwick's queerness is discovered, and inheres, in the network of permeable relation itself, the transpersonal field so large it confounds epistemology modeled on the scale of a single consciousness.

Dialogue's queer network undermines the self's narcissistic desire for infinite reciprocity. The self cannot calculate a return on its investment, nor can it "*know*," finally, whether the system is open or closed; yet this knowledge is irrelevant to "valuing/all the transformations," the dynamic movements within and among subjects and beyond them.[87] (This is why Sedgwick coins the word *trans-i-ness*, lowercasing the "I" and placing it within a prefix and suffix of unspecified becoming.) "Falling in love" in this network is therefore not "sexual" but rather an experience of

suddenly, globally, "knowing" that another person represents your only
access to some vitally
    transmissible truth
    or radiantly heightened
    mode of perception,
and that if you lose the thread of this intimacy, both your soul and your
whole world might subsist forever in some desert-like state of ontological
impoverishment.[88]

Here the other is a window that clears a line of sight to the ontological
fiber of impersonal relationality. The "impoverishment" of non-relation
signals Sedgwick's displacement of reciprocity within the post-Proustian
network of love. While the circuit is not symmetrical or calculable, it
requires mutual participation. Hence Sedgwick's personal "image of hell"
is glimpsed when she nearly abandons her cat, Harpo, in a graveyard.[89]
Likewise, one of her most painful experiences of breast cancer occurs
when she is "ignored for a couple of hours in the hospital ... and couldn't
get the attention of the horrid nurses" despite weeping.[90] These experiences haunt Sedgwick as representations of abandonment in which one
has abdicated, or been severed from, a nourishing relation with the other.
Although Sedgwick admits it is "easier for me to feel [abandonment] than
'I am afraid,'" her dread at images of desertion suggests that abandonment condenses the existential fear she has of "los[ing] the thread" of
relational intimacy.[91]

The counter to abandonment, in *Dialogue*'s lexicon, is "holding."
As Van Wey explains, Sedgwick experiences a "warm and quiet environment as part of therapeutic transference instead of the anger, suspicion,
mortifying self-loss she had imagined."[92] Sedgwick specifies this environment by comparing therapy to a

    —Bath into which I
    slowly lower my great bulk,
      to be supported
in some medium less human than "holding" (in Winnicott's famous image
of the therapeutic relation) would suggest.
    That is, there's something about being *impersonally* held.[93]

Here Sedgwick's "great bulk"—a fraught metaphor because of the
Kosofsky family's denigration of her weight—is "supported." But Van
Wey does not hold her; rather, it is the impersonal relation between them

that enables Sedgwick to access "support like buoyancy in water—there, unfailing, not caring."[94] Holding is the correlative affect of Sedgwick's permeable and impersonal network of relation. To be sure, the passivity of holding is fraught with potential violence. One might be dropped and abandoned. Yet *Dialogue* affirms holding as a way to produce a mode of recognition wherein the self is successfully held in the other, embracing the self as it is but not so tightly that it arrests becoming otherwise. Indeed, Sedgwick takes pleasure in figures from Buddhism that produce "the recognition of personally specific things" in another while also "deindividuat[ing]" them.[95]

Held in this way, the self can experiment with inhabiting the other's reparative perspectives. With Van Wey, Sedgwick experiences this "circuit of reciprocity between these holding relations: your ability to hold me inside you, and mine to hold you inside me" as "nourish[ing]."[96] Sedgwick is pleasantly unsettled, for instance, on hearing that she "exist[s] on weekends" for Van Wey when he admits to thinking about her.[97] This "—ontological/net" comforts Sedgwick because she finds relief in the prospect of living on in others after death.[98] But in *Dialogue*'s present, intersubjective holding enables Sedgwick to internalize a voice that mitigates the anxiety she feels about dying. *Dialogue*'s final lines intone both valences when Van Wey observes that Sedgwick has "come to be able to hear a voice like my voice inside herself when it is quiet that she can trust and have confidence in. I can imagine the voice telling her she can stop."[99] Note the *mise-en-abyme* layered within this line: Sedgwick has chosen this moment from Van Wey's notes to conclude the memoir, giving him the last word; yet these words perform his imagining her imagining a voice "like" his, but not his. And this voice says what Sedgwick has yearned to hear since childhood—that she can die.[100] That Sedgwick reads Van Wey's words in the abbreviated version of this material presented in her Kessler lecture evidences her desire to performatively inhabit a compassionate voice *like* Van Wey's, even if only for a moment.[101]

Rather than represent Sedgwick's inhabitation of Van Wey's position within a unidirectional model of transference, *Dialogue* highlights the extent to which the therapist shares in the patient's experience. By doing so, the memoir underscores the potential for holding to produce transformation for both participants. Thus, Van Wey echoes Sedgwick's own yearning to be held by him. He admits that "being really seen by you is something that matters to me. Not that I just get narcissistically recirculated back to myself through your eyes, which happens all the time—but that I'm changed to myself in some way as I see that you see me."[102] While *Dialogue* depicts the intractability of projection—particularly in Sedgwick's initial disparagement of Van Wey's intellect—the memoir affirms overcoming these dynamics in favor of mutual holding, in which both subjects become recognized and, through recognition, "transfigure[d]."[103] Of course, therapy provides such durable relations because it is premised on the therapist's financial and medical commitment to the patient. In non-therapeutic exchanges, the need for durability is no less present, though it is far less guaranteed. Holding is thus a relation that must be chosen, cultivated, and sustained—in short, practiced as an ethic. As we will see, Sedgwick stresses the stratified conditions under which queer communities enact such commitments, but she insists that a homophobic environment only amplifies the need for queer modes of collective holding.

Dialogue extends impersonal holding to its readers, soliciting us to hold Sedgwick and Van Wey. *Dialogue* frames the stakes for our response when Sedgwick requests Van Wey's session notes. The risk, Van Wey paraphrases, is that her reading will be "sadistic" and consequently "spoil me as a source of nurturance for her."[104] We can see the roots of Sedgwick's reparative reading here. But far from sponsoring "better" reading, as Berlant puts it, reparative reading simply offers a different motive for reading—specifically, focalizing the other.[105] Indeed, Sedgwick finds Van Wey's notes reassuring because they attempt to inhabit her point of view, reparatively reading her.

Sedgwick enacts a similar focalization when, in the course of writing *Dialogue*, she edits the writings of Gary Fisher, her former student who dies of AIDS. Sedgwick literally dreams "*as*" Fisher, nightly inhabiting "world[s] clothed in the restless, elastic skin of his beautiful idiom."[106] We should take pause at Sedgwick's metaphor here, inasmuch as it risks effacing Fisher's racial difference. Without disavowing this problematic intonation, I wish to point out that it is characteristic of a premise valorized throughout Sedgwick's work—namely, that "*The paths of allo-identification are likely to be strange and recalcitrant.*"[107] Indeed, *Dialogue* notes Sedgwick's confusion around her nourishing identifications with gay men, as well as her ambivalence about being a white woman "patronizing" Fisher's racially and sexually charged writing.[108] Acknowledging she might be "the wrong person to be promoting this [Fisher's] material," Sedgwick nonetheless feels an "investment in making that work, or in demonstrating the interest of that border-crossing position."[109] This is perhaps why Sedgwick compares reading Fisher to falling asleep while reading and dreaming one's own "mental semantics into the sentence structure of the author."[110] Given up in such an experience is the illusion that our idioms are ever truly extricable from those that inhabit us. Sedgwick thus affirms the unruly circuits of identification as a potential source for relationality, and possibly political solidarity, across the boundaries of social difference.

Dialogue consequently embraces difference as productive for holding relations. For example, Van Wey's gender initially poses a problem for Sedgwick. She describes him as looking like someone "for whom, maybe—unlike me or most anyone I love—his entitlement to exist, the OK-ness of being who and as he is, has never seemed very seriously questionable."[111] At stake in Sedgwick's desire for a feminist, non-homophobic therapist is not a "laundry list or a litmus test" of personal preference.[112] Rather, these are political values that underwrite the possibility of their having an ethical encounter in which Sedgwick can learn from Van Wey. Male privilege, buttressed by the affect of "entitlement," presents an obstacle to their intersubjective relation insofar as it forestalls the focalization required for holding. Sedgwick wonders, "How could someone like that have learned to think or feel?"[113]

However, Van Wey's sexual difference ultimately presents an "opportunity" for focalization.[114] First presuming he was "like a stereotype [*sic*] male with easily accessible and quickly on-and-off sexual feelings," Sedgwick later focalizes Van Wey, wondering if he identifies with her confusions around sexuality.[115] Precisely because social difference never leaves *Dialogue*'s exchange, the memoir affirms permeable identification as enabling an ethical insight similar to one Sedgwick values in Mahayana pedagogy—namely, that the other is *"not other than oneself."*[116] Here Sedgwick echoes Francisco Varela, who also draws from Buddhism and psychoanalysis for an ethical pedagogy. Central to the analytic scene, Varela underscores, is "learning to see ourselves and others as inescapably transitory and fragmented."[117] Sedgwick stresses, though, that one cannot eternally inhabit this space of fragmentation. Doing so sacrifices the non-identical reintegration necessary for one to offer a pedagogical relation to others. This is why *Dialogue* carves out a space for subjective agency within permeable intersubjectivity.

THE MIDDLE RANGES OF AGENCY IN FLESH AND FANTASY

Insofar as *Dialogue* insists on the self as permeable, it would seem to sacrifice a recognizable conception of agency. Of course, agency has been a long-standing problem for queer theory. As Butler summarizes, "some would say that to be a split subject ... is precisely *not* to have the grounds for agency."[118] Butler's solution, however, ultimately troubles Sedgwick. Butler famously claims that "the agency of the subject appears to be an effect of its subordination. Any effort to oppose that subordination will necessarily presuppose and reinvoke it."[119] For Sedgwick, this formulation hews too closely to a constricting understanding of Foucault's repressive hypothesis. If one cannot study and critique repression without contributing to it, Sedgwick fears that critique becomes dualistic—compressed into the polar limits of acceptance or refusal. While Sedgwick does not yearn for a utopian outside to power, she affirms "ways of understanding human desire that might be quite to the side of prohibition and repression."[120] Indeed, a significant realization for Sedgwick in *Dialogue* is that "agency ... may not lie only in extremes of grandiosity or abjection."[121] This realization underwrites Sedgwick's subsequent affirmation of the "middle ranges of agency," which perceive power as a "form of relationality that deals in, for example, negotiations (including win–win negotiations), the exchange of affect, and other small differentials."[122] These embodied exchanges allow for "effectual creativity and change" that fall between the extremes of repression or liberation.[123] More significantly, Sedgwick's redefinition of agency challenges the location of queer agency in the performative subversion of norms and places it instead in affective embodiment.

Dialogue crystallizes the negotiation of embodiment as a mode of agency when a foot pain leads Sedgwick to fear that her cancer has returned. The terror evacuates Sedgwick's "interiority," making her feel that her "whole materiality has flattened."[124] As a solution, Van Wey suggests that they push against one another: "So up rise I, in lieu of answer; and up rises Shannon. And planting our feet and ourselves about a yard apart, we place hand against hand, his and mine, and push with our little might to force each other a step or two backward."[125] Afterward, Sedgwick feels "embodied in quite/a new way; dimensional, /powerful. /*Not scared*."[126] At stake in this scene of reciprocal touching are two polarities of agency. Their hands evidence Sedgwick's point that the sensation of touching undermines any "dualistic understanding of agency and passivity."[127] Both touch and are touched, reciprocally. Yet their touching nonetheless creates a site of agency for Sedgwick. That agency does not result from an exercise of conscious self-determination. On the contrary, it emerges from an experience that prioritizes affective embodiment over conscious thought. As Sedgwick and Adam Frank insist, following Silvan Tomkins, "inefficiency" exists among cognition, affect, and the drives.[128] This "productive opacity" is the locus of "learning, development, continuity, differentiation" as well as "freedom."[129]

Since Sedgwick has "no idea what to expect" from this embodied encounter, subjective change emerges for her.[130] She cannot intellectualize, and thereby tame, the "dangerous threshold" of embodied relation that she initially perceives as "out of bounds."[131] Afterward, Sedgwick is "disquieted at this tectonic shift in what I've presumed were the fixed zones of permission and prohibition."[132] This shift underlies *Dialogue*'s affirmation of opacity as a condition of subjective possibility. But more specifically, it demonstrates that some prohibitions are, in fact, only presumptions that can be turned into opportunities for relation. After all, Van Wey has not "articulated ... a rule that sex talk is inevitable. Any more than he's ever told me—what? that we can't touch, or I must say whatever's in my head."[133] What emerges in their affective encounter is a surprise, a loosening of Sedgwick's projective assumptions; she discovers that what she thought was fixed is open, what appeared to be a prohibition was only a habit that can be worked around.

To articulate the ethical significance of these affective negotiations, Sedgwick turns to Klein to suggest that these small differentials point toward reparative modes of agency. But in doing so, does she sacrifice the social constitution of power that queer theory values for its political critique? After all, Butler incisively critiques Klein for ignoring the social nature of psychic violence. Diverging from Klein's conception of an "innate desire to triumph," Butler argues that "certain forms of love entail the loss of the object" because they "fail to qualify as objects of love."[134] These objects are "marked for 'death'" by social forces antagonistic to their persistence.[135] Because Butler insists on the inexorability of prohibition as the structuring force of subjectivity and agency, her performative politics are based on the immanent contestation of the norms that mark certain groups for death, exclusion, or abjection. This is one reason that Butler finds the conjunction of Freud with Foucault so productive, because Freud enables her to claim that internalizing prohibition is constitutive of psychic life. Yet Sedgwick wishes to turn from precisely this premise of psychoanalysis, and she looks to Klein to do so. After all, repression and the Oedipal complex are secondary mechanisms in Klein,

subordinate to the primary defenses of splitting, introjection, and projection. Thus, a key factor in Sedgwick's turn to Klein lies in her desire to
elaborate non-Oedipal accounts of psychic life and agency that circumvent
the foundational role of prohibition.

Without minimizing this motivating force, I wish to highlight
Sedgwick's somewhat inconsistent reading of Klein to demonstrate the
ethical insights into queer politics she derives from Klein.[136] My point
is not that Sedgwick is "wrong" in her interpretation of Klein but that
she has a specifically ethical investment in her reading. That investment is
most clear in Sedgwick's preference for Klein's description of the psyche in
terms of positions. "Positions" signal for Sedgwick an alternative to structural, developmental, and essentialist models of psychology. Sedgwick
equates positions with "critical *practices*" insofar as both offer "changing
and heterogeneous relational stances."[137] At some moments, Sedgwick
acknowledges Klein's description of the positions as progressively developmental, yet she tends to de-emphasize this interpretation in favor of a
less "fixed" model.[138] However, as Meira Likierman notes, it is not at all
clear that Klein saw the depressive position as her followers do—namely,
as a "more permanent feature of adult mental life" that we reinhabit.[139]
More fundamentally, it is not clear that Klein saw the position as one we
can *choose* to inhabit. Yet Sedgwick clearly does. At stake in doing so is
Sedgwick's desire to access affective motives for queer critique that attenu-
ate the collective anxiety that instigates paranoid defenses.

In Sedgwick's view, the "intense dread" that structured queer communities in the late 1980s and early 1990s "imprint[ed] a paranoid structura-
tion onto the theory and activism of that period."[140] This is unsurprising,
she notes, because of the collective repression enacted by a homophobic nation. Precisely because paranoid modes of being were "enforced,"
Sedgwick perceives them as "impoverishing, and humiliating," even if
paranoia was constructive for queer activism.[141] Though Klein does not
link paranoia to a specific historical context, she describes it as a reaction,
a primary defense against the ego's fundamental endogenous anxiety, and
she counterposes the paranoid/schizoid position to the anxiety-mitigating,
reparative strategies of the depressive position. By aligning long-term
political commitments with the "mature ethical dimension of the depressive position," then, Sedgwick aims to carve out a space for queer activism
that does not prioritize the impoverishing paranoid/schizoid defenses.[142]
These defenses obstruct intersubjectivity because their fantasies of extreme
abjection and omnipotence disable, in advance, a reparative focalization of
the other.

Though Sedgwick's theory might suggest that she wholly rejects the paranoid/schizoid position for queer sexual politics, *Dialogue* draws on its space of fantasy for intersubjective negotiations of social power by displaying Sedgwick's masturbatory fantasies of sexual violence. *Dialogue* affirms the performative exhibition of sexual fantasy as a way to negotiate social power because fantasy is productively, if painfully, pitched between intrapsychic and external reality. In this respect, *Dialogue* is inspired by Klein's view of the psyche as "populated, not with ideas, representations, knowledges, urges, and repressions, but with *things*, things with physical properties, including people and hacked-off bits of people."[143] By insisting on the literality of psychic objects (and again, their bits), Sedgwick conceives of fantasy as an active negotiation of reality. We see the implications for this concept in *Dialogue* when Sedgwick grapples with the sadomasochism of her masturbation fantasies. Their dynamics include, among other elements, an institutional setting with a "hierarchy," a spectator to the scene of punishment, and "some speech or action of coerced consent from the person being punished."[144] Sedgwick tends to identify with the latter figure, "at that fold of wanting to withhold consent but being forced to perform it."[145] While she experiences "Warm. Golden. /Intoxicating" affects during masturbation, the fantasies that accompany it are suffused with "Violence and pain. /Humiliation. Torture. /Rape, systematic."[146] Sedgwick is quick to insist that "these fantasies stay in their place. ... They don't connect with real life."[147] Yet they become displaced, and disappear as sources of nourishment, when Sedgwick undergoes breast cancer treatment. The treatment undermines the otherwise stable line between fantasy and reality. These "two, utterly separate worlds" touch when a nurse gets irritated at Sedgwick while attempting to draw her blood.[148] With the muted cries of another patient in the distance, Sedgwick, as she lies on the bed in pain, can "feel every pulse of her [the nurse's] impatience."[149]

This bleeding of fantasy into reality instigates Sedgwick's desire to share her fantasies of abjection with Van Wey, and as a result of articulating them, she experiences a return of sexual desire. One could read her experience as a classic example of the repressive hypothesis—a fantasized liberation from repression purchased through confession. After all, in Van Wey's words, "it is here at the place of talking about the experience, the S/M [sadomasochistic] fantasies, not within the fantasies, that the sense of an enjoying subject with agency is possible/permitted."[150] Yet *Dialogue* forestalls the repressive reading by making explicit that the return of Sedgwick's genitally based sexuality is predicated on the "place of talking," the intersubjective scene of narration. By doing so, *Dialogue* reveals a key discursive technology by which sexual subjectivity is consolidated. Further, Sedgwick solicits her readers as participatory witnesses, thereby undermining our identification as masochists or voyeurs, the two positions that Leigh Gilmore suggests "autobiography about trauma forces the reader to assume."[151] Rather than being "superior, privileged eavesdroppers," we are invited to—as Sedgwick once wrote of Henry James—partake in the "exhibitionistic enjoyment and performance of a sexuality organized around shame … [as] an audience desired."[152] That Sedgwick desires an audience, that the telling of her fantasies performs a sexuality, is key to *Dialogue*'s creation of a participatory space for the affective negotiation of sexual agency outside the polarities of abjection and omnipotence.

The performative sharing of fantasy results in the return of "sensual reality and sense of possibility … of the reality of my own [Sedgwick's] body."[153] This return has feminist significance, insofar as Sedgwick is no longer defined as an "object for others to satisfy their touch needs, not mine."[154] *Dialogue* thus suggests that fantasies of masturbation can provide desperately needed nourishment for an objectified self, as they do in Sedgwick's childhood, making her feel "safe—almost … held."[155] *Dialogue* also enacts a mode of queer performativity by exhibiting fantasies otherwise experienced as shameful; queer performativity is, in Sedgwick's conception, a "strategy for the production of meaning and being, in relation to the affect shame."[156] Shame, for Sedgwick, is underwritten by the desire to "reconstitute the interpersonal bridge" that is frustrated when we fail to elicit another's positive interest.[157] *Dialogue*'s telling of Sedgwick's fantasies is thus motivated by her desire to performatively reconstitute this bridge and to quell her humiliation without denying the experience of shame. Sedgwick's exhibitionism is therefore not reductively narcissistic; rather, it exemplifies the ethic that Michael Warner defines as the basis for queer "sociability," specifically the "acknowledgment of all that is most abject and least reputable in oneself."[158]

Sedgwick's turn to therapy for this relationality is part of a broader queer project that seeks ethical insight within the psychoanalytic encounter. Despite their divergences elsewhere, Sedgwick's depiction of fantasy converges with Leo Bersani's recent suggestion that "perhaps the therapeutic secret of psychoanalysis lies in its willingness to entertain any possibility of behavior or thought as only possibility."[159] The virtuality of psychoanalytic narration illuminates why Sedgwick does not feel herself to be uttering "Gothic projectiles/into the long void" but instead "giddily welcoming/speculation of//what words may arise/and at what instant they may, /bubbling, between us."[160] Loosened from constraint, "suspended in the real," Sedgwick's discussion of her fantasies with Van Wey feels like an "experiment" that produces a relieving sense of being "a very routine/patient."[161] Their therapeutic relation engenders an experimental scene that allows Sedgwick's subjectivity to be, at once, pleasurably unsettled, comfortingly impersonal, and utterly ordinary. Both Sedgwick and Bersani insist that the relational modalities enabled by therapeutic encounters should not be "sequestered" from the world.[162] For precisely this reason, Sedgwick claims that the ethical value of sadomasochistic performativity is that it is *not* disjoined from the social. Indeed, Sedgwick critiques the "hygienic dislinkages" that seek to redeem S/M as pure fantasy, and she resists affirmations of its negotiation of "power, consent, and safety" as simply an alternative to mainstream sexual cultures.[163] Rather, Sedgwick values "the richness of experimental and experiential meaning in these scenes," which is amplified if one understands that they are "neither simply continuous with, nor simply dislinked from the relations and histories that surround and embed them."[164] Without these assumptions, one can see S/M dramatizing power dynamics and creating a space for the performative working through of those relations outside the institutional contexts of therapy. At stake in this analogy is not the sanitization of sex and fantasy as therapy. Rather, Sedgwick eroticizes therapy, framing it as an equally "potent, body-implicating, and time-bending representational [project]" as S/M.[165] These embodied representational spaces enact incipiently social modes of agency that produce subjective change through the intersubjective negotiation of affect. To understand the ethical principle that guides the emergence and defines the values of these changes for queer communities, I turn to *Dialogue*'s location of intersubjective possibility within the transitional space of dying.

Queer Belonging in Mortality

Dialogue is steeped in a confrontation with mortality. By its close, Fisher has died of AIDS, Sedgwick's doctor has an AIDS-related infection, her brother-in-law has metastatic melanoma, her mother has melanoma, Van Wey requires cardiac catheterization, and Sedgwick's cancer has metastasized to her spine. As Sedgwick suggests, these "brutal foreshortening[s]" of life define the "deroutinized" temporality of queer relationality—lovers and friends die without "'normal' generational narrative[s]" to organize their collective identification.[166] The pressure of cross-generational mortality results in an ethical relationality premised on the present. "Whatever else we know," Sedgwick states, "we know there isn't time to bullshit. ... It is one another immediately, one another as the present fullness of a becoming whose arc may extend no further, whom we each must learn best to apprehend, fulfill, and bear company."[167] In addition to Sedgwick's Buddhism here, we can sense the skepticism about claims to the future that is central to queer theory's post-AIDS structure of feeling.[168]

Where mainstream LGBTQ movements have sought to supplant the cultural equivalence of queerness with death, some see queerness's negativity as its most critical force. Edelman, for example, argues that queers might undermine the ideological coherence of "reproductive futurism" and the social order it buttresses by embracing their figuration as harbingers of the death drive.[169] In his framework, nearly all social appeals based on positive affect, particularly compassion, underwrite phantasmic interpellations of subjects into narcissistic identifications with conservative images of the future that perpetuate sameness. Sedgwick challenges the view that fantasy provides "narcissistic solace" that secures the ego's "fix[ation] to fixity."[170] But she also suggests that the desire for future happiness need not be a "defense against the ego's certain end"; it can enable the ego's reconciliation with finitude, and its relational cultivation can produce the imagination of social possibilities foreclosed by the paranoid fear of contingency.[171]

As *Dialogue* concludes, Sedgwick becomes interested in Buddhist thought that conceives death as an "ethical" skill.[172] She values the idea that "some passage of discontinuity like death can be the occasion of enlightenment, if you do it right, i.e., if you can be in a place to recognize a love that is you and is also toward you."[173] While Sedgwick does not define the content of this enlightenment, she embraces Buddhist concepts for traversing discontinuity: "nondualism, spaciousness, an intimate and nonlinear relation to mortality, an alert pedagogical relationality free of projection, an emptying of the concept of self, and at the same time a primary emphasis on happiness."[174] As the phrase *at the same time* suggests, Sedgwick wishes to balance a permeable relation to non-being with the subjective experience of felicity. The seemingly innocuous first sentence of *Dialogue* foregrounds both dispositions: "Apparently it's as a patient that I want to emerge."[175] In a progressive temporality, one wants to stop being a patient as soon as possible. Here that desire is reversed; the locus of possibility lies in becoming a patient. "Patient" signals, on the one hand, Van Wey's inflexibility. Despite the profession's shift to "client," he uses "patient" because "that's the way they taught us, back in graduate school—seems like too much trouble to change."[176] Rather than focus on

Van Wey's intransigence, Sedgwick affirms "patient" as a disposition they share—an openness to the future without grasping at what is to come. This is why Sedgwick redefines patient as a

> modest

> > word that makes no claim
> > to anything but—wanting
> > to be happier

> and wanting, it's true, someone else to shoulder a lot of agency in the matter of my happiness.[177]

Patience expresses Sedgwick's desire for some future with happiness and for help in accessing it while she "learn[s] to unbe a self."[178] The modesty of Sedgwick's "claim" lies in its contingency, evidenced in the statement: "I'm good, if I am, because I'm lucky enough to be happy (if I am)."[179] Sedgwick's conditional "if" captures the non-causal relatedness of each variable in this equation, in which happiness contributes to, rather than provides evidence of, one's goodness. Sedgwick's contingent happiness forestalls the inverse proposition: "I am lucky and happy because I am good."[180] *Dialogue*'s insistence on the immanent ethical value of positive affect anticipates Michael D. Snediker's theory of "queer optimism," which extricates positive affects from promissory and utopian temporalities allergic to contingency.[181] Following Snediker's claim that positive affects are not given but "theoretically mobilizable," we might read *Dialogue* as redefining the ethical repertoire of happiness—happiness becomes a disposition realized through the reparative care of the other that enables the self to become "[u]ngreedy, unattached, unrageful, unignorant."[182]

Sedgwick claims that this relationality can incite the imagination of ethical and political change. Through reparative relations, one realizes that "the future may be different from the present ... [and] that the past, in turn, could have happened differently from the way it actually did."[183] This is why Sedgwick claims that "activist politics, even more than pedagogy," straddle the threshold between the paranoid/schizoid and depressive positions.[184] While she admits that her activism drew much energy from the former position, Sedgwick claims the latter is more capable of conceptualizing change. The depressive position provides resources to admit, "We, like those others, are subject to the imperious dynamics of *ressentiment*," and then ask, "[n]ow how can the dynamics themselves become different?"[185]

Sedgwick's ethics thus seek to reimagine intersubjectivity as such, limiting projective blame and amplifying mutual preservation to engender the imagination of collective change. Sedgwick cautions that, at any point within the depressive position, the psyche might succumb to thought-crushing depression, anticipatory projection, or "manic escapism."[186] But she argues that the inaugural realization of the position also provides the resources for working through these affects—namely, a "guilty, empathetic view of the other as at once good, damaged, integral, and requiring and eliciting love and care."[187] While Sedgwick's ethic might inspire activism, it cannot be a model of politics as such—she does not specify the material conditions necessary for producing collective nourishment. Yet political commitment requires a durable investment in preserving a collective into the future and the ability to articulate the prospect of a future different from the past. In a world where queerness—rather than a sadistic culture of homophobia and sexism—is framed as an illness, Sedgwick's ethic aims to repair the psychic violence enacted by heteronormative cultures. This violence prevents the incipiently social imagination of queer change by eroding value in oneself and one's relations. By defining nourishment as the condition for imagining collective possibility, Sedgwick rewrites queerness as a project of cultivating intersubjective care.

Despite the hope in Sedgwick's ethics, I would qualify José Esteban Muñoz's correlation of reparation with utopianism.[188] Rather than affirm a utopian temporality, Sedgwick locates reparative possibility in the eroding present of dying. The value of this transitional space, for Sedgwick, is that it offers a pedagogy that can contribute to queer activism. Sedgwick characterizes the space between life and death in terms of the Buddhist *bardo*, wherein one confronts mortality and recognizes the impermanence of life.[189] When asked whether a politics lies in the *bardo*, Sedgwick admits that it "doesn't, ideally, seem to involve mobilizing rage or grievance," affects conventionally congenial to activism.[190] Yet Sedgwick notes that this liminal state "potentiated AIDS activism" and remains a source of "potential for activism as well as reflection around other slow-acting diseases."[191] The *bardo's* potential is that minority communities will recognize their impermanence as a common condition. This is why *Dialogue's* final entry notes that another of Sedgwick's friends has breast cancer. Sedgwick is not alone in her confrontation with mortality, and the reparative work that *Dialogue* models will have to go on without Sedgwick or Van Wey. Though it affirms the contingency of relations, *Dialogue* insists on the need for durable reparative care extending into the future, beyond the bounds of any one particular life.

Dialogue crystallizes this affirmation in its concluding image, when Sedgwick trips on the "shrubby border" between the parking lots of Van Wey's office and a gas station.[192] As she walks back toward his office, Sedgwick glimpses Van Wey walking ahead of her. She writes, "I see him gather up from the pavement the clumps of pine mulch I kicked down as I was teetering on the brink. Then bobbing up gently, he pats it back into place, his hands briefly smoothing it in with the other mulch."[193] For Sedgwick, this scene is a "time-lapse graphic."[194] It enables "Shannon [to] occupy the place where I was, encountering my ghost without recognition, unmaking my mistake—me, turning back, seeing it."[195] Van Wey unknowingly inhabits Sedgwick's position, offering, in her friend's words, "An immediate, involuntary substitution."[196]

Undoubtedly, this narrative condenses *Dialogue*'s key tropes—contiguous spatiality, permeable inhabitation, corporeal negotiation, and impersonal care; indeed, Sedgwick "love[s] that his care for me was not care for *me*."[197] In this sense, the image evidences how "reparative work" persists when we are gone, performed by others related to us only in the queerest sense, others who may never realize who inhabits them or for whom they substitute.[198] Whenever she feels "frustration or fear," Sedgwick turns "inward toward" this "object of reflection" and "smile[s]."[199] In its content, and as an experience held inside her, this image provides a tactical position for Sedgwick to experience nourishment, relationality, and the possibility for change even in moments of (un)becoming.

As I have argued throughout, *Dialogue* similarly offers these affective relations to its readers. Though it is a dialogue, the memoir insists that relations, incipiently social, always fan out beyond the two. Holding, nourishing, loving, touching; reparation, happiness, possibility—these terms constellate a series of queer relations key to the form and expressive content of *Dialogue*. But more fundamentally, they chart an ethical itinerary in permeable intersubjectivity, one that might teach us ways to realize life's possibilities for one another in the face of our ever-present endings.

NOTES

1. Eve Kosofsky Sedgwick, *Touching Feeling: Affect, Pedagogy, Performativity* (Durham: Duke University Press, 2003), 123–51.
2. See Sharon Marcus and Stephen Best, "Surface Reading: An Introduction," *Representations* 108, no. 1 (2009): 1–21.
3. Eve Kosofsky Sedgwick, "Melanie Klein and the Difference Affect Makes," *South Atlantic Quarterly* 106, no. 3 (2007): 625–42. This essay

has subsequently been republished with minor edits in *The Weather in Proust*, ed. Jonathan Goldberg (Durham: Duke University Press, 2011). Here I refer to the original publication and pagination of the essay, in part because Sedgwick herself completed the edits for this essay and because the context for the essay highlights Sedgwick's thinking about the past and future(s) of queer theory. The special issue of *SAQ* was entitled "After Sex? On Writing Since Queer Theory," and it was edited by Janet Halley and Andrew Parker. For critiques of the disavowal of the AIDS crisis that converge with Sedgwick's, see Douglas Crimp, "Melancholia and Moralism," in *Loss*, ed. David Eng and David Kazanjian (Berkeley: University of California Press, 2003), 188–202; Judith Butler, "Melancholy Gender/Refused Identification," in *The Psychic Life of Power* (Stanford: Stanford University Press, 1997), 132–50; and Michael Warner, "Something Queer about the Nation-State," in *Publics and Counterpublics* (New York: Zone Books, 2002), 209–23.
4. Sedgwick, "Melanie," 640.
5. Ibid.
6. In this chapter, I use "positive" and "negative" as descriptors of affective states to denote Silvan Tomkins's influence on Sedgwick and his division of affects into positive (interest/excitement, enjoyment/joy), resetting (surprise/startle), and negative (distress/anguish, fear/terror, shame/humiliation, anger/rage, contempt, and disgust). Thus shame is technically a "negative" affect in which Sedgwick finds much positive ethical value. At the same time, I use negative to highlight Sedgwick's critique of the affects associated with Melanie Klein's paranoid/schizoid position insofar as they obstruct the queerness of intersubjectivity.
7. For example, note the title of the gay-marketed show *Glee*, which braids together positive affective discourse with a message of liberal tolerance and self-celebration.
8. Heather Love, *Feeling Backward: Loss and the Politics of Queer History* (Cambridge: Harvard University Press, 2007), 30.
9. For the former, see Sedgwick's critique of D. A. Miller and Judith Butler in *Touching Feeling*, 123–51. For the latter, see her interview with Michael D. Snediker, "Queer Little Gods: A Conversation," *Massachusetts Review*, nos. 1–2 (2008): 194–218.
10. Eve Kosofsky Sedgwick, *A Dialogue on Love* (Boston: Beacon, 1999).
11. A key influence on Sedgwick's *haibun* is her reading of *Japanese Death Poems*, ed. Yoel Hoffman (Tokyo: Tuttle Publishing, 1986). Hoffman's introduction provides an insightful analysis of the haiku form and situates its usage within the cultural history of Japanese death practices and poetics. Sedgwick's use of the *haibun* is not unique to American literature. For American appropriations of the form, see *Journey to the Interior: American Versions of Haibun*, ed. Bruce Ross (Tokyo: Tuttle Publishing, 1988).

12. Sedgwick, "Melanie," 642.
13. Ibid., 640.
14. Eve Kosofsky Sedgwick, "Teaching Depression," *Scholar and Feminist Online* 4, no. 2 (2006), accessed August 7, 2016, http://sfonline.barnard.edu/heilbrun/sedgwick_01.htm, original emphasis.
15. Sedgwick, *Touching*, 13.
16. Sedgwick, *Dialogue*, 60.
17. Ibid.
18. Ibid.
19. Ibid., 109. For a relevant reading of Sedgwick's queer conception of temporality, see Jane Gallop, "Sedgwick's Twisted Temporalities, 'or even just reading and writing,'" in *Queer Times, Queer Becomings*, eds. E.L. McCallum and Mikko Tuhkanen (Albany: State University of New York, 2011), 47–74.
20. Eve Kosofsky Sedgwick, "Teaching 'Experimental Critical Writing,'" in *The Ends of Performance*, ed. Peggy Phelan and Jill Lane (New York: New York University Press, 1998), 115.
21. *Dialogue* is inspired by James Merrill's poetry, particularly "The Prose of Departure" and "The Book of Ephraim." For other influences, see Jason Edwards, *Eve Kosofsky Sedgwick* (London: Routledge, 2009), 121–66.
22. Sedgwick, "Teaching Depression."
23. Ibid.
24. Ibid.
25. For a succinct overview of this critique, see Jonathan Culler, *On Deconstruction: Theory and Criticism After Structuralism* (Ithaca: Cornell University Press, 2007), 39. Also see the introduction.
26. Cynthia G. Franklin, *Academic Lives: Memoir, Cultural Theory, and the University Today* (Athens: University of Georgia Press, 2009), 242–43.
27. Sedgwick, *Dialogue*, 194.
28. Ibid., 210.
29. Ibid., 130.
30. Ibid., 194.
31. Ibid.
32. Ibid.
33. For helpful formal insights into the *haibun*, see Edwards, *Eve*, 131; and Katy Hawkins, "Woven Spaces: Eve Kosofsky Sedgwick's *A Dialogue on Love*," *Women and Performance: A Journal of Feminist Theory* 16, no. 2 (2006): 251–67.
34. Sedgwick, *Dialogue*, 207.
35. Sedgwick, *Touching*, 3.
36. Sedgwick, *Dialogue*, 207.
37. Ibid., 199, original emphasis.

38. Renu Bora, "Outing Texture," in *Novel Gazing: Queer Readings in Fiction*, ed. Eve Kosofsky Sedgwick (Durham: Duke University Press, 1997), 123.
39. See Eve Kosofsky Sedgwick, "A Poem Is Being Written," in *Tendencies* (Durham: Duke University Press, 1993), 177 214.
40. Ibid., 186.
41. Hawkins, "Woven," 255.
42. Sedgwick, *Dialogue*, 199.
43. Sedgwick and Snediker, "Queer Little Gods," 198.
44. Ibid.
45. Sedgwick, *Dialogue*, 105.
46. Ibid.
47. Ibid., 204.
48. Ibid., 8.
49. Ibid.
50. Ibid., 116.
51. Sedgwick, *Touching*, 6.
52. Sedgwick, *Dialogue*, 205.
53. Ibid., 137.
54. Brian Massumi, *Parables for the Virtual: Movement, Affect, Sensation* (Durham: Duke University Press, 2002), 32.
55. Ibid., 28. Massumi complicates this narrative in his more recent work on affect. See Brian Massumi, *Politics of Affect* (Malden: Polity Press, 2015), especially 212–13.
56. Ibid., 61.
57. For a queer approach to the materiality and animacy of language, see Mel Y. Chen, *Animacies: Biopolitics, Racial Mattering, and Queer Affect* (Durham: Duke University Press, 2012).
58. Sedgwick, *Touching*, 6.
59. Ibid.
60. Ibid., 7.
61. Ibid., 6.
62. Ibid., 18.
63. Ibid., 23.
64. Edwards, *Eve*, 131.
65. This is an apt example of the "torsion" between performativity and reference that Sedgwick describes above.
66. Sedgwick, *Touching*, 8.
67. Ibid.
68. Stephen M. Barber and David L. Clark, "Queer Moments: The Performative Temporalities of Eve Kosofsky Sedgwick," in *Regarding Sedgwick: Essays on Queer Culture and Critical Theory*, eds. Stephen M. Barber and David L. Clark (New York: Routledge, 2002), 7, original emphasis.

69. Nancy K. Miller, "Reviewing Eve," in *Regarding Sedgwick: Essays on Queer Culture and Critical Theory*, eds. Stephen M. Barber and David L. Clark (New York: Routledge, 2002), 219.

70. Lauren Berlant, *Cruel Optimism* (Durham: Duke University Press, 2011), 125. For Berlant's subsequent, and richly insightful, reappraisal of Sedgwick's memoir and her notions of reparation, see Lauren Berlant and Lee Edelman, *Sex, or the Unbearable* (Durham: Duke University Press, 2014), especially 35–61. Berlant's reading here converges in many respects with mine, particularly her assertion that, for Sedgwick, "the very shifting of the subject in response to its own threat to its self-attachment can be the source of an affective creativity that is not just a fantasmatic toupée, but also the possibility of a recalibrated sensorium" (61). My understanding of this creativity includes this sensorium but, as I elaborate below, focuses more specifically on the discovery of relational agencies that do not presume the subject as their foundation.

71. Ibid.

72. Ibid.

73. Ibid., 124–25.

74. Ibid., 159.

75. Sedgwick, *Touching*, 160.

76. Ibid., 162, 159.

77. Ibid., 160.

78. Ibid., original emphasis.

79. Sedgwick, *Dialogue*, 215.

80. For a helpful introduction to these divergent traditions, see *The Buddhist Tradition: In India, China and Japan*, ed. William Theodore de Bary (New York: Random House, 1972); and *Essential Tibetan Buddhism*, ed. Robert A.F. Thurman (San Francisco: HarperSanFrancisco, 1995). The classic Tibetan text on the Bodhisattva is Śāntideva, *A Guide to the Bodhisattva Way of Life*, trans. Vesna A. Wallace and B. Alan Wallace (Ithaca, NY: Snow Lion Publications, 1997). For an introductory gloss on this text, see Dalai Lama, *For the Benefit of All Beings: A Commentary on The Way of the Bodhisattva*, trans. Padmakara Translation Group (Boston: Shambhala, 1994). Key Mahayana texts that inspire Sedgwick's interpretation of Buddhist pedagogy include *The Holy Teaching of Vimalakirti: A Mahayana Scripture*, trans. Robert Thurman (University Park: Pennsylvania State University Press, 1976) and *A Treasury of Mahāyāna Sūtras: Selections from the Mahāratnakūta Sūtra*, ed. Garma C. C. Chang, trans. Buddhist Association of the United States (University Park: Pennsylvania State University Press, 1983). Sedgwick's argument about Tibetan Buddhist pedagogy is heavily influenced by her reading of Sogyal Rinpoche, *The Tibetan Book of Living and Dying* (New York: HarperCollins, 2002).

81. Sedgwick, *Dialogue*, 215.
82. Ibid., 106.
83. Ibid., 113.
84. Ibid., 114, original emphasis.
85. Ibid., 115.
86. Ibid., original emphasis.
87. Ibid., 114, original emphasis.
88. Ibid., 168.
89. Ibid., 96.
90. Ibid., 88.
91. Ibid., 88, 168.
92. Ibid., 83.
93. Ibid., 66–67, original emphasis.
94. Ibid., 139. Note that the queer relationality of care is not premised on subjective recognition. It is a relational holding premised on impersonality—a caring that is not "not caring" in the sense of caring about *her* but caring as a practice of nurturance that does not make excessive demands on the other to *be* a certain self, to mirror back a certain kind of relationality. Hence, the liquid metaphors of Sedgwick's haiku underscore the transitivity of the form that this relation takes. Sedgwick qualifies that this relation is "less human" than Winnicott's language of holding suggests, thereby stressing that the queer relationality of care is *not* reducible to the liberal-humanist model of recognition. It rests on an ambient, atmospheric, or spatial model of relations that do not necessarily cohere into selves while also not being radically and temporally oriented toward the masochistic annihilation of the self. On the concept of holding in object relations, see especially D.W. Winnicott, *Playing and Reality* (New York: Routledge, 2005); *The Child, Family, and the Outside World* (New York: Perseus Publishing, 1992); and Adam Phillips, *Winnicott* (Cambridge: Harvard University Press, 1988). For a different approach to impersonal relationality in queer theory, see Leo Bersani and Adam Phillips, *Intimacies* (Chicago: The University of Chicago Press, 2008), particularly Bersani's conception of impersonal narcissism.
95. Ibid., 215.
96. Ibid., 164–65.
97. Ibid., 38.
98. Ibid.
99. Ibid., 220.
100. Ibid., 16.
101. See Eve Kosofsky Sedgwick, "A Dialogue on Love," in *Queer Ideas: The David R. Kessler Lectures in Lesbian and Gay Studies* (New York: Feminist Press at the City University of New York, 2003), 137–68.
102. Sedgwick, Dialogue, 163.

103. Ibid., 38.

104. Ibid., 200.

105. Berlant, *Cruel*, 124. As the memoir suggests, the question of reparative work is not a transcendental ethical or moral imperative; Sedgwick does not position reparation as "better" reading at the top of a hierarchy of good reading. Rather, she foregrounds the distinct affective motivations behind different modalities of readerly and aesthetic relation, which are infused by qualitatively specific affective atmospherics. The question of reading, then, is ethical insofar as we must consider the contextual conditions that shape the scene of reading, and we must reflect on the affective and relational potentialities we (readers and writers) hope reading will foster. This is why Sedgwick is so acutely concerned about the relationship between the contexts of contemporary queer theory and the affective motivations that will infuse queer reading in her present. It is also, I believe, a reason that she experiments with a range of aesthetic idioms, such as experimental writing and textile art, to see if their distinct means may be able to foster reader relations that differ from those elicited through critical theory.

106. Eve Kosofsky Sedgwick, "Afterword," in *Gary in My Pocket*, ed. Eve Kosofsky Sedgwick (Durham: Duke University Press, 1996), 291. Sedgwick's use of idiom is informed by the work of Christopher Bollas, *Being a Character: Psychoanalysis and Self Experience* (New York: Routledge, 1992).

107. Eve Kosofsky Sedgwick, *The Epistemology of the Closet* (Berkeley: University of California Press, 1990), 59.

108. Sedgwick, *Dialogue*, 179. On Sedgwick's notion of mobile identification, also see "White Glasses," *Tendencies* (Durham: Duke University Press, 1993), 252–66.

109. Sedgwick, *Dialogue*, 179.

110. Sedgwick, "Afterword," 291.

111. Sedgwick, *Dialogue*, 10.

112. Ibid., 9.

113. Ibid., 10.

114. Ibid., 202.

115. Ibid., 195.

116. Sedgwick, *Touching*, 168.

117. Francisco J. Varela, *Ethical Know-How: Action, Wisdom, and Cognition* (Stanford: Stanford University Press, 1999), 65.

118. Judith Butler, *Giving an Account of Oneself* (New York: Fordham University Press, 2005), 64.

119. Butler, *Psychic*, 12.

120. Sedgwick, *Touching*, 10.

121. Sedgwick, *Dialogue*, 203.
122. Sedgwick, "Melanie," 631–32.
123. Sedgwick, *Touching*, 13.
124. Sedgwick, *Dialogue*, 92.
125. Ibid., 93.
126. Ibid., 94, original emphasis.
127. Sedgwick, *Touching*, 14.
128. Eve Kosofsky Sedgwick and Adam Frank, "Shame in the Cybernetic Fold: Reading Silvan Tomkins," in *Shame and Its Sisters: A Silvan Tomkins Reader*, ed. Eve Kosofsky Sedgwick and Adam Frank (Durham: Duke University Press, 1995), 14.
129. Ibid., 13–14.
130. Sedgwick, *Dialogue*, 93.
131. Ibid.
132. Ibid., 94.
133. Ibid., 43.
134. Butler, *Psychic*, 26–27.
135. Ibid., 27.
136. For a reading of Klein's positions that supports Sedgwick's, see Deborah P. Britzman, "Theory Kindergarten," in *Regarding Sedgwick: Essays on Queer Culture and Critical Theory*, eds. Stephen M. Barber and David L. Clark (New York: Routledge, 2002), 121–42.
137. Sedgwick, *Touching*, 128, original emphasis.
138. Eve Kosofsky Sedgwick, Stephen M. Barber, and David L. Clark, "This Piercing Bouquet: An Interview with Eve Kosofsky Sedgwick," in *Regarding Sedgwick: Essays on Queer Culture and Critical Theory*, eds. Stephen M. Barber and David L. Clark (New York: Routledge, 2002), 247. See also Sedgwick, "Melanie," 636–38.
139. Meira Likierman, *Melanie Klein: Her Work in Context* (London: Continuum, 2001), 116.
140. Sedgwick, "Melanie," 639.
141. Ibid.
142. Ibid., 638.
143. Ibid., 629.
144. Sedgwick, *Dialogue*, 172.
145. Ibid.
146. Ibid., 45, 46.
147. Ibid., 46.
148. Ibid., 48.
149. Ibid., 49.
150. Ibid., 189.
151. Leigh Gilmore, *The Limits of Autobiography: Trauma and Testimony* (Ithaca: Cornell University Press, 2001), 22.

152. Sedgwick, *Touching*, 54.
153. Sedgwick, *Dialogue*, 175.
154. Ibid., 206.
155. Ibid., 76.
156. Sedgwick, *Touching*, 61.
157. Ibid., 36.
158. Michael Warner, *The Trouble with Normal: Sex, Politics, and the Ethics of Queer Life* (Cambridge: Harvard University Press, 1999), 35.
159. Bersani and Phillips, *Intimacies*, 28.
160. Sedgwick, *Dialogue*, 183–84.
161. Bersani and Phillips, *Intimacies*, 29; Sedgwick, *Dialogue*, 184–85.
162. Bersani and Phillips, *Intimacies*, 30.
163. Sedgwick, "Afterword," 282.
164. Ibid., 282–83. Notably, Sedgwick asserts that this conception of S/M is "underarticulated outside of fiction," thereby amplifying the significance of queer experimental literature, such as Fisher's and her own, to complexly perform and embody it (Ibid., 282).
165. Ibid., 283.
166. Sedgwick, *Touching*, 148.
167. Ibid., 149.
168. A significant exception is José Esteban Muñoz, who persuasively defines futurity as constitutive of queerness. See *Cruising Utopia: The Then and There of Queer Futurity* (New York: New York University Press, 2009).
169. Lee Edelman, *No Future: Queer Theory and the Death Drive* (Durham: Duke University Press, 2004).
170. Ibid., 33.
171. Ibid., 34.
172. Sedgwick, *Dialogue*, 210.
173. Ibid., 215.
174. Sedgwick, Barber, and Clark, "This Piercing Bouquet," 259. The greatest influence on Sedgwick's conception of Buddhist happiness is the American Buddhist scholar Robert Thurman, particularly his introduction to *The Tibetan Book of the Dead*, trans. Robert A.F. Thurman (New York: Bantam Books, 1994), which Sedgwick quotes at length in *Dialogue* (210). For a fuller account of the interdependence between Buddhism and positive affect, see Thurman, *Inner Revolution: Life, Liberty and the Pursuit of Real Happiness* (New York: Riverhead Books, 1998); and *Infinite Life: Awakening to Bliss Within* (New York: Riverhead Books, 2004). Underlying Sedgwick's emphasis on the solicitous discourse of happiness is her dissatisfaction with Stephen Batchelor's contemptuous and judgmental rhetoric in *Buddhism without Beliefs: A Contemporary Guide to Awakening* (New York: Riverhead Books, 1997). While Sedgwick's approach to Buddhist concepts is indebted to both Thurman's

and Batchelor's agnosticism, which does not demand decisive beliefs regarding Buddhist dogma, Sedgwick's *aesthetics* of Buddhism clearly contrasts Batchelor's stricter "disdain for *consolation*" (*Touching*, 179, original emphasis).

175. Sedgwick, *Dialogue*, 1.
176. Ibid.
177. Ibid.
178. Sedgwick, *Touching*, 179.
179. Sedgwick, *Dialogue*, 216.
180. Ibid. Insofar as Sedgwick insists on the fortuitous nature of happiness, she contributes to recovering the contingency at the etymological root of the term. Doing so, Sara Ahmed argues, is a queer project when it challenges the conflation of happiness, social virtue, and heteronormativity. For her incisive analysis of how heteronormativity coercively deploys the speech acts of happiness, *The Promise of Happiness* (Durham: Duke University Press, 2010), especially 88–120.
181. Michael D. Snediker, *Queer Optimism: Lyric Personhood and Other Felicitous Persuasions* (Minneapolis: University of Minnesota Press, 2009), 2.
182. Snediker, *Queer Optimism*, 30; Sedgwick, *Dialogue*, 216.
183. Sedgwick, *Touching*, 146. For a less sanguine reading of reparation, see Leo Bersani, *The Culture of Redemption* (Cambridge: Harvard University Press, 1990). For a reclamation of Kleinian negativity, see Jacqueline Rose, *Why War? Psychoanalysis, Politics, and the Return to Melanie Klein* (Oxford: Blackwell, 1993), 137–90.
184. Sedgwick, "Teaching Depression."
185. Ibid.
186. Sedgwick, "Melanie," 637.
187. Sedgwick, *Touching*, 137.
188. Muñoz, *Cruising*, 11–12.
189. Sedgwick's understanding of the *bardo* is based primarily in her reading of Rinpoche, *Tibetan Book of Living and Dying*. Rinpoche explains that bardo "simply means a 'transition' or a gap between the completion of one situation and the onset of another" (106). Sedgwick tends to employ the bardo in this expansive sense of being in between, laying particular emphasis on the insights that can arise in this transitional space. See Ibid., 106–14, for a brief gloss of the term and its history. In addition to Rinpoche's exegesis of the different bardo states described in the *Bardo Thödol*, or *The Tibetan Book of the Dead*, see Lama Lodü, *Bardo Teachings: The Way of Death and Rebirth* (Ithaca: Snow Lion Publications, 1982). For an insightful synthesis of Sedgwick's interpretation of the *bardo* with queer theories of lesbian identity, see Melissa Solomon, "Flaming

Iguanas, Dalai Pandas, and Other Lesbian Bardos (A Few Perimeter Points)," in *Regarding Sedgwick: Essays on Queer Culture and Critical Theory*, eds. Stephen M. Barber and David L. Clark (New York: Routledge, 2002), 201–16.

190. Sedgwick, Barber, and Clark, "This Piercing Bouquet," 256. Here Sedgwick suggests that we define "the bardo of dying" broadly "as the space between diagnosis and physical death."

191. Ibid.

192. Sedgwick, *Dialogue*, 218.

193. Ibid., 219. Sedgwick's description of "bobbing" recalls Van Wey's notion of a "bobbing-like-a-cork strategy" for her to endure the "waves" of anxiety (136, 126). Notably, this strategy entails Sedgwick "feeling 'not together' … Temporarily disarticulating my different worlds from each other, my faculties, my past from present from future" (136). Bobbing provides an alternative to Sedgwick's desire for Van Wey to "glue me to the ground so I don't just get buffeted away" (126). Indeed, as Van Wey notes, "If I glue you to the ground, you'll drown in a minute" (Ibid). Bobbing, then, recalls the impersonal and asubjective "medium" of holding (the "bath" that affords buoyancy), and it is an analogue for the affective relation and temporality of a mode of queer survival that pertains in the face of omnipresent anxiety and dread (66).

194. Ibid.

195. Ibid.

196. Ibid., 220.

197. Ibid., 219, original emphasis.

198. Ibid., 220.

199. Ibid., 219. Note Sedgwick's own caveat about "uncritical" affect—and an uncritical *susceptibility* to that affect—that emerges in this passage: "I'm wary of such sudden condensations of sweetness, the kind that, in the past, have made me fall in love." She adds, "But I don't resist, either, secretly fingering this enigmatic pebble. I can't quite figure out what makes its meaning for me." Sweetness is an important affect for bad reading because it is not apparently assaultive, transgressive, or shattering— but, it is nonetheless "bad" because of its association with uncritical sentimentality. Yet Sedgwick's "secretly fingering" this image underscores the affective relations of queer eroticism, particularly masturbatory solipsism, that often frame narratives of bad reading. Sedgwick's giving in to these pleasures affords an incipiently social queer relationality to an infinite range of impersonal others across time.

CHAPTER 6

Conclusion: The Queerness of Aesthetic Agency

In 2003, Chuck Palahniuk uploaded an angry voicemail to his website. Afraid that an entertainment reporter would out him as a homosexual in a forthcoming article, Palahniuk pre-emptively outed himself.[1] He recorded the voicemail on the writer's phone, and then he shared the recording with his reading public. For years, rumors had circulated about Palahniuk's sexuality, particularly after it was revealed in 1999 that Palahniuk lied to the press about having a wife.[2] Thus, Palahniuk's coming out was generally perceived as a defensive act. In the words of one blogger, Palahniuk continues to be seen as "reluctantly gay."[3] Yet the locus of this reluctance remains a point of speculation for the gay press. In 2008, for example, *The Advocate* noted with some frustration that Palahniuk continues to respond with secrecy and ambiguity when pressed about his sexuality. Palahniuk "clearly does care, and deeply, about the perimeter of his privacy and the ability to turn off the lights when he wants to ... Palahniuk is not in the closet. The whole question misses the point. But a part of him seems to recognize the utility of shadows, the function of mystery. He does not want to be known."[4] The interviewer does not question whether Palahniuk's sexuality can be encapsulated within the parameters of the coming-out narrative or whether Palahniuk would consent to the conflation of his sexuality with the identity category "homosexual." Instead, in a particularly paranoid reading, the interviewer concludes that the "utility of shadows" lies in their strategic ability to preserve the consumer interest

© The Author(s) 2017
T. Bradway, *Queer Experimental Literature*,
Palgrave Studies in Affect Theory and Literary Criticism,
DOI 10.1057/978-1-137-59543-0_6

of Palahniuk's devoted heterosexual male readership, which he acquired as a result of the film adaptation of *Fight Club* (1999). The "perimeter of privacy"—and Palahniuk's ambivalence about it—is collapsed to a story about the gay author's economic incentive to manage the heteronormative anxieties of male readers as they confront texts with profoundly queer themes: transgender characters; queer depictions of masturbation, orgies, and sex clubs; complex homoeroticism; and an arch camp aesthetic. The interviewer does not consider the more radical and equally likely possibility—that these readers are attracted to and affectively invested in Palahniuk's fiction *precisely because* of its queer figurations.

At the same time that Palahniuk uploaded his voicemail, he began to perform a short story in public that would come to rival *Fight Club* in notoriety and popularity. At readings for his novel, *Lullaby* (2002), Palahniuk performed a story entitled "Guts," which was later published in *Playboy* magazine and in the collection *Haunted* (2005).[5] "Guts" graphically describes three incidents of male masturbation that result in public humiliation and, in two cases, horrific bodily trauma. A lubricated carrot used for masturbatory anal eroticism disappears from a boy's room, and it haunts his relationship with his family for decades; a teenager inserts a thin candle into his urethra, and it ultimately becomes stuck inside his bladder and requires painful surgery; and most famously, the narrator masturbates in a swimming pool and, while simulating anilingus with the pool's suction valve, accidentally pulls his intestines out through his anus during orgasm. The content of these stories echoes grotesque depictions of sexuality we have seen in queer experimental literature by William S. Burroughs, Samuel R. Delany, and Kathy Acker, a tradition that clearly influences Palahniuk. The images are absurd, surreal, and provocative. Likewise, the narrative's focus on scenes of masturbation recalls its significant figural role in queer experimental literature, as discussed in the introduction and glimpsed in my analyses of Alison Bechdel, Acker, and Eve Kosofsky Sedgwick. However, the controversy around "Guts" has not focused on the queerness of its content but, rather, on the number of faintings that Palahniuk's performance of "Guts" has provoked in his readers. Palahniuk claims that, thus far, hundreds of people have fainted during his public readings.[6] In his essay on the phenomenon, "The 'Guts' Effect," Palahniuk depicts "Guts" as a kind of shocking performance art, and he describes the growing crowds attending his international book tour that hope to witness or experience the event.[7]

Palahniuk claims that the popularity of the story and its visceral effects on readers testifies to the enduring, if marginal, agency of literature. Whereas mass media such as film and television "have to maintain a certain decorum in order to be broadcast to a vast audience," Palahniuk claims that books are "as private and consensual as sex. A book takes time and effort to consume—something that gives a reader every chance to walk away. Actually, so few people make the effort to read that it's difficult to call books a 'mass medium.' No one really gives a damn about books. No one has bothered to ban a book in decades."[8] Palahniuk is being less than sincere in this representation of books as "private and consensual as sex," given that all the private masturbation in "Guts" invariably becomes public, and its publicity is a source of ironic anguish and dark humor. For example, the "slippery, filthy" carrot that a boy uses to anally masturbate disappears from his room when his mother does his laundry.[9] The boy "waits months under a black cloud, waiting for his folks to confront him. And they never do. Ever. Even now he's grown up, that invisible carrot hangs over every Christmas dinner, every birthday party. Every Easter-egg hunt with his kids, his parents' grandkids, that ghost carrot is hover-ing over all of them."[10] It is tempting to reduce the carrot to the secret truth that homosexuality invariably signifies for Western culture.[11] Yet this would miss the satirical twist that Palahniuk makes here, in which the proverbial carrot and stick of anal pleasure becomes inverted; it's not that the boy pursues the carrot but the carrot that pursues him and his fam-ily, like a ghostly disembodied specter.[12] The carrot is, itself, an affective form—a structure of relation that constitutes the family *as a queer family*, stuck together through unspeakable pleasure. If reading is as "private and consensual" as *this* figuration of sex, then books are not so much carrots on sticks, beckoning promises of guaranteed satisfaction, but rather lubri-cated carrots that hover in unpredictable and ineffable ways, forging a queer relationality in space and time that did not pre-exist its emergence.

Perhaps it is better, then, to say that Palahniuk is being completely earnest in his claim that books are "as private and consensual as sex," but that his narration of "sex" demands a queer redefinition of the suppos-edly consensual, private, disembodied, and cerebral relations that typically pertain to reading. In "Guts," queer sexuality is represented as, at once, deeply seductive and abject, impossible to resist and rife with shattering consequences. Akin to Lee Edelman's conception of the *sinthomosexual*, the story positions queer experimentation as a threat to reproductive futu-rity, the stability of the nuclear family, and the coherence and solidity of the subject.[13] Stuck in the pool, drowning as his intestines are sucked into the drain, and prevented from reaching the water's surface for air, the narrator imagines life after his death:

> What my folks will find after work is a big naked fetus, curled in on itself. Floating in the cloudy water of their backyard pool. Tethered to the bottom by a thick rope of veins and twisted guts. The opposite of a kid hanging himself to death while he jacks off. This is the baby they brought home from the hospital thirteen years ago. Here's the kid they hoped would snag a football scholarship and get an M.B.A. Who'd care for them in their old age. Here's all their hopes and dreams. Floating here, naked and dead. All around him, big milky pearls of wasted sperm.[14]

This scene literalizes heteronormativity's worst fears. The "wasted sperm" stands in for the wastedness of non-reproductive sexuality and, of course, of the wasted life of the child that strayed from the path of heteronormative futurity, which would have produced the proper integration into masculinity and middle-class labor alike (football and an M.B.A.). Instead, the queer child has become an aborted fetus stuck in a figural womb.[15] Although the narrator survives in the conclusion of the story, his "wasted" sperm inadvertently impregnates his sister when she later swims in the pool. Masturbation turns into incest; private sex turns into public sex; and bodily fluids violate bodily boundaries. In "Guts," the horror of queerness is less the corruption of masculine heterosexuality than the revelation of queer experimentation to heteronormativity's public gaze, which is literalized here as non-agential bodily permeability. Hence, when a wave of teenage suicides results from failed (or, one might argue, all too *successful*) experiments with autoerotic asphyxiation, their parents "cleaned up. They put some pants on their kid. They made it look ... better. Intentional at least. The regular kind of sad, teen suicide."[16] Heteronormativity must deny the intentional desire to experiment with queer pleasure, preferring a tragic rather than an ecstatic scene for this becoming public of queer pleasure.

How, then, should we read the relationship between Palahniuk's ambivalent publication of his sexual identity alongside this story about queer publicness? How should we read the fainting bodies and gathering crowds that "Guts" conjures in the aftermath of its "gay" author being forced to "come out"? Clearly, I have stacked the deck, setting us up for a paranoid reading that dialectically inverts *The Advocate*'s paranoid reading. After all, isn't Palahniuk's story—and its visceral assault on readers in public—a kind of sublimated aggression for his own being "outed"?[17] As ambulances arrive to the scene of one of Palahniuk's performances, one of the fainters angrily asks the author: "Was [your] goal just to humiliate [me] in public? To make [me] faint in front of so many people … ?"[18] The paranoid reading would answer in the affirmative—claiming that, to invoke Burroughs, Palahniuk is "giving [him] the horrors," reversing the gaze of heteronormative culture to face its own corporeal susceptibility to queer fantasies.[19] In this reading, the story's invocation of "That something too awful to name" is, quite simply, Palahniuk's homosexuality, and the story and its performance are both horror narratives in which straight men find themselves unwittingly and distressingly seduced, and ultimately violated, by their contact with queer pleasures. "Guts" would be a symptom, then, of an omni-present and intractable gay shame: Palahniuk's, the reader's, and the culture's.

There are a number of drawbacks to such a "strong" affective reading, which *Queer Experimental Literature* has redressed by attending to bad reading—to the perverse agency of aesthetic objects to unfurl queer affective relations within, around, and beneath the existing structures of the public sphere.[20] My claim has been that queer experimental literature catalyzes forces of social imagination that cannot be understood through the idioms of paranoid or reparative reading alone. The former privileges the masterful critic's exposure of symptomatic causality whereas the latter relies on the empathetic critic's gestures of protection and hermeneutic care. In either case, the critic's epistemic and affective agency predominates over the agency of the aesthetic object itself. I have suggested, to borrow the words of Jennifer Doyle, that we "focus instead on what that work is taking on, using *its* terms to understand the nature of its intervention."[21] Unlike the artists in Doyle's archive, Palahniuk's performance art is avowedly apolitical; he claims no other purpose beyond sharing the story of "three true anecdotes," and "Guts" presents itself as a documentary account of factual events.[22] Yet the story's intervention lies in its narration—and performance—of queer pleasure as an affective experiment, a testing of the body's orifices and capacities, a rewriting of pleasure's zones and attachments and supplements. If "reading" and "sex" are analogous within the prism of "Guts," as Palahniuk claims, then reading becomes an experiment with affect that is "consensual" but unpredictable. Readers have "every chance to walk away." But, like the rumors and tales that elicit the protagonists' autoerotic experimentations, the seductiveness of reading can be too strong to resist. It whispers of new affective possibilities and relations that cannot be codified in definitive terms, promising to open the body to thresholds that cannot be predicted in advance. In this respect, "Guts" recoils against hetero- *and* homonormative narrative structures in which sexuality must be reduced to, and disclosed as, identity rather than erotic practice, pleasure, and experiment.

Thus, we should resist the temptation to reduce the affective relationality of "Guts" to "humiliation" or, indeed, any *one* affective referent, whether it is disgust, shame, or impish glee. At the same time, it is important to recuperate, as I have done throughout *Queer Experimental Literature*, the affirmative potentialities of queer pleasure, which are too often discounted as naïve fantasies of anarchic liberation or intimate privacy. Indeed, I want to stress that Palahniuk's readers are drawn to this affective event, at least in part, *because they want to faint*. They want erotic and ecstatic contact with text's affective effects, and the interest of the game rests on not knowing whether or not or how the text will affect them so—whether the text will *stick* to them, too. This fact does not diminish the agency of the text itself. On the contrary, it foregrounds the audience's investment—and intentional participation—in configuring a dramatic scene where the text's virtual affects can become actualized. Doyle's wonderful description of the audience that gathers for the performance art of Ron Athley could well apply to Palahniuk's reading public: "They knew what they were getting into, even if they didn't know exactly what was going to happen. [The artists] are giving them something that they want. Or something that they think they might want."[23] The opacity of the "something" here should not lead us to focus on the obscure *object* of desire that the performance may or may not signify, however incompletely, for an audience. Instead, the "something" is atmospheric and emergent, opaque because of its diffuseness and relational potentiality. In this sense, we might think of Palahniuk's "Guts" as narrating and configuring a scene for queer eroticism. As I argued in the introduction, queer eroticism is a scene for experimenting with the body's openness to perverse forms of recombination and adhesion. Whereas desire is premised on "belief," as Elizabeth Freeman writes, queer erotics is more interested in "encounter, less in damaged wholes than in intersections of body parts, less in loss than in novel possibility (will this part fit into that one? what's my gender if I do this or that to my body?)."[24] This is precisely the curious ethos that inspires the experimentation of "Guts's" wayward protagonists, but it also captures the way that Palahniuk invites his readers into an encounter with affective becoming. Indeed, the aesthetic object is *itself* part of the scene of queer eroticism, a vector for surface contact in an affective experiment that is curiously oriented toward seeing what a body can do—toward how it might become with other bodies.

Within this perversely permeable scene, the empty abstraction "the reader" (much like the abstraction "the subject") cannot pertain as the operative grammar for mapping aesthetic-object relations. Like the bodies in "Guts," readers are unspooled from inside, literally turned inside out, and like the narrator, they may not recognize themselves in their insides. When he sees his intestines floating beside him, the narrator thrashes at them and thinks that this scene "doesn't make sense. This thick rope, some kind of snake, blue-white and braided with veins, has come up out of the pool drain and it's holding on to my butt. ... That's the only way this makes sense. Some horrible sea monster, a sea serpent, something that's never seen the light of day, it's been hiding in the dark bottom of the pool drain, waiting to eat me."[25] To make "sense" of this scene, the body resists, with horror and disgust, refusing to see its own corporeality. The proliferation of metaphors—rope, snake, vein, monster, and serpent—attempt to crystallize a position of externality for the narrator, an expulsion of himself from his body. He cannot bear to see his body folding in, like Acker's labyrinthine languages of the body, and "holding" itself together through forces and relations that he does not control, vulnerable to an affection that can push the body further than he (knew he) wanted to go. Similarly, Palahniuk's readers might resist; they may blame the author and disavow their affective implication in the story as "humiliation," refusing to see their affective insides becoming outsides, splayed for others to see. Yet how could the story cause readers to faint if they were not, in some sense, deeply invested in its affects and figurations?

The point, then, is not to ask *what* the reader or the narrator "wants" from the encounter with queer experimental literature—which, in any case, is rarely any clearer after the event is over, after its potentialities have washed away. Rather, the point is to understand these co-existent potentialities as composing the affective atmospherics of the event of reading; these potentialities promise an encounter that cannot really be known in advance of its unfolding. This encounter is underscored—and preserved— by the strange subtitle for Palaniuk's essay about the effect of "Guts," "An Afterword (or Warning) of Sorts." What, precisely, does Palahniuk have to warn readers about? After all, we have already read the story—this essay is placed at the end of *Haunted* and "Guts" is placed at the beginning—and we have either fainted or not, thrown the book down in disgust or not. A warning placed at the outset would be a prologue to the encounter. Undoubtedly, a warning solicits curiosity and the desire to transgress, but it also relies on a specifically paranoid relation to the reading public: it anticipates and names, in advance, what the affective effect will be; it codifies and hails "the reader" as a certain kind of affective and social subject; and it implies, however fictively, that the reader's cognition can blunt the effects of the text's affective agency. A warning as prologue, then, would violently circumscribe (although by no means extinguish) the affective relations in play. This is precisely why Palahniuk makes a "warning" and an "afterword" performatively analogous. The warning is a warning "of sorts," because Palahniuk will not sort out the relations of before and after, inside and outside, public and private, in the dramatic scene of the "Guts" effect. To do so would delimit, retrospectively and proleptically, the question of *whose* desires and *which* feelings are in circulation when the story's intensities are unfurled in public. At the same time, Palahniuk implies that warnings are *always* retroactive, emerging only after an unexpected becoming has taken place.

The becoming of "Guts" persists—the number of fainters rises, the crowds continue to amass. Yet this queer public is not legible under the sign of a particular identity or social cause. The readers of "Guts" are a kind of perverse mirror of Sedgwick's post-Proustian network of permeability, dynamized around ecstatic disgust (or disgusting ecstasy) rather than love.[26] They are not a political collective in any traditional sense and may never crystallize into such terms. In this respect, "Guts" exemplifies queer experimental literature's fomenting of *incipiently social* modes of queer belonging. On the one hand, these texts recreate, through the affective relations of reading, the reader relations that structure their reception; in doing so, they experiment with queer configurations of aesthetic and erotic belonging, which absolutely have a political resonance. On the other hand, these texts meditate on their intractable *distance* from the proper spheres of political collectivity; they are incapable of generating a critical subject or a critical form of social imagination within the existing structures for representing political collectivity. These structures demand the sacrifice of queer relationality. Indeed, they repress the putatively uncritical investment in affect and dismiss figural mappings of the political onto the erotic, the sexual, the genital, or the intimate (and vice versa). Thus, queer experimental literature claims the liminal threshold between the "merely" affective and the "properly" social as its (improper) domain.

The bad readings that it elicits cannot be redeemed into the existing terms of aesthetic politics. To do so would be to obscure the potentiality harbored within the incipiently social domain of bad reading, the transitional affective scene that underlies the subject and the social alike and allows for experiments in reimagining social belonging in queerer idioms.

This book has explored such idioms through the affective relations of bad reading solicited by queer experimental literature. As I conclude, it is important to underscore that the critic's—particularly the literary or cultural critic's—relation to the text has *not* been the primary vector for these idioms. While literary studies has now recovered "reading" as an area of concern, it bears repeating that the professional critic should not be the privileged hero in the dramatic scene of reading. I share Lauren Berlant's caution against "idealizing, even implicitly, any program of better thought or reading."[27] As I argued in the introduction, too often such "programs" fail to acknowledge the normative social imaginary that underlies their narrative about the "good reader." It should be no surprise that the good reader leads us back to the protocols of the good citizen-subject, one who properly adheres to the logics of disembodied rationality, reproductive futurity, and heteronormative coherence. In academic definitions of reading, the good reading is typically the most cognitively masterful and the most counterintuitive, and the putative agency of its criticality lies in the dramatic agency of epistemic effects. In Berlant's words, "Those of us who think for a living [i.e. institutionally located academics] are too well-positioned to characterize certain virtuous acts of thought as dramatically powerful and right, whether effective or futile; we are set up to overestimate the proper clarity and destiny of an idea's effects and appropriate affects … [S]uch dramas can produce strange distortions in the ways we stage agency as a mode of heroic authorship, and vice versa."[28]

Queer Experimental Literature has displaced attention from the critic's idioms for reading to reinvigorate an attention to the agencies that aesthetic objects offer within their own terms. This methodology is particularly important for queer experimental literature because of the presumption that it lacks any agency whatsoever. Its aesthetic politics have been overlooked because they look too much like solipsism or degraded fantasy, and their investment in affect, particularly positive affects, cuts against poststructuralism's narration of agency as anti-essentialist demystification. By no means do I wish to deny the import of this mode, but I do wish to contest its exemplary status as an analogue for "queer critique." As much as they subvert and slant existing norms, queer aesthetics also create new affective relations and horizons of belonging. By attending to these fecundities, bad reading pluralizes the idioms for queer agency that can emerge within the event of reading. Each chapter has shown that bad reading can be an idiom for contesting hegemonic definitions of "critical reading" (or "critical language," in Acker's case). Yet, as postcritical methodologies become increasingly central to literary criticism, scholars must remember that they are, often unknowingly, inheriting a longer para-academic history of affective reading. Indeed, *Queer Experimental Literature* reveals the historical and political contingency of critical reading and demonstrates that a plurality of affective modalities for queer reading have been produced in the minor scene of experimental writing. Therefore, this book should be seen as a step in locating postcritical methods alongside and within their broader cultural histories, so that we do not perpetuate the mistake of staging aesthetic agency in terms that solely map onto academic idioms.

The idiom of bad reading does not promise "better" reading, nor does it propose to displace the hermeneutics of suspicion at the top of a hierarchical structure of reader relations.[29] On the contrary, bad reading describes an affective event staged within queer experimental literature—although it is by no means consigned to this archive—that is singular, deeply bound to the intersection of sexual and aesthetic politics in the postwar period. By granting that aesthetic surfaces speak in different languages than literary criticism, bad reading broadens the aesthetic forms that count as "critically queer" and the ways in which queer critique emerges through the affective forces of aesthetic form. It asks us to attend to the dialogic and dynamic affective torsions between aesthetic objects and their social worlds. As Freeman argues, aesthetic style "neither transcends nor subsumes culture but pries it open a bit, rearranges or reconstitutes its elements, providing glimpses of an otherwise-being that is unrealizable as street activism or as blueprint for the future."[30] When we conflate aesthetic agency with instrumentalism (blueprints or street activism) or the idioms of academic criticism, we miss this affective potentiality, this "otherwise-being," that cannot promise social transformation but can preserve and provoke its becoming.

Thus, bad reading breaks with other postcritical methodologies—particularly "surface reading"—when those methods oppose affective surfaces to political agency. Echoing Berlant, Stephen Best and Sharon Marcus personify political critique in the figure of the literary-critical "hero."[31] They critique political critics for their identification of "heroic texts" and the attribution of "heroism ... to the artwork due to its autonomy from ideology."[32] Yet in narrowly defining the politics of aesthetics as an ideology of heroism, Best and Marcus foreclose a broader conception of how aesthetic surfaces possess political agency—how, in short, aesthetic objects marshal the queer forces of affect through their surfaces. *Queer Experimental Literature* has suggested that, to borrow Best and Marcus's words, "a true openness to all the potentials made available by texts is also a prerequisite to an attentiveness that does not reduce them to instrumental means to an end."[33] Such openness must suspend the assumption that a text's potentials will be recognizable to the interpretative idioms that we use to read them. Yet openness to "all potentials" must *also* include the new modes of agency that aesthetic surfaces bring into being. These agencies may not always be legible in the terms that political criticism influenced by poststructuralism has valued (subversion, shattering, disruption, negation). This is because the aesthetic offers its own distinct idioms—often knowingly elaborated against postmodern and post-structural discourse—for dreaming up new relations between aesthetic objects and their incipiently social worlds.

Therefore, *Queer Experimental Literature* does not exemplify what Jeffrey J. Williams has recently characterized as the "new modesty in literary criticism."[34] On the contrary, I have charted queer relations of bad reading that immodestly dream up new modes of belonging, however prohibited, obstructed, or impossible these relations may be. Although often depicted as the poster child of paranoid reading, it is important to remember that Michel Foucault similarly stressed the necessity of an immodest affirmation of the affective potentialities unleashed by queer aesthetics.[35] Foucault characterized gay cultures as "creative force[s]" engaged in epistemological, political, and social invention; and he affirmed sadomasochistic cultures, in particular, for teaching us that "we can produce pleasure with very odd things ... in very unusual situations," and this production of "new possibilities for pleasure ... [is] a kind of creation, a creative enterprise."[36] It might seem surprising to hear the language of creation emerge here. Yet Foucault's call to "create culture" and to "realize cultural creations" was, in part, a challenge to the emergent identity politics of the lesbian and gay movement.[37] Indeed, he stressed: "I don't know what we would do to form these creations, and I don't know what forms these creations would take. For instance, I am not at all sure that the best form of literary creations by gay people is gay novels."[38] Perhaps like Palahniuk's putative "reluctance" to embrace a gay identity, we can see Foucault's hesitancy to provide an index for a "gay aesthetic" as one mode of queer agency. If queer culture must not reproduce the heteronormative law of identity, then Foucault's demurral holds open the possibility for unprecedented becomings to flourish and to provoke, engendering forms that are unrecognizable within the current schemes of aesthetic interpretation. This is an immodest modesty or, perhaps, a modest guise for an immodest dream; it is surely a stranger, more perverse form of immodesty than the masterful and egotistical critic that Best, Marcus, Berlant, and others rightly refute. After all, immodesty need not only be heroic; it can be abject and indecent, brazenly refusing to satisfy the dictates of decency, decorum, and good behavior.[39] Rather than shove aside and silence with the sanction of knowing better, the immodest reader might—like queer experimental literature—beckon and beg for more, experimenting to see what might still be possible, making room so that others can join in, clearing space to see who might faint next.

What if, following Foucault and Palahniuk, reading is less like criticism and more like sex? We would have to grant that aesthetics are "odd things" that produce pleasure in unusual situations; and we would have to suppose that aesthetic pleasures, like sexual pleasures, create immodest and unforeseen possibilities for becoming and belonging together. The aesthetic, like sex, may not be equivalent to political agency, but it is no less queer, no less related to power, and no less open to fostering collective potentials for otherwise-being. Must it be immodesty to crave an idiom for reading that can do justice to the affective forces of aesthetic agency in their loving and agonistic entanglements? For now, this idiom may read as uncritically queer. But in the meantime, its relations will work on and through us, despite ourselves.

NOTES

1. The author did not, in fact, out Palahniuk. See Karen Valby, "Chuck Palahniuk Does Not Attend Fight Club," *Entertainment Weekly*, September 26, 2003, accessed August 3, 2016, http://www.ew.com/article/2003/09/26/chuck-palahniuk-does-not-attend-fight-club.
2. See Austin Bunn, "Open Book," *The Advocate*, May 12, 2008, accessed August 3, 2016, http://www.advocate.com/news/2008/05/21/open-book.
3. Jay Barmann, "Reluctantly Gay Author Chuck Palahniuk 'Remixes' His Gayest Book, Comes to Castro Theater," *SFist*, July 6, 2012, accessed

   August 3, 2016, http://sfist.com/2012/07/06/reluctantly_gay_author_
   chuck_palahn.php.
 4. Bunn, "Open."
 5. Chuck Palahniuk, "Guts," in *Haunted* (New York: Anchor Books, 2005),
   12–21.
 6. Joshua Chaplinsky, "Strange But True: A Short Biography of Chuck
   Palahniuk," *Chuck Palahniuk.net*, accessed August 3, 2016, http://
   chuckpalahniuk.net/author/strange-but-true-a-short-biography-of-chuck-
   palahniuk.
 7. Chuck Palahniuk, "The Guts Effect: An Afterword (or Warning) of Sorts,"
   in *Haunted* (New York: Anchor Books, 2005), 404–11.
 8. Ibid., 410.
 9. Palahniuk, "Guts," 13.
10. Ibid.
11. See Eve Kosofsky Sedgwick, *Epistemology of the Closet* (Berkeley: University
   of California Press, 1990); and Lee Edelman, *Homographesis: Essays in Gay
   Literary and Cultural Theory* (New York: Routledge, 1994).
12. On the aesthetics and politics of queer spectrality, see Chap. 1.
13. Lee Edelman, *No Future: Queer Theory and the Death Drive* (Durham:
   Duke University Press, 2004), 33–66.
14. Palahniuk, "Guts," 19.
15. On the queerness of the child, see Kathryn Bond Stockton, *The Queer
   Child: On Growing Sideways in the Twentieth Century* (Durham: Duke
   University Press, 2009).
16. Palahniuk, "Guts," 14, ellipsis in original.
17. On the aggressiveness of Palahniuk's fiction, see Kathryn Hume, *Aggressive
   Fictions: Reading the Contemporary American Novel* (Ithaca: Cornell
   University Press, 2012); and Robin Mookerjee, *Transgressive Fiction: The
   New Satiric Tradition* (New York: Palgrave Macmillan, 2013).
18. Palahniuk, "Guts Effect," 410, ellipsis original.
19. See Chap. 1.
20. On the differences between strong and weak affect theories, see Eve
   Kosofsky Sedgwick and Adam Frank, "Shame in the Cybernetic Fold:
   Reading Silvan Tomkins," in *Shame and Its Sisters: A Silvan Tomkins
   Reader*, eds. Eve Kosofsky Sedgwick and Adam Frank (Durham: Duke
   University Press, 1995), 1–28.
21. Jennifer Doyle, *Hold It Against Me: Difficulty and Emotion in Contemporary
   Art* (Durham: Duke University Press, 2013), 13, original emphasis.
22. Palahniuk, "Guts Effect," 405.
23. Doyle, *Hold It*, 27.
24. Elizabeth Freeman, *Time Binds: Queer Temporalities, Queer Histories*
   (Durham: Duke University Press, 2010), 13–14.

25. Palahniuk, "Guts," 18.
26. On the post-Proustian network of love, see Chap. 5.
27. Lauren Berlant, *Cruel Optimism* (Durham: Duke University Press, 2011), 124.
28. Ibid.
29. For an account of the turn to affect that differs from mine, see Robyn Wiegman, "The Times We're In: Queer Feminist Criticism and the Reparative 'Turn,'" *Feminist Theory* 15 no. 1 (2014): 4–25.
30. Freeman, *Time Binds*, xix.
31. Sharon Marcus and Stephen Best, "Surface Reading: An Introduction," *Representations* 108, no. 1 (2009): 1–21.
32. Ibid., 13.
33. Ibid., 16.
34. Jeffrey J. Williams, "The New Modesty in Literary Criticism," *The Chronicle of Higher Education*, January 5, 2015, accessed August 3, 2016, http://chronicle.com/article/The-New-Modesty-in-Literary/150993/.
35. Michel Foucault, "Sex, Power, and the Politics of Identity," in *Ethics: Subjectivity and Truth*, ed. Paul Rabinow, trans. Robert Hurley (New York: The New Press, 1997), 163–73.
36. Ibid., 164, 165.
37. Ibid., 164.
38. Ibid.
39. For a convergent approach, see Kathryn Bond Stockton, "Surfacing (in the Heat of Reading): Is It Like Kissing or Some Other Sex Act?" *J19: The Journal of Nineteenth-Century Americanists* 3, no. 1 (2015): 7–13.

INDEX[1]

A

Acéphale society, 115

Acker, Kathy. *See also* Acker, postmodernity and languages of the body

and academic codifications, 92

and affect as anti-human force, xxxii

and Artaud, 140n87

on art criticism, 119

on art in England and New York, 108–9

and "avant-garde" concept, xliv

and Bataille, 103, 115, 118, 138n65

on Baudrillard, 109, 110

on bodybuilding, 120

and Burroughs, 6, 112, 116, 123

on the colon, 115

and conceptual art, 107, 108, 110–13, 116, 122–3, 131

and deconstruction, 107, 108, 112, 131

and Deleuze/Guattari, 106, 107, 109

and feminism, 138n59, 138n64

and feminist criticism, 108

and Foucault, 106, 109

"I'm not writing for the reader" quote, 104

and Irigaray, 114, 138n59, 139n69

on joys and new models of society, 118

on Kristeva, 138n59

and narcissism, 129

and neoliberalism, 105–7, 124

and Palahniuk's "Guts" stories, 234, 239

and patriarchy, 103, 106, 113–15, 125–6, 131

plagiarism case, 123

and politics, xliv, 128–32

and postmodernism, ix, 106–10

and poststructuralism, 106, 109–10, 113, 122, 131, 132

and provocative representation of queer eroticism, 133

[1] Note: Page numbers followed by 'n' refer to foot notes.

© The Author(s) 2017

T. Bradway, *Queer Experimental Literature*,

Palgrave Studies in Affect Theory and Literary Criticism,

DOI 10.1057/978-1-137-59543-0

Acker, Kathy (*cont.*)
and sadomasochism, 122
SAMOIS affiliation, 141n109
on society's "post-cynical"
phase, 110
works; *The Adult Life of Toulouse
Lautrec*, 123; *Bodies of Work*,
113; "Critical Languages"
(*Bodies of Work*), 118, 242;
Empire of the Senseless, 110–13,
122, 158; *Hannibal Lecter, My
Father*, 103–4; *In Memoriam to
Identity*, 122–3, 128–30, 132;
My Mother: Demonology, 138n65;
"Against Ordinary Language:
The Language of the Body"
(*Bodies of Work*), 116; "Seeing
Gender" (*Bodies of Work*),
113–15, 131; *Young Lust*, 123
Acker, postmodernity and languages of
the body. *See also* Acker, Kathy
Acker and unreadability, 103–8,
116, 129–30, 133
Acker's languages of the body; and
critics, 105–6; and French
feminism, 107; and
neoliberalism, 105–7; and
poststructural literary theory,
106–7
Acker's relationship to theory,
106–7
against "deconstruction"; Acker's
"deconstruction" of canonical
fictions, 108; England,
New York, and gentrification
of conceptual art, 108–9;
rejection of depoliticizing
postmodernism, 109–10; shift
towards affirmative aesthetics,
110–11; turn to "actual flesh"
and break with conceptualism,
111–13
chapter overview, xii

languages of the body and
thresholds of becoming; *Bodies
of Work* and rethinking of
poststructuralism, 113;
bodybuilding, failure, and
unpredictable thresholds of
becoming, 120–1; languages
of intensity, affect and
thresholds of indistinction,
116–17; languages of the
body, joys, and new models of
political belonging, 117–18;
languages of the body and
reinvigoration of art criticism,
118–19; masturbatory writing,
thresholds of indistinction, and
affective becoming, 119–20;
queerness, Bataille, Acéphale
Society and Nietzsche,
115–16; "Seeing Gender" and
Butler's "Bodies That Matter"
essay, 113–14; "Seeing
Gender" and *écriture féminine*,
114, 131; "Seeing Gender"
and the mother and the pirate,
114–15
queering the author–reader contract;
Hume's "author-reader
contract" theory, 121–2; *In
Memoriam to Identity* and
plagiarism case, 122–3, 131; *In
Memoriam to Identity* and
political significance of
imagination, 128–31; *In
Memoriam to Identity* and
unreadability, 129–30;
neoliberalism and gentrification,
124; "Rimbaud" and fucking
without dreaming, 124–6;
"Rimbaud" and languages of
the body, 127–8; suicide in
"Rimbaud" and *In Memoriam
to Identity*, 126–7, 130–1

stopping reading; Acker's demystification of ideological codes, 131–2; critics on politics of Acker's aesthetics, 132; languages of the body and experimenting with failure/becoming, 132–3
adhesion, and queerness, xlv–xlvi, 238
Adler, Alfred, 7, 9
The Advocate, Chuck Palahniuk interview, 233–4, 236–7
affect. *See also* affective relations; affect theory; Winterson's queer exuberance and politics of positive affect
 as anti-human force, xxxii
 vs. emotion, xli, 203
 and phenomenology, xxxviii
 and political organizations (Burroughs), 28
 and politics, 153–4
 positive affect and queer theory, 150–3, 155–6, 192n210
 positive vs. negative affect, 196, 223n6
 and psychoanalysis, xxxviii, 180
 and reader-response criticism, xxxv
affective fallacy (New Criticism), xxxv
affective history. *See* Delany's AIDS novels and queer hermeneutics as affective history
affective reading. *See* Sedgwick's memoir and queer theory's rediscovery of affective reading
affective relations. *See also* affect; affect theory; empathy; hermeneutics of suspicion
 and humanism, xxxi–xxxiii
 and LGBT movements, 195
 and queer aesthetic politics, 6
 "queering" of, v
 and queer relationality, xlii
 and reading, v, xxvii–xxviii, xxix

affect theory. *See also* affect; affective relations
 and cruelness of positive effects, 150–1
 and emotion vs. affect, 203
 and joy, 118
 and literary criticism, vii–viii
 and prioritizing specific literary forms, xxxv–xxxvi
 'theory from above' and 'suspicion/empathy' dichotomy, xxxi
affirmation, politics of, 133, 156, 180–1
agency. *See also* Palahniuk's "Guts" and queerness of aesthetic agency
 and Butler, 213, 214
 and fantasy, 216–17
 and instrumentalism, 242–3
 and queer theory, 197, 213, 214
 and Sedgwick, 213–18
Ahmed, Sara, 151, 196, 231n180
AIDS crisis. *See also* Delany's AIDS novels and queer hermeneutics as affective history; epidemic of signification
 and LGBT movement, 195
 literary response to, 98n68
 and paranoid/reparative reading, xxix, 56
 and queer theory, 92
Altieri, Charles, xxxv
anarchism, and experimental writing, xliv, xlv
Andermahr, Sonya, 149, 189n115
"anti-social" thesis, xiiin4, 136n40
Aristotle, xxxvi, 103
art. *See also* conceptual art
 Acker on, 108–9, 118–19
 Grosz on, xxxix, xl, 162
 and politics, 162
 and post-structuralism, xxxix
 and subjectivity, 162–3
 Winterson on, 161, 165, 171, 179

Artaud, Antonin, 76, 140n87
Athley, Ron, 238
Attridge, Derek, xxxv, xxxvii–xxxviii
Augustine, St., 2
Author–reader contract, x, 121–2,
    124, 129–30
Autonomia, 109
avant-garde
    and experimental writing,
        xliii–xliv
    gentrification of queer avant-garde, xi

B
bad reading and the incipiently social.
    See also preface
    "bad" *vs.* "good" reading; affective
        relations *vs.* "good" reading
        norms, xxvii–xxviii, xxix;
        Frankenstein as bad reader,
        xxviii–xxix; "incipiently social"
        concept, xxxii–xxxiii, lxn78;
        paranoid/reparative reading
        (Sedgwick), xxix–xxx; "perverse
        reader" concept (Sedgwick),
        xxxiii–xxxiv; public agency and
        "counterpublic discourse"
        (Warner), xxxii; queer reading
        practices outside academia, xxx;
        rejection of humanist paradigm,
        xxxi–xxxii; social contexts and
        critical politics of reading, xxx;
        suspicion/empathy *vs.* aesthetic
        object's affective agency, xxx–
        xxxi; viscerality and historicity,
        xxxiv–xxxv
    readerly feeling and literary theory;
        affect and reader-response
        criticism, xxxv; "affective
        fallacy" and New Criticism,
        xxxv; affect theory and
        prioritizing specific literary
        forms, xxxv–xxxvi; Attridge,
        xxxv, xxxvii–xxxviii;

    Nussbaum, xxxv, xxxvi;
        psychoanalysis, xxxviii
    reader relations as effective
        becomings; art as autonomous
        field of sensation (Deleuze/
        Guattari), xxxix; queer
        relationality and "affective
        relation" phrase, xlii; sensations
        and signifiers (Massumi and
        Grosz), xxxix–xl; subjectivity
        and emotions as obstacle, xl–xli;
        subjectivity and futurity, xli–xlii;
        text, reader and plane of
        immanence, xl; "zone of
        proximity" and becoming
        (Deleuze), xl
    reading, affective relations and
        queer experimental literature;
        écriture féminine and critique
        of, xlii–xliii; "fantasy" as
        aesthetic idiom, xlvi–xlvii;
        queer adhesion *vs.* corrosion,
        xlv, xlvi; queer eroticism *vs.*
        desire, xlv–xlvi; queer
        experimental writing and
        avant-garde, xliii–xliv; queer
        experimental writing and
        patriarchy, xliii; queer
        experimental writing and
        politics, xliv–xlv; queerness,
        aesthetic politics of, xlv–xlvi
    reading and intimations of
        relationality, Bechdel's *Fun
        Home*, xlviii–lii
Bakhtin, Mikhail
    The Dialogic Imagination, 53
    notion of the carnivalesque, 75–6
Balakrishnan, Gopal, 159
Barber, Stephen M., 206
bardo (in Buddhism), 221
Barthes, Roland, 108
Bataille, George, 103, 115, 118,
    138n65
Batchelor, Stephen, 230n174

Baudelaire, Charles, 73
Baudrillard, Jean, 106, 109, 110, 132
Beardsley, Monroe, xxxv
Beat fiction, 45n80
Bechdel, Alison, 234
    Fun Home, xlviii–lii
Beckett, Samuel, 116
Benjamin, Walter, *Arcades Project*, 53
Berlant, Lauren
    on academia and idealizing programs
        of "better" reading, 241
    on fantasy, lxiin103
    on leftists' "traumatic identity" and
        optimism, 156–7
    on multiple localities of queer
        theory and practice, liv(11)
    and "new modesty" in literary
        criticism, 244
    on politics and affect amelioration,
        153–4
    and positive affect, 196
    on positive affect vs. queer
        flourishing, 151
    on projects of queer optimism,
        192n210
    on queer commentary and
        "mongrelized" genres, lxii(95)
    on queer commentary's various
        forms, lvn28
    on queer culture and its politics,
        lxin89
    on reparative reading as "better"
        reading, 211
    on Sedgwick's work and
        "orientation toward interiority"
        problematic, 206
Bersani, Leo, xlv, 217, 218
Best, Stephen, xxx, xxxi, 96n37, 244
biopower, xi, xxxiv, 26, 27, 154, 157–8
black experimental writing, x
Bogue, Ronald, lixn72
Bollas, Christopher, 228n106
Bora, Renu, 201
Brande, David, 139n72

Brennan, Teresa, lxn80
Brennan, William J., Justice, 1–2
Brown, Wendy, 155
Buddhism. *See* Sedgwick, Eve Kosofsky
Burroughs, William S. *See also*
        Burroughs's queer spectrality and
        obscene relationality
    and Acker, 6, 112, 116, 123
    and affect as anti-human force, xxxii
    and "avant-garde" concept, xliv
    "cut-up fold-in" method, 5, 19–20,
        23–4, 29, 30, 35
    and fantasy; "Is this literal?" question,
        11–12, 18, 20, 25; and *Naked
        Lunch* obscenity trial, 1–4, 36–7;
        spectral fantasy, 6–7; and *The
        Wild Boys*, 48n132
    fetishism and race/racism, 44n56
    homophobia and Orientalist fantasy,
        14–16
    homophobic traits in writings, 13, 18
    misogyny, xliii, 18
    "The Name is Burroughs" essay, 22–3
    and Palahniuk, 6
    and Palahniuk's "Guts" stories,
        234, 237
    patriarchy, xliii
    possession, 6, 9, 14, 16–17, 19,
        25–6, 29, 38–9
    and provocative representation of
        queer eroticism, 133
    quotes on; cut-up fold-in method,
        5; electric brain stimulation and
        sexual excitement, 27; Freud's
        theories, 46n94; Mexico City's
        appeal, 14–15; *Naked Lunch*
        title, 13; *Naked Lunch* trial,
        41n15; narrative routines, 11;
        organization of cut-up novels,
        20; "other cheek routine" and
        Cory, D. W., 44n59; political
        organizations and affect, 28;
        possession concept, 38; *Queer*
        not to be published, 10

Burroughs's queer spectrality and obscene relationality. *See also* Burroughs, William S.

Burroughs's turn to experimental literature; from *Junky* to "cut-up fold-in" trilogy, 4; prevailing criticism of cut-up novels, 5

chapter overview, xi

form and "bad" queer reading, 5–6

"Is this literal?" question, 11–12, 18, 20, 25

1966 Naked Lunch obscenity trial; definitions of obscenity, 1–2; hallucination *vs.* imagination, 2; novel as scientific, 38; politics and social fantasies, 2–4, 36–7

Queer spectrality; homophobia, spectrality and homoeroticism, 6–7; homosexuality, spectrality and queer theory, 7–8; *"I'm not queer-I'm disembodied"* quote, 1; invisibility, Mexico and homophobia, 14–15; "naked lust" and depiction of gay men as perverts, 12–13; narrative form and spectrality, 8–9; photography, "real men" and racism, 17, 23; queer spectrality and judgment, 9; sadism *vs.* reciprocity, 16; search for "telepathic contact" in *Junky*, 44n68; "shadowy line of boys" and impossibility of contact, 10–11; "Skip Tracer" dream and futility of material coercion, 16–17; spectral disembodiment and "boys on rubbish heap" passage, 15–16; spectrality and frustrated homosexual relationality, 10–12, 23; spectrality, homoeroticism and "imaginary hand" passage,

13–14; story narrative and plot, 9–10; yearning for queer sociality, 17–18

returning it to the "white reader"; cut-ups and language, 19–22; humanity and "fag" horror in *Naked Lunch* and cut-up novels, 19; images of eroticism and control mechanisms in *Nova Express* and *The Soft Machine*, 27; institutional control *vs.* spontaneity, 19; *Junky*'s "gives me the horror" and liberation from word locks, 18–20; *Naked Lunch* and cancer as metaphor for control, 47n127; *Naked Lunch*'s "examination" routine and biopower, 25–7; *Naked Lunch*'s "talking asshole" routine and spectrality, 28–30; *Naked Lunch*'s "The Word will leap on you" and queering of readers, 21–2; *Nova Express*'s *"Nothing Is True–Everything Is Permitted,"* 20; *The Soft Machine*'s hanging routines and fantasy/reality line, 24–5; *The Soft Machine*'s "Pants down to the ankle" and cut-up style, 23–4; spectral readers and liberation from control, 27–8; "White Reader" in *The Soft Machine, Naked Lunch* and *Queer*, 22–3

sociability; Burroughs as anti-social writer, 30–1; *Junky* and ambivalence about sociality, 31–2; *Naked Lunch*'s "Hassan's Rumpus" routine and becoming-relational, 35–6; *Queer*'s "loneliness" passage, 31; queer sociality and agglutination

of words, 34–6; queer sociality and cut-up fold-in method, 35–6; *Queer*'s "one gweat big blob" and queer collectivity, 30, 35; "There are no good relationships" (*The Ticket That Exploded*), 30; *The Ticket That Exploded* and ghostly permeability, 33–4; *The Ticket That Exploded* and indistinct communalism, 36 solipsism and sociality; *Naked Lunch*'s "return it to the white reader" and readerly solipsism, 37–8; *Naked Lunch* trial and solipsistic mind of junkie, 36–7; rejection of judgment and new relationality, 39; spectrality and queerness-relationality entwinement, 38–9
Butler, Judith
 and Acker, 106
 on agency, 213, 214
 on agency, Klein, Freud and Foucault, 214
 Bodies That Matter, 113–14
 "Critically Queer" (in Bodies That Matter), 151
 on critical promise of drag, 152–3
 and Freud's theory on homosexuality, 175–6
 on melancholia, 151
 and positive affect, 196
 Sedgwick's critique of, 223n9
 "Uncritical Exuberance" (online essay), 150–1, 180, 181

C
Camus, Albert, li
capitalism. *See also* neoliberalism
and Acker's writing, 111, 117, 123, 132
and Burroughs's writing, 14
and Delany's writings, 88
and happiness, 159
and "waning of affect" in postmodernism, 154
and Winterson's writing, 159–61, 164–5, 168
carnivalesque, as subversive, 75–6
Carroll, Lewis, 113
"carrot-on-the-stick" approach to reading, x
chapter overview, xi–xiii. *See also* preface
Cixous, Hélène, xlii, 114
Clark, David L., 206
Clune, Michael, 105–6
Colebrooke, Claire, 137n56
conceptual art, and Acker, 107, 108, 110–13, 116, 122–3, 131
corrosion, and queerness, xlv
Cory, D. W., 44n59
Crimp, Douglas, 196
critical reading
and bad reading, v, xxix
and deconstruction, livn13
and hermeneutics of suspicion, xxix
and liberal humanism, xxxii
and Marxism, livn13
and postcritical reading, x–xi
and psychoanalysis, livn13
and symptomatic reading, livn13
critical theory. *See also* literary criticism; queer theory
and hermeneutics of suspicion, xi, xxix
and queer reading practices outside academia, xxx
Cusset, François, xxx, liiin2, 96n45
Cvetkovich, Ann, 196
Cynic philosophers, 87

D

Damasio, Antonio, xlii, lviiin51
Dean, Tim, xlv
deconstruction
  and Acker, 107, 108, 112, 131
  and critical reading, livn13
  and Delany's hermeneutics, 55,
    57–66, 79
  and double reading, 123
  and estrangement, xxxvii
  and hermeneutics of suspicion, 60, 70
  and paranoid reading, 60
  and Sedgwick, 204
deconstructive resignification, ix, 8,
  107, 116, 149
Defoe, Daniel, *A Journal of the Plague
  Year*, 76
de Grazia, Edward, 2, 38
DeKoven, Marianne, 187n72
Delany, Samuel R. *See also* Delany's
  AIDS novels and queer
  hermeneutics as affective history
  and "avant-garde" concept, xliv
  on metaphoric structure
    and AIDS, 79
  on Nevèrÿon series, 69
  and Palahniuk's "Guts" stories, 234
  and postmodernism, ix
  and provocative representation of
    queer eroticism, 133
  "radical" reader concept, 54–5,
    57–9, 60, 66, 74, 77
  "vigilant reader" concept, 60–1,
    64–6
  works; *The Jewel-Hinged Jaw*, 56;
    The Motion of Light on Water,
    52; *Nevèrÿon* series, 56–7,
    61–2, 66, 69; "Reading at
    Work, and Other Activities
    Frowned on By Authority" (on
    Haraway's "A Cyborg
    Manifesto"), 64–6; *Starboard
    Wine*, 56; *Times Square Red*, 52;
    Trouble on Triton, 97n65

Delany's AIDS novels and queer
  hermeneutics as affective history.
  See also Delany, Samuel R.
  AIDS and queer reading as affective
    inheritance, 92–3
  chapter overview, xi–xii
  Delany and experimental writing;
    'Delany's para-academic
    experimentation, 52–3;
    Delany's "radical reader" and
    queer hermeneutics for AIDS,
    54–5; 1994 OutWrite
    Convention's rejection of
    experimental writing, 51–2;
    para-academic mode,
    hermeneutics, and affective
    history, 53–4
  Delany and hermeneutics;
    hermeneutics of suspicion and
    paranoid reading, 55–6;
    semiotics and Delany's
    alternative hermeneutics, 56–7;
    shift to "radical reader" and
    deconstructive hermeneutics in
    Tale of Plagues and Carnivals,
    55, 57–9
  Delany and theory of
    deconstruction; "radical reader"
    and blurring of fiction and
    theory, 66; readerly "vigilance"
    vs. "masterful" reader, 60–1;
    Ryan, "language and power"
    debate, and affective suffering,
    61–3; *The Tale of Plagues and
    Carnivals*, affective dimension
    of linguistic displacement, and
    readerly relations, 63–4; *The
    Tale of Plagues and Carnivals*
    and metafictive meditation on
    activist and academic readers, 64;
    "vigilant" reading and "reading"
    of Haraway, 64–6
  The Mad Man; disclaimer and
    criticism of dearth of research

on AIDS, 81; eroticism, queer
sexual acts, and narrative of
uncertainty, 81–2;
hermeneutics of pleasure and
dissatisfaction with
deconstruction, 79–80;
hermeneutics of pleasure and
para-academic *vs.* academic
discourses, 55, 83–5, 87, 91;
hermeneutics of pleasure and
queer erotic economies, 88–9;
hermeneutics of pleasure *vs.*
"safe sex" discourses, 81–2;
historical pornographic novel,
80–1; historical structure and
gay affective experience, 82–3;
mixture of minor literary
forms, 53; official/unofficial
social/sexual systems and
queer sociality space, 84–6;
orgy one-penny game as
challenge to capitalistic
hierarchies, 87–8; pornotopia,
EKPYROSIS (apocalypse) and
sexual revelation, 86–7; queer
erotic economies, The Pit, and
violence, 88–9; rape scene and
"questionable" readings, 90–1
The Tales of Plagues and Carnivals;
ancillary status and structure of
novel, 66–7; criticism of
Bakhtin's carnivalesque as
subversion, 75–7; mixture of
minor literary forms, 53;
Noyeed, impossible dialog and
space for future readings, 78;
psychoanalytic reading trope,
99n105; reference "anxiety"
and "Bridge of Lost Desire"
section, 67–9; reference,
formalism, art and activism,
69–70; sex advice to gay men in
postscript, 80; text's
allegorizing of feelings and

Kermit's and Leslie's debate,
70–1; "unfinished" writing and
historical crisis of
representation, 72–3;
"unfinished" writing and
readers' uncertain
"completion" of Pheron, 73–4;
violence of para-academic text
vs. Master's academic
rewritings, 74–5
de Lauretis, Teresa, xlv, 57,
lxiin103
Deleuze, Gilles
and affect as a force, xlii
and becoming, 153
on belief in the world, 118
on difference-as-dialectic, 140n88
and Dionysian intoxication
metaphors, liiin8, 9
and invisibility, 14
on judgment, 9, 39
on "powers of the false" or
aesthetics of illusion, 164
and reader relations as affective
becomings, xxxix
on subjective "escape" as aim of
literature, xli
and subjectivity as obstacle, xl–xli
on "zone of proximity" and
becoming, xl
Deleuze, Gilles and Guattari, Félix
and Acker, 106, 107, 109
on art and sensations, xxxix
on Burroughs's cut-up fold-in
method, 5, 35
on fabulation, xlvi–xlvii
on Kafka, xlvii
de Man, Paul, 63
D'Emilio, John, 48n139
Derrida, Jacques, xxxvii, 8, 9, 96n45,
106, 109, 173 4
de Sade, Marquis, 103
de Saussure, Ferdinand, 57, 113
descriptive reading, xxxi, 93

desire
  in Burroughs's *Queer*, 13–14, 16
  vs. eroticism, xlv–xlvi, 238
  Freud's theory, xxxviii
Dewey, John, 2
Dickens, Charles, 164
Dillard, Annie, *Living By
  Fiction*, 69
Diogenes, 53, 87
disembodiment, and queerness,
  15–16
double reading, 123
Doyle, Jennifer, xliv–xlv, 237, 238

E
écriture féminine, xlii–xliii, 114, 131
ecstasy taking, and queer time
  (Muñoz), xlii, li
Edelman, Lee
  on compassion and reproductive
    futurity, 151, 219
  and disruption of representation, xlv
  on fantasy, xlvi
  and positive affect, 196
  on queer irony *vs.* symbolic order,
    180, 181
  and the *sinthomosexual*, 235–6
Edwards, Jason, 204–5
Edwards, John, 199
Ellison, Ralph, *Invisible Man*, 14
Emerson, Carol, 76
emotion
  vs. affect, xli, 203
  as obstacle, xl–xli
empathy
  in Nussbaum's theory, xxxvi
  vs. suspicion, vii, xxix, xxxi
epidemic of signification
  concept, xi, 55–6
  and Delany, 57, 58, 60, 62, 78, 79,
    91, 92

eroticism
  and "cut-up fold-in" technique, 5
  vs. desire, xlv–xlvi, 238
  and fantasy, 4, 16
estrangement
  and Acker's writing, 104, 131
  and deconstruction, xxxvii
  and Sedgwick's writing, 200, 202
ethical responsibility, and queer
  spectrality, 9
experimental writing
  and anarchism, xliv, xlv
  black experimental writing, x
  and feminist criticism, xlii–xliii
  and 1994 OutWrite Convention,
    51–2
  relevance of, ix–x
exuberance. *See* Winterson's queer
  exuberance and politics
  of positive affect

F
fantasy
  as aesthetic idiom, xlvi–xlvii
  and agency, 216–17
  Berlant on, lxiin103
  and Burroughs; "Is this literal?"
    question, 11–12, 18, 20, 25;
    and *Naked Lunch* obscenity
    trial, 1–4, 36–7; spectral fantasy,
    6–7; and *The Wild Boys*, 48n132
  and eroticism, 4, 16
  and Lacan, xlvi
  and. narcissism, xliv, xlvi, xlvii
  and psychoanalysis, 43n44
Faulkner, William, 122
Felski, Rita, x, xxx, xxxi
feminism
  and Acker, 138n59, 138n64
  and Kristeva, 138n59
  and Sedgwick, 217

feminist criticism. *See also écriture
féminine*; French feminism
and Acker, 108
and Deleuze/Guattari's
concepts, xxxix
and experimental writing, xlii–xliii
and Freud, xxxviii
and literary instrumentalism,
xxxvii–xxxviii
post-structural feminism, xliii
Fight Club (film), 234
Fish, Stanley, xxxv, lviin45
Fisher, Gary, 211–12, 218, 230n164
Fitterman, Robert, 111–12, 137n46
Foucault, Michel
and Acker, 106, 109
on "*bios philosophicus*" and
Diogenes's public
masturbation, 87
Butler on, 214
on creating culture and gay
aesthetic, 243–4
on gay and sadomasochistic
cultures, 243
on historical contingency and power
relations, vi
McCann's and Szalay's critique of,
140n83
and paranoid reading, 243
on repressive hypothesis, 197, 213
Frank, Adam, xxxi, xxxviii, 214
Frankenstein, Victor (fiction
character), xxviii–xxix, xxxiii, xlii,
xlviii, li
Franklin, Cynthia G., 199
Freccero, Carla, 8, 9
Freedman, Estelle B., 48n139
Freeman, Elizabeth, vi, xliv, xlv–xlvi,
53–4, 91, 238, 242
French feminism, xlii–xliii, 107. *See
also* écriture féminine
Freud, Sigmund. *See also*
psychoanalysis

Burroughs on, 46n94
and Burroughs's *Naked Lunch*
obscenity trial, 2
Butler on, 175–6, 214
desire theory and queer/feminist
criticism, xxxviii
and internalization of prohibition,
214
and interpretations of symbols, xlviii
"the loss of some abstraction"
quote, 169
and Massumi's emotion/subjectivity
theory, xli
on narcissism and homosexuality, 175
Sedgwick on, 204
Friedman, Ellen G., 136n38
Fun Home (graphic novel, Alison
Bechdel), xlviii–lii
futurity
and queerness, vi–vii, xlii, xlvi, 151,
218–19
and subjectivity, xli–xlii

G
Ganteau, Jean-Michel, 149
gay liberation movement, 3. *See also*
LGBTQ movements
gay pride, 152
Gilbert, Sandra M., *The Madwoman in
the Attic* (Gilbert and Gubar),
119–20
Gilmore, Leigh, 217
Ginsberg, Allen, 2, 3, 10, 40n11,
43n48, 47n129
Glass, Loren, lviin43
Glee (show), 223n7
Goldsmith, Kenneth, 111
Gonzalez, Alberto, 199
Grosz, Elizabeth
on art as political, 162
on art unleashing a "pure
intensity," xxxix

Grosz, Elizabeth (*cont.*)
  "artworks don't signify" quote, xl
  and Deleuze/Guattari's concepts,
    xxxix
  on Hegelian tradition in queer
    theory, 185n32
  on Kristeva and feminism, 138n59
  on politics and pleasure, 161–2
  on sensation and future, xli–xlii
Guattari, Félix. *See* Deleuze, Gilles and
    Guattari, Félix
Gubar, Susan, *The Madwoman in the
    Attic* (Gilbert and Gubar),
    119–20

H
haibun (in Sedgwick's *A Dialogue on
    Love*), 197, 200–2
Halberstam, Jack, 120, 196
hanging routines, in Burroughs's *The
    Soft Machine*, 24–5
happiness. *See also* joy; optimism
  and Acker/Burroughs, 112
  and capitalism, 159
  and queer theory, 151–2
  and Sedgwick's writing, 198,
    219–20
  and Winterson's writing, 181–2
Haraway, Donna, "A Cyborg
    Manifesto" and Delany, 64–6
Hardt, Michael, *Empire* (Hardt and
    Negri), 105, 154, 159
Harris, Andrea, 149
Hassan, Ihab, 5
Hawkins, Katy, 202
Hayles, Katherine, 5
Hegel, Georg Wilhelm Friedrich, 53,
    85, 118, 153, 185n32
Heidegger, Martin, 116
Heraclitus, 86

hermeneutics of pleasure. *See also*
    pleasure
  and Delany, 55, 79–4, 87–9
  and queer experimental
    literature, x
hermeneutics of suspicion
  and critical reading, xxix
  and deconstruction, 60, 79
  vs. Delany's hermeneutics, 54–5,
    61, 84
  and modes of interpretation,
    xxx–xxxi
  and philosophy discipline, 87
  vs. postcritical reading, xi
  and queer reading of AIDS, 92
  and queer theory, xi, xxix, 193, 194,
    242
Hocquenghem, Guy, 7–9
Hoffman, Yoel, 223n11
Holquist, Michael, 76
Holzer, Jenny, 109
homonormativity
  and biopower, xi, xxxiv
  perceived as non-oppositional, vi
homophobia
  and bad reading as survival, xxxiii
  and Burroughs's Orientalist fantasy,
    14–16
  in Burroughs's writing, 13, 18
  and narrative of medical
    secularization, 38
  and spectrality, 6–7
  and trauma, 181–2
Huber, Irmtraud, 110
humanism
  and affective relations of reading,
    xxxi–xxxiii
  vs. estrangement in reading, xxxvii
  and Nussbaum's theory, xxxvi
Hume, Kathryn, x, xliv, 121–2,
    126–7

I

imagination
  vs. hallucination (Burroughs's *Naked Lunch* obscenity trial), 2
  political significance of (in Acker), 128–31
immanence, plane of, xl
"incipiently social" concept, xxxii–xxxiii, lxn78. *See also* bad reading and the incipiently social
instrumentalism
  and aesthetic agency, 242–3
  literary instrumentalism, xxxvii–xxxviii
invisibility, and queer spectrality, 14–15
Irigaray, Luce, xlii, 106, 113, 114, 138n59, 139n69

J

James, Henry, xlv, 217
Jameson, Fredric, lvin42, 66, 93, 99n93, 167
Japanese Death Poems, 223n11
Johnson, Barbara, viii, 57, 76
joy. *See also* happiness; optimism
  and affect theory, 118
Joyce, James, xlviii, li, 2
judgment, and queer spectrality, 9, 39

K

Kafka, Franz, xlvii
Kazin, Alfred, 30–1
Kerouac, Jack, 43n48, 45n80
Kesey, Ken, 45n80
Klein, Melanie, 199, 214–16, 223n6
Konstantinou, Lee, 132, 135n20, 136n40
Kristeva, Julia, xlii, xliii, 106, 114, 138n59, 202

L

Lacan, Jacques, xlvi, 192n210
Laplanche, Jean, xxxviii
Le Guin, Ursula K., 172
lesbian literature, reception of in UK compared to US, 183n9
Levinas, Emmanuel, xxxvii
Levine, Sherri, 109
LGBTQ movements
  and affective relations and AIDS crisis, 195
  and equivalence of queerness with death, 219
  and queer theory, 152
Likierman, Meira, 215
literary criticism. *See also* critical theory; queer theory
  and affect theory, vii–viii
  "new modesty" in, xiii, 203, 243–4
  and postcritical reading, 242
  and queer reading practices outside academia, xxx
  and readerly feeling problem, xxxv
literary instrumentalism, xxxvii–xxxviii
Love, Heather, xxxi, 93, 196
Lydenberg, Robin, 19, 22, 45n88

M

Mailer, Norman, 2
Marcus, Sharon, xxx, xxxi, 96n37, 242–4
Marxism
  and critical reading, livn13
  and literary instrumentalism, xxxvii–xxxviii
Massumi, Brian
  and affect theory, xxxv
  on affirmative reading, critique, and question of dosage, 80
  on emotion *vs.* affect, xli, 203

Massumi, Brian (*cont.*)
  on "intemperate arrogance of
    debunking" of critique, 92
  on joy, 118
  on reading and incipient action,
    lxn78
  on reading and sensations, xxxix–xl
  on signification preceding bodily
    process, 153
  use of "emotion" term, lviiin51
masturbation
  Diogenes's public masturbation, 87
  masturbation and ghostly carrots
    (Palahniuk), 235
  masturbation fantasies (Sedgwick),
    216–18
  masturbatory reading (Bechdel), xlix–l
  masturbatory solipsism, 232n199
  masturbatory writing (Acker),
    119–20
McCallum, E. L., 153
McCann, Sean, 117, 119
McHale, Brian, 167, 171–2
McKeon, Michael, 188n98
melancholia
  Butler on, 151
  and leftist activism, 155
  and queer theory, 151
  and Winterson's critique of
    modernity, 168–9
  and Winterson's critique of "original
    self" concept, 173–4
Merrill, James, 203, 224n21
metafiction, ix
  and Delany's writing, 53, 57, 64,
    67, 72–3
  and Winterson's writing, 164–5
Michaels, Walter Benn, 105
Miller, D. A., 223n9
Miller, Nancy K., xlii–xliii, 206
Millet, Kate, li
Mintcheva, Svetlana, 142n133
misogyny, in Burroughs, xliii, 18

modesty, "new modesty" in literary
    criticism, xiii, 203, 243–4
Muñoz, José Esteban, vi–vii, xlii, li,
    165, 181, 221, 230n168
Murphy, Timothy, 14, 17, 30

N
narcissism
  and Acker's writing, 129
  and counterpublic texts (Warner), 31
  and fantasy, xliv, xlvi, xlvii
  Freud on, 175
  and Sedgwick's writing, 199, 208,
    210–11, 217, 219
  and subjectivity, xlvii
  and Winterson's writing, 168, 175,
    180, 181
Negri, Antonio, *Empire* (Hardt and
    Negri), 105, 154, 159
neoliberalism. *See also* capitalism
  and Acker, 105–7, 124
  and affect, 150
  and biopolitical codification of
    feelings, 158
  and commodification of queer
    radical aesthetics discourses, xi
  and "fucking without dreaming"
    (Acker), 126
  and gentrification of artistic
    community, 124, 132
  and gentrification of queer avant-
    garde, xi
  and homonormativity perceived as
    non-oppositional, vi
  and poststructural theories, 132
  and punk culture, 132
  and state-sanctioned forms of gay
    relationality, 148
  and Winterson's aesthetic conceit,
    156–7
New Criticism, affective fallacy, xxxv
Ngai, Sianne, xxxv, 21, 49n154, 107

Nietzsche, Friedrich, 53, 82, 109, 115–16, 118, 140n88, 153, 174
Nussbaum, Martha, xxxv, xxxvi

O

Obama, Barack, and "Uncritical Exuberance" (Butler), 150–1, 180
obscenity. *See also* Burroughs's queer spectrality and obscene relationality
    laws in pre-Stonewall America, xi
    Naked Lunch obscenity trial, 1–4, 36–7, 38
    Supreme Court's new definition, 1–2
Ohi, Kevin, xlv
optimism
    and leftists' "traumatic identity" (Berlant), 156–7
    queer optimism, 152, 192n210, 220
Orientalism, and Burroughs, 14–16
OutWrite Convention (1994), 51–2

P

Palahniuk, Chuck. *See also* Palahniuk's "Guts" and queerness of aesthetic agency
    Burroughs's influence on, 6
    Fight Club, 234
    "The 'Guts' Effect" (essay), 234
    Haunted, 234, 239
    Lullaby, 234
    and postmodernism, ix
Palahniuk's "Guts" and queerness of aesthetic agency. *See also* Palahniuk, Chuck
    chapter overview, xiii
    Palahniuk; coming out and *The Advocate* interview, 233–4, 236–7; "Guts" public readings and faintings, 234;

masturbation and ghostly carrots, 235; notion of books as private and consensual as sex, 235; paranoid/reparative reading of public reading faintings, 236–7; seductiveness of reading and wanting to faint, 237–9; warning as afterword and unexpected becoming, 239–40; "wasted sperm" passage and queer sexuality as threat to reproductive futurity, 235–6
queer aesthetics and Foucault, 243–4
queer experimental literature and incipiently social modes of queer belonging, 240–1
queer experimental literature *vs.* "new modesty" in literary criticism, 243–4
queer idioms and bad reading *vs.* literary/cultural criticism, 241–2
surface reading, political agency and new modes of agency, 242–3
Panagia, Davide, 177
para-academic mode
    concept, x, xxx
    and Delany, 52–3, 64–6, 73–4, 83–4, 92
    and queer theory, 53–4
    and Sedgwick, 92
paranoia, and Sedgwick, xxix, xxx, 56, 195–7, 215–16
paranoid reading. *See also* reparative reading
    and AIDS crisis context (Sedgwick), xxix, 56
    critique of Sedgwick's paranoid/ reparative reading dichotomy, viii–ix, xxix–xxx, 236–7
    and deconstruction, 60
    and Delany's writing, 54, 80, 93
    and Foucault, 243

patriarchy. *See also* Winterson, Jeanette
  and Acker's writing, 103, 106,
    113–15, 125–6, 131
  and Burroughs's writing, xliii
  and experimental writing, xliii
  and French feminism, xliii
Patton, Cindy, 56
Peirce, Charles Sanders, 57
"people who are missing" concept,
  108, 135n24
phenomenology, xxxviii, xxxix
philosophy, and Delany's hermeneutics
  of pleasure, 87
Place, Vanessa, 111–12, 137n46
Plato, 113, 200
pleasure. *See also* hermeneutics of
  pleasure
  and politics, 161–2
  and therapy, 202–3
politics
  and Acker, xliv, 128–31, 132
  and affect, 28, 153–4
  and affect amelioration (Berlant),
    153–4
  and art, 162
  and melancholia, 155
  and pleasure, 161–2
  and queer experimental writing,
    xliv–xlv
  and social fantasies (Burroughs's
    Naked Lunch obscenity trial),
    2–4, 36–7
Pontalis, Jean-Bertrand, xxxviii
pornography, and academia, 91
possession (in Burroughs), 6, 9, 14,
  16–17, 19, 25–6, 29, 38–9
postcritical reading, x–xi, 242
postmodernism
  and Acker, ix, 106–7, 108–10
  characteristics of postmodern
    fiction, 167, 171–2
  and language, 117–20
  and queerness, ix, 6

  and Realism, 188n98
  and turn to the self, 168
  "waning of affect" and political
    economy, 154
  and Winterson, ix, 167–8
poststructural feminism, xliii
poststructural theory
  and Acker, 106, 109–10, 113, 122,
    131, 132
  and art, xxxix
  and neoliberalism, 132
  and queer theory, 193, 241
  and Realism, 188n98
  and Sausserian semiotics, 113
preface. *See also* bad reading and the
  incipiently social
  experimental writing and race/
    sexual politics, ix–x
  pleasure and queer experimental
    literature, x
  postcritical reading, x–xi
  postmodernism and queerness, ix
  queer negativity *vs.* creative queer
    relationality, v–vi
  queer relationality and queerness as
    collectivity, vi–vii
  reading, affect theory and literary
    criticism, vii–viii
  reparative/paranoid vs. affective
    queer reading, viii–ix
  summaries of book chapters, xi–xiii
Prince, Richard, 109
Proust, Marcel, "post-Proustian" love
  and Sedgwick, 207–8, 209, 240
psychoanalysis. *See also* Freud,
  Sigmund
  and affect, xxxviii
  vs. Buddhism and
    interconnectedness, 200
  and critical reading, livn13
  and Delany's *The Tales of Plagues
    and Carnivals*, 99n105
  and fantasy, 43n44

and internalization of prohibition, 214

and positive affects as identifications with normative ideals, 180

and queer search for ethical insight, 217

punk culture, 104, 108, 132, 136n40

Q

queerness

and adhesion, xlv–xlvi, 238

aesthetic politics of, xlv–xlvi

and "affective relation" phrase, xlii

as collectivity, vi–vii

as consumer identity, xi

and corrosion, xlv

and disembodiment, 15–16

as force of subversion *vs.* creative queerness, v–vi

and futurity, vi–vii, xlii, xlvi, 151, 218–19

and postmodernism, ix, 6

Sedgwick's definition of, 206

queer optimism, 152, 192n210, 220

queer theory. *See also* Sedgwick's memoir and queer theory's rediscovery of affective reading

and affective reading, 6

and affirmation, 180–1

and agency, 197, 213, 214

and "critical" vs. "uncritical" feelings, 147–8

and Delany's work, 52–3

and Deleuze/Guattari's concepts, xxxix

and eroticism *vs.* desire, xlv–xlvi

and French feminism, xliii

and Freud, xxxviii

and happiness, 151–2

and Hegelian tradition, 185n32

and hermeneutics of suspicion, xi, xxix, 193, 194, 242

and historical relationship to AIDS crisis, 92

and Lacanian understanding of fantasy, xlvi

and LGBT politics, 152

and melancholia, 151

and para-academic writing, 53–4

and positive affect, 150–3, 155–6, 192n210

and poststructural theory, 193, 241

and queer spectrality, 8

and Winterson's work, 148–9

R

racism

and Burroughs's portrayal of Mexicans, 15

and Burroughs's racialized fetishism, 44n56

photography and racist white masculinity, 17, 23

reader-response criticism, xxxv, xxxvii, xxxix

reading. *See also* bad reading and the incipiently social; critical reading; paranoid reading; reparative reading

and affective relations, v, xxvii–xxviii, xxix

author-reader contract, x, 121–2, 124, 129–30

carrot on the stick approach to, x

descriptive reading, xxxi, 93

double reading, 123

masturbatory reading, xlix–l

postcritical reading, x–xi, 242

"radical" reader (Delany), 54–5, 57–9, 60, 66, 74, 77

surface reading, xxx, 242–3

symptomatic reading, xxx, livn13

"vigilant reader" (Delany), 60–1, 64–6

Réage, Pauline, 103
Realism
    and postmodernism, 188n98
    Winterson on, 163–4
Reed, Anthony, *Freedom Time: The Poetics and Politics of Black Experimental Writing*, ix–x, xliv
Renaissance, Winterson on, 166
reparative reading. *See also* paranoid reading
    critique of Sedgwick's paranoid/reparative reading dichotomy, viii–ix, xxix–xxx, 236–7
    and Delany's writing, 80
    and Sedgwick's memoir, 92, 194–5, 197, 206, 211
ressentiment, 118, 169, 178, 220
Rice, Condoleezza, 199
Rimbaud, Arthur, "Rimbaud" in Acker's *In Memoriam to Identity*, 122, 124–8
Rinpoche, Sogyal, 226n80, 231n189
Robbins, Harold, *The Pirate*, 123
Rock, Catherine, 126
Rohy, Valerie, xlvii
Romanticism, 53, 111, 163
Rousseau, Jean-Jacques, 173–4
Rubin, Gayle, 141n109
Russell, Jamie, 41n18, 45n78
Ryan, Michael, 57, 61–2

S
sadomasochism, 16, 122, 198, 216, 218, 243
SAMOIS, 141n109
Schulman, Sarah, 107, 140n85, 148
Scott, Darieck, 81
Sedgwick, Eve Kosofsky. *See also* Sedgwick's memoir and queer theory's rediscovery of affective reading
    on affect, xxxviii

on affective pedagogy, 187n63
on binary between positive and negative affects, 151
and Buddhism; *bardo*, 221; contribution to therapy, 198; death as "ethical" skill, 219; interconnectedness, 200; pedagogy and dissolvent relationality, xlv, 207; pedagogy and evasion, 187n63; pedagogy and permeability, 206–7, 210, 212; permeable intersubjectivity, 196
on Butler, 223n9
on deconstructive analyses of nonverbal reality, 204
and feminism, 217
on Freudian sublimation, 204
and *haibun* (in *A Dialogue on Love*), 197, 200–2
on James, Henry, 217
and narcissism, 199, 208, 210–11, 217, 219
on the novel, 200
and Palahniuk's "Guts" stories, 234, 240
and paranoia, xxix, xxx, 56, 195–6, 197, 215–16
on paranoia and queer activism in late 1980s-early 1990s, 215
on paranoid and reparative queer reading, viii–ix, xxix–xxx, 236–7
on paranoid reading and hermeneutics of suspicion, 56
Permeable We! 196
on "perverse reader" concept, xxxiii–xxxiv
and range of affective idioms, lxn76
and reparative reading in her memoir, 92, 194–5, 197, 206, 211
on "space of high anxiety" and reading novels, 46n93

works; Kessler lecture, 210; "Melanie Klein and the Difference Affect Makes" (essay), 222n3; "Paranoid Reading and Reparative Reading" (essay), 193; "Queer Little Gods: A Conversation" (interview), 223n9; "Teaching 'Experimental Critical Writing" (essay), 199; *Touching Feeling*, 223n9

Sedgwick's memoir and queer theory's rediscovery of affective reading. *See also* Sedgwick, Eve Kosofsky

affective relations and queer theory; queer critics' emphasis on negative affect, 196; Sedgwick on LGBT movement, AIDS and positive affect, 195–6; Sedgwick's *A Dialogue on Love* and permeable intersubjectivity, 196–8

chapter overview, xii–xiii

A Dialogue on Love; *Dialogue*'s narrative form and permeable first person, 198–9; *Dialogue*'s typographic space and affective relationality, 204; Japanese *haibun* and absence of first person, 199–202; modesty and potentiality for change, 203; spaciousness, affect, and intersubjectivity, 202; therapy and pleasure, 202–3; wordlessness, language, and emotion, 203–4

A Dialogue on Love and agency; Butler's take on agency, 213, 214; "middle ranges" of agency, 213; negotiation of embodiment as mode of agency, 213–14; queer activism and paranoia, 215–16;

sadomasochist masturbation fantasies and affective negotiation of agency, 216–18; turn to Klein, 214–16

A Dialogue on Love and pedagogy of permeability; affect, pedagogy, and queerness, 206; Berlant's critique of Sedgwick's conception of impersonality, 206; Buddhist pedagogy and impersonal intersubjectivity, 206–7; love redefined and permeability, 207–9; reading Gary Fisher, circuits of identification, and relationality, 211–12; relational holding and embracing difference, 209–12; reparative reading and focalizing the other, 211

A Dialogue on Love and queer belonging in mortality; death and queer futurity, 218–19; death as "ethical" skill in Buddhism, 219, 221; patience, happiness, and goodness, 220; "patient" *vs.* "client" terminology, 219–20; reparative relations, *bardo*, and imagination of collective change, 220–2

introduction; bad reading, experimental literature, and queer theory, 193–4; context of Sedgwick's turn to affect, 193–4

semiotics and Delany's hermeneutics, 56–7 Sausserian semiotics and poststructuralism, 113

Shelley, Mary, Victor Frankenstein character, xxviii–xxix, xxxiii, xlii, xlviii, li

Showalter, Elaine, 149

sinthomosexual, 235–6
Skerl, Jennie, 47n130
Smith, Adam, xxxvi
Snediker, Michael D., 152, 220
solipsism
  and Burroughs's writing, 6, 7, 11,
    12, 22, 31, 37–8, 39
  and queer experimental literature, v,
    xliv, xlvii, 241
  and Sedgwick's writing, 199,
    232n199
  and Winterson's writing, 146, 149,
    156, 166
Sontag, Susan, *AIDS and its
  Metaphors*, 79
spectrality. *See* Burroughs's queer
  spectrality and obscene
  relationality
Spinoza, Baruch, 118, 120
Spivak, Gayatri, 57
spontaneity, *vs.* institutional control, 19
Stein, Gertrude, 20–1
stickiness. *See* adhesion
Stonewall, xi, 3, 30
Strauss, Richard, *Rosenkavalier*, 166
subjectivity
  and art, 162–3
  and conceptual art, 111
  and futurity, xli–xlii
  and narcissism, xlvii
  as obstacle, xl–xli
surface reading, xxx, 242–3
suspicion. *See also* hermeneutics of
  suspicion
  vs. empathy, vii, xxix, xxxi
symptomatic reading, xxx, livn13
Szalay, Michael, 117, 119

T
Terada, Rei, lixn61
Thomas, Clarence, 199

Thurman, Robert, 230n174
Tomkins, Silvan, xxxviii, 214, 223n6
Tompkins, Jane, xxxv
Tomso, Gregory, 92
trauma, and homophobia, 181–2
Treichler, Paula, 55
trigger warnings, 40n6
Tucker, Jeffrey Allen, 56–7, 69
Tuhkanen, Mikko, 153

U
US Supreme Court, on new definition
  of obscenity, 1–2
utopianism, vi–vii, 149, 156, 165,
  192n219, 221

V
Van Wey, Shannon (in Sedgwick's *A
  Dialogue on Love*)
  "bobbing up gently" scene, 222
  embodiment as mode of agency,
    213, 214
  first person's constraints, 201
  his gender and permeable
    identification, 212
  his illness, 218
  holding relations, 209–11
  hope for family's reunification and
    Sedgwick's resistance, 200
  intersubjective relationality, 207
  "patient" *vs.* "client" terminology,
    219–20
  relationality and positive affect, 202,
    204, 205
  sadomasochist fantasies and agency,
    216, 218
  session notes in Sedgwick's
    text, 199
  "turning out different" therapeutic
    goal, 198

Varela, Francisco, 212
Verlaine, Paul, in Acker's "Rimbaud"
   (*In Memoriam to Identity*), 122,
   124–8

W
Wallace, David Foster, 106–7
Warner, Michael
   counterpublic discourse and
      orientation to futurity, lxn78
   counterpublic discourse and public
      agency, xxxii
   counterpublic texts read as debased
      narcissism, 31
   cultural construction of AIDS-
      related discourses, 55–6
   Fear of a Queer Planet, 56
   modern hierarchy of faculties and
      imagination, 36
   multiple localities of queer theory
      and practice, livn11
   queer commentary and mongrelized
      genres, lxiin95
   queer commentary's various
      forms, lvn28
   queer culture and its politics, lxin89
   queer sociability and experience
      of shame, 217
   The *Trouble with Normal* and
      Diogenes, 101n159
Waters, Sarah, 183n9
Weber, Samuel, 76
Whiting, Frederick, 39n1
Whitman, Walt, 35
Williams, Jeffrey J., 243
Wimsatt, W. K., xxxv
Winnicott, D. W., 209, 227n94
Winterson, Jeanette. *See also*
   Winterson's queer exuberance and
   politics of positive affect

on art as creation, 161
on art as intimacy and public
   declaration, 171
on art not being therapy, 179
on art *vs.* capitalism, 165
and "avant-garde" concept, xliv
on language and experimental
   aesthetics, 171
on love as an intervention, 145,
   150, 158
on love-parallel, 160
and narcissism, 168, 175,
   180, 181
and patriarchy; and biopolitical
   instrumentation of sexuality,
   157–8; and fear of affective
   exposure, 146, 147, 177–8;
   and "Handel character" in *Art
   and Lies*, 169–70; and ideology
   of lack, 159; and medicine,
   170; and narcissism, 175; and
   power of art, 167; and romance
   traditions, 149, 150; and
   suppression of complex
   emotion, 160; and suppression
   of desire, 168
and positive affect, 133
and postmodernism, ix, 167–8
on queer culture, 163
and queer theory, 148–9
on realistic aesthetics, 163–4
on the Renaissance, 166
on Romanticism, 163
works; *Art and Lies*, 165–80; *Art
   Objects: Essays on Ecstasy and
   Effrontery*, 159, 165, 166; *The
   Stone Gods*, 145, 150, 157–8,
   172, 173; *Why Be Happy
   When You Could Be Normal?*
   181–2; *Written on the Body*,
   145–7, 173

Winterson's queer exuberance
and politics of positive affect.
See also Winterson, Jeanette
chapter overview, xii
introduction; gender/sexuality as
social fictions in *Written on the
Body*, 145–6; visceral
transmission of affect in *Written
on the Body*, 146–7; Winterson's
focus on emotion and queer
theory, 147–8; Winterson's
mainstream and academic
publics, 148–9; Winterson's
queer exuberance, love as
"intervention" and queer
becoming, 149–50
politics of queer affect; Butler's
"Uncritical Exuberance"
notion, 150–1; politics, political
economy and affect, 153–4;
positive affect and queer theory,
151–3; queer theory and
politics of affirmation, 155–6;
Winterson's sentimentality and
desire for new relational
structures, 156–7
visceral aesthetics and biopolitics;
affect and love as
"intervention" *vs.* political
codification of sexuality, 157–8;
art, pleasure, and politics,
161–2; art outside subjective
experience, 162–3; art's
rebelliousness and consumer
culture, 159–61; non-
representational aesthetics *vs.*
realism and consumer

capitalism., 163–5; turn to
experimental aesthetics and *Art
and Lies*, 165–6
Winterson's *Art and Lies*; characters
and structure of novel, 166–7;
consumerist homogeneity and
"effacement" of the individual,
167–8; medicine as objectifying
patriarchal discipline, 169–70;
melancholic attachment to the
past and perpetuation of
oppression, 168–9; non-
representational aesthetics,
politics and social becoming,
176–80; queerness and sexual
difference, 175–6; queer
relationality and reciprocal
energetics of the Word, 170–2;
sentimentality and grammar of
second person, 172–3; shock of
affect and non-existent original
self, 173–4; violence, rape, and
visceral aesthetics, 174–5
Winterson's *Why Be Happy When
You Could Be Normal?*;
affirmation and queer theory,
180–1; happiness, "wound" of
homophobia, and queer
potentiality, 181–2
Wittgenstein, Ludwig, 116
Wittig, Monique, xlii, 114
women's writing. *See écriture féminine*
Wong, Norman, 51

Z
"zone of proximity" (Deleuze), xl

Made in the USA
Columbia, SC
04 September 2021